Reading and Understanding
The Acts of the Apostles, The New Testament Letters, and the Book of Revelation

D0863911

Dr. Thomas B. Lane

outskirtspress
DENVER, COLORADO

Outskirts Press, Inc.
http://www.outskirtspress.com

ISBN: 978-1-4327-9496-5

Library of Congress Control Number: 2012910797

Outskirts Press and the "OP" logo are trademarks belonging to Outskirts Press, Inc.

PRINTED IN THE UNITED STATES OF AMERICA

Reading and Understanding the Acts of the Apostles, the New Testament Letters, and the Beginning of the Church is the third volume in a three part series on reading and understanding the Bible. The first volume published is titled *Reading and Understanding the Old Testament: The Foundation of Judaism, Christianity, and Islam.* The second volume is titled *Reading and Understanding the Gospels: Who Jesus Is, What He Teaches, and the Beginning of Christianity.*

I am dedicating these writings to Andrea, my very supporting wife, Lee Anne, and Lana my two wonderful daughters who for many years kept encouraging me to write, and to my best buddy, my first grandson, my little guy, Samuel Lane Durkee, who was born three months early at two pounds five ounces. He was excited to come into this world so he decided to come early. May he bless his creator and the world as he has blessed us. My hope is that when he is old enough, he will read this humble attempt that begins to reveal the one God and will develop a relationship with that one God. I am also dedicating this series of books to Lila Lane Fortier, who has just entered the world four weeks early at 4 pounds 12 ounces and 19 inches long. Her eyes were wide open and alert and ready to begin life. May God use both Samuel and Lila as two of his very special people.

A special thanks goes to my wife Andrea, Samuel and Lila's "grandra," for the many hours she took going through all three manuscripts to help me proofread and correct my writing. Her editorial writing has been absolutely invaluable. Without her corrections and additions this complete series would not be anywhere near its final results. Also, a tribute is due to my loving, caring parents, Don and Pat, who gave me my first Bible and raised me and my sister Marsha in the church. A final tribute is appropriate to the one who originally inspired me to learn more about the Scriptures, Roy Ruckman, from whom I took my initial courses in the Old and New Testaments with my two very good friends John Wiberg and Carl De Caspers one summer a long time ago at the University of Texas-El Paso.

Table of Contents

INTRODUCTION: PURPOSE AND METHODS OF INTERPRETATION

This book is written for anyone who is interested in acquiring basic knowledge and understanding of the content in the New Testament letters, which include the Acts of the Apostles and the book of Revelation. Even though this book is a verse by verse study, it is primarily written for the beginning student in the university, or adults who have never read through these books or given them any in-depth study, but also for anyone who wants to expand their understanding. Therefore it is not an advanced scholarly study but is designed to supply a foundation that will enable one to eventually read, meditate, and think intelligently about the content that is within the books, and possibly even motivate one to continue to a more advanced scholarly study. The goal is simply to help those interested gain basic literacy of the content of the New Testament beyond the four Gospels to enable the reader to understand the books describing the beginning and development of the Christian church. This book is for anyone seeking to know who Peter, Paul,

James, and John are, and what they did and said as the church began to develop.

This book is a canonical-synchronic study that takes into account modern scholarship. Canonical and synchronic means that the books of the Bible as they are completed contain all of God's inspired word, and that all parts need to be understood according to their structure and meaning, and in unity with the whole of all the books. The writer stresses a theological and religious approach rooted in the scholarship of historical and literary analysis based upon the message of the content as understood by practicing Christians. A theological and religious approach is integrated into the historical and literary analysis because the writers of the New Testament were theologians. To ignore that aspect is to misunderstand the content. Here, the author accepts St Anselm of Canterbury's definition of theology as faith seeking understanding.

Taking into account modern scholarship means that this writer attempts to utilize in a practical and applied way the principles of modern scholarship, even though this book is not about modern scholarship. In a beginning study of the content of the New Testament this writer does not want to overwhelm the reader with the methodology, intricacies, and debates of higher scholarship. It is preferable that beginning students see how a writer with faith applies scholarship in a practical way, as they read and attempt to understand the content. After the content is basically understood then the reader will be more prepared to deal with scholarship's intricacies and challenges.

In order to study modern scholarship's challenge to the New Testament such as historical and literary criticism, archeology, methodology and research, Hebrew and Greek word studies, who wrote the books, when they were written, why they were written, to whom they were written, how they were originally put together, and such debates, as well as other scholarly concerns, one will have to consult other works, and the reader is encouraged to do so.

This book will stay with the purpose of helping readers gain a basic understanding and application of the New Testament content. That means at times there will be an attempt to interpret and apply to our lives in a practical way some of these writings. This writer will do so in an attempt to clarify some underlying meanings and themes and to challenge and enable the readers to begin to make some of their own applications as well as to perhaps disagree with this author. In disagreeing the reader is encouraged to always show reasoning based upon Scripture and not personal preferences.

Until modern times the Bible was basically studied in order to better understand and serve God. With the coming of the Age of Enlightenment scholars soon allowed the historical critical method to dominate the serving God approach to the point that the Bible was broken into small pieces, dissected, and left there. Their primary purpose was to discover how the Bible came about and what was historically real and what was not.

This served a purpose and will continue to do so, but it is now time to put the Scriptures back together again into a unified whole to enable readers to once again better understand and serve God; thus the reason for the canonical-synthetic, theological, and religious approach. In the process we can not ignore the advances of biblical scholarship, and the fact that we now live on this side of the Enlightenment in a Post-Modern Age. The historical critical method does have an important part to play, even though it will no longer dominate.

It will be obvious to the reader that the writer is a Christian living in twenty-first century America. It will also be obvious that the author respects the historical method but sees the need to build upon that approach in a practical way, so that once again people can see that the Bible has much to say to people living in these times today.

For Christians the Bible consists of an Old Testament and a New Testament where the word *testament* is also translated as law or covenant. In general Jews do not use the term Old Testament, for they do not accept the New Testament. For Jews, Torah, Tanakh, and Bible are what they call the Old Testament. Torah means the law or the teachings. For Christians the New Testament is based upon the Old Testament but is also a reinterpretation of some of it, which is one reason why it is called the New Testament. Jesus came to bring the old to a climax, to fulfill it, and institute a new covenant. God forming a people is like parents raising a child. Some things during infancy are permitted that later are prohibited or changed because of the development of God's plan and the increasing maturity of people.

This writer appreciates the statement made by the Second Vatican Council, in paragraphs 15 and 16 of the Dogmatic Constitution on Divine Revelation that says, "God, the inspirer and author of the books of both testaments, in his wisdom has so brought it about that the New should be hidden in the Old and that the Old should be made manifest in the New. For, though Christ founded the New Covenant in his blood, still the books of the Old Testament all of them caught up in the gospel message, attain and show forth their full meaning in the New Testament, and in their turn, shed light on it and explain it." Jesus said that he came to fulfill the law, to fill it full, to bring it to a climax, or to bring it to its deepest meaning and intention.

Jews reject the New Testament as Scripture since they do not believe Jesus was the Messiah, the Son of God, who rose from the dead. For many Jews, Jesus was simply a prophet. Jews have a writing that is based upon the Torah but in a sense also reinterprets much of the Old Testament and adds to it. Talmud is the name they give to those writings. Islam accepts some of the Old Testament and New Testament, but only what the Qur'an accepts from both books. The Qur'an basically reinterprets those books for Muslims, and it also adds to it. This writer has discussed those things in detail in his previous book: *Reading and Understanding the Old Testament: The Foundation of Judaism, Christianity, and Islam.*

This writer's methodology is from the perspective of Catholicism and main line Protestantism, and those who call themselves moderate Evangelical, but it is not from the perspective of the Fundamentalist churches, or even the approach of some of the more conservative Evangelical churches. The difference centers on methods of approaching the Bible and interpreting it. This writer does believe the Bible to be inspired of God, and he does take the Bible seriously but not always literally as defined by Fundamentalists and some conservative Evangelicals. Literal does not mean, "The Bible says what it means and means what it says," or "The Bible says it; I believe it; that settles it," meaning there is nothing to interpret. These are two fundamentalist sayings, which this writer rejects because these sayings basically are teaching that there is nothing to interpret.

All writing and all historical writings are interpreted writings. Even as translators change the original writings of Hebrew, Aramaic, and Greek Scripture to English, interpretations are often necessary. Another item of importance is to note that most writers when they discuss Jesus emphasize what his death should mean to his people, but this writer, while including such, will emphasize what his life should mean to his people. This will be understood better as one reads through these writings.

Literal means the author's original sense, or as John Calvin said the plain sense, as an attempt to understand the underlying meaning of what the biblical writers intended. The next step is applying it in today's world in order to better understand and serve God. This includes understanding the history, the different metaphors and literary forms the biblical writers used to express their intention and purpose, and the theology of the writer. Consequently, the New Testament is seen as a living book not a dead historical document. It has as its purpose to tell the truth about God and the truth about ourselves with respect to our relationship with God, ourselves, others that God created, and his created order.

As we read the New Testament we must also keep in mind that the ancient writers did not write history as we moderns write it. Therefore to understand the ancient writers, we must understand their two thousand year old methodology and not try to force our modern day methodologies, ideologies, and historiography onto their writings. In approaching the New Testament it is important to understand that the writings are more concerned with why things happened not how things happened; whereas we moderns are more concerned with the exact details of what and how things happened with its chronology. The Bible is not designed to be an exact history or science book as moderns understand history and science, even though there is basic history in it, and the whole story of God's people is in the context of real history. Exact historical and scientific facts, based on our modern day method of analysis and thinking, was not the way of thinking, methodology, or purpose of ancient writers.

We must also understand that God chose humans to carry his inspired message, and he allowed them to put it into their human forms. Some of the many different types of literature discovered by scholars are the following: historical narratives (stories), actual history, myths, legends (religious myths and legends contain inspired truths), short stories, sermons, genealogies, chronicles, songs, meditations, letters, blessings and curses, legal sayings and codes of law, prophetic sayings, proverbial sayings, poetry and poetic dialogue, gospels, letters, epistles, parables, allegories, hymns, and other forms of literature. Each form of literature contains God's inspired truths. In addition in religious literature literary forms such as myths and legends do not rule out the fact that some actual history may be involved but the stories have been embellished for the same reason that Jesus often spoke in hyperboles.

For certain, we must look at the literary forms in their historical context, and then attempt to analyze the different types of literature authors used in the historical context to establish their purpose and meaning. It is especially important to analyze as far as possible what the particular biblical author is attempting to do, and how he is doing it. Even though the Bible is God inspired, it was still written by human authors, using different styles and different forms of literature in order to express God's inspired theological and religious truths.

In order to understand Scripture, one must understand the world view of those writing and how writings were passed along. There were no printing presses and copy machines, and very few could read and write. The writers were simply responding by faith to God working in their every day lives, and then expressing it in a manner appropriate with their culture. Today we are more concerned with the now, the present, the details of what happened, the chronology of something, and the immediate cause and effect. In that era they were more concerned with underlying meanings and ultimate purposes. The biblical writers wrote to preserve the teachings and actions of Jesus and the first apostles and their converts as they planted and dealt with the newly formed churches. Their writings are faith documents based within an historical context to show that God is working his plan in history.

We must always keep in mind that the Bible is not a book to tell us everything we would like to know but to give us what we need to know. It is important to emphasize that the Bible is primarily a book of faith, spiritual direction, a type of catechism, a book of theological and religious truths embedded in the context of the lives of real people. Therefore look more for the essential religious truths, the theological and moral themes, the virtues and values God approves, and vices not approved, as well as God's overall vision, rather than a detailed chronology, exact historical description of events, exact rules to follow, and personal ideologies or moralisms.

There are many issues that have developed in today's world to which the Bible does not give exact answers, but it does give us a way to begin to think through new issues and find answers. The promise is that the Spirit will lead the church. Some examples of a few modern day issues not mentioned in the Bible are the following: genetic issues such as determining the sex of a child, artificial insemination, surrogate parenting, same sex marriages and their adoption of children, organ transplants, artificial life support, abortion, contraception, euthanasia, just warfare, plus many other modern day issues.

A shock to most people is that the Bible does not even mention abortion, contraception, and euthanasia. In order to declare them sinful, it is necessary to assume God wants life in all instances, and then carry that assumption over to abortion, contraception and even euthanasia. That is not saying that those things are wrong, but it is pointing out what is biblical content and what is not, and how some groups reach their conclusions. Those facts do not mean there are no answers, but the truth must be faced that the Bible, including the New Testament, does not give exact answers to all of life's problems.

Serious study and thought need to be given by people in the

churches as well as the churches in consultation with each other as they stay open to the Holy Spirit in seeking answers to new issues that develop. Sometimes answers take years.

We will also see that many of the Bible's teachings will adapt and develop. In order to understand these writings as well as to apply them to our lives today, we need to see and understand their development within different contexts, and understand that some of the issues are no longer issues. Also, we need to understand that even though numerous issues in our world today are not dealt with in the Bible, the virtues, values, and principles of how to deal with today's issues in most cases are there.

It is important to understand that the Gospels were written after the Apostle Paul's writings. The Apostle Paul writing in the AD fifties and sixties was earlier than the writings of Matthew, Mark, Luke, and John. Most of the writings of Paul as well as Peter, James, and John are letters to churches dealing with local, situational happenings. Even though there are many things in those letters that apply to believers of all ages, it is dangerous to isolate verses and create timeless laws from everything read in these books. It is also important to note that there are issues Paul, Peter, James, and John wrote about that are never mentioned by the later gospel writers. That does not mean these issues should be ignored, but it is important to be careful, and remember that all things are summed up in loving God and neighbor. This is just one reason to study Scripture in groups with those educated in Scripture and methods of interpretation.

As the reader goes through the books and chapters of the New Testament exact verses that contain the information discussed will be used. This is done with the hope that the reader will get a sense of the Scriptures themselves, and at times open the Bible, turn to the chapter, and read the account, or at least some of the account in more detail and even meditate and reflect upon it.

There is no better way to learn about the Bible and be confronted by God's word than by actually reading it. Even though the purpose is to acquaint the novice reader with the Bible's content, this writer's goal is also to have readers eventually get into the books and read them for themselves. Most important this book will be ideal for group Bible study. The biblical books do not need to be read and studied in order.

This writer will have an introduction to each of the books that gives the essence of each book. Therefore in addition to reading through the book there are other options. The introductions to all the books can be read first in order to get a sense of what each book is about. Then, one can go back to a more in depth reading of the books to learn about their details. Finally, one can then go to the Bible itself and read it in an in depth manner. None of this needs to be done all at once, but accomplished at one's level of readiness, as one builds upon portions of knowledge gained. This book can also be used as a reference guide.

Reading and Understanding the Acts of the Apostles, the New Testament Letters, and the book of Revelation is also designed to enable the instructor of Scripture, or the leader of Bible study, or the adult or young adult church school teacher, to take all of the students through a book while the students follow using different translations of the Bible. In that way the student gets more familiar with the biblical text. This text book then becomes a secondary resource while the Bible is the primary resource. The instructor and the student can also use this book together as the instructor takes the student through its different parts.

Depending on the level of the students, the instructor may want to use the text as a reading assignment to discuss during class time. This writer has used all of these methods at many different levels, including adult church studies, as well as at the college and university level where he taught over a thirty year period. The way this book is structured is basically the way this writer taught Biblical Studies courses, always insisting the students be exposed to the actual verses of Scripture. This writer is convinced that there is a basic lack of understanding of Scripture because too many have no experience in using a Bible, never really experiencing the Scripture verses in context. They may have read portions of some of the books and heard sermons on different ideas, themes, and Scriptures, but never experienced the books as a whole for themselves. This writer is convinced that it is important for learners to experience the New Testament books for themselves, which is why this book is structured as it is.

Also, it must be stated that where this writer learned much of his information over the years is no longer remembered. Much of it is taken from professors in different courses as well as personal readings. The bibliography is an attempt to give credit to the information gleaned from personal study. Over the years many of the things learned were written into different Bibles and included within notes used in teaching.

These notes, accumulated over the years, usually do not cite the exact resources from which they came. This writer does not take much credit for original thinking about the text, other than the way this text is put together and the personal applications. He apologizes when something in this text is taken from someone else and could not remember where it came from. Hopefully, at the least, it is included in the bibliography. A special appreciation is for the writings of N T Wright, James D G Dunn, Allen Verhey, Jim Wallis, Luke Timothy Johnson, Marcus Borg and many challenging Protestant and Roman Catholic biblical scholars. In some places within the text, rather than long, numerous footnotes and endnotes, parentheses will be used to refer to the author listed in the bibliography of sources. This is done in order to produce easier reading for beginning students not yet ready to examine long footnotes.

Most of the modern day applications of these verses are the thinking of this author. It is how the author applies Scriptures to the times in which we live. It is not expected that everyone will agree, but they are the thoughts and opinions of the author used to help the reader to begin to think about modern day applications. It will make for good classroom discussion as to why students agree or disagree with the author's comments on the Scriptures.

It would be nice to be able to write an objective account without any bias or presuppositions, but pure objectivity by anyone is not possible. Even so, this author has attempted to read the Scriptures inductively, and as objectively as possible, and apply them to our modern era. The goal is to go only where the biblical verses lead attempting to view things today as Christ would. It is the author's hope that the reader will do the same, and when there is disagreement, let the discussion stay with reasoning based upon Scripture.

The author does believe the Scriptures are still alive and will illuminate its readers. Even though this book is about how many Christians think about the New Testament, one does not have to be a Christian to benefit from this book. A non-Christian will learn how many Christians understand their religion. For those who are Christians, group study is highly encouraged. This is so one can bounce ideas off others and have direction from church leaders, especially those who can lead students to think more deeply about the different verses and relate them to the vast storehouse of thinking contained in the church throughout its long history.

In this work when this writer gives the Scripture or the sense of Scripture, the *New Revised Standard Version* is used. This version is acceptable to Roman Catholics, the Orthodox, and numerous Protestant groups, especially the mainline Protestant Church. Other than the biblical text, capitalization and spelling used in this writer's comments are from the *Society of Biblical Literature (SBL) Handbook of Style for Ancient Near Eastern, Biblical and Early Christian Studies.* As one reads it will be noticeable that the different Bible translations use their own system of capitalization, punctuation, and style that is sometimes very different from both the SBL Handbook and contemporary style. One example is the capitalization of (Sabbath). The SBL Handbook uses a capital S, but the NRSV does not capitalize (sabbath). The same is with the word Scripture, which is capitalized in the SBL Handbook but not so in the NRSV (scripture).

Because much of what is written is basically to highlight what the Bible says, there will not be quotation marks when the Letters are quoted. This may be somewhat rare, but according to the *Chicago Manuel of Style* (14th Edition) under alternatives to quotation marks it is acceptable. The reader will be able to tell most of the time what is from Scripture. Often what is quoted follows the word, say or said. The chapter and verses will always be noted in order for the reader to examine. Many times the reader will see a parenthesis ( ) with a number inside which will indicate the verse or verses referenced. This approach is taken in the belief that constantly looking at pages filled with quotation marks is too cumbersome for the reader as well as the writer. But where quotation marks are used in Scripture, they will be used in this book.

Dr Thomas B. Lane

NECESSARY BACKGROUND
RELATED TO
INTERPRETATION ISSUES

The New Testament is probably the most revered book in the modern world, but like the Old Testament its real contents are basically unknown and little understood by the masses of people. This may be considered an affront by people who have heard sermons most of their lives, but listening to sermons does not necessarily mean one is now educated in the Bible. It may mean one is educated only in certain parts and certain verses of the Bible. Or it may mean one is educated in a certain clergyperson's understanding of certain verses. Although different people do interpret Scripture in different ways, for serious Christian scholars of Scripture, even though there are differences, there is much agreement on basic content.

The Old Testament includes many different authors covering a period of approximately fifteen hundred or more years. The New Testament is a collection of twenty-seven books written by different authors over a period of about fifty years. The New Testament covers about one hundred years, the first century AD. The first book was written in the early AD fifties and the last one in the AD nineties.

This is the time the Roman Empire controlled most of the known world including the area known as the Holy Land, later named Palestine by the Romans.

The Old Testament focuses on the nation of Israel while the New Testament focuses on a person belonging to that nation, Jesus the Christ, a Jew, who Scripture says was crucified and rose from the dead, and then established a church to which all nations are called. Christ is a Greek word meaning Anointed, while the Hebrew word for Anointed is Messiah. His first name is Jesus, but his last name is not really Christ, even though some write as though it is. He is Jesus the Christ. The first Christians who were Jews believed he was the Christ, the Anointed, the Messiah.

The word testament means covenant or law. So new and old covenants have to do with agreements God has made with his people. The old covenant was basically for one nation, and according to Jews there is still only one covenant. They are still looking for the Messiah and the new covenant. But according to Christians, Jesus, the Messiah, initiated the new covenant for a new age. This new age is to be permeated by the kingdom of God that has broken into the world with Jesus and will grow and spread like a mustard seed until he comes again to make it complete. All people of all nations are invited to participate.

There was a need for a new covenant for a number of reasons, one is that the teachings and prophecy in the first covenant needed to be fulfilled or brought to completion. Another reason is that the Jews failed in their mission to bring God and his message to all the peoples of the world. In fact they had developed a system that kept the people of the nations from being part of God's people. The people of Judea were actually separating themselves from the world to the point that God's people and the nation had become completely isolated from the world.

God had called his people to be a light shining in the darkness, a city set upon the hill, and to make God's light known to the world, but his people rejected God's mission. Their attitude was expressed in the prophet Jonah, who detested the foreigners God sent him to preach repentance to. God's people were to inform the world who God is and what his message is, and to be a moral example to the people of the world. They were not to become like the pagans but a beacon of light for them. Unfortunately, they refused the mission God gave them.

The new covenant for people of all nations was prophesied in the Old Testament, especially through Jeremiah (31:31-34) and Ezekiel (36:22-29, 37:24-28). The Gospel writers inform us that through Jesus the new covenant and the new age are beginning. This does not mean that all aspects of the old are thrown away. For example, the vision is still there as are the virtues, values, and many of the principles retained. The idea in Genesis 17:6-8 that I will be your God and you will be my people is also retained. All things will now be summed up in and through the words and actions of Jesus.

The first four books of the New Testament, Matthew, Mark, Luke, and John are called the Gospels. Gospel is a word meaning good news. The good news is that God's kingdom is now breaking into the world through Jesus. The good news is that Christ, the Messiah, the expected Davidic king has come (Ezekiel 37:24-28). Jews from the second temple onward, the time of Ezra and Nehemiah, including all the post-exilic writings, believed as long as they were dominated by a foreign power, they were still in exile, and the sins of the nation had not been forgiven (Daniel 9, Ezra 9, and Nehemiah 9). This was so even though the Assyrian and Babylonian exiles were over, and they were living in their own land.

The good news is that the old is passing away, a new age has begun, the new kingdom is breaking into the world, just as the prophets foretold. The nation's sins are forgiven, the exile is over, God has returned to his people. The problem is that none of it happens in the manner they thought it would. The disciples will integrate Jesus' interpretation of the prophets with the church, which after the death of Jesus becomes the announcer of the kingdom.

The church will then take the place of the nation of Israel as the new Israel of God. Christ will be the new Torah and new temple where God's presence lives, and where sins are forgiven. From Jerusalem of Judea the message of good news will be proclaimed throughout the world. The New Testament letters will tell the story of the church and its development. Most of the letters are written to specific churches about specific issues occurring in the early church.

It is important to note that this kingdom begins with Jesus. Its official beginning seems to be confirmed in two parts with the fulfillment of two of his prophecies. After Jesus' death and resurrection, he goes to the right hand of the Father and sends the Holy Spirit to his disciples as he said he would. This happens on the day of Pentecost when Peter preaches the first sermon and three thousand are baptized. On this day the Spirit is deposited within the church (Acts chapter 2).

Then in AD 70 Jesus' second major prophecy is fulfilled when Rome destroys Jerusalem and the temple with its sacrificial system. This opens the way for the rapid advancement of Christianity. The Jews will have to reorganize, and the Judaism that develops will be mainly through the activity of the Pharisees and the development of a religion without the temple. The other Jewish groups seem to disappear with the destruction of Jerusalem and the temple.

Jesus had warned the people to change their violent agenda toward Rome, or they would be destroyed. With the fall of the great city and the temple Jesus' prophecy is confirmed and he is vindicated. It will take Judaism a long time to recover. In the meantime the Jewish Christians with their kingdom and Jewish King Jesus will invite Gentiles into the new kingdom, and the movement will greatly expand. The Father will now attempt to rule the world through his Son and the kingdom he establishes. Jesus tells his followers that he came to preach the kingdom (Lk 4:43), and after his death and resurrection he sends his followers out to continue his mission. The New Testament letters will describe the events that take place as they continue his mission of expanding the kingdom.

Colossians 1:13-14 says, He (God) has rescued us from the power of darkness and transferred us into the kingdom of his beloved Son, in whom we have redemption, the forgiveness of sins. This new beginning and hope for a sinful world that involves transformation and renewal of both individuals and the world in which they live, just as the prophets described, will be completed when Christ returns and all things are made new. This is good news, and the beginning of the transformation. It all centers around Jesus and the kingdom he came to preach (Lk 4:43, 9:62). It must be noted that the kingdom is not just about eternal life in the future; it is about abundant life now (Jn 10:10). It is about renewal of individuals and the world and its institutions now. It is about God's plan, the kingdom, being put into operation until Christ comes again to complete the plan, making all things new. This is the story of the New Testament letters.

The first four books of the New Testament, Matthew, Mark, Luke, and John, called the Gospels are the topic of the second book in this series on the Bible. Even though each has its own emphasis, they are four complementary accounts of the life and teachings of Jesus. The topic of this third book is what follows the life, death, and resurrection of Jesus. It begins with the book of Acts, which is a brief history of the beginning, development, and spread of the early church. Acts is followed by letters to the newly established churches from Paul, Peter, James and John, usually dealing with situational problems, even though there are many principles that can be taken and applied to life today. The New Testament writings contain the heart and core of Christianity.

It must be remembered that most of the New Testament letters were written before the Gospels. Paul writes the first New Testament book when he writes to the Thessalonians in the early 50s AD with the rest of his books written from 52-66 AD. That means thirty five years pass before the first gospel is written, which is the Gospel of Mark and approximately twenty years pass before Paul writes his first letter.

During that period of time, what Jesus said and did was mainly being passed on orally in narrative and drama form. It is thought that the accounts of the trial, crucifixion, and resurrection accounts were probably passed on from community to community in play acting form. All four Gospels are faith accounts and remembrances of what Jesus said and did, even though when put into writing they are biographies as defined by the ancient world. The four Gospels all have a different theological emphasis even though they are united in telling the same basic story. Their similarities are as important as their differences.

Matthew, Mark, and Luke are called Synoptic Gospels because they are similar. In one sense they describe Jesus from the point of view leading up to the crucifixion and resurrection emphasizing a view of Jesus from his human side. Scholars call this a Christology from below. John's gospel views Jesus from his divine side emphasizing his divinity from a more theological and mystically oriented position. John looks at Jesus more from this side of the crucifixion and resurrection. Scholars call this a Christology from above. Both sides are true yet different.

Before the Gospels were written, the teachings and actions of Jesus circulated orally and in writing for thirty-five plus years. It is during this time that the Letters were written. This author believes there were many more oral sources than written sources. Then bits and pieces began to be put into writing. How the written sources originated and came together to form the written Gospels and the Letters is called Source Criticism. How the oral forms originated and came together is called Form Criticism. Criticism is just another word for analysis. The four evangelists collected the oral and written pieces and combined them into the Gospels. Tradition Criticism attempts to trace how the different forms developed until finally written. Textual Criticism is making sure we have the best Greek text available for the complete New Testament. The New Testament writings were all in the Greek language, the main language of the Roman Empire.

Rhetorical and Literary Criticism seek to analyze the different literary forms the writers of the New Testament used in putting their writing together. It seeks to understand the different literary forms and their purpose as well as who wrote them, to whom, why, when and how. This leads to Canonical Criticism, which analyzes how it all fits together into a unity and the whole of Scripture. Then scholars seek to discover how much of the book is written by a single author, and how much of the book is edited, and what the particular emphasis is of the author or editors. Each of the four Gospels and the Letters has its own point of view adapted to the special groups to whom they are writing. The study of how the writers and editors used what they had and for what purpose is called Redaction Criticism.

It is also interesting to note that none of the Gospels tell us who the writer is. It was later that the early Christians added the names Matthew, Mark, Luke, and John to the writings. It is different for the letters where the writer is identified. Another interesting point is that the chapters and verses were not added until the Middles Ages. In fact everything was in capital letters, and there was no punctuation, which makes adding the chapters, verses, and punctuation a human effort that involves not only translation from Greek to English but also interpretation. A quick example explains. The text would be as follows. The Hebrew or Greek text is written GODISNOWHERE. Is that to be translated God is now here, or God is nowhere?

For the most part the Bible is basically a narrative, a story supporting a particular world view through the use of history, literature, and theology. Understanding the history, literature, and theology are also interpretation issues. All history, and all literature, and all theology are interpretive issues, which is why it is important to study the Bible with a learned believer associated with a church community. The writings of Paul, John, Peter and James are basically situational writing, while Luke the writer of Acts is an historical narrative; the writers are both preserving the core of Christianity and dealing with particular problems in the churches of that time.

Studying the Bible in the university has both advantages and disadvantages. In doing so it must be noted that most university professors are historians, anthropologists, or sociologists, and not theologians. Therefore they are not really concerned with faith and often times do not believe the Scriptures are God inspired, or if they do, it is not their concern. Most of them are trained only in the methods of modern scientific history. In their study of the Bible, most are only concerned with research in a very narrow area and are not really interested with how things fit together for inspired, theological purposes. If anyone is interested, the bibliography includes numerous sources that explore in detail these different issues, criticisms, and translation issues. Their emphasis is not all bad, for it does serve a very important historical purpose, but it usually has little benefit and even less interest for the beginning student or the average person who takes his religion and spiritual development seriously and is taking the course to add understanding to faith.

Because, in many situations the study of religion does not include the faith aspect and how people's faith influences their decisions, we remain basically illiterate in understanding the faith of different people, how it affects their thinking and their lives, and why people do what they do. This also is a major reason that many mistakes in U. S. foreign policy and world affairs have been made.

For those of faith, Christians believe the New Testament Scriptures are inspired by the Holy Spirit as the word of God, but they do not always agree on what inspiration exactly means. Even so, these Scriptures are written in the Greek language by humans using their own personal style. They are not magical books dropped from heaven written in sixteenth century King James English as the uneducated seem to think. As we explore these different forms of analysis in a practical way the reader will better understand the New Testament Gospels and Letters. Understanding the different Christian approaches to the inspiration and infallibility of Scripture is thoroughly explored in a book by Gabe Fackre, *The Christian Story: Authority of Scripture, vol 2.*

As one reads through the New Testament, the serious reader will see what appear to be numerous differences and what are called apparent contradictions. Many of these, center on small details in describing incidents. In attempting to explain those differences, we will understand that ancient writers in an oral society did not write history as we moderns do. Again, this writer emphasizes that the Bible is not meant to be a history book as we moderns understand history, even though basic history is involved. Quite often the problem appears when one attempts to understand what was said in an ancient culture through the thinking and practices of one's current culture. This is one major way Scripture is misinterpreted.

In looking at these differences, we will also notice how humans see things from different perspectives, and how this has its positive aspects. It is also important to understand that the writings of Scripture are both human and divine, and they do not always fit into a neat little package of rational analysis. Jesus and the Bible are considered both divine and human, even at times mystical. We humans have difficulty dealing with that concept. The perfect God inspired a message through imperfect people, and in the process let them free to express God's inspired message through their imperfections. Humans sometimes have difficulty dealing with that idea. Because it is God's word, they want to make the human aspect of the writing perfect also.

It is also true that at the same time God is near us, he is also beyond us. Here we have two opposite ideas integrated. This is a mystery. Unfortunately, because of the Age of Enlightenment, scientific rationalism is the main methodology that many university scholars are concerned with, which eliminates the mystical, the theological, and the miraculous. This also leads to a distortion and misinterpretation of God's word. In order to attempt to interpret the meaning of the original writers, it is important to integrate the historical, the literary, and the theological. Remember that the original writers were first of all theologians, and they were very human.

It may sound like this author opposes the work of university scholars in their historical and scientific methods, but that is not true. They serve a very important need. It is important to verify as much history as possible in order to show that faith is based in reality, but scientific history has a difficult time dealing with mystery, the miraculous, and theological issues. Again, one must realize the purpose of many university professors is not to promote faith, even though some may have faith.

This writer's point is that there are many factors to be taken into consideration in order to better understand and make sense of the Scriptures. We must deal with the fact that God is also mystery, and the writers of the Scriptures used different forms of literature to express their teachings and theology. Along with this thinking is the theological diversity in the Bible. The New Testament documents not only express a variety of New Testament themes, but sometimes they speak in different ways on the same theme. As we will see sometimes a statement is true in one situation but not so in another. Understanding how a different verse in a different context functions is important. It is like the root of a tomato plant that produces a number of different tomatoes; they all come from the same root, but are not always the same.

Context of a particular theme or verse in its different situations is the key to understanding, and is why it is dangerous to take anything out of context to prove a point. Because of these numerous factors, anyone interested in learning the Scriptures from a deeper perspective needs to study in a group with a leader who is informed and takes the Scriptures seriously. To read or study the Bible by oneself is fine for spiritual and meditation purposes, but it can result in the distortion of the intended meaning of Scripture.

Stanley Hauerwas (1993, 15-18) believes that when individual American Christians read and interpret the Bible without instruction from a qualified instructor apart from the church, manipulation and distortion will be the norm and not the exception. It is easy for the Bible to become a vehicle for a person's presuppositions, religion, ideology, politics, and social concerns that are quite different from the religion, politics, economics, and social concerns expressed within the Scriptures. Actually what happens in America is that many readers read their culture of democratic freedom and capitalism and other interests into the Scriptures that say nothing about those issues. When that happens, the Scriptures become distorted, and then they are used mainly for one's current politics, economics, social engineering, and ideology. In interpreting Scripture, context is of utmost importance.

As stated it is fact the there is much diversity in Scripture. George Forell in his book titled *The Protestant Faith* (1989, 57-61) explains that some of the diversity is best explained or understood by a concept borrowed from physics known as the principle of complementarity. Briefly stated, it means that the various ideas or pictures used to describe systems of atoms are adequate to certain experiments, yet mutually exclusive. For example, an atom can be described as a planetary system or as a nucleus surrounded by waves, whose frequency is decisive. These different pictures are complementary to each other. While they seem to contradict each other, they are both correct if used properly. Similarly, in theology we often get at the truth by saying two things simultaneously that seen on the surface seem to be contradictory, but the difference helps us to get a deeper insight into the Christian message.

In a book titled *God was in Christ* by D M Baillie (1948, 109-110) he sums up the idea perfectly. Baillie says, The attempt to put our experience of God into theological statements is something like the attempt to draw a map of the world on a flat surface, the page of an atlas. It is impossible to do this without a certain degree of falsification, because the surface of the earth is a spherical surface whose pattern can not be produced accurately on a plane. And yet the map must be drawn for convenience's sake. Therefore an atlas meets the problem by giving us two different maps of the world which can be compared to each other. The one is contained in two circles representing two hemispheres. The other is contained in an oblong, Mercator projection. Each is a map of the whole world, and they contradict each other to some extent in every point. Yet they both are needed, and taken together they correct each other.

The different projections would be either misleading or mystifying to anyone who did not know that in their different ways they represent the surface of a sphere. But they can serve their useful purpose for anyone who understands that they are intended simply to represent in portable form the pattern covering the surface of this round earth which one knows in actual experience.

The point is to illustrate that the Bible is somewhat limited in what it says because it is written in human words. That does not mean we can not understand it, but it does mean that we have to use words in different ways in different situations in order to try to understand the full truth. On this side of the divide we will never see or understand completely or perfectly. Now we see in part; we see in a mirror dimly, but then we will see face to face (1 Cor 15:12-13).

So it is with the paradoxes of faith which often involve mystery. They are inevitable, not because the divine reality is self-contradictory, but because when we objectify it into an either-or analysis, all our judgments are in some measure falsified. The higher truth which reconciles them cannot always be fully expressed in words, though it is experienced and lived in the I-Thou relationship of faith towards God. Eliminating the mystery only falsifies and complicates the issue more.

The following are some biblical examples: The two creation accounts in Genesis where the emphasis in one is the transcendent God who is beyond all, while the emphasis in the other is the immanent God who is very near to us, even within us. Other examples are the Bible is human, the Bible is divine; God is love,

God is wrath; God is just, God is merciful; do not judge but there are times when judgments must be made; God has predestined, or God is sovereign, yet humans have free will; Jesus is divine, Jesus is human; God is Father, God is Son, and God is the Holy Spirit; salvation is by grace through faith and is a gift of God as stressed in Jn 3:16, Rom 3:19-26, and Gal 2:16, and salvation is by obedience and works as stressed in Mt 7:21, 25:31-46, Jn 3:36, Jas 2:14-24, Lk 10:25-28, Rev 22:12. Christ came to save the world not to judge the world Jn 3:17-18, but Christ also came to judge the world Jn 12:48, Lk 19:11-28, Mk 8:38.

Leonard Sweet (1994, 31) in Edmund Keller's book *Some Paradoxes of Paul* notes the response to Jesus' ministry in Lk 5:26, "We have seen strange things today," literally translates as, "We have seen paradoxes today." The sixteenth century reformer Sebastian Frank built his theology on the 280 paradoxes he found within the Bible. Niels Bohr, nuclear physicist and Nobel Laureate said, "No paradox, no progress." The early Christians talked about strength in weakness (2 Cor 12:9), living through dying (Jn 12:24), wisdom through foolishness (1 Cor 1:25), self-confidence by self-emptying (Phil 2:7-9), losing self to find self (Mt 10:39), exaltation in humility (Mt 23:12), seeing by looking at the unseen (2 Cor 4:18). Finding truth is negotiating the paradoxes.

They seem to be contradictions, but they are not. It is not a matter of picking one and ignoring the other as some religious groups do. First of all, it is a matter of reading what is said in context. The four Gospels are an excellent example of how the principle of complementarity can function. Some see all this as contradictory, but only because they are not educated in the nature of Scripture and understanding the importance of context and how to interpret it. They refuse to see Scripture as the inspired word of God. That does not mean everyone must see everything exactly the same, but there is much that can be agreed on, and even historically verified. The close reader will notice numerous differences as the Gospels are read. The challenge is how to make sense of these inspired differences.

In the previous comparisons we have a picture of opposites that historically have divided believers and non-believers, as well as dividing the different religious groups. One side is chosen as the truth while the opposite is ignored like it does not exist. The problem seems to be simplistic thinking while wanting to force God's truth or non-truth into preconceived notions or narrow boxes, as well as attempting to eliminate all mystery from Scripture. In our modern scientifically ordered society that tends to de-emphasize the humanities and the arts, we humans tend to attempt to fit everything into a rational logic that can be scientifically controlled.

The principle of complementarity says that there is truth in both ends of paired opposites. Both are needed to get the complete or total picture. They must be taken together in their different contexts, and they correct each other by integrating the opposite ends. The extreme ends that sometimes abuse the truth are defused, and one is able to get a deeper insight into the whole message. Often, a higher or deeper truth reconciles the paradox which sometimes is difficult to put into human words, but can be explained to some extent by thinking about the different map projections as noted. Ideas such as this are important in understanding the New Testament. In the end we are still dealing with the mystery of God.

By focusing on only one aspect, the total picture is missed. The different details expressed in the birth accounts, the trial and crucifixion accounts, and the resurrection accounts can be compared to an automobile accident where three people see it, but they all see it from a different angle or perspective. When they are called into court to explain what happened, their stories seem to conflict. Is one person telling the truth, and the other not telling the truth? Most of the time the answer is no, they simply saw the accident from different perspectives, and add things they believe are important. Or even in telling the story they highlight different perspectives, sometimes because of their own presuppositions. It takes someone else looking at the total picture and the different contexts to put things together. Humans see things through different lens, but as they do, the basic truth is there, if they are open to see it.

Understanding that these Scriptures are from a basic oral culture, a culture totally different from twenty-first century America, a culture that knew nothing about the individualism of a representative democratic republic or capitalism, and knew nothing or very little about a middle class, the main issues or major truths are more easily discovered. In understanding Scripture one can not view the culture of the ancients by forcing twenty-first century issues upon it.

The New Testament letters may be read in any order without having to read from front to back, but this book will present them in order beginning with the book of Acts, which was written by Luke, who is the writer of the Gospel of Luke. In fact the book of Acts is a sequel to his gospel. It is a story about those who had no idea that Jesus would rise from the dead, but when he did, they spent their lives advancing his mission willing to put their lives on the line to do his will.

Dr Thomas B. Lane

ACTS OF THE APOSTLES

This is the second volume of Luke's two volume work. The first is titled the Gospel of Luke. The book of Acts is about the beginning and development of the church. In chapter 1 after the resurrection Jesus ascends to the Father, but before he ascends he tells the apostles to wait in Jerusalem, for he will send the Holy Spirit upon them. The book's real title could be the Acts of the Holy Spirit, for it is the Holy Spirit who does the acting by working through the apostles. In chapter 2 the Spirit falls upon the church on the Day of Pentecost and they are all filled with the Spirit and speak in languages that Jews from different parts of the world can understand. Peter gives the first sermon concerning Jesus' death and resurrection. The people, who are all Jews, ask what they are to do. He tells them to repent and be baptized for the forgiveness of sins and receive the gift of the Holy Spirit. Three thousand respond, and the church begins. This is the official day for the beginning of the church.

In chapter 3 the apostles go out into the known world preaching the *Kerygma*, which is the death, burial, resurrection, and return of Christ in judgment. He is the Messiah, the one promised to come from a descendent of King David. The apostles are given the power to perform miracles just as Christ did.

In chapter 4 the authorities are annoyed because the apostles are teaching that Jesus rose from the dead. The authorities arrest the apostles and warn them to stop preaching, but they reply that they can not stop preaching their message. Eventually they are released, and when gathered with their friends, they pray for the boldness to keep preaching. The first Christians held all things in common, and there were no needy among them.

In chapter 5 Ananias and his wife lie about giving everything to the common purse and consequently are struck dead for lying to the Holy Spirit. Then Peter and some of the apostles are arrested again, and they are warned again to stop teaching and preaching the resurrection. Their answer is they are to obey God, not human authority. In the meantime the number of disciples is multiplying.

In chapter 6 deacons are established to serve the needs of the people, so the apostles can spend time in prayer, teaching, and preaching. In chapter 7 Stephen, a deacon and the first martyr, is killed, and Saul, a Jew trained to be a Pharisee, who later becomes the Apostle Paul, holds the coats of those who stone Stephen to death. Because the church experiences persecution in Jerusalem, the Christians scatter to Samaria, Antioch of Syria, and into Asia Minor, today known as Turkey.

In chapter 8 as a result of the persecution the apostles leave Jerusalem and go to other areas to spread the word. In the meantime Philip, another deacon, is directed to an Ethiopian eunuch who is trying to understand the book of Isaiah. Philip teaches him by explaining the Scriptures, and he is baptized.

In chapter 9 Christ appears to Paul and he is blinded as he is on the road to Damascus to persecute Christians. He is led to Damascus by those who are with him. Another believer named Ananias is called by God to heal him and baptize him as a Christian. After a period of time, probably three years, eventually a disciple named

Barnabas takes him to Jerusalem and introduces him to Peter. Many of the Christians in the area are afraid of Paul because of his former reputation; therefore, to let things calm down he is sent to his home area in Tarsus of Cilicia in Asia Minor (Turkey). In the meantime Peter raises a lady named Dorcus from the dead.

In chapter 10 Peter is then sent to preach to a Gentile, a Roman commander named Cornelius, a good man who did much for the Jews. Cornelius has had a vision from God to call Peter to his house. Peter also has a vision to meet Cornelius, and in Peter's vision God tells Peter to eliminate all the Old Testament food laws, for they no longer will be valid. They meet, and after Cornelius listens to Peter's message about Christ, he is the first Gentile to become a Christian by being baptized. Peter is given the responsibility to lead both the first Jews and the first Gentiles to Christ.

In chapter 11 the church in Antioch of Syria becomes a major church. The same Barnabas that introduced Paul to Peter in Jerusalem is called by the church to do mission work, so he goes to Tarsus in Cilicia and takes Paul to Antioch where he spends one year.

In chapter 12 King Herod Agrippa, grandson of Herod the Great, has James the brother of John killed as a martyr, and then he has Peter arrested, but an angel miraculously sets Peter free and leads him to the house of Mary the mother of Mark where they are praying for Peter's release. This is the Mark whose name will be put on the Gospel of Mark. In the meantime Herod dies of a disease brought on by an angel because he delighted in people calling him god.

In chapter 13 the church in Antioch ordains Barnabas and Paul and sends them on a mission trip. They go to Cyprus and the first missionary journey of the Apostle Paul begins. From Cyprus they go into Asia Minor (Turkey) and they plant churches in some key areas. They then go to Perga and Antioch of Pisidia in Asia Minor. They always go into the synagogue first where both Gentiles and Jews listen to them. Always some of each group responds, but some Jews then stir up trouble against them, which causes them to move on to the next area. Meanwhile a small church is usually planted.

In chapter 14 they go to Iconium, Lystra, and Derbe all in Asia Minor. They speak boldly about the death and resurrection of Jesus, and the same pattern occurs. Then they retrace their steps and return to Antioch of Syria.

In chapter 15 they go to Jerusalem to meet with the church leaders. It appears that James the brother of Jesus emerges as the most important leader of the Jerusalem church. Some Jews from Jerusalem who have become Christians decide that Gentiles coming into the church will have to first become Jews by being circumcised and observe the Old Testament food, purity, and Sabbath laws. Obviously they are not aware of Peter's vision, or if so, they dismiss it as a wild dream. Paul rejects this belief and convinces the Council to reject it also, even though a few stipulations are added to appease the Jews, so Jew and Gentile can at least fellowship with one other as Christians.

Paul and Barnabas will go back to Antioch, and then begin a new missionary journey, but they split with each other and go in opposite paths. Barnabas will take John Mark with him. He is the later writer of the Gospel of Mark and had gone with them on the first missionary journey. Apparently, on that journey he became homesick and went home. At this time Paul does not believe Mark is worthy to go on another missionary journey, which is why Barnabas takes him, and they go in different directions. This breach will be healed later. This split is a good thing for more places are evangelized. Paul will go with Silas, one of the leaders in Jerusalem, who is sent with Paul to explain the ruling that Gentiles do not

need to be circumcised and become a Jew, and then follow the
Jewish food laws in order to become a Christian.

In chapter 16 and through the rest of the book of Acts, Luke,
the writer of both the Gospel of Luke and the Acts of the Apostles
will concentrate on Paul, Timothy, and Titus. Paul and some of the
disciples will go back into Asia Minor (Turkey) ordaining elders to
carry on the work. Then they find Timothy in Lystra who will join
them. As previously stated the pattern continues to repeat itself.
They first preach in the synagogues to the Jews and when rejected,
they speak to the Gentiles. Many are converted, and a church is
planted. But Paul and those with him are greatly persecuted, and
they are jailed numerous times.

After (Asia Minor) they go into Greece where churches are
planted in Philippi, Thessalonica, Beroea, Athens, and Corinth.
Wherever they go, the same pattern is repeated; they are persecuted
both physically and mentally. Paul goes on three main missionary
journeys, and then he returns to Jerusalem where he is arrested
again and jailed for two years. Then, because he is a Roman citizen
he is able to go to Rome to appeal his case to the Emperor. There he
will eventually be put to death. Even so the church is planted from
Jerusalem as far as Europe, and Christianity is well on its way. Some
believe Paul was set free in Rome, and then went to Spain and other
areas before he was again imprisoned in Rome and put to death
with Peter. But it is very difficult to know for sure.

Acts is a theological history, which is a form of history different
from what the modern world is used to seeing. Peter is the hero
in the first part of the book and Paul the second part. There are
18 speeches in Acts making up one-forth of the book. All these
speeches center on the crucified and risen Christ. One time in
particular Peter and his friends are threatened by the authorities
with death for preaching that there is no salvation outside of Christ,

and their answer is, "We must obey God rather than man." Let us go back to Acts chapter one and look in more detail at what took place after the resurrection of Jesus the Messiah.

The question many ask is why were these early Christians persecuted and made martyrs for the first three hundred years of Christianity? One answer is the Jews persecuted them for religious reasons, but that is not the only reason there were so many martyrs. The Romans were the reason for most of the martyrs, and the reasons were political.

Many of the Roman emperors claim to be a god. They are to be worshiped as the lord and savior who brings peace to the kingdom, which is the Roman Empire. But now the followers of Christ are going throughout the empire preaching that the kingdom of God has now broken in upon the earth and there is a new king who is the real Lord and Savior. This true Lord and Savior is bringing peace to the earth with no violence, which is contrary to the way the Roman emperor makes and keeps peace. And the kingdom of the real Lord and Savior which has already broken into the world will have no end.

When the emperors, who are not interested in any regime change, hear this message they become very concerned. It is for this same reason that the leaders put Jesus to death. When the leaders of Rome see the values of the kingdom of God challenging the values of the worldly kingdom of Rome, sparks fly. This is especially so when they see throngs of people being converted to Christ and the teachings of his kingdom. The ground is set for much martyrdom. With so many people becoming Christians, idol worship begins to diminish. This becomes an economic issue because a major part of a town's economy is built around the temples and shrines of the many pagan gods and most important it is built around the temples and shrines to honor the emperor. When what is preached comes into conflict with the economy of a local area, problems will surface. An example illustrating the issue is chapter 19:8-41.

◈

Acts chapter 1:1-3 says, In the first book, Theophilus, I wrote about all that Jesus did and taught from the beginning until the day when he was taken up to heaven, after giving instructions through the Holy Spirit to the apostles whom he had chosen. After his suffering he presented himself alive to them by many convincing proofs appearing to them forty days and speaking to them about the kingdom of God.

After proving to his apostles that he has risen from his crucifixion he emphasizes the importance of the kingdom. Luke 4:43 has Jesus coming into the world and stating that to preach the good news of the kingdom of God is the purpose of his coming. The kingdom of God is explained in detail in this author's book titled *Reading and Understanding the Gospels: Who Jesus Is, What He Teaches, and the Beginning of Christianity.*

Since the Acts of the Apostles is Luke's second volume, let us look at how Luke begins the Gospel of Luke in his first volume. Luke chapter 1:1-4 says, Since many have undertaken to set down an orderly account of the events that have been fulfilled among us (promises of Scripture are fulfilled), just as they were handed on to us by those who from the beginning were eyewitnesses and servants of the word, I too decided, after investigating everything carefully from the very first, to write an orderly account for you, most excellent Theophilus, so that you may know the truth concerning the things about which you have been instructed.

Luke in addition to being a physician is a serious historian in the ancient sense. Luke tells us that the writers of the Gospels used sources of information that can no longer be located. Luke is saying his information was received from eyewitnesses who also taught and preached the word and that his account is an orderly account. What he means by an orderly account is not certain. Possibly he is indicating that from all the different oral and written accounts circulating, he is putting themes and chronology together more thoroughly.

Luke is telling us he is a second generation Christian like his readers. He writes in classical Greek which indicates he is an educated convert like many of his readers who are scattered throughout the Roman Empire. Luke wants to help his non-Jewish converts trace their roots back to the historic Jesus to better understand his actions and teachings, and to follow the growth and development of the early church. He wants everyone to thoroughly understand the gospel's Jewish roots, to see that the new covenant is rooted in the old covenant, and to see that everyone's humanity goes back to Adam.

In both volumes he writes to Theophilus. We do not know exactly who he is. An educated guess is that he is a God-fearer. Those called God-fearers attended a Jewish synagogue because they were tired of the different pagan religions and were impressed with the one God belief and the teachings of the Jews. Most God-fearers had not converted officially to the religion of the Jews, even though they consistently attended the assembly. This writer would imagine that adult circumcision was always somewhat of a hindrance to completing conversion. This gives us a brief origin and purpose of Luke's writing.

Luke continues in Acts with Jesus appearing to the apostles after his resurrection. Acts 1:4-5 says, While staying with them, he (Jesus) ordered them (apostles) not to leave Jerusalem, but to wait there for the promise of the Father. "This," he said, "is what you have heard from me; for John baptized with water, but you will be baptized with the Holy Spirit not many days from now." (John said he baptized with water, but the one to come would baptize with the Holy Spirit, Mk 1:8, Mt 3:11, Lk 3:16, Jn 1:33. Humans can baptize with water, but only Jesus can include the Holy Spirit with water baptism.)

Verses 6-8 say, So when they had come together, they asked him, "Lord, is this the time when you will restore the kingdom to Israel?" He replied, "It is not for you to know the times or the periods that the Father has set by his own authority. But you will receive power when the Holy Spirit has come upon you; and you will be my witnesses in Jerusalem, in all Judea and Samaria, and to the ends of the earth."

Since the Messiah was promised the throne of David in the Old Testament, which was confirmed in Lk 1:32 in the angel's message to Mary, the disciples are wondering when it will take place. They are looking for the finalized political kingdom where the Romans are expelled from the land and the Jews have the political power. Jesus basically tells them to focus on his instructions and wait for the power that will come upon them through the Holy Spirit. But Luke is linking Jesus' answer to the kingdom promised in Daniel 7:13-14 as he describes the ascension of Jesus to the right hand of God in the following verses.

Verses 9-11 say, When he had said this, as they were watching, he was lifted up, and a cloud took him out of their sight. (In Scripture God is often symbolized by clouds. According to Luke this is Jesus' answer to their question. Israel's God is restoring his kingdom to his people as promised in Daniel, but it was not in the way they were expecting. It would be a good idea for the reader to now look up Daniel 7:13-14.)

While he was going and they were gazing up toward heaven, suddenly two men in white robes stood by them. They said, "Men of Galilee, why do you stand looking up toward heaven? This Jesus, who has been taken up from you into heaven, will come in the same way as you saw him go into heaven." (The angel is saying that this Jesus who is Lord and one in being with the Father will return.)

Verses 12-14 say, Then they returned to Jerusalem from the mount called Olivet, which is near Jerusalem, a sabbath day's journey away. When they had entered the city, they went to the room upstairs where they were staying, Peter, and John, and James, and Andrew, Philip and Thomas, Bartholomew and Matthew, James son of Alphaeus, and Simon the Zealot, and Judas son of James. All these were constantly devoting themselves to prayer, together with certain women, including Mary the mother of Jesus, as well as his brothers. (Mary and his brothers, James, Joseph, Simon, and Judas, Mt 13:55, who were formerly skeptics concerning Jesus, are now joined with the apostles.)

In verses 15-20 Luke tells us that sometime during those days Peter speaking to a crowd of one hundred twenty persons said that the scripture had to be fulfilled (Pss 69:25, 109:8) concerning Judas' betrayal as well as the need for someone to take his place. Meanwhile Peter in (18) mentions that Judas died after buying a field with traitor's money by falling headlong, bursting open in the middle and all his bowels gushed out.

Matthew 27:5 says he hanged himself. The differences on how Judas died come from an oral culture passing along stories about Jesus over a fifty year period before Luke puts it in writing. The common agreement is that he took his life. Keep in mind an exact detailed history is not the purpose of ancient writers. God used imperfect people to preserve his inspired message (theology). Verse 19 states that the field was called Hakeldama or Field of Blood.

In verse 20 Peter quotes the Psalms to show all this was foretold, even that another should be appointed to take the place of Judas.

In verses 21-26 Peter says that the replacement has to be someone who was with them from the beginning with John's baptism and who witnessed the resurrection. The choice is narrowed down in (23) between Joseph called Barsabbas, who is also known as Justus, and Matthias. After praying and casting lots, the lot fell to Mathias, and he is added to the eleven apostles. (The symbolism of twelve replaces the twelve tribes of Israel to show the new Israel is being reconstituted.)

Chapter 2:1-4 says, When the day of Pentecost had come, they were all together in one place. (Pentecost is fifty days after Passover. The Jewish tradition says that Moses received the law on the Feast of Pentecost.) And suddenly from heaven there came a sound like the rush of a violent wind, and it filled the entire house where they were sitting. Divided tongues, as of fire appeared among them, and a tongue rested on each of them. All of them were filled with the Holy Spirit and began to speak in other languages, as the Spirit gave them ability. (Fire symbolizes the presence of God as in God appearing to Moses in a bush, Ex 3:1-6, and a tongue of fire resting on each one symbolizes the Spirit of God touching them and causing them to speak in a way they previously never spoke.)

The wind (Spirit) as in Genesis 1 is creating once again. The languages are foreign languages, or as the disciples spoke, somehow it came to the listeners' ears in their native languages. Language is now uniting the people as opposed to the tower of Babel incident when language brought disunity separating the people (Gen 11:1-11). The message is that the one God is making an effort to bring people together in unity and peace with him and each other.

Verses 5-13 say, Now there were devout Jews from every nation under heaven living in Jerusalem. And at the sound the crowd gathered and was bewildered, because each one heard them speaking in the native language of each. Amazed and astonished, they asked, "Are not all these who are speaking Galileans? And how is it that we hear, each of us, in our own native language? Parthians, Medes, Elamites, and residents of Mesopotamia, Judea and Cappadocia, Pontus and Asia, Phrygia and Pamphylia, Egypt and the parts of Libya belonging to Cyrene, and visitors from Rome, both Jews and proselytes, Cretans and Arabs—in our own languages we hear them speaking about God's deeds of power." All were amazed and perplexed, saying to one another, "What does this mean?" But others sneered and said, "They are filled with new wine." (In other words they have been drinking too much alcohol.)

In verses 14-21 Peter said, "Men of Judea and all who live in Jerusalem, let this be known to you, and listen to what I say. Indeed these are not drunk, as you suppose, for it is only nine o'clock in the morning. (It is too early for anyone to be drunk.) No, this was what was spoken through the prophet Joel: 'In the last days it will be, God declares, that I will pour out my Spirit on all flesh, and your sons and daughters shall prophesy, and your young men shall see visions, and your old men shall dream dreams. Even upon my slaves, both men and women, in those days I will pour out my Spirit; and they shall prophesy. And I will show portents in the heaven above and signs in the earth below, blood, and fire, and smoky mist. The sun shall be turned to darkness and the moon to blood, before the coming of the Lord's great and glorious day. Then everyone who calls upon the Lord shall be saved.'

Peter quotes from Joel 2:28-30. Verse 17 notes that it is now the last days. The last days date from the time Christ is risen to the right hand of God and the sending of the Spirit, which is the beginning of the church age, and it lasts until the last judgment and the new heaven and the new earth. Therefore, according to Scripture, we have been in the last days for over two thousand years. The Spirit is poured out on both men, women, and even slaves. For the first time in history the symbolism is that all are one, even women and slaves. The sun turning to darkness, the moon to blood is Old Testament apocalyptic language symbolizing a time of judgment and great change.

Peter continues his message in verses 22-28 by informing them that Jesus was attested by God with deeds of power, wonder, and signs that God did through him. This was according to his plan and foreknowledge. Then Peter tells them that they crucified and killed this Jesus, the one chosen by the Father. "But God raised him up having freed him from death, for it was impossible for him to be held in its power." Peter then quotes David from Ps 16:8-11 where he speaks of the Messiah who makes known the way of life and would not be abandoned to corruption.

Peter continues in verses 29-36 saying, "Fellow Israelites, I may say to you confidently of our ancestor David that he both died and was buried, and his tomb is with us to this day. Since he was a prophet, he knew that God had sworn with an oath to him that he would put one of his descendants on his throne. Foreseeing this, David spoke of the resurrection of the Messiah, saying, 'He was not abandoned to Hades, nor did his flesh experience corruption.' This Jesus God raised up, and of that all of us are witnesses. Verse 33 says, "Being therefore exalted at the right hand of God, and having received from the Father the promise of the Holy Spirit, he has poured out this that you both see and hear. For David did not ascend into the heavens, but he himself says, 'The Lord said to my Lord, "Sit at my right hand, until I make your enemies your footstool." ' (Peter quotes Ps 110:1.) "Therefore let the entire house of Israel know with certainty that God has made him both Lord and Messiah, this Jesus whom you crucified."

That they crucified the one who is both God and the Messiah basically concludes Peter's preaching. Actually, 1 Corinthians 2:8 says, the rulers of this age killed him, but in Scripture what the group leaders do is also associated in some way with all who belong to the group. A modern day example would be the following: Because the President and the nation went along with declaring war on Iraq on the basis of false information where 4500 American soldiers were killed and over one hundred thousand people of Iraq were killed, all Americans are in some way responsible. That is contrary to the way most Americans think, but it is the thinking of Scripture.

Verses 37-42 say, Now when they heard this, they were cut to the heart and said to Peter and the other apostles, "Brothers, what should we do?" Peter said to them, "Repent, and be baptized every one of you in the name of Jesus Christ so that your sins may be forgiven; and you will receive the gift of the Holy Spirit. For the promise is for you, for your children, and for all who are far away, everyone whom the Lord our God calls to him." And he testified with many other arguments and exhorted them, saying, "Save yourself from this corrupt generation." (The ways of the world are always called a corrupt generation.) So those who welcomed his message were baptized, and that day three thousand persons were added. They devoted themselves to the apostles' teaching and fellowship, to the breaking of bread and the prayers.

After listening to Peter's message about the crucifixion and resurrection, they repent of their sins, and are baptized for the forgiveness of their sins, and receive the gift of the Holy Spirit. As they receive the gift of the Holy Spirit their sins are washed away. In the New Testament the Holy Spirit and baptism go together usually in the order stated (see Titus 3:4-7, 1 Peter 3:21-23). Peter is preaching the first sermon as the Father through Christ and in the power of the Holy Spirit establishes the church. The Holy Spirit creates the church and from the church the Holy Spirit will be given to individuals. Each person who responds will be given the Holy Spirit, which was not the case in the Old Testament. The Holy Spirit wipes away their sins and gives gifts to them in order to build up the church and give glory and praise to God (Eph 4:11-13).

There are times the Spirit falls upon people, and then they are baptized in water, but that usually is a miraculous falling of the Spirit for all to see. In these incidents God's purpose is to send a message to the apostles to make them understand that God is accepting those on whom the Spirit is falling. Jews, even Jews who became the first Christians, had a difficult time learning that God accepts non-Jews.

It is important to note what they do after being baptized. They devote themselves to the apostles' teachings, are in fellowship with each other, taking care of each other's needs, praying, and having the Eucharist after eating together (pot luck suppers?). This is the heart of the purpose of the church. Are these actions the primary activity of today's churches?

Verses 43-47 say, Awe came upon everyone, because many wonders and signs were being done by the apostles. All who believed were together and had all things in common; they would sell their possessions and goods and distribute the proceeds to all, as any had need. Day by day, as they spent much time in the temple, they broke bread at home and ate their food with glad and generous hearts, praising God and having the good will of all people. And day by day the Lord added to their number those who were being saved.

They met each other's needs because Christ met their needs. Is this a timeless model of how to put into action the call of Christ to take care of the needs of people, their own and others? The answer is no; it is just one way and possibly not the best way. This does present a problem to the literalists who believe there should be no additions or subtractions from the Bible and if anyone deviates from Scripture, they are not true believers.

∽◦◡

Chapter 3:1-3 says, One day Peter and John were going up to the temple at the hour of prayer, at three o'clock in the afternoon. And a man lame from birth was being carried in. People would lay him daily at the gate of the temple called the Beautiful Gate so that he could ask for alms from those entering the temple. When he saw Peter and John about to go into the temple, he asked them for alms.

Verses 4-10 say, Peter looked intently at him, as did John, and said, "Look at us." And he fixed his attention on them, expecting to receive something from them. But Peter said, "I have no silver or gold, but what I have I give you; in the name of Jesus Christ of Nazareth, stand up and walk." And he took him by the right hand and raised him up; and immediately his feet and ankles were made strong. Jumping up, he stood and began to walk, and he entered the temple with them, walking and leaping and praising God. All the people saw him walking and praising God, and they recognized him as the one who used to sit and ask for alms at the Beautiful Gate of the temple; and they were filled with wonder and amazement at what had happened to him.

The apostles are going to carry on Christ's mission, and with it they will be given the power to perform some of the same miracles that Jesus performed in order to jump-start the movement. Like Jesus a high priority for these early Christians is healing and concern for a person's health. The man is described as jumping up, walking, leaping, and praising God, which is the fulfillment of Israel's promised restoration, Isa 35:1-10. The eyes of the blind will be opened, the ears of the deaf will be unstopped; the lame will leap like a deer, and the speechless sing for joy.

Verses 11-13 say, While he clung to Peter and John, all the people ran together to them in the portico called Solomon's Portico, utterly astonished. When Peter saw it, he addressed the people, "You Israelites, why do you wonder at this, or why do you stare at us, as though by our own power or piety we had made him walk? The God of Abraham, the God of Isaac, and the God of Jacob, the God of our ancestors has glorified his servant Jesus, whom you handed over and rejected in the presence of Pilate, though he had decided to release him. (Peter connects Jesus to all of Israel's history and by calling him God's servant, the suffering servant of Isa 52:13-53:12 is recalled.)

Then reminding them of Jesus being put to death in (14) he involves them in the death of Jesus by saying, "But you rejected the Holy and Righteous One and asked to have a murderer given to you, and you killed the Author of life, whom God raised from the dead. To this we are witnesses.

Jesus is called the Author of life. Col 1:15-20 informs us that Jesus with the Father authored creation; all things were created by him and for him in order to bring all things under him and to reconcile everything to the Father through him. Then, by being part of Israel in some way, they are implicated in Jesus being put to death, see 2:33. As previously stated being in some way responsible for what the group you belong to does, even if you did not participate, is a biblical principle that Americans, because of our individualistic attitude, basically do not accept. For example, all Americans are responsible for the bombings of Hiroshima and Nagasaki, the war in Iraq, and other activity that may be frowned on by Christ. The biblical principle is sound, for it then puts responsibility on the people to challenge and correct those who are making decisions for the group.

Peter in verses 16-18 says, "And by faith in his name, his name itself has made this man strong, whom you see and know; and the faith that is through Jesus has given him this perfect health in the presence of all of you. And now friends, I know that you acted in ignorance, as did also your rulers. In this way God fulfilled what he had foretold through all the prophets, that his Messiah would suffer."

All is fulfilled because God allows people to act in ignorance when, if he chooses, he can stop them. This principle of making God responsible is normal through Scripture. It is not saying that God is controlling everything by working his puppet strings, and it is not defining the concept of *predestination* by saying that God literally makes things happen overriding freedom of choice. It is simply a way of stating that God is sovereign. He has the power to stop something, but in most cases he allows freedom of choice to work. The same principle applies to Pharaoh in Egypt and the betrayal of Judas.

Peter in verses 19-21 then says, "Repent therefore, and turn to God so that your sins (plural meaning all your violations of God's teachings) may be wiped out so that times of refreshing may come from the presence of the Lord, and that he may send the Messiah appointed for you, that is Jesus, who must remain in heaven until the time of universal restoration that God announced long ago through his holy prophets." (The restoration has begun through the kingdom but will not be completed until he returns at the end time to make all things perfect.)

Notice he says repent to have your sins wiped out, not just covered as in the Old Testament, so when Jesus comes in the end for the final judgment, one may be cleansed to enter the new heaven and new earth, for no one will enter heaven unclean, Rev 21:27. It is important to note that being forgiven of sins is not a one time process; it is a life long process.

Then Peter in (22-23) says, Moses said, 'The Lord your God will raise up for you from your own people a prophet like me. You must listen to whatever he tells you. And it will be that everyone who does not listen to that prophet will be utterly rooted out of the people.' (Moses was referring to Jesus. This goes back to verses 19-21. Then Peter relates it all to God's plan for the ages expressed through his prophets.)

Verses 24-26 say, "And all the prophets, as many as have spoken, from Samuel and those after him, also predicted these days. You are the descendants of the prophets and of the covenant God gave to your ancestors, saying to Abraham, 'And to your descendants all the families of the earth shall be blessed.' (This is a reference to Gen 12:1-3.) When God raised up his servant, he sent him first to you, to bless you by turning each of you from your wicked ways." (The message of repentance and the kingdom is to go first to Israel and then to the world.)

Chapter 4:1-4 says, While Peter and John were speaking to the people, the priests, the captain of the temple, and the Sadducees came to them, much annoyed because they were teaching the people and proclaiming that in Jesus there is the resurrection of the dead. So they arrested them and put them in custody until the next day, for it was already evening. But many of those who heard the word believed; and they numbered about five thousand. (Since only males are counted, the number is considerably larger.)

The priests in charge are mainly Sadducees from the line of Aaron, Moses' brother. All priests are supposed to come from the line of Aaron. Sadducees do not believe in a bodily resurrection including the resurrection of Jesus, nor do they believe in spirits or angels. Many do not believe in a life after death, but a few do believe in a resurrection of the spirit, but not a bodily resurrection. Their main interest is to maintain the status quo for the powerful and wealthy because they greatly benefit from it. They are in control of the temple treasury, the key banking center of the nation. The captain of the temple is in charge of protecting the temple, the priests, and Levites. He is a very powerful individual. Moses and Aaron came from the tribe of Levi. Those Levites not in the line of Aaron are the priests' helpers in the temple.

Annas is high priest at the time, and after him Caiaphas, his son-in-law will become the high priest. They are now appointed by Rome, which upsets the masses of Jews because it is a violation of their law. Annas ruled from 6-15 AD and Caiaphas from 18-36 AD. They are in charge of the Sanhedrin, which is the religious and political ruling body, which is a theocracy. Rome allows considerable leeway in local rule, so the Sanhedrin has local power as long as they submit to Rome. The Sanhedrin consists primarily of the Sadducees, but also a few Pharisees and scribes, as well as elders. They also control the temple which is the primary banking system for the economy. Horsley (2003, 91-104) discusses this in detail.

Verses 5-7 say, The next day their rulers, elders, and scribes assembled in Jerusalem, with Annas the high priest, Caiaphas, John, and Alexander, and all who were of the high-priestly family. (This is probably a meeting of the full Sanhedrin. Scribes are those who are proficient in writing and in the Old Testament law, both written and the oral tradition. Many of them are Pharisees, who believe in a bodily resurrection, angels, and spirits. The elders are wealthy lay people who are mainly the business leaders who are part of the Sanhedrin.)

Verses 7-12 say, When they had made the prisoners stand in their midst, they inquired, "By what power or by what name did you do this?" Then Peter, filled with the Holy Spirit, said to them, "Rulers of the people and elders, if we are questioned today because of a good deed done to someone who was sick and are asked how this man has been healed, let it be known to all of you, and to all the people of Israel, that this man is standing before you in good health by the name of Jesus Christ of Nazareth, whom you crucified, whom God raised from the dead. This Jesus is 'the stone that was rejected by you, the builders; it has become the cornerstone.' There is salvation in no one else, for there is no other name in heaven given among mortals by which we must be saved."

Peter speaks not his own words, but the words of the Holy Spirit. His quote is from Ps 118:22. Salvation refers both to the physical healing of the lame man, and salvation from judgment, which includes the final judgment. For Luke salvation is physical, social, and spiritual, and salvation is not through the Roman emperor as the emperor claimed. Real salvation is only through Jesus and the kingdom he came to preach. This got Jesus in trouble with the Roman and Jewish authorities, and the same will occur with his apostles and disciples. It is one of the reasons for the death of many of the early martyrs. Their claim was that the Roman emperor was not king of the kingdom, god to be worshiped, or the great peacemaker as the Romans taught and people of the land were to believe. Those titles belong only to Jesus and he is the one to be worshiped not the emperor.

Verses 13-18 say, Now when they saw the boldness of Peter and John and realized that they were uneducated ordinary men, they were amazed and recognized them as companions of Jesus. When they saw the man who had been cured standing beside them, they had nothing to say in opposition. So they ordered them to leave the council while they discussed the matter with one other. They said, "What will we do with them? For it is obvious to all who live in Jerusalem that a notable sign has been done through them; we cannot deny it. But to keep it from spreading further among the people, let us warn them to speak no more to anyone in this name." So they called them and ordered them not to speak or teach at all in the name of Jesus.

Verses 19-22 say, But Peter and John answered them, "Whether it is right in God's sight to listen to you rather than to God, you must judge; for we cannot keep from speaking about what we have seen and heard." After threatening them again, they let them go, finding no way to punish them because of the people, for all of them praised God for what had happened. For the man on whom this sign of healing had been performed was more than forty years old. (The same thing that happened to Jesus over healing is now occurring with his disciples.)

In verses 23-30 the disciples are released, and they gather together to pray. In (29) they pray, "Lord, look at their threats, and grant your servants to speak your word with all boldness, while you stretch out your hand to heal, and signs and wonders are performed through the name of your holy servant Jesus." When they had prayed, the place in which they were gathered together was shaken; and they were all filled with the Holy Spirit and spoke the word of God with boldness. (This is symbolizing God presence and his answering their prayer. It is like a second Pentecost, and they are filled with the Spirit.)

Verses 32-37 say, Now the whole group of those who believed were of one heart and soul, and no one claimed private ownership of any possessions, but everything they owned was held in common. With great power the apostles gave their testimony to the resurrection of the Lord Jesus, and great grace was upon them all. There was not a needy person among them, for as many as owned lands or houses sold them and brought the proceeds of what was sold. They laid it at the apostles' feet, and it was distributed to each as any had need. There was a Levite, a native of Cyprus, Joseph, to whom the apostles gave the name Barnabas (which means "son of encouragement"). He sold a field that belonged to him, then brought the money, and laid it at the apostles' feet (see Deut 15:4-11). (We will hear more about this man soon.)

These early Christians had an intense concern for each other's welfare. They are not forced to do this; they do it by their own free will. They want to establish a covenant community where justice, peace, and righteous are both practiced and produced. Their only purpose is to support each other in order to get the message about Jesus, his resurrection, and his kingdom out to others.

In chapter 5:1-11 Ananias and his wife sell a piece of property and hold back some of the proceeds. They are not required to give any of it, but they lie to the apostles saying that they are giving all of it to the common fund. They are putting the Spirit of the Lord to a test. In verse 3 Peter asked, "why has Satan filled your heart to lie to the Holy Spirit and to keep back part of the proceeds of the land?" Satan is associated with their premeditated actions. Both die because of their actions. The apostles are representing the Holy Spirit and the church, Jn 14:26, 16:13. Verse 11 says, And great fear seized the whole church and all who heard of these things. (This is the first mention of the word church.)

Verses 12-16 say, Now many signs and wonders were done among the people through the apostles. And they were all together in Solomon's Portico. None of the rest dared to join them, but the people held them in high esteem Yet more than ever believers were added to the Lord, great numbers of both men and women, so that they even carried out the sick into the streets, and laid them on cots and mats, in order that Peter's shadow might fall on some of them as he came by. A great number of people would also gather from the towns around Jerusalem, bringing the sick and those tormented by unclean spirits, and they were all cured. (Serious Christians have always been concerned with healing and people's health. This incident with Peter's shadow, along with miracles that occur through Paul's handkerchiefs and aprons in 19:11, are the background of the cult of the relics that became so popular in Europe.)

Verses 17-21 say, Then the high priest took action; he and all who were with him being filled with jealousy, arrested the apostles and put them in the public prison. But during the night an angel of the Lord opened the prison doors, brought them out, and said, "Go, stand in the temple and tell the people the whole message about this life." When they heard this, they entered the temple at daybreak and went on with their teaching. Then through verse 27 the Sanhedrin and the captain of the temple learn that they are no longer in jail but in the temple teaching. So they sent for them and had them brought before them so the high priest could question them.

In verses 28-29 he said, "We gave you strict orders not to teach in this name, yet here you have filled Jerusalem with your teaching and you are determined to bring this man's blood on us." But Peter and the apostles answered in 29-32 "We must obey God rather than any human authority. The God of our ancestors raised up Jesus, whom you had killed by hanging him on a tree. God exalted him at his right hand as Leader (translated Author in 3:15) and Savior that he might give repentance to Israel and forgiveness of sins. And we are witnesses to these things, and so is the Holy Spirit whom God has given to those who obey him." (Notice obedience and not just belief is necessary to receive the Holy Spirit.)

Notice repentance is first for the nation of Israel, and then it is offered to individuals who obey God. Forgiveness of sins comes to those who obey God. This probably is a reference to belief, repentance, and baptism, 2:38, 2 Peter 1:10, 2 Thess 2:13-15. Faith is never belief only, for even the demons believe (James 2:19).

Verse 33 says, when they heard this, they were enraged and wanted to kill them. (This is the same thing that happened to Jesus. No matter how many miracles were done, they still opposed Jesus, just as they are again doing with his apostles.) In verses 33-39 a Pharisee named Gamaliel, a member of the Sanhedrin, encouraged caution. He gave as examples two incidents of the past as his reasoning. A man named Theudas and another named Judas the Galilean had great followings, but both failed and their followers were dispersed. In (38-40) he said, " So in the present case, I tell you, keep away from these men and let them alone; for if this plan or this undertaking is of human origin, it will fail; but if it is of God, you will not be able to overthrow them—in that case you might even be found fighting against God!" They were convinced by him, and when they had called in the apostles, they had them flogged. Then they ordered them not to speak in the name of Jesus, and let them go.

Verses 41-42 say, As they left the council, they rejoiced that they were considered worthy to suffer dishonor for the sake of the name. And every day in the temple and at home they did not cease to teach and proclaim Jesus as the Messiah. (Oh, for the same courage in our time. How many Christians does the reader know who consider it worthy to suffer dishonor for the name of Christ?)

❦

Chapter 6:1-6 says, Now during those days, when the disciples were increasing in number, the Hellenists complained against the Hebrews because their widows were being neglected in the daily distribution of food. (The issue is between Greek speaking Jews from the Dispersion, who had become followers of Christ and Hebrew speaking Jews that had become Christian. The apostles gathered together to solve the problem.)

In verse 2 they said, "It is not right that we should neglect the word of God in order to serve tables. Therefore, friends, select from among yourselves seven men of good standing, full of the Spirit and of wisdom, whom we may appoint to this task, while we, for our part, will devote ourselves to prayer and to serving the word."

This begins a division of labor according to the different gifts given by God. Choosing seven indicates it is a big job seeing all the people are fed. Naturally problems develop and ways to solve them need to be developed. The apostles needed to devote their time in prayer and serving the word. The names of the seven chosen are listed as Stephen, Philip, Prochorus, Nicanor, Timon, Parmenas, and Nicolaus, a proselyte of Antioch. Tradition calls them the first deacons. Verses 6-7 say, They had these men stand before the apostles, who prayed and laid their hands on them. The word of God continued to spread; the number of disciples increased greatly in Jerusalem, and a great many of the priests became obedient to the faith. (There is no such thing as believing without being obedient. These were priests from the old covenant.)

One of the persons chosen to deliver food to the widows is Stephen. Verse 8 says, Stephen, full of grace and power, did great wonders and signs among the people. In verses 9-12 those of the synagogue of the Freedman made up of Greek speaking Jews (not followers of Christ) from outside of Jerusalem but now in Jerusalem argued with Stephen, but verse 10 says, they could not withstand the wisdom and the Spirit with which he spoke. They secretly instigated men to lie about him saying, he spoke blasphemous words against Moses and God. Then they stirred up the people and brought him before the Sanhedrin.

In verses 13-15 they say, "This man never stops saying things against this holy place and the law; for we have heard him say that this Jesus of Nazareth will destroy this place and will change the customs that Moses handed on to us." And all who sat in the council looked intently at him, and they saw that his face was like the face of an angel.

Chapter 7:1 says, the high priest asked him, "Are these things so?" In verses 2-50 Stephen replies with a long speech about Israel's history. The purpose of the speech is summed up in verses 51-53. After reviewing some of Israel's history, these verses have Stephen saying, "You stiff necked people, uncircumcised in heart and ears, you are forever opposing the Holy Spirit, just as your ancestors used to do. Which of the prophets did your ancestors not persecute? They killed those who foretold the coming of the Righteous One, and now you have become his betrayers and murderers. You are the ones that received the law as ordained by angels, and yet you have not kept it."

Verses 54-60 say, When they heard these things, they became enraged and ground their teeth at Stephen. But filled with the Holy Spirit, he gazed into heaven and saw the glory of God and Jesus standing at the right hand of God. "Look," he said, "I see the heavens opened and the Son of Man standing at the right hand of God!" But they covered their ears, and with a loud shout all rushed together against him. Then they dragged him out of the city and began to stone him; and the witnesses laid their coats at the feet of a young man named Saul. (This is he who eventually becomes the Apostle Paul.) While they were stoning Stephen, he prayed, "Lord Jesus, receive my Spirit." Then he knelt down and cried out in a loud voice, "Lord, do not hold this sin against them." When he had said this, he died.

Luke is comparing what happened to Jesus with Stephen. Both were unfairly put to death, and both asked God to forgive their persecutors. It is interesting to note that any territory under Roman jurisdiction is required to get approval from the Romans to put anyone to death. This law was followed in putting Jesus to death but not for Stephen.

∾ ॰ ॰

Chapter 8:1-2 says, Saul approved of their killing him. That day a severe persecution began against the church in Jerusalem, and all except the apostles were scattered throughout the countryside of Judea and Samaria. (With persecution the church is forced to expand into other areas.) Verse 3 says, But Saul was ravaging the church by entering house after house; dragging off both men and women, he committed them to prison. (Saul, soon to be the Apostle Paul, is a committed Jewish Pharisee, who feels it is his duty to squash these renegades who are distorting the religion of the Jews.)

Verses 4-8 say, Now those who were scattered went from place to place, proclaiming the word. Philip (like Stephen is a Hellenistic Jew) went down to the city of Samaria (Shechem) and proclaimed the Messiah to them. The crowds with one accord listened eagerly to what was said by Philip, hearing and seeing the signs that he did, for unclean spirits, crying with loud shrieks, came out of many who were possessed; and many others who were paralyzed or lame were cured. So there was great joy in that city. (Luke's point is that there is a spirit world behind this physical world that causes havoc for those who do not have Christ and the Holy Spirit within them.)

In verses 9-13 a magician named Simon who had amazed Samaria for a long time with his magic is brought into the picture. In (12) the people heard Philip proclaim the good news about the kingdom of God and the name of Jesus Christ, and they were baptized both men and women. (Under Jewish law women were not taught, but now they hear the teaching and respond.) Verse 13 says, Even Simon himself believed. After being baptized he stayed constantly with Philip and was amazed when he saw the signs and great miracles that took place. (He was amazed because he knew well the difference between these miracles and magic.)

In verses 14-17 after the apostles hear that Samaria accepts the word of God, they send Peter and John to them; they go and pray that they may accept the Holy Spirit. Luke adds that the Spirit had not yet come upon them; they have only been baptized in the name of the Lord Jesus. Verse 17 says, Then Peter and John laid their hands on them, and they received the Holy Spirit.

Everything has to be coordinated with the church and under the direction of the apostles and their teachings, which is why they are sent. Independent churches doing what they want and keeping separated from the whole church is not the way Christianity is to function in the New Testament. It must be seen by all that the Samaritans are approved by God to receive the things of God and that everything is in unity with the apostles. Historically, like the Gentiles Jews did not believe that God would also want the Samaritans as his people. Thus the reason for baptism and the Spirit being in reverse order. God is showing the apostles and the whole church that this is all part of his plan to go into the world to all people. Another reason the Spirit is withheld is to show all people that God has designed the church and its leadership to be his instrument. Yes, God works outside the church, but all is to eventually be brought under the unity of the apostolic church.

Verses 18-24 once again involve Simon. He is impressed with the coming of the Spirit with the apostles laying on hands, so he offers them money in order to have the same power. In (20-24) Peter said, "May your silver perish with you, because you thought you could obtain God's gift with money! You have no part or share in this, for your heart is not right before God. Repent therefore of this wickedness of yours, and pray to the Lord that, if possible, the intent of your heart may be forgiven you. For I see that you are in the gall of bitterness and the chains of wickedness." Simon answered, "Pray for me to the Lord, that nothing of what you have said may happen to me." Verse 25 says, Now after Peter and John had testified and spoken the word of the Lord, they returned to Jerusalem, proclaiming the good news to many villages of the Samaritans.

The following contains the story of Philip and the Ethiopian eunuch to show how the mission went to Africa. In ancient times eunuchs were given important positions in kingdoms, especially when women were involved. Verses 26-28 say, Then an angel of the Lord said to Philip, "Get up and go toward the south to the road that goes down from Jerusalem to Gaza." (This is a wilderness road.) So he got up and went. Now there was an Ethiopian eunuch, a court official of the Candace, queen of the Ethiopians, in charge of her entire treasury. (Candace was a title used for the Nubian queen.) He had come to Jerusalem to worship and was returning home; seated in his chariot, he was reading the prophet Isaiah. (He must have heard about Jesus and the resurrection. He was in Jerusalem on the day of Pentecost, so he must have been an Israelite or at least a convert.)

Verses 29-31 say, Then the Spirit said to Philip, "Go over to this chariot and join it." So Philip ran up to it and heard him reading the prophet Isaiah. He asked, "Do you understand what you are reading?" He replied, "How can I, unless someone guides me?" And he invited Philip to get in and sit beside him.

Being guided in understanding the Bible is important. Teaching as many years as this writer has taught in many different groups, both Catholic and Protestant, this writer has discovered that many people have attempted to read the Scriptures on their own, but somewhere along the line stopped. Practically everyone mentioned the reason they stopped was that they needed help; they needed someone to guide them through reading and understanding the Bible. This, of course, is the purpose behind this series of books the author is writing.

Verses 32-34 say, Now the passage of the scripture that he was reading was this: "Like a sheep he was led to the slaughter, and like a lamb silent before its shearer, so he does not open his mouth. In his humiliation justice was denied him. Who can describe his generation? For his life is taken away from the earth." (The passage quoted is Isa 53:7-8 in the Septuagint version. It is about God's servant who suffers.) The eunuch asked Philip, "About whom, may I ask you, does the prophet say this, about himself or about someone else?"

Verses 35-40 say, Then Philip began to speak, and starting with this scripture, he proclaimed the good news about Jesus. As they were going along the road, they came to some water; and the eunuch said, "Look, here is water! What is to prevent me from being baptized?" He commanded the chariot to stop, and both of them, Philip and the eunuch, went down into the water, and Philip baptized him. When they came up out of the water, the Spirit of the Lord snatched Philip away; the eunuch saw him no more, and went on his way rejoicing. But Philip found himself at Azotus, and as he was passing through the region, he proclaimed the good news to all the towns until he came to Caesarea. (The first baptisms were by immersion, which is why they went down into the water. For Luke the Spirit is always creating and acting. Later church tradition says that the eunuch became the first missionary to Africa.)

Chapter 9 is the conversion of Saul to the Apostle Paul. Chapter 9:1-2 says, Meanwhile Saul, still breathing threats and murder against the disciples of the Lord, went to the high priest and asked him for letters to the synagogues at Damascus, so that if he found any who belonged to the Way, men or women, he might bring them bound to Jerusalem. (The believers were first called followers of the Way. It is a new Way of thinking and a new Way of living religious life.)

Verses 3-9 say, Now as he was going along and approaching Damascus, suddenly a light from heaven flashed around him. He fell to the ground and heard a voice saying to him, "Saul, Saul, why do you persecute me?" He asked, "Who are you, Lord?" The reply came, "I am Jesus, whom you are persecuting. But get up and enter the city, and you will be told what you are to do." The men who were traveling with him stood speechless because they heard the voice but saw no one. Saul got up from the ground, and though his eyes were open, he could see nothing; so they led him by the hand and brought him to Damascus. For three days he was without sight, and neither ate nor drank.

Verses 10-11 say, Now there was a disciple in Damascus named Ananias. The Lord said to him in a vision, "Ananias." He answered, "Here I am, Lord." The Lord said to him, "Get up and go to the street called Straight (the major east-west corridor, possibly today named Darb el-Mostakim), and at the house of Judas look for a man of Tarsus named Saul. (This is the first time Saul is identified as being from Tarsus, the capital of the Roman city of Cilicia in Asia Minor, which is modern day Turkey.)

At this moment he is praying, and (12-16) says, he has seen in a vision a man named Ananias come in and lay his hands on him so that he might regain his sight." (There are many visions from God in the book of Acts.) But Ananias answered, "Lord, I have heard from many about this man, how much evil he has done to your saints in Jerusalem; and here he has authority from the chief priests to bind all who invoke your name." (All believers are called saints.) But the Lord said to him, "Go, for he is an instrument I have chosen to bring my name before Gentiles and kings and before the people of Israel; I myself will show him how much he must suffer for the sake of my name." (God uses his people as instruments for his purposes.)

Verses 17-20 say, So Ananias went and entered the house. He laid his hands on Saul and said, "Brother Saul, the Lord Jesus, who appeared to you on your way here, has sent me so that you may regain your sight and be filled with the Holy Spirit." And immediately something like scales fell from his eyes, and his sight was restored. Then he got up and was baptized, and after taking some food he regained his strength. For several days he was with the disciples in Damascus, and immediately he began to proclaim Jesus in the synagogues, saying, "He is the Son of God." (There are three accounts of Saul's conversion; each one is slightly different, see also 22:4-16, and 26:9-18 for comparison.)

Verses 26-28 say, When he had come to Jerusalem, he attempted to join the disciples; and they were all afraid of him, for they did not believe he was a disciple. But Barnabas took him, brought him to the disciples, and described for them how on the road he had seen the Lord, who had spoken to him, and how in Damascus he had spoken boldly in the name of Jesus. (Other accounts say this occurred three years later, see Gal 1:18-19.)

So he went in and out among them in Jerusalem, speaking boldly in the name of the Lord. He spoke and argued with the Hellenists (Jews who speak Greek and live or had lived in the Diaspora, meaning outside Judea.); but they were attempting to kill him. When the believers learned of it, they brought him down to

Caesarea and sent him to Tarsus. Meanwhile the church throughout Judea, Galilee, and Samaria had peace and was built up. Living in the fear of the Lord and in the comfort of the Holy Spirit, the church increased in numbers.

Verses 32-35 shift back to Peter who goes to Lydda where he healed Aeneas, a paralytic, who had been bedridden for eight years. Verse 35 says, All the residents of Sharon and Lydda saw him and turned to the Lord. (Does the reader think that "all" is literal or hyperbolic? Sharon is the plane on which Lydda is located. It is located west of Jerusalem.)

In verses 36-43 in Joppa there is a disciple named Tabitha, which in Greek is Dorcus. She is devoted to good works and charity. She dies and is laid in an upstairs room while two men are sent to Peter requesting him to come. When he comes to the upper room all the women are displaying clothing Dorcus has made for people. Verse 40 says, Peter put all of them outside, and then he knelt down and prayed. He turned to the body and said, "Tabitha, get up." Then she opened her eyes, and seeing Peter, she sat up. He gave her his hand and helped her up. Then calling the saints and widows, he showed her to be alive. This became known throughout Joppa, and many believed in the Lord. Meanwhile he stayed in Joppa for sometime with a certain Simon, a tanner. (A tanner works with dead animal carcasses and according to the Jews he is defiled and ritually unclean. This shows Peter is no longer bound to the purity laws of the old law.)

❧

Chapter 10:1-2 says, In Caesarea there was a man named Cornelius, a centurion of the Italian Cohort, as it was called. (Caesarea is on the coast and is where the Roman government offices are located.) He was a devout man who feared God with all his household; he gave alms generously to the people and prayed constantly to God.

Verses 3-8 say, One afternoon about three o'clock he had a vision in which he clearly saw an angel of God coming in and saying to him, "Cornelius." He stared at him in terror and said, "What is it Lord?" He answered, "Your prayers and your alms have ascended as a memorial before God. Now send men to Joppa for a certain Simon who is called Peter; he is lodging with Simon, a tanner whose house is by the seaside." When the angel who spoke to him had left, he called two of his slaves and a devout soldier from the ranks of those who served him, and after telling them everything, he sent them to Joppa.

Verses 9-16 say, About noon the next day, as they were on their journey and approaching the city, Peter went up on the roof to pray. He became hungry and wanted something to eat; and while it was being prepared, he fell into a trance. He saw the heaven opened and something like a large sheet coming down, being lowered to the ground by its four corners. In it were all kinds of four footed creatures and reptiles and birds of the air Then he heard a voice saying, "Get up, Peter; kill and eat." But Peter said, "By no means, Lord; for I have never eaten anything that is profane or unclean." The voice said to him again, a second time, "What God has made clean, you must not call profane." This happened three times, and the thing was suddenly taken up to heaven. (The message God is giving to Peter is that all the Old Testament dietary laws are no longer valid. Under the new covenant it is now acceptable to eat what was formerly not.)

While Peter is contemplating the vision in (17-24) those Cornelius sent appeared at the house. The Spirit appears to Peter and tells him to go meet them, for he has sent them. They tell Peter the vision Cornelius had and that an angel directed him to send for Peter. The next day they set out for Joppa with some of the believers, and the following day they arrive at Joppa. Verses 25-29 say, On Peter's arrival Cornelius met him, and falling at his feet worshiped him. But Peter made him get up, saying, "Stand up; I am only a mortal." And as he talked with him, he went in and found many had assembled; and he said to them, "You yourselves know that it is unlawful for a Jew to associate with or to visit a Gentile; but God has shown me that I should not call anyone profane or unclean. So when I was sent for, I came without objection. Now may I ask why you sent for me?"

Not being permitted to associate with a Gentile is not an Old Testament teaching, but had become such with the teaching of the Pharisees and the oral law. This oral teaching had become so entrenched among the Jews that it is taking this special divine revelation to make them aware that it was not in the purposes of God. The Jews did not believe Gentiles could ever be accepted by God. Much of this had developed because of the deduction they made from their dietary and purity laws.

In verses 30-33 Cornelius relates the incident he had with the man who suddenly appeared to him in dazzling clothes and how he had told him to send for Peter. Verse 33 says, "Therefore I sent for you immediately, and you have been kind enough to come. So now all of us are here in the presence of God to listen to all that the Lord has commanded you to say."

Verses 34-41 say, Then Peter began to speak to them: "I truly understand that God shows no partiality, but in every nation anyone who fears him and does what is right is acceptable to him. You know the message he sent to the people of Israel, preaching peace by Jesus Christ — he is Lord of all. That message spread throughout Judea, beginning in Galilee after the baptism that John announced: how God anointed Jesus of Nazareth with the Holy Spirit and with power; how he went about doing good and healing all who were oppressed by the devil, for God was with him . . ." (Luke continued by summarizing the ministry of Jesus, his death and resurrection, and Jesus' post resurrection appearances.) In verses 42-43 Peter says, "He commanded us to preach to the people and to testify that he is the one ordained by God as judge of the living and the dead. All the prophets testify about him that everyone who believes in him receives forgiveness of sins through his name."

The message is that God shows no partiality. All who fear God and do what is right are acceptable to Jesus, who came to bring peace with God and peace with each other. The emphasis is on how the whole world is reconciled to God and each other. Forgiveness of sin, reconciliation, and peace through the resurrected Jesus to all peoples of the world is the revelation God gives to Peter.

Verses 44-48 say, While Peter was still speaking, the Holy Spirit fell upon all who heard the word. (The Holy Spirit works through the word and upon those who hear the word.) The circumcised believers (Jews who had become followers of Christ) who had come with Peter were astounded that the gift of the Holy Spirit had been poured out upon the Gentiles, for they heard them speaking in tongues and extolling God. (This is God's proof to them that he is accepting Gentiles also.) Then Peter said, "Can anyone withhold the water for baptizing these people who have received the Holy Spirit just as we have?" (They received it in a miraculous way as they had on the day of Pentecost, Acts 2.) So he ordered them to be baptized in the name of Jesus Christ. Then they invited him to stay for several days. (This is to receive more teaching on the Way.)

The Holy Spirit fell upon the Gentiles before baptism, which is exactly the way it happened when the Samaritans believed. This is necessary in order to show the Jews that God is including those who the Jews did not believe God would accept. Therefore it is God's way of showing them that it acceptable for these people to be baptized. The Gentiles also are to become a part of the one family of God. Cornelius is the first Gentile convert. Peter is the one in charge, preaching the first sermon to the Jews on the day of Pentecost when the church began. He is now the one to preach to the first Gentiles that come into the church. The importance of Peter as the leader of the original apostles as the church is established can not be denied.

Chapter 11:1-4 says, Now the apostles and the believers who were in Judea heard that the Gentiles had also accepted the word of God. So when Peter went up to Jerusalem, the circumcised believers criticized him, saying, "Why did you go to uncircumcised men and eat with them?" Then Peter began to explain it to them. Verses 4-18 are basically Peter telling the same story that he experienced in Chapter 10. (Hebrew style includes much repetition, especially when something is important.)

Verses 19-26 say, Now those who were scattered because of the persecution that took place over Stephen traveled as far as Phoenicia, Cyprus, and Antioch, and they spoke the word to no one except Jews. But among them were some men of Cyprus and Cyrene who, on coming to Antioch, spoke to the Hellenists (probably Greek Gentiles) also, proclaiming the Lord Jesus. The hand of the Lord was with them, and a great number became believers and turned to the Lord.

Verses 22-26 say, News of this came to the ears of the church in Jerusalem, and they sent Barnabas to Antioch. When he came and saw the grace of God, he rejoiced, and he exhorted them all to remain faithful to the Lord with steadfast devotion; for he was a good man, full of the Holy Spirit and of faith. And a great many people were brought to the Lord. Then Barnabas went to Tarsus to look for Saul, and when he found him, he brought him to Antioch. So it was for an entire year they met with the church and taught a great many people, and it was in Antioch that the disciples were first called "Christians." (From the beginning of Paul's conversion Barnabas is Paul's advocate recommending him to Peter in Jerusalem and now getting him in Tarsus.)

Verses 27-30 say, At that time prophets came down from Jerusalem to Antioch. One of them named Agabus stood up and predicted by the Spirit that there would be a severe famine over all the world; and this took place during the reign of Claudius. The disciples determined that according to their ability, each would send relief to the believers living in Judea; this they did, sending it to the elders by Barnabas and Saul. (Always the concern of Christians is for people to have their basic physical and material needs met.)

Chapter 12:1-5 says, About that time King Herod laid violent hands upon some who belonged to the church. He had James, the brother of John, killed with the sword. (This was Herod Agrippa, the grandson of Herod the Great, who also had John the Baptist killed. Claudius made him king in AD 41.) After he saw that it pleased the Jews, he proceeded to arrest Peter also. (This was during the festival of Unleavened Bread.) When he had seized him, he put him in prison and handed him over to four squads of soldiers to guard him, intending to bring him out to the people after the Passover. While Peter was kept in prison, the church prayed fervently to God for him.

Verses 6-11 say, The very night before Herod was going to bring him out, Peter bound with two chains, was sleeping between two soldiers, while guards in front of the door were keeping watch over the prison. Suddenly an angel of the Lord appeared and a light shone in the cell. He tapped Peter on the side and woke him saying, "Get up quickly." And the chains fell off his wrists. The angel said to him, "Fasten your belt and put on your sandals." He did so. Then he said to him, "Wrap your cloak around you and follow me." Peter went out and followed him; he did not realize that what was happening with the angel's help was real; he thought he was seeing a vision . . . Then Peter came to himself and said, "Now I am sure that the Lord has sent his angel and rescued me from the hands of Herod and from all that the Jewish people were expecting."

Verses 12-17 say, As soon as he realized this, he went to the house of Mary, the mother of John whose other name was Mark, where many had gathered and were praying. (Later tradition notes this as the author of the Gospel of Mark.) When he knocked at the outer gate, a maid named Rhoda came to answer. On recognizing Peter's voice, she was so overjoyed that, instead of opening the gate, she ran in and announced that Peter was standing at the gate. They said to her, "You are out of your mind!" But she insisted that it was so. They said, "It is his angel." Meanwhile Peter continued knocking; and when they opened the gate, they saw him and were amazed. He motioned to them with his hand to be silent, and described for them how the Lord had brought him out of prison. And he added, "Tell this to James and to the believers." Then he left and went to another place. (James is the brother of Jesus.)

Verses 18-19 say, When morning came, there was no small commotion among the soldiers over what had become of Peter. When Herod had searched for him and could not find him, he examined the guards and ordered them to be put to death. Then he went down from Judea to Caesarea and stayed there. (The Romans have a law that if a prisoner escapes, the guards are to get the sentence the prisoner had.)

In verses 20-23 Herod delivers a public address to the people of

Tyre and Sidon, and the people declare him a god. Verse 23 says, And immediately, because he had not given the glory to God, an angel of the Lord struck him down, and he was eaten by worms and died. (Josephus in Antiquities 19.343-52 confirms this incident concerning the death of Herod Agrippa. He said he lingered five days from an intestinal disease.)

Verses 24-25 say, But the word of God continued to advance and gain adherents. Then after completing their mission Barnabas and Saul returned to Jerusalem and brought with them John, whose other name was Mark. (Luke emphasizes the connection between the church in Jerusalem and the church in Antioch and the mission of Paul and Barnabas. It is difficult to see where these last verses fit chronologically. This seems to be a summary of Paul's first missionary journey that Luke has yet to mention, but will mention in the next chapter. But the information docs not seem to fit with what happened to Mark following the first missionary journey.)

❧❧

Chapter 13:1-3 says, Now in the church at Antioch there were prophets and teachers: Barnabas, Simeon who was called Niger, Lucius of Cyrene (Libya), Manaen a member of the court of Herod the ruler, and Saul. (This is Herod Antipas, a son of Herod the Great, who ruled Galilee and Perea.) While they were worshiping the Lord and fasting, the Holy Spirit said, "Set apart for me Barnabas and Saul for the work to which I have called them." Then after fasting and praying they laid their hands on them and sent them off.

Verses 4-7 say, So, being sent out by the Holy Spirit, they went down to Seleucia (port city for Antioch on the Orontes River); and from there they sailed to Cyprus. When they arrived at Salamis (eastern port of Cyprus), they proclaimed the word of God in the synagogues of the Jews. And they had John Mark (Barnabas' cousin, Col 4:10) also to assist them. When they had gone through the whole island as far as Paphos, they met a certain magician, a Jewish false prophet, named Bar-Jesus. He was with the proconsul, Sergius Paulis, an intelligent man, who summoned Barnabas and Saul and wanted to hear the word of God. (A proconsul is a governor of senatorial rank appointed by the Roman senate usually for one year only, in a place that is stable with no need for troops.)

Verses 8-12 say, But the magician Elymas (for that is the translation of his name) opposed them and tried to turn the proconsul away from the faith. But Saul also known as Paul, filled with the Holy Spirit, looked intently at him and said, "You son of the devil, you enemy of all righteousness, full of all deceit and villainy, will you not stop making crooked the straight paths of the Lord? And now listen — the hand of the Lord is against you, and you will be blind for awhile, unable to see the sun." Immediately mist and darkness came over him, and he went about groping for someone to lead him by the hand. When the proconsul saw what happened, he believed, for he was astonished at the teaching about the Lord. (In the beginning of the church and its mission miracles are for the advancement of the message about Christ and the church. Once the church is established Luke insinuates in Lk 16:29-31 that we have the scriptures so listen to them.)

Verses 13-17 say, Then Paul and his companions set sail from Paphos and came to Perga in Pamphylia. (Today this is in southern Turkey.) John (Mark), however, left them and returned to Jerusalem; but they went on from Perga and came to Antioch in Pisidia. (Antioch is a Roman colony where many Jews settled. It is located high up in the mountains. Today is near the modern Yalovach. No one knows why John Mark leaves, but we do know Paul is not happy about it.)

On the sabbath day they went into the synagogue and sat down. After the reading of the law and the prophets, the officials of the synagogue sent them a message, saying, "Brothers, if you have any word of exhortation for the people, give it." So Paul stood up and with a gesture began to speak: "You Israelites, and others who fear God, listen. The God of this people Israel chose our ancestors and made the people great during their stay in the land of Egypt, and with uplifted arm he led them out of it. Then from verses 18-39 he gives a summary of their history to take them through John the Baptist to the crucifixion and resurrection with verse 26 telling them that the message of this salvation has been sent.

In verses 38-41 Paul says, "Let it be known to you therefore, my brothers, that through this man forgiveness of sins is proclaimed to you; by this Jesus everyone who believes is set free from all those sins from which you could not be freed by the law of Moses. Beware, therefore, that what the prophets said does not happen to you: 'Look you scoffers! Be amazed and perish, for in your days I am doing a work, a work that you will never believe, even if someone tells you.' " (This is a quote from Hab 1:5.)

Verses 42-43 say, As Paul and Barnabas were going out, the people urged them to speak about these things again the next sabbath. When the meeting of the synagogue broke up, many Jews and devout converts to Judaism followed Paul and Barnabas, who spoke to them and urged them to continue in the grace of God.

Verses 44-47 say, The next sabbath almost the whole city gathered to hear the word of the Lord. But when the Jews saw the crowds, they were filled with jealousy; and blaspheming, they contradicted what was spoken by Paul. Then both Paul and Barnabas spoke out boldly, saying, "It was necessary that the word of God should be spoken first to you. Since you reject it and judge for yourselves to be unworthy of eternal life, we are now turning to the Gentiles. For the Lord has commanded us, saying, 'I have set you to be a light for the Gentiles, so that you may bring salvation to the ends of the earth.' " (This is a quote from Isa 49:6.)

Verses 48-51 say, When the Gentiles heard this, they were glad and praised the word of the Lord; and as many as had been destined for eternal life became believers. Thus the word of the Lord spread throughout the region. But the Jews incited the devout women of high standing and the leading men of the city, and stirred up persecution against Paul and Barnabas, and drove them out of the region. So they shook the dust off their feet in protest against them, and went to Iconium. (Shaking the dust off their feet is a cultural expression stating that the hearers are responsible for the consequences of their actions.) Verse 52 says, And the disciples were filled with joy and with the Holy Spirit.

Chapter 14:1-2 says, The same thing occurred in Iconium, where Paul and Barnabas went into the Jewish synagogue and spoke in such a way that a great number of both Jews and Greeks became believers.

Iconium is modern day Konya. At one time it was the capital of the Seljuk Turks during the Ottoman empire. It was located on the main east-west route between Asia and Syria and was a prosperous market town with copper mines nearby. It was claimed to be the first city established after the ancient flood during the time of Noah.

Verses 3-7 say, they remained for a long time, speaking boldly for the Lord, who testified to the word of his grace by granting signs and wonders to be done through them. But the residents of the city were divided; some sided with the Jews, and some with the apostles. And when an attempt was made by both Gentiles and Jews, with their rulers, to mistreat them and to stone them, the apostles learned of it and fled to Lystra and Derbe, cities of Lycaonia, and to the surrounding country; and there they continued proclaiming the good news. (Lystra is modern day Hatun-Serai in modern day Turkey. Derbe is probably Kerti, a mound near Beydilli.)

In verses 8-14 Paul heals a man crippled from birth. The people are amazed and in (11-12) believe Paul is Hermes and Barnabas is Zeus. They believe the gods have come to them in human form. The priest of Zeus, whose temple is outside the city, came with people and wanted to offer sacrifice. But in (15-17) they say, "Friends, why are you doing this? We are mortals just like you, and we bring you good news, that you should turn from these worthless things to the living God, who made the heaven and the earth and the sea and all that is in them. In past generations he allowed all the nations to follow their own ways; yet he has not left himself without a witness in doing good — giving you rains from heaven and fruitful seasons, and filling you with food and your hearts with joy." Verse 18 says, Even with these words, they scarcely restrained the crowds from offering sacrifice to them.

Verses 19-20 say, But Jews came there from Antioch and Iconium and won over the crowds. Then they stoned Paul and dragged him out of the city, supposing that he was dead. But when the disciples surrounded him, he got up and went into the city. The next day he went on with Barnabas to Derbe. (Crowds can be quite fickle as we already learned when studying the events in the last week of Jesus' life on earth before his crucifixion.)

Verses 21-23 say, After they had proclaimed the good news to that city and had made many disciples, they returned to Lystra, then on to Iconium and Antioch. There they strengthened the souls of the disciples and encouraged them to continue in the faith, saying, "It is through many persecutions that we must enter the kingdom of God." And after they had appointed elders for them in the church, with prayer and fasting they entrusted them to the Lord in whom they had come to believe.

Verses 24-28 say, Then they passed through Pisidia and came to Pamphylia. When they had spoken the word in Perga, they went down to Attalia. From there they sailed back to Antioch, where they had been commended to the grace of God for the work that they had completed. When they arrived, they called the church together and related all that God had done with them, and how he had opened a door of faith for the Gentiles. And they stayed there with the disciples for some time. (This ends the first missionary journey.)

Chapter 15:1 says, Then certain individuals came down from Judea and were teaching the brothers, "Unless you are circumcised according to the custom of Moses, you cannot be saved." After Paul and Barnabas debated the issue with them, they were appointed to go to Jerusalem to discuss the issue with the apostles. On the way they reported the conversion of the Gentiles to the church in Phoenicia and Samaria bringing great joy to them. Verses 4-5 say, When they came to Jerusalem, they were welcomed by the church and the apostles and the elders, and they reported all that God had done with them. (Credit and glory is always given to God; they never take credit for themselves.) But some believers who belonged to the sect of the Pharisees stood up and said, "It is necessary for them to be circumcised and ordered to keep the law of Moses."

Verses 6-11 say, The apostles and the elders met together to consider this matter. After there had been much debate, Peter stood up and said to them, "My brothers, you know that in the early days God made a choice among you, that I should be the one through whom the Gentiles would hear the message of the good news and become believers. And God who knows the human heart, testified to them by giving them the Holy Spirit, just as he did to us; and in cleansing their hearts by faith he has made no distinction between them and us. Now therefore why are you putting God to the test by placing on the neck of the disciples a yoke that neither our ancestors nor we have been able to bear? On the contrary, we believe that we will be saved through the grace of the Lord Jesus, just as they will."

Verses 12-18 say, The whole assembly kept silence, and listened to Barnabas and Paul as they told of all the signs and wonders that God had done through them among the Gentiles. After they finished speaking, James replied, "My brothers, listen to me. Simeon has related how God first looked favorably on the Gentiles, to take from among them a people for his name. This agrees with the words from the prophets, as it is written, 'After this I will return, and I will rebuild the dwelling of David, which has fallen; from its ruins I will rebuild it, and I will set it up, so that all other peoples may seek the Lord — even all the Gentiles over whom my name has been called. Thus says the Lord, who has been making these things known from long ago.' (This is from the Septuagint, the Greek Old Testament, Amos 9:11-12.)

Verses 19-21 say, "Therefore I have reached the decision that we should not trouble those Gentiles who are turning to God, but we should write to them to abstain only from things polluted by idols and from fornication (with the gods at the pagan temples) and from whatever has been strangled and from blood (see Lev 3:17, 17:10-14). (We are not sure what being strangled means. It could be a reference to animals not properly slaughtered and not kosher in accordance with Lev 17:3, 19:26, Deut 12:16, 23-27.) For in every city, for generations past, Moses has had those who proclaim him, for he has been read aloud every sabbath in the synagogues."

These should not necessarily be seen as timeless laws, but more as a way to promote easier fellowship between Jewish and Gentile

Christians at a time when the relationship between the two was very strained.

In verses 22-29 the apostles and elders with the consent of the whole church choose Judas called Barsabbas and Silas, leaders among the brothers, with a letter stating their decision. They are to go with Paul and Barnabas to Antioch. The letter is addressed to the believers of Gentile origin in Antioch, Syria, and Cilicia. (Silas also called Silvanus will become a partner with Paul and even be seen with Peter.)

Verses 30-35 say, So they went off and went down to Antioch. When they gathered the congregation together, they delivered the letter. When its members read it, they rejoiced at the exhortation. Judas and Silas, who were themselves prophets, said much to encourage and strengthen the believers. After they had been there for sometime, they were sent off in peace by the believers to those who had sent them. But Paul and Barnabas remained in Antioch, and there, with many others, they taught and proclaimed the word of the Lord.

Verses 36-41 say, After some days Paul said to Barnabas, "Come, let us return and visit the believers in every city where we proclaimed the word of the Lord and see how they are doing." Barnabas wanted to take with them John called Mark. But Paul decided not to take with them one who had deserted them in Pamphylia and had not accompanied them in the work. The disagreement became so sharp that they parted company; Barnabas took Mark with him and sailed away to Cyprus. But Paul chose Silas and set out, the believers commending him to the grace of the Lord. He went through Syria and Cilicia, strengthening the churches.

Chapter 16:1-2 says Paul went on also to Derbe and Lystra,

where there was a disciple named Timothy, the son of a Jewish woman who was a believer; but his father was Greek. He was well spoken of by the believers in Lystra and Iconium. Verse 3 says, Paul wanted Timothy to accompany him; and he took him and had him circumcised because of the Jews who were in those places, for they all knew his father was a Greek.

Being born of a Jewish woman, makes Timothy a Jew. Paul never rejects his Jewishness so for Jewish men, they are to be circumcised. As Christians these first believers are Jewish Christians. Circumcising Timothy will give him more credibility among the Jews; it will make it easier to bear witness to the Jews about the need for Christ. It has nothing to do with salvation but is a witness to the Jews that they do not have to reject their culture in becoming a Christian.

Verses 4-5 say, As they went from town to town, they delivered to them for observance the decisions that had been reached by the apostles and elders who were in Jerusalem. So the churches were strengthened in the faith and increased in numbers daily.

Verses 6-10 say, they went through the region of Phrygia and Galatia, having been forbidden by the Holy Spirit to speak the word in Asia. (Apparently, it is time to go elsewhere.) When they had come opposite Mysia, they attempted to go into Bithynia but the Spirit of Jesus would not allow them; so passing by Mysia, they went down to Troas. (The Spirit of Jesus is the Holy Spirit; the Spirit is leading them.) During the night Paul had a vision (divine communication); there stood a man of Macedonia pleading with him and saying, "Come over to Macedonia and help us." When he had seen the vision, we immediately tried to cross over to Macedonia, being convinced that God had called us to proclaim the good news to them. (The shift here to the first person plural "*we*" extends through 16:17. See also 20:5-15, 21:1-18, 27:1-28:16. Most scholars believe that Luke is personally with Paul in these passages. So he must have been living in this area.)

Verses 11-12 say, We set sail from Troas (near ancient Troy where the famous battle with the Trojan horse took place) and took a straight course (across the Aegean Sea) to Samothrace (an island), the following day to Neapolis (port for Philippi), and from there to Philippi, which is a leading city of the district of Macedonia and a Roman colony. We remained in this city for some time. (They are now in Greece in the continent of Europe leaving Asia Minor, or Turkey.)

Verses 13-15 say, On the sabbath day we went outside the gate by the river, where we supposed there was a place of prayer; and we sat down and spoke to the women who had gathered there. A certain woman named Lydia, a worshiper of God (a Gentile who worshiped the Jewish God), was listening to us; she was from the city of Thyatira (in Asia Minor, listed in Rev 2:18-29) and a dealer in purple cloth. The Lord opened her heart to listen eagerly to what was said by Paul. When she and her household were baptized, she urged us, saying, "If you have judged me to be faithful to the Lord, come and stay at my home." And she prevailed upon us.

Purple cloth is the clothing for kings and the wealthy. Thyatira is known for the purple dye that colored the cloth. The dye is taken drop by drop from a certain shellfish, thus making the cloth expensive. A place of prayer is a place where Jews gather for prayer when there are not ten males to form a synagogue. The household may include just her particular family or all who work for her, even children. As a merchant of purple, she would have a high social and economic status. The fact that she is called a mistress indicates she is not married.

In verses 16-17 a slave girl with a spirit of divination, who had made her owners much money though her fortune telling (magic) kept following them saying, "These men are slaves of the Most High God, who proclaim to you a way of salvation." Paul in (18) orders the spirit out of her. (Because she is a fortune teller, the evil spirit that gives her that ability is cast out by Paul.) Verses 19-21 say, But when her owners saw that their hope of making money was gone, they seized Paul and Silas and dragged them into the marketplace before the authorities. When they had brought them before the magistrates, they said, "These men are disturbing our city; they are Jews and advocating customs that are not lawful for us as Romans to adopt or observe." (Their charge is that they are opposed to Roman authority.)

Whenever Christianity attacks vested interest, trouble always follows. It is characteristic of humans that if their profits are threatened, trouble is sure to follow. Note the anti-semitism in their statement. Every person should ask themselves if what they are doing is helping or exploiting their fellow humans. Is the money made worth the price when it comes time to answer to God?

Verses 22-24 say, The crowd joined in attacking them, and the magistrates had them stripped of their clothing and ordered them to be beaten with rods. After they had given them a severe flogging, they threw them into prison and ordered the jailer to keep them securely. Following these instructions, he put them in the innermost cell and fastened their feet in the stocks.

Verses 25-28 say, About midnight Paul and Silas were praying and singing hymns to God, and the prisoners were listening to them. Suddenly there was an earthquake, so violent that the foundations of the prison were shaken; and immediately all the doors were opened and everyone's chains were unfastened. When the jailer woke up and saw the prison doors wide open, he drew his sword and was about to kill himself, since he supposed that the prisoners had escaped. (If a guard lost a prisoner, it could be death for the guard.) Paul shouted in a loud voice, "Do not harm yourself, for we are all here."

In verses 29-34 the jailer fell down before Paul and Silas and said, "Sirs, what must I do to be saved?" They answered, "Believe on the Lord Jesus, and you will be saved, you and your household." They spoke the word of the Lord to him and to all who were in his house. At the same hour of the night he took them and washed their wounds; then he and his family were baptized without delay. He brought them up into the house and set food before them; and he and his entire household rejoiced that he had become a believer in God. (As a general rule the word is to be heard, then belief in the word is necessary, then repentance for sin, and baptism follows, see Acts 2:37-42. Keep in mind even the demons believe, James 2:19.)

In verses 35-40 the magistrates sent the police to tell the jailer saying that they were to be freed, but Paul replied, "They have beaten us in public, uncondemned, men who are Roman citizens, and have thrown us into prison; and now they are going to discharge us in secret? Certainly not! Let them come and take us out themselves." The police reported these words to the magistrates, and they were afraid when they heard that they were Roman citizens; so they came and apologized to them. Paul then went to Lydia's house to encourage all the believers, and then they departed. (We do not know how Paul had obtained Roman citizenship, but because of it, he had certain rights. Here he takes advantage of those rights in order to make sure that when he leaves, the believers will not be harassed.)

❦

Chapter 17:1-4 says, After Paul and Silas had passed through Amphipolis and Apollonia, they came to Thessalonica, where there was a synagogue of the Jews. And Paul went in, as was his custom, and on three sabbath days argued with them from the scriptures, explaining and proving that it was necessary for the Messiah to suffer and rise from the dead, and saying, "This is the Messiah, Jesus whom I am proclaiming to you." Some of them were persuaded and joined Paul and Silas, as did many of the devout Greeks (Gentiles) and not a few of the leading women.

They are traveling on the famous Egnatian Way, the famous road from Rome to the Middle East. The highway goes right through the middle of Thessalonica. Paul always proceeds to the synagogue because the Jews had to first hear the message that in Jesus, who was crucified and rose from the dead, the old covenant has been fulfilled and the new has begun. The kingdom of God, the new age, the last age, has begun. The other reason for going to the synagogue is that the God-fearers are there. These people are Gentiles who have rejected the pagan gods for the one God of the Jews. These people are very open to becoming followers of Jesus. They, along with Jews believing in Jesus, are the first Christians.

Verses 5-9 say, But the Jews became jealous, and with the help of some ruffians in the marketplaces they formed a mob and set the city in an uproar. (The Jews are jealous because both Jews and Gentiles are leaving Judaism and going to be followers of Christ.) While they were searching for Paul and Silas to bring them out to the assembly, they attacked Jason's house. (Apparently Jason is a follower of Christ and provided his house for the Christians to meet and even for Paul and Silas to stay. We do not know where Timothy is at this point.) When they could not find them, they dragged Jason and some believers before the city authorities, shouting, "These people who have been turning the world upside down (quite a reference) have come here also, and Jason has entertained them as guests. They are all acting contrary to the decrees of the emperor, saying that there is another king named Jesus." The people and the city officials were disturbed when they heard this, and after they had taken bail from Jason and the others, they let them go. (Again, the charge is that they are rejecting Roman authority.)

Turning the world upside down says much about their accomplishments and their reputation spreading throughout the whole area. The charge against them is political. They are declaring that Jesus is King; it is not a false charge. This very charge got Jesus put to death, for the Romans will not tolerate anything they think might be a revolution. But this revolution is not one of violence or one to politically rule on earth. It is a peaceful revolution dealing with a way of thinking and living and has nothing to do with Christians politically governing the world, even though they challenge the thinking of the political authorities. This is the usual misunderstanding about the nature of the kingdom. Therefore Paul needs to be careful of not being charged as a political revolutionary. Unfortunately, he will later be put to death by the Roman government just as Jesus was.

Verses 10-12 say, That very night the believers sent Paul and Silas off to Beroea; and when they arrived, they went to the Jewish synagogue. These Jews were more receptive than those in Thessalonica, for they welcomed the message very eagerly and examined the scriptures every day to see whether these things were so. (The Old Testament is their Scripture, and the first Christians use it to show people that Jesus is the one Moses and the prophets foretold. These people would not accept the teaching unless it could be shown in Scripture.) Many of them therefore believed, including not a few Greek women and men of high standing. (Examining the Scriptures is what every Christian and every church should constantly be doing.)

Verses 13-15 say, But when the Jews of Thessalonica learned that the word of God had been proclaimed by Paul in Beroea as well, they came there too, to stir up and incite the crowds. Then the believers immediately sent Paul away to the coast, but Silas and Timothy remained behind. Those who conducted Paul brought him as far as Athens; and after receiving instructions to have Silas and Timothy join him as soon as possible, they left him.

Verses 16-21 describe Athens. The city is filled with idols. There are many Epicurean and Stoic philosophers. The Epicureans did not believe in any religion. If a few did believe in any form of religion, it would be deism, meaning God is not involved in the affairs of the world. They live a life in detachment from desire and let things go as they may. The Stoic goal is to align their will with the reason of the universe. All is according to natural law. Their approach to God, if any, would be pantheism, meaning that God is everything. The two groups are alive today but with different names. Paul went to both the synagogue and the marketplace, and in verse 18 they said, "What does this babbler want to say?" Others said, "He seems to be a proclaimer of foreign divinities." In (19) they asked him, "May we know what this new teaching is that you are presenting? It sounds rather strange to us, so we would like to know what it means." Verse 21 says, Now all the Athenians and the foreigners living there would spend their time in nothing but telling or hearing something new. (This is typical of what happens in the modern world and even to many biblical scholars of today.)

Verses 22-28 say, Then Paul stood in front of the Areopagus and said, "Athenians, I see how extremely religious you are in every way, for as I went through the city and looked carefully at the objects of your worship, I found among them an altar with the inscription, 'To an unknown god.' What therefore you worship as unknown, this I proclaim to you. The God who made the world and everything in it, he who is Lord of heaven and earth, does not live in shrines made with human hands, nor is he served by human hands, as though he needed anything, since he himself gives to all mortals life and breath and all things. From one ancestor he made all nations to inhabit the whole earth, and he allotted the times of their existence and the boundaries of the places where they would live, so that they would search for God and perhaps grope for him and find him — though indeed he is not far from each one of us. For 'In him we live and move and have our being'; as even some of our own poets have said, 'For we too are his offspring.' (The first quote is from Epimenedes and the second is from Aratus, a Greek poet from Cilicia, who was a Stoic.)

Verses 29-31 continue, "Since we are God's offspring, we ought not to think that the deity is like gold, or silver, or stone, an image formed by the art and imagination of mortals. While God has overlooked the times of human ignorance, now he commands all people everywhere to repent, because he has fixed a day on which he will have the world judged in righteousness by a man whom he appointed, and of this he has given assurance to all by raising him from the dead."

This very same message is appropriate even for today. While on earth God overlooks the ignorance of humans when they have not been informed and looks at the heart (Rom 2:14-16). There will be a judgment day, so Paul mentions the importance of repentance; they have now been informed, so they are now responsible.

Verses 32-34 say, When they heard of the resurrection of the dead, some scoffed; but others said, "We will hear you again about this." At that point Paul left them. But some of them joined him and became believers, including Dionysius the Aeropagite and a woman named Damaris, and others with them.

Chapter 18:1-4 says, After this Paul left Athens and went to

Corinth. There he found a Jew named Aquila, a native of Pontus, who had recently come from Italy with his wife Priscilla, because Claudius had ordered all Jews to leave Rome. Every sabbath Paul would argue in the synagogue and would try to convince Jews and Greeks. (Claudius is the Roman Emperor in 41-54 AD, who expelled the Jews from Rome around 49 AD. It may be that Jews rejecting Jesus and Jews accepting Jesus were in conflict, and because Rome is in political turmoil Claudius found the Jews could be used as a scapegoat.)

Paul went to see them because he was of the same trade, he stayed with them, and they worked together — by trade they were tentmakers. They became fellow tentmakers and workers for Christ. The Greek word can also be translated leather maker. As a rabbi Paul is required to have a trade. Therefore he does not need to take any money for his teachings about Christ and the kingdom of God. Paul stayed with Priscilla and Aquila while in Corinth.

Corinth is about fifty miles south of Athens. It is the capital of Achaia and lies near a narrow isthmus that is three and a half miles wide. Because of this Corinth has two ports and is a natural commercial and trade center. It was a stopping point for many sailors. The city is filled with shrines to the Greek gods, the emperor, and the temple of Aphrodite. Polhill (1999, 215) says that at one time it had a thousand sacred prostitutes.

At this point Judaism consists of Jews who do not accept Jesus as rising from the dead or the one who forgives sin. Forgiveness came at the temple through the system of animal sacrifices and the Day of Atonement.

Verses 5-6 say, When Silas and Timothy arrived from Macedonia, Paul was occupied with proclaiming the word, testifying to the Jews that the Messiah was Jesus. When they opposed and reviled him, in protest he shook the dust from his clothes and said to them, "Your blood be upon your own heads! I am innocent. From now on I will go to the Gentiles." (This is reminiscent of Ezekiel's words about the sentinel or watchman, Ezek 33:1-7. The peoples' souls are the watchman's responsibility, if the souls are not warned, but if they are warned then their destruction is their own responsibility.)

Verses 7-8 say, Then he left the synagogue and went to the house of a man named Titius Justus, a worshiper of God; his house was next door to the synagogue. Crispus, the official of the synagogue, became a believer in the Lord, together with all his household; and many of the Corinthians that heard Paul became believers and were baptized. (Titius is a Gentile and a believer. An official of the synagogue like Crispus becoming a believer would be a shock to the Jewish community.)

Verses 9-11 say, One night the Lord said to Paul in a vision, "Do not be afraid, but speak and do not be silent; for I am with you, and no one will lay a hand on you to harm you, for there are many in this city who are my people." He stayed there a year and six months, teaching the word of God among them. (Visions are directions from God. For those today thinking they receive a vision from God, it is important to know that it is never to display self-importance or self-aggrandizement, and it will not be anything contrary to Scripture.)

Verses 12-17 say, But when Gallio was proconsul of Achaia, the Jews made a united attack on Paul and brought him before the tribunal. They said, "This man is persuading people to worship God in ways that are contrary to the law." Just as Paul was about to speak, Gallio said to the Jews, "If it were a matter of crime or serious villainy, I would be justified in accepting the complaint of you Jews; but since it is a matter of questions about words and names and your own law, see to it yourselves; I do not wish to be a judge of these matters." And he dismissed them from the tribunal. Then all of them seized Sosthenes, the official of the synagogue, and beat him in front of the tribunal. But Gallio paid no attention to any of these things.

An archeological find shows that Gallio was proconsul in Corinth in 51-53 AD. He was the brother of Seneca, a Roman philosopher, a Stoic, and tutor of the future emperor Nero. A proconsul is the chief administrator of a senatorial province. The charge against them was not just a religious charge but also a political one, which was the same as Jesus, but Gallio rejects those charges saying it is an internal problem of the Jews.

In verse 18 after staying there a considerable time Paul with Priscilla and Aquila sailed for Syria. At Cenchrea, one of the ports of Corinth, he had his hair cut, for he was under a vow. (On the Nazirite vow, see Num 6:1-21.) This conveys Paul's continuity of Jewish practices. Paul never rejects the fact that he is a Jew. He is a Jew who becomes a follower of Jesus. Jews are never required to give up their culture or religious practices, but Paul teaches that these customs simply do not save anyone, for only Christ and his blood save a person.

Verse 19-23 say, When they reached Ephesus (a port in Asia Minor), he left them there, but first he himself went into the synagogue and had a discussion with the Jews. When they asked him to stay longer, he declined; but on taking leave of them, he said, "I will return to you, if God wills." Then he set sail from Ephesus. When he had landed at Caesarea, he went up to Jerusalem and greeted the church, and then went down to Antioch. After spending some time there he departed and went from place to place through the region of Galatia and Phrygia, strengthening the disciples. (This ends the second missionary journey and begins the third.)

Verses 24-26 say, Now there came to Ephesus a Jew named Apollos, a native of Alexandria. He was an eloquent man, well versed in the scriptures. (This means the Old Testament because the new is not yet written.) He had been instructed in the Way of the Lord, and he spoke with burning enthusiasm and taught accurately the things concerning Jesus, though he knew only the baptism of John. (He understood well the passages in the Old Testament and how they applied to Jesus as the Messiah and the one foretold by the prophets.) He began to speak boldly in the synagogue; but when Priscilla and Aquila heard him, they took him aside and explained the Way of God to him more accurately. (How many of us need the Way of God explained to us more accurately? We must always be open to a correction of our beliefs and deeper insight. First Corinthians 13:2 tells us that we now see in a mirror dimly and only know in part. We will know in fullness when Christ returns at the end time.)

Verses 27-28 say, And when he wished to cross over to Achaia the believers encouraged him. On his arrival he greatly helped those who through grace had become believers, for he powerfully refuted the Jews in public, showing by the scriptures that the Messiah is Jesus.

In chapter 19:1-7 Paul returns to Ephesus and finds twelve of John the Baptist's disciples who are baptized into John's baptism but have not heard about the Holy Spirit. Apparently, they need to be informed that the one John said is greater than he, has now come. In verses 5-6 they were baptized in the name of the Lord Jesus, and Paul laid his hands on them, the Holy Spirit came upon them, and they spoke in tongues and prophesied. Peter and John conveyed the Holy Spirit in this same way (8:17). (This is not the norm but for exceptional situations, and it shows that what the apostles did is necessary and legitimate and puts them under the authority of the apostolic faith.)

In verses 8-10 Paul enters a synagogue and for three months speaks boldly and argues persuasively about the kingdom of God. (Notice the message is the kingdom of God, which is the primary kingdom followers are to live under, Phil 3:20.) When some stubbornly refuse to believe and speak evil of the Way, Paul leaves and argues daily in a lecture hall of Tyrannus. Verses 10-12 say, This continued for two years, so that all the residents of Asia, both Jews and Greeks heard the word of the Lord. (All the residents of Asia is another hyperbole.) God did extraordinary miracles through Paul, so that when the handkerchiefs or aprons that had touched his skin were brought to the sick, their diseases left them, and the evil spirits came out of them (see 5:15, Mk 5:25-29, 6:56).

Note that the emphasis is always on God's power, even though he uses his created beings or the material creation as his instruments. This leads to the cult of relics that was popular in the Middle Ages. This can not be described as magical or superstitious as some have tried to do, for as explained it is the power of God working. Lourdes for some people may be a possible modern day explanation.

Verses 13-17 say, Then some itinerant Jewish exorcists tried to use the name of the Lord Jesus over those who had evil spirits, saying, "I adjure you by the Jesus whom Paul proclaims." Seven sons of a Jewish high priest named Sceva were doing this. (There is no record of this high priest.) But the evil spirit said to them in reply, "Jesus I know, and Paul I know; but who are you?" Then the man with the evil spirit leaped on them, mastered them all, and so overpowered them that they fled out of the house naked and wounded. (In understanding this we must say that in this time at the beginning of Christianity with the planting of the first churches, the Holy Spirit worked somewhat differently from how it works today. One possible explanation is that in an age of magic these miracles were necessary to establish Christianity. Now that it is established, it does not continue. As Luke said, Lk 16:29-31, they have the scriptures.)

In verses 17-20 all the people are awestruck by what is happening and the name of the Lord Jesus is praised. A number of those who practiced magic burned their books of magic in public. Their value is calculated at fifty thousand coins. Verse 20 says, So the word of the Lord grew mightily and prevailed. (These magicians saw the difference between their magic and the miracles being performed by the apostles and the apostles clothing that had touched those who had been healed. The writer is saying God is making clear what is from him and what is not from him.)

Verses 21-22 say, Now after these things had been accomplished, Paul resolved in the Spirit to go through Macedonia and Achaia, and then go on to Jerusalem. He said, "After I have gone there, I must also see Rome." So he sent two of his helpers, Timothy and Erastus, former treasurer of Corinth, to Macedonia, while he himself stayed for sometime longer in Asia.

In verses 23-27 Demetrius, a silversmith, who made miniature silver shrines of the temple of Artemis gathered together the workers of the same trade. (Artemis is a virgin goddess who gives help to women in childbirth. The temple is a massive structure and one of the seven architectural wonders of the ancient world. It is a major financial institution, accepting sacrifices, deposits, and making loans as most of the pagan temples did in the ancient world. This one is the largest banking center in Asia and is central to the civic pride and commercial well-being of the city. Paul is charged with violating the interests of those devoted to their temples, and upsetting the economy because he is proclaiming their gods as false.)

In verses 25-27 Demetrius says, "Men, you know that we get our wealth from this business. You also see and hear that not only in Ephesus but in almost the whole of Asia this Paul has persuaded and drawn away a considerable number of people by saying that gods made with hands are not gods. And there is danger not only that this trade of ours may come into disrepute but also that the temple of the great goddess Artemis will be scorned, and she will be deprived of her majesty that brought all Asia and the world to worship her." (What does the reader think his primary concern is? How different is that from our times?)

Verses 28-31 say, When they heard this, they were enraged and shouted, "Great is Artemis of the Ephesians!" The city was filled with confusion; and people rushed together to the theater, dragging with them Gaius and Aristarchus, Macedonians who were Paul's travel companions. Paul wished to go into the crowd, but the disciples would not let him; even some officials of the province of Asia, who were friendly to him, sent him a message urging him not to venture into the theater.

In verse 33 a Jew named Alexander tried to speak, but (34) says, they would not let him speak, and for two hours they shouted in unison. "Great is Artemis of the Ephesians!" Hays (1996, 128) says, "To transfer this story . . . into our situation, we might think of the silversmiths as defense contractors worried that the Christians will put them out of business by turning everybody into pacifists. The mob chant then—instead of great is Artemis of the Ephesians— would simply be U-S-A, U-S-A, U-S-A! (What does the reader think of that analysis?)

In verses 35-41 the town clerk quiets them down by telling them if Demetrius and his people have a complaint, they have a channel to go through. The courts are open and there are proconsuls; let them bring charges there against one another. He tells them that if there is anything further they want to know, settle it in the regular assembly, for they are all in danger of being charged with rioting. When he had said this, he dismissed the assembly. (If the Romans see a riot, they rush in troops and destroy the area and many are killed. The town would also lose some or all of local control.)

⌒◞◞◟◟⌒

Chapter 20:1-3 says, After the uproar had ceased, Paul sent for the disciples; and after encouraging them and saying farewell, he left for Macedonia. After he had gone through those regions and had given the believers much encouragement, he came to Greece, where he stayed for three months. He was about to set sail for Syria when a plot was made known against him by the Jews, and so he decided to return through Macedonia (Philippi). Some of the disciples went ahead and were waiting for him in Troas. Luke in (6) says, but we sailed from Philippi after the days of Unleavened Bread (Passover), and in five days we joined them in Troas, where we stayed for seven days.

Verses 7-9 say, On the first day of the week, when we met to break bread (Holy Communion?), Paul was holding a discussion with them; since he intended to leave the next day, he continued speaking until midnight. There were many lamps in the room upstairs where we were meeting. A young man named Eutychus, who was sitting in the window, began to sink off into a deep sleep while Paul talked still longer. Overcome by sleep, he fell to the ground three floors below and was picked up dead. (He is the first person, with many more to follow throughout the years, to fall asleep during a long sermon. The fact that even Paul put someone to sleep should be encouragement to modern day preachers.) Verses 10-12 say, But Paul went down, and bending over him took him in his arms, and said, "Do not be alarmed, for his life is in him." (Like Peter in 9:36-42, he raises him from the dead. Then Paul went upstairs, and after he had broken bread and eaten, he continued to converse with them until dawn; then he left. Meanwhile they had taken the boy away alive and were not a little comforted.

In verses 13-17 they set sail for Miletus, which was past Ephesus. (Miletus is about thirty miles south of Ephesus and at one time was the biggest city in Asia. It still is a major commercial area with excellent harbors.) Verses 18-23 say, From Miletus he sent a message to Ephesus, asking the elders of the church to meet him. When they came to him he said to them: "You yourselves know how I lived among you the entire time from the first day that I set foot in Asia, serving the Lord with all humility and with tears, enduring the trials that came to me through the plots of the Jews. I did not shrink from doing anything helpful, proclaiming the message to you and teaching you publically and from house to house, as I testified to both Jews and Greeks about repentance toward God and faith toward our Lord Jesus. And now as a captive to the Spirit, I am on my way to Jerusalem, not knowing what will happen to me there, except that the Holy Spirit testifies to me in every city that imprisonments and persecutions are waiting for me.

Verses 24-28 continue, "But I do not count my life of any value to myself, if only I may finish my course and the ministry that I received from the Lord Jesus, to testify to the good news of God's grace. And now I know that none of you, among whom I have gone about proclaiming the kingdom, will ever see my face again. Therefore I declare to you this day that I am not responsible for the blood of any of you, for I did not shrink from declaring to you the whole purpose of God. Keep watch over yourselves and over all the flock, of which the Holy Spirit has made you overseers, to shepherd the church of God that he obtained with the blood of his own Son. (The word overseers is also translated bishops. Luke also calls them elders or presbyters.)

Verses 29-35 continue, "I know that after I have gone, savage wolves will come in among you, not sparing the flock. Some even of your own group will continue distorting the truth in order to entice the disciples to follow them. Therefore be alert, remembering that for three years I did not cease night or day to warn everyone with tears. And now I commend you to God and to the message of his grace, a message that is able to build you up and to give you the inheritance among all who are sanctified. I coveted no one's silver or gold or clothing. You know for yourselves that I worked with my own hands to support myself and my companions. In all this I have given you an example that by such work we must support the weak, remembering the words of the Lord Jesus, for he himself said, 'It is more blessed to give than to receive.' "

That statement is not found in the Gospels, but this is the nature of Paul's ministry, which is giving oneself to and remembering the weak, the poor, and those not favored by the wealthy and powerful. Does this characterize your church or those the reader is familiar with today?

Verses 36-38 say, When he had finished speaking, he knelt down with them and prayed. There was much weeping among them all; they embraced Paul and kissed him, grieving especially because of what he had said, that they would not see him again. Then they brought him to the ship.

In chapter 21:1-3 they sailed to Syria and landed at Tyre. Verse 4 says, We looked up the disciples and stayed there for seven days. Through the Spirit they told Paul not to go on to Jerusalem. In (5-9) they prayed together, and then got back on the ship, sailed to Ptolemais where they stayed with believers for one day, then went to Caesarea where they stayed with Philip the evangelist, one of the seven, who had four unmarried daughters with the gift of prophecy.

In verses 10-12 after staying there several days a prophet named

Agabus came down from Judea and told them the Jews in Jerusalem will put him in chains. The people urged him not to go. Verses 13-14 say, Then Paul answered, "What are you doing weeping and breaking my heart? For I am ready not only to be bound but even to die in Jerusalem for the name of the Lord Jesus." Since he would not be persuaded, we remained silent except to say, "The Lord's will be done."

In verses 17-25 they arrive in Jerusalem and the next day visit James and the elders. (James has emerged as the leader of the Jerusalem church.) Paul relates what God is doing through the Gentiles, and they praise God. Then they tell Paul there are thousands of Jews zealous for the law in Jerusalem, who believe he is teaching against Moses and the law. So they encourage him to join with four of them under a vow to go through the rite of purification and pay for the shaving of their heads. That way they will see there is no truth to the rumor about him and that he still observes the law. (This would be to demonstrate that he is not rejecting his people or his culture.) Verse 26 says, Then Paul took the men, and the next day, having purified himself, he entered the temple with them, making public the completion of the days of purification when the sacrifice would be made for each of them.

In verses 27-34 after the seven days are almost completed, Jews from Asia see him in the temple and stir up the crowd against him. They call other Israelites and tell them that he is the one teaching everywhere against the law of Moses. (This is how bad rumors spread. Paul does not reject the law of Moses, but he teaches how it is fulfilled in Jesus. When people reject anything new and reject change, problems are sure to come.) The city is aroused, and they seize Paul and drag him into the temple. While they were trying to kill him, word comes to the military officer in charge that all Jerusalem is in an uproar. When the soldiers arrive, they arrest him, put him in chains, and inquire what he did. There is such an uproar, they can not find out what he did, so they take him to their barracks. Verse 35 says, When Paul came to the steps, the violence of the mob was so great that he had to be carried by the soldiers. The crowd that followed kept shouting, "Away with him!"

In verses 37-40 Paul asks the military officer if he can say something to him. The officer is surprised that he speaks Greek and that he is not the Egyptian, a pseudo-messiah, who planned to lead a revolt against Rome leading four thousand assassins into the wilderness around 52-59 AD (see Josephus, War ii.13.5.). Paul tells him that he is a Jew from Tarsus in Cilicia, a Roman city, and that he is a Roman citizen. Paul begs him for permission to speak, and is given permission. He then addresses them in the Hebrew language.

In chapter 22:1-21 he rehearses his history as previously mentioned. Chapters 22-26 are filled with speeches, as Paul gives his defense in various settings. Here as a Jew, he wants to appeal to things Jewish. He begins his speech by addressing the crowd as brothers and sisters exactly as Stephen did in Acts 7:2. Their charges that Paul violated both law and temple are the same charges brought against Stephen in Acts 6:13. He states who he is and where he is from and that he was brought up in Jerusalem and educated in the Mosaic law under Gamaliel. He mentions how he persecuted the Way, and on the way to Damascus how Jesus appeared to him.

The three accounts of his conversion (9:1-19, 22:3-16, 26:4-18) differ to some extent because of different contexts. The reader can compare the following account with the other two to see the differences. Verses 6-11 say, "While I was on my way and approaching Damascus, about noon a great light from heaven suddenly shone about me. I fell to the ground and heard a voice saying to me, 'Saul, Saul, why are you persecuting me?' I answered, 'Who are you, Lord?' Then he said to me, 'I am Jesus of Nazareth whom you are persecuting.' Now those who were with me saw the light but did not hear the voice of the one who was speaking to me. I asked, 'What am I to do, Lord?' The Lord said to me, 'Get up and go to Damascus; there you will be told everything that has been assigned to you to do.' Since I could not see because of the brightness of the light, those who were with me took my hand and led me to Damascus."

In verses 12-16 he continues, "A certain Ananias, a devout man according to the law and well spoken of by all the Jews living there, came to me, and standing beside me, he said, 'Brother Saul, regain your sight!' In that very hour I regained my sight and saw him. Then he said, 'The God of our ancestors has chosen you to know his will, to see the Righteous One and to hear his voice; for you will be his witness to all the world of what you have seen and heard. And now why do you delay? Get up, be baptized, and have your sins washed away, calling on his name.' (This complies with Acts 2:38.)

Verses 17-21 say, "After I had returned to Jerusalem and while I was praying in the temple, I fell into a trance and saw Jesus saying to me, 'Hurry and get out of Jerusalem quickly, because they will not accept your testimony about me.' And I said, 'Lord, they themselves know that in every synagogue I imprisoned and beat those who believed in you. And when the blood of your witness Stephen was shed, I myself was standing by, approving and keeping the coats of those who killed him.' Then he said to me, 'Go, for I will send you far away to the Gentiles.' "

Verses 22-27 say, Up to this point they listened to him, but then they shouted, "Away with such a fellow from the earth! For he should not be allowed to live." And while they were shouting, throwing off their cloaks, and tossing dust in the air, the tribune

(Roman military leader) directed that he was to be brought into the barracks, and ordered him to be examined by flogging, to find out the reason for this outcry against him. But when they tied him up with thongs, Paul said to the centurion who was standing by, "Is it legal for you to flog a Roman citizen who is uncondemned?"

In verse 28 Paul told them he was born a Roman citizen. Verses 29-30 say, Immediately those who were about to examine him drew back from him; and the tribune also was afraid, for he realized that Paul was a Roman citizen and that he had bound him. (This action is not permitted to be done to a Roman citizen under these circumstances.) Since he wanted to find out what Paul was being accused of by the Jews, the next day he released him and ordered the chief priests and the entire council to meet. He brought Paul down and had him stand before them.

Chapter 23:1-5 says, While Paul was looking intently at the council he said, "Brothers, up to this day I have lived my life with a clear conscience before God." Then the high priest Ananias (high priest and in charge of Sanhedrin from 48-66 AD) ordered those standing near him to strike him on the mouth. At this Paul said to him. "God will strike you, you whitewashed wall (see Ezek 13:10-16, Mt 23:27)! Are you sitting there to judge me according to the law, and yet in violation of the law (Deut 28:22) you order me to be struck?" Those standing nearby said, Do you dare to insult God's high priest?" And Paul said, "I did not realize, brothers, that he was high priest; for it is written, 'You shall not speak evil of a leader of your people.' " (It is difficult to understand why Paul did not recognize the high priest, but it gives Paul an opportunity to demonstrate his respect for their Scriptures as he cites Ex 22:27-28, which is a critique of any leader who does not obey the law.)

Verses 6-11 say, When Paul noticed that some were Sadducees and others were Pharisees, he called out in the council, "Brothers, I am a Pharisee, a son of Pharisees. I am on trial concerning the hope of the resurrection of the dead." When he said this, a dissension began between the Pharisees and the Sadducees, and the assembly was divided. (The Sadducees say there is no resurrection, or angels, or spirits; but the Pharisees acknowledge all three.) Then a great clamor, and certain scribes of the Pharisees' group stood up and contended, "We find nothing wrong with this man. What if a spirit or an angel has spoken with him?" When the dissension became violent, the tribune, fearing that they would tear Paul to pieces, ordered the soldiers to go down, take him by force and bring him into the barracks. That night the Lord stood near him and said, "Keep up your courage! For just as you have testified for me in Jerusalem, so you must bear witness also in Rome."

Verses 12-15 say, In the morning the Jews joined in a conspiracy and bound themselves by an oath neither to eat nor drink until they had killed Paul. There were more than forty who joined in this conspiracy. They went to the chief priests and elders and said, "We have strictly bound ourselves by an oath to taste no food until we have killed Paul. Now then, you and the council must notify the tribune to bring him down to you, on the pretext that you want to make a more thorough examination of his case. And we are ready to do away with him before he arrives."

In verses 16-22 the son of Paul's sister heard about this and told Paul. Paul told the military officer, who took his nephew to another officer, and the officer was told of the plot. In (23-30) the tribune summoned two of the centurions and said, "Get ready to leave by nine o'clock tonight for Caesarea with two hundred soldiers, seventy horsemen, and two hundred spearmen. Also provide mounts for Paul to ride, and take him safely to Felix the governor." Then he

(Claudius Lysias) wrote a letter to Felix, the Roman procurator, stating what had happened and saying that he had not found him guilty of anything deserving death or imprisonment. (Felix is in power from 52-58 AD.)

Verses 31-35 say, So the soldiers according to their instructions, took Paul and brought him during the night to Antipatris. The next day they let the horsemen go on with him, while they returned to the barracks. When they came to Caesarea and delivered the letter to the governor, they presented Paul also before him. On reading the letter, he asked what province he belonged to, and when he learned that he was from Cilicia, he said, "I will give you a hearing when your accusers arrive." Then he ordered that he be kept under guard in Herod's headquarters.

In chapter 24:1-8 Ananias with elders and an attorney named Tertullus came five days later. Paul is summoned and Tertullus begins by smooth talking Felix the governor saying "Your Excellency, because of you we have long enjoyed peace, and reforms have been made for this people because of your foresight. We welcome this in every way and everywhere with utmost gratitude." In (5-6) he begins to accuse Paul by saying, "We have, in fact, found this man a pestilent fellow, an agitator among all the Jews throughout the world, and a ringleader of the sect of the Nazarenes. He even tried to profane the temple, and so we seized him. By examining him yourself you will be able to learn from him concerning everything of which we accuse him."

In verses 10-13 Paul makes his defense telling the governor that they can not prove anything, but in (14-21) he says, "But this I admit to you, that according to the Way, which they call a sect, I worship the God of our ancestors, believing everything laid down according to the law or written in the prophets. I have a hope in God — a hope that they themselves also accept — that there will be a resurrection of both the righteous and the unrighteous. Therefore I do my best always to have a clear conscience toward God and all people. Now after some years I came to bring alms to my nation and to offer sacrifices. While I was doing this, they found me in the temple, completing the rite of purification, without any crowd or disturbance. But there were some Jews from Asia — they ought to be here before you to make an accusation, if they have anything against me. Or let these men here tell what crime they had found when I stood before the council, unless it was this one sentence that I called out while standing before them, 'It is about the resurrection of the dead that I am on trial before you today.' "

In verses 22-23 Felix, who is well informed about the Way, adjourned the hearing until Lysias the tribune gets there. He orders the centurion to keep him in custody, but to give him some liberty, and to let his friends take care of his needs.

Verses 24-26 say, Some days later when Felix came with his wife Drusilla (the daughter of Herod Agrippa I, who left her husband to marry Felix), who was Jewish, he sent for Paul and heard him speak concerning faith in Jesus Christ. And as he discussed justice, self control, and the coming judgment, Felix became frightened and said, "Go away for the present; when I have an opportunity, I will send for you." At the same time he hoped that money would be given to him by Paul, and for that reason he used to send for him very often and converse with him. (Unfortunately, money is often the controlling factor in almost everything.) Verse 27 says, After two years had passed, Felix was succeeded by Porcius Festus; and since he wanted to grant the Jews a favor, Felix left Paul in prison.

Many of our government officials do the same today. While in office, they make sure they take care of those who will take care of them when they are no longer in office. That is how our special interest system works in Congress and state legislatures. Any more in America just making it to Congress or the presidency guarantees the elected official comfort for life. Specials interests hire these officials after they are no longer in office as thanks for taking care of them while they were in office, and to use their influence. Of course, the elected officials all deny this, but statistics and their voting records deny their plea of innocence.

In chapter 25:1-7 Festus goes to Jerusalem where the chief priests and leaders of the Jews give him a report against Paul. (Festus comes to power around 59 AD and is assassinated in 66 AD.) They ask for Paul to be transferred to Jerusalem because they are planning an ambush to kill Paul just as they had planned two years ago. Festus invites them to come to Caesarea and accuse him. After staying among them for eight or ten days he goes back to Caesarea and orders Paul to be brought to him. The Jews surround him bringing many serious charges against him, which they can not prove. In verse 8 Paul said in his defense, "I have in no way committed an offense against the law of the Jews, or against the temple, or against the emperor."

Verses 9-12 say, But Festus, wishing to do the Jews a favor, asked Paul, "Do you wish to go up to Jerusalem and be tried there before me on these charges?" Paul said, "I am appealing to the emperor's tribunal; this is where I should be tried. I have done no wrong to the Jews, as you very well know. Now if I am in the wrong and have committed something for which I deserve to die, I am not trying to escape death; but if there is nothing to their charges against me, no one can turn me over to them. I appeal to the emperor." Then Festus, after he conferred with the council, replied, "You have appealed to the emperor; to the emperor you will go."

Only Roman citizens can appeal to the emperor, and once there is an appeal, it can not be changed. Also, if their case is judged against the person, the result is death. Eventually Paul will be put to death by the Romans. The charge can be none other than crimes against the state.

In verse 13 King Agrippa and Bernice arrived at Caesarea to welcome Festus. (Agrippa II is the son of Agrippa I, who is the grandson of Herod the Great. Bernice is his sister. Both are children of Agrippa I. It is said that Agrippa and Bernice are in an incestuous relationship.) Festus explained Paul's case to the king in (14-21). In verse 22 Agrippa said to Festus, "I would like to hear the man myself." "Tomorrow," he said, "you will hear him."

In verses 23-27 the next day Agrippa and Bernice come with great pomp. Paul is brought in. Festus tells Agrippa that he has examined him and found he has done nothing deserving death. He said that he has nothing definite to write to the emperor and wants Agrippa to examine Paul so he may have something to write to the emperor.

In chapter 26:1-5 Agrippa gives Paul permission to speak. He tells Agrippa he feels fortunate to present his case before him because he is familiar with the customs and controversies of the Jews. Then Paul presents his background and the background of the situation including his experience of Jesus. In verses 6-8 Paul says, "I stand here on trial on account of my hope in the promise made by God to our ancestors, a promise that our twelve tribes hope to attain, as they earnestly worship day and night. It is for this hope, your Excellency, that I am accused by Jews! Why is it thought incredible by any of you that God raises the dead?"

Concerning his experience of Jesus in verses 13-18 Paul says, "I saw a light from heaven, brighter than the sun, shining around me and my companions. When we had all fallen to the ground, I heard a voice saying to me in the Hebrew language, 'Saul, Saul, why are you persecuting me? It hurts you to kick against the goads.' (Kicking against the goads means a stubborn resistance against divine prodding.) I asked, 'Who are you, Lord?' The Lord answered, 'I am Jesus whom you are persecuting. But get up and stand on your feet; for I have appeared to you for this purpose, to appoint you to serve and testify to the things in which you have seen me and to those in which I will appear to you. I will rescue you from your people and from the Gentiles — to whom I am sending you to open their eyes so that they may turn from darkness to light and from the power of Satan to God, so that they may receive forgiveness of sins and a place among those who are sanctified by faith in me.'

Verses 19-23 say, "After that King Agrippa, I was not disobedient to the heavenly vision, but declared first to those in Damascus, then in Jerusalem and throughout the countryside in Judea, and also to the Gentiles, that they should repent and turn to God and do deeds consistent with repentance. For this reason the Jews seized me in the temple and tried to kill me. To this day I have had help from God, and so I stand here, testifying to both small and great, saying nothing but what the prophets and Moses said would take place: that the Messiah must suffer, and that, by being the first to rise from the dead, he would proclaim light both to our people and the Gentiles."

In verses 24-26 Festus exclaims that Paul's learning has driven him insane, but Paul disagrees noting that Agrippa knows what Paul is talking about. In verses 27-29 Paul says, "King Agrippa, do you believe the prophets? I know that you believe." Agrippa said to Paul, "Are you so quickly persuading me to become a Christian?"

Paul replied, "Whether quickly or not, I pray to God that not only you but also all who are listening to me today might become such as I am — except these chains."

Verses 30-32 say, Then the king got up, and with him the governor and Bernice and those who had been seated with them; and as they were leaving, they said to one another, "This man is doing nothing to deserve death and imprisonment." Agrippa said to Festus, "This man could have been set free if he had not appealed to the emperor." (Jesus was declared innocent by Pilate three times also. Most of what happened to Jesus also happens to Paul. Agrippa and Festus declare him innocent, but Paul originally appealed to Rome, 25:9-10, because Festus was going to turn him over to the Jews. Under Roman law the appeal can not be changed.)

Chapter 27:1-3 says, When it was decided that we were to set sail for Italy, they transferred Paul and some other prisoners to a centurion of the Augustan Cohort, named Julius. Embarking on a ship of Adramyttium that was about to set sail to the ports along the coast of Asia, we put to sea, accompanied by Aristarchus, a Macedonian from Thessalonica. The next day we put in at Sidon; and Julius treated Paul kindly, and allowed him to go to his friends to be cared for. (Remember in all the "we" verses it is Luke who is writing.)

In verses 4-8 They sail under the lee of Cyprus because of the wind, go by Cilicia and Pamphylia and then go to Myra in Lycia. Myra is a major port in grain traffic from Egypt to Rome. At Myra they get on a ship from Alexandria going to Italy. Because of the wind, they sail slowly and arrive off Cnidos, and then because the wind is against them they sail under the lee of Crete of Salmone. Sailing past it with difficulty, we came to a place called Fair Havens, near the city of Lasea. (Fair Havens is a place with a Christian population even today.)

In verses 9-20 because of the winter, sailing became dangerous. Paul advises they would lose much cargo and many lives if they continue, but the pilot and the owner of the ship believe the harbor is not suitable for spending the winter. They put to sea with the hope of reaching Phoenix, a harbor of Crete. In (13-21) a violent wind comes upon the ship and moves it under the lee of Cauda. The storm pounds them violently, so they begin to throw some of the cargo overboard. (When grain gets wet, it gets very heavy and will sink them.) For many days there was no sun or stars, and all hope of being saved is abandoned.

In verses 21-26 Paul stands up and says, "Men, you should have listened to me and not have set sail from Crete and thereby avoided this damage and loss. I urge you now to keep up your courage, for there will be no loss of life among you, but only of the ship. For last night there stood by me an angel of the God to whom I belong and whom I worship, and he said, 'Do not be afraid, Paul; you must stand before the emperor; and indeed, God has granted safety to all those who are sailing with you.' So keep up your courage, men, for I have faith in God that it will be exactly as I have told you. But we will have to run aground on some island."

In verses 27-38 after fourteen days they think they may be getting near land, Paul tells them to take some food, and tells them they will survive. We learn that there are two hundred seventy-six people on the ship. In verses 39-44 they see land, and the ship strikes a reef and begins to break up. The soldiers plan to kill the prisoners so none can escape, but the centurion wishing to save Paul orders them not to do so. He orders people overboard to make it to shore. Some swim, others use planks and pieces of the ship; all make it safely to shore.

In chapter 28:1-6 they are on the island of Malta, and the people show them unusual kindness. It begins to rain and is cool, so they make a fire. Paul gathers some firewood and builds a fire, and in the process a viper bites him. Paul shakes off the snake into the fire and suffers no harm (see Lk 10:18-19 and Mk 16:18), and the people declare Paul a god.

In verses 7-11 we learn that Publius, the leading man of the island, entertained them hospitably for three days. His father is sick with fever and dysentery, and Paul heals him by praying and laying his hands on him. Paul heals many on the island. (Good health is always a priority of the early Christians.) When they are ready to sail the people of the island provide them with all the provisions they need. After three months of winter, they set sail on an Alexandrian (Egypt) ship with the Twin Brothers as a figurehead (Castor and Pollux, sons of Zeus are associated with safety on the seas. Many of today's fundamentalists would not have boarded the ship.)

In verses 12-16 they go to Syracuse, Rhegium, and Puteoli. There they find believers and stay seven days. Then they go to Rome. The believers from Rome came from as far as the Forum of Appius (a market town forty-three miles from Rome) and Three Taverns (a watering hole thirty-three miles from Rome) to meet us. On seeing them, Paul thanks God and takes courage. On arriving in Rome Paul is allowed to live by himself, with the soldier who is guarding him.

In verses 17-22 after three days, Paul calls together the local leaders of the Jews and relates the story of what happened to him in Jerusalem and why he is here. They tell him they have heard nothing about him, but in (22) they tell him they would like to hear from him about the sect that everywhere is spoken against. (Contrary to most scholarship, this indicates that Paul is planting the church in Rome.) Verses 23-24 say, After they had set a day to meet with him, they came to him at his lodgings in great numbers. From morning until evening he explained the matter to them, testifying to the kingdom of God and trying to convince them about Jesus both from the law of Moses and from the prophets. Some were convinced by what he had said, while others refused to believe.

Verses 25-28 say, So they disagreed with each other; and as they were leaving, Paul made one further statement: "The Holy Spirit in saying to your ancestors through the prophet Isaiah, 'Go to this people and say, You will indeed listen, but never understand, and you will indeed look, but never perceive. For this people's heart has grown dull, and their ears are hard of hearing, and they have shut their eyes; so that they may not look with their eyes, and listen with their ears, and understand with their heart and turn — and I would heal them.' Let it be known to you then that this salvation of God has been sent to the Gentiles; they will listen." (Paul in I Corinthian 2:14 says, those who are unspiritual do not receive the gifts of God's Spirit, for they are foolishness to them, and they are unable to understand them because they are spiritually discerned.)

Verses 30-31 say, He lived there two whole years at his own expense and welcomed all who came to him, proclaiming the kingdom of God and teaching about the Lord Jesus Christ with all boldness and without hindrance. (It is important to note what is proclaimed, Jesus and the kingdom of God that has broken in upon the earth. See the author's book on the Gospels to understand the importance of the kingdom of God, for that is what Jesus came to proclaim, Lk 4: 43, 9:62.)

There is much that Luke does not tell us such as what happens after this. Luke's main concern in the book of Acts is the spread of the message of Christ, the kingdom, and the church. This is how

Paul got to Rome; now the message will go throughout the whole Roman Empire, and within three hundred years, and after many martyrs, the Roman empire will become Christian. Perhaps Luke intended to end Acts in an open-ended way to say the story is not over, for the rest is up to you in the same manner Mark ended his gospel. Of course, we would like to know more, but most people do not even read this small book of Acts let alone an encyclopedia of happenings.

What happens next? Does Paul appear before the emperor? Is he set free? Some say there was a statute of limitations of two years. If the accusers do not appear for trial, the case will be dismissed. Others say the trial did not go well, so Luke does not mention it because he wants to end on a positive note. Tradition says that both Paul and Peter are martyred in Rome under Nero, but Nero comes a little later. Some of the early Christians like Clement believed he is released and goes to Spain. Eusebus writes he is released, goes to Spain and elsewhere, and later is martyred with Peter under Nero. But the evidence of Eusebus comes two hundred years later. Also, if Paul did plant the church in Rome as this chapter seems to indicate, then his letter to the Romans would have to come after being released from prison in Rome at this particular time.

Some believe the Pastoral Letters, 1 and 2 Timothy and Titus come after Paul's imprisonment in Rome as do a number of things Paul says about himself in other letters not mentioned in Acts. No one really knows. Luke's primary concern is that the good news has reached Rome, and from Rome seeds will be planted throughout the whole known world.

As a way of review list some of the most important verses or thoughts Luke makes in the book of Acts.

THE LETTER TO THE ROMANS

Romans is the Apostle Paul's letter to the church in Rome. It is a letter containing much theology. There was probably more than one church in Rome. The Roman Catholic Church believes Peter established the church in Rome, which is possible but difficult to prove. Acts 28:17-25 seems to indicate it was Paul who planted the church in Rome, but that has its problems also. Tradition says that both Peter and Paul were martyred in Rome. The letter was probably written between 54-58 AD from the city of Corinth, and it is the longest of Paul's letters.

In 1:16 he writes I am not ashamed of the gospel; it is the power of God for the salvation to everyone who has faith, to the Jew first and also to the Greek. The gospel is the good news from God about Jesus and the kingdom of God to both Jew and Gentile.

In that same chapter Paul discloses the natural law when he says we can know there is a God by looking at his creation. In verse 20 he says, Ever since the creation of the world his eternal power and divine nature, invisible though they are, have been understood and seen through the things he has made. Therefore those who reject God and his ways have no excuse when they worship the things of the world (creation) and not the Creator. By acting like this they claim to be wise, but they are fools for doing so.

He then lists the foolish things people do. Among them are greed, envy, arrogance, and homosexuality. His point in mentioning these actions is to ask people why one would point out anyone of them without pointing out their own foolish actions, and to make everyone understand that they are without excuse when they judge the sins of others (called their foolishness) and overlook their own. Homosexuality is included in Paul's list and will be discussed in more detail in chapter 1.

Chapter 2 mentions God's judgment on the basis of works, obedience to Christ, and the idea that it is not the hearers of the law who will be justified but the doers of the law. This is an aspect of the New Testament that many church theologians seem to ignore. This chapter also mentions that those who do not have the teaching about who Christ is and what he teaches will be judged by their heart, which is another aspect that seems to be glossed over by too many.

From the middle of chapter 3 to chapter 5 Paul shows how everyone is what Scripture calls a sinner and needs Christ, for only Christ can eliminate sin. We learn that both Jew and Gentile are justified or made right with God only by faith in Christ. Many scholars believe the best translation of "faith in Christ" is "the faith of Christ." The reason is that one's faith is not what really eliminates sin; Christ's faith is what eliminates sin. It is his faith in doing the Father's will by accepting the cross that sin was defeated. It is true one must have faith in Christ and what he did, but, according to Scripture, even that faith is God's gift.

An example of justifying faith in chapter 4 is Abraham who trusted God. In all aspects God is the initiator of all grace, and humans either let it work in and through them or reject it. The idea in the book of Romans is that God's righteousness in Christ is transferred to us by the Holy Spirit. Justification and sanctification are two sides of the coin while both are the work of God through his grace. Initial justification begins with God accepting people as they are, but total justification does not stop when one first responds to God. In the process we learn that faith does not stop with belief. Biblical faith includes belief, trust, and obedience through love where God's grace works in and through his people by his gifts of faith, hope, and love.

Philippians 2:12-13 says, work out your own salvation with fear and trembling; for it is God who is at work in you, enabling you both to will and to work for his good pleasure. It is God who is doing the work. People simply give him permission to use them as his instruments or as a channel for his work. As St Augustine said, In crowning our merits God is actually crowning his own gifts, for everything we have is his gift.

Chapter 5 continues along the same line mentioning the peace his people have with God comes from being justified by God's gift of grace through both Christ's faith and the gift of faith God gives his people. Verse 5 says, God's love has been poured into our hearts through the Holy Spirit that has been given to us. This is the same Spirit that also works by bearing God's fruit through God's people (Jn 15, Gal 5:22-26). Next what Adam did and what Christ did and the effects on humans are compared. Verse 19 says, For just by the one man's disobedience the many were made sinners, so by the one man's obedience the many will be made righteous. The question is: How are the many made disobedient by Adam and righteous by Christ?

Chapter 6 explains the meaning of baptism. As Christ died to sin, his followers die to sin; as Christ rose to new life with the Father, his followers rise to new life by becoming a new creation in union with him and each other. God's people now yield their bodies to Christ as weapons of righteousness leading to sanctification (holiness). Paul tells the church that now they are freed from death, for the wages of sin is death, but the free gift from God is eternal life. As Adam transferred his sin to humanity, humanity then confirms sin by their actions. But Christ transfers his righteousness to his people granting new life. His followers then confirm that transfer by a new life and obedient heart. The question different religions debate is over the meaning of transfer. Is it a real transfer or a transfer by the act of confirming? Or is it by both?

In chapter 7 Paul says the old law was holy and good, but it was imperfect, which is why Christ fulfilled the law. But the old was good because it revealed God and his ways. It told us who God is, who we are as his created people, how we are to relate to God, ourselves, his other created humans, and his created order. And it taught what sin is. Because the old law could not do anything about sin other than cover it, a new law was needed to eliminate it, which is one of the major reasons for the incarnation (taking on human flesh) of Christ. An important part of the chapter is Paul discussing his own battle with sin, something all people who are serious about following Christ can identify with.

In chapter 8 Paul says there is now no condemnation for those who are in union with Christ Jesus, for the law of the Spirit of life in Christ Jesus has freed us from the law of sin and death. Now his followers live according to the Spirit and not according to the flesh, and those who live by the Spirit are now members of God's family adopted by God. The Spirit now nurtures, helps, and leads, and even prays for us when we do not know how to pray. Life in the flesh and life in the Spirit are compared. One leads to death; the other leads to life and peace. For those who love God Paul says that nothing can now separate us from God but ourselves. No one can condemn us or separate us from the love of God in Christ Jesus our Lord.

In chapters 9-11 he discusses his love and hope for Israel knowing that a remnant will be saved as God has done throughout their history. The chapters are somewhat controversial because the future of the Jews is discussed. Will they be saved because they were first chosen by God, or must they also turn to Christ for salvation? Scholars are mixed on the answer. The answer according to most Christians was rather definite until the guilt many non-Jews carry with respect to the Holocaust brought on by Nazi Germany. How much influence should this horrific event have on what the Bible is saying?

In chapters 12-13 some duties of Christians are discussed as followers of Christ offer themselves to God conforming themselves to him instead of the world. Paul calls this way of life our spiritual worship. Rom 12:1-2 calls for God's people to present their bodies as a living sacrifice, holy and acceptable to God, which is called one's spiritual worship. The call is not to be conformed to this world, but be transformed by the renewing of your mind, so that the will of God is discerned, what is good, acceptable, and perfect.

In chapters 14 and 15 Paul sets guidelines on how Christians who disagree with each other can get along together and benefit each other. In verses 20-21 Paul states that his calling is to take the message of Christ where it has not been and to plant a church for others to build upon. In verses 26-27 he talks of sharing resources with the poor in Jerusalem and the necessity of sharing and being of service in material things. The religion of Jesus Christ, if it follows his example is as much about material things, as it is about spiritual things. Finally, in chapter 16 Paul sends his greetings to 26 people in the church, many are women and one, according to most scholars is a woman diakonos (deacon).

Romans chapter 1:1-7 begins by saying, Paul, a servant of Jesus Christ, called to be an apostle, set apart for the gospel of God, which he promised beforehand through his prophets in the holy scriptures, the gospel concerning his Son, who was descended from David according to the flesh and was declared to be Son of God with power according to the spirit of holiness by resurrection from the dead, Jesus Christ our Lord, through whom we have received grace and apostleship to bring about the obedience of faith among all the Gentiles for the sake of his name, including yourselves who are called to belong to Jesus Christ, To all God's beloved in Rome, who are called to be saints: Grace to you and peace from God our Father and the Lord Jesus Christ.

The Apostle Paul, Christ's servant (actually the word is slave) who received God's grace as an apostle, is the author of this book, and he is writing to the saints in Rome. The saints are all the serious, dedicated believers who are obedient to the faith. He gives a brief summary of the good news that Jesus is the son of David, as foretold by the prophets, installed in his position to the right hand of God (Dan 7:13-14) by his resurrection.

There is much in these first seven verses. Paul is stating that the promises God made to Abraham have been fulfilled by the sending of God's Son. Creation is being renewed, the covenant is being renewed as foretold, the new and final age is beginning, and God has confirmed this by raising his Son from the dead. God's people are now all who are in Jesus through faith, but true faith means an obedient faith. The world has been blessed through Abraham just as God promised Abraham (Gen 12:1-3). God has done what he said he would do.

Paul always includes a statement of grace and peace to whom he is writing. Grace means the gift of unmerited favor that comes from God, and with grace comes a reconciliation peace with God and peace with each other. Paul is saying that the real Lord and Savior who brings peace is the one God and his Son Jesus. It is not the Roman emperor, the one who also claims to be the lord and savior that brings peace to the world. The peace the emperor claims to bring is brought by fear and military might; the peace Jesus brings is through grace in the spirit of love.

In verses 8-15 Paul is thankful because their faith is proclaimed throughout the world. He tells them that he always remembers them in his prayers, and prays that he will eventually succeed in coming to them, so they can mutually be encouraged by each other's faith. Paul tells them that he desires to proclaim the gospel to them and to share with them some spiritual gift in order to strengthen them and reap some harvest among them as he has done with the rest of the Gentiles. As Paul says in verse 15, hence my eagerness to proclaim the gospel to you who are in Rome.

Paul in verses 16-17 tells them, I am not ashamed of the gospel; it is the power of God for salvation to everyone who has faith, to the Jew first and also to the Greek. For in it the righteousness of God is revealed through faith for faith; as it is written, "The one who is righteous will live by faith."

The righteousness of God is revealed through the faith of Christ in order for people to have faith. By their obedience of faith they will reveal that they have been made righteous by Christ. At a time when people are being martyred for the faith, Paul states he is not afraid of standing with the gospel, which is the good news that Christ has died, Christ has risen, the kingdom of God has begun, and Christ will come again. He will come for all who are created new, both Jew and Gentile. God is now ruling the world through his Son, Jesus, and his followers; the kingdom of God has broken into the world. A new creation and transformation of individuals, the world, and the world's institutions has begun through the Spirit

Jesus sends to work in and through his people. The problem of sin and evil is dealt with and is reversed.

The good news is that Jesus is Lord, and God is ruling the world through Jesus and those who submit to him. The Caesars of the world are being defeated. Evil has been taken care of individually and corporately; evil will not prevail. It has been defeated, and it is in the process of being defeated for both individuals and the world, and it will finally be defeated when Christ comes again perfecting all things in a new heaven and new earth (1 Cor 15:20-28).

This good news is for everyone who has faith, both Jew and Gentile. Paul says that in the gospel the righteousness of God, meaning his faithfulness to his covenant is revealed through faith for faith. Paul is saying the covenant God made through Abraham has now been fulfilled. God told Abraham he would bless the world through him and Abraham's offspring, and Abraham believed, and it was reckoned to him as righteousness, meaning that he and God entered into a right relationship. Now both Jew and Gentile become God's people through the faithfulness of God, and like Abraham they receive the blessing of a relationship of being God's people by grace through faith just like Abraham.

As they live in this world God's people are called to confirm their part of the covenant through the obedience of faith accomplished by the grace of the Holy Spirit. The righteous, those made righteous by the faith of Christ, will now live by faith (Hab 2:4). This is also interpreted as the one who is righteous by faith will live.

Dunn (2005, 206-210) compares the different meanings of the word *righteousness* between the Greco-Roman tradition, which is also the European-American concept of righteousness, with the Hebrew concept of righteousness and its root words justice and justification. In the Greco-European-American definition righteousness and justice are ideal concepts or absolute ethical norms against which particular claims and duties are measured as a standard set by the ideal of individual justice. But in Hebrew thought righteousness is something one has in one's relationship as a *social* being. People are righteous when they meet the claims which others have on them by virtue of their relationship. In a court the responsibility of the judge is to recognize what these obligations are within the people and to judge them accordingly.

The same is true of God's righteousness. In this case the relationship is the covenant that by God's grace he chooses Israel as his people and enters into relationship with Israel through Abraham. He tells Abraham he will make a great nation from him. He will give them land, and he will bless the world through him (Gen 12:1-30). The one God (Yahweh) will be their God, and they will be his people chosen to take his light to the world. According to Deuteronomy 27-30 he will bless them if they obey him, and will curse them if they are disobedient.

In Scripture the message is primarily about group responsibility, the nation's responsibility to God. In Exodus and Leviticus the sacrificial system is established whereby upon repentance they will be forgiven when their obedience falls short. They were never expected to be perfect, but they were expected to always remain faithful to God and each other. But throughout their history neither the nation nor many individuals within the nation remained faithful to the God that called them. In western thought justice is more about a person paying the price for what he did. In eastern or biblical thought justice is more about what we owe each other.

As we go through Romans Paul will emphasize how the reversal of the decline and decay of being made in God's image takes place. Paul will also examine the Jewish national boast that only they are God's people and because of that should have special favor based on election and the covenant. He will point out their unfaithfulness in refusing the call to be God's light to the Gentiles, and how they actually kept Gentiles from coming to God's light because of their nationalistic arrogance.

When the righteous live by faith God is honored, but when those who call themselves God's people ignore God's commands and live by a system of their own creation, and a philosophy and way of life of their own creation, God is not honored. Not only is God not honored, but his light does not penetrate the world. In the following many sins are listed, which are the sins of all humans. Paul believes humanity can know God through creation and through faith and thus realize their reason for being created, but instead they make idols out of creation, and because of that, they degrade themselves and ignore their reason for being created.

Verses 18-23 say, For the wrath of God is revealed from heaven against all ungodliness and wickedness of those who by their wickedness suppress the truth. (Because of their wickedness, God's truth and light are impeded from making an impact.) For what can be known about God is plain to them, because God has shown it to them. Ever since the creation of the world his eternal power and divine nature, invisible though they are, have been understood and seen through the things he has made. (God reveals himself through his created order, his natural law.) So they are without excuse; for though they knew God, they did not honor him as God or give thanks to him, but they became futile in their thinking, and their senseless minds were darkened. (As they reject God's light, they fall into darkness.) Claiming to become wise, they became fools; and they exchanged the glory of the immortal God for images resembling a mortal human being or birds or four-footed animals or reptiles.

Humanity should know and believe in God just by being aware of God's creation that surrounds them, but they reject that God created what they see and experience; thus they worship God's creation instead of the Creator. They make themselves and the things of the world their god. Meanwhile, they claim to be wise in their decision, but actually they have become fools, and because of that, they will bear the wrath of God. (Moderns do not like to hear anything about the wrath of God, but Scripture makes it very plain.)

Verses 24-25 say, Therefore God gave them up (let them go) in the lusts of their hearts to impurity, to the degrading of their bodies among themselves, because they exchanged the truth about God for a lie and worshiped and served the creature rather than the Creator, who is blessed forever! Amen. For this reason God gave them up to degrading passions. (They created God in their own image, and God allowed them free will to do what they wanted.)

The following from verses 26-28 shows some of the ways they degraded themselves as they worshiped the things of this world. Their women exchanged natural intercourse for unnatural, and in the same way also the men, giving up natural intercourse with women, were consumed with passion for one another. Men committed shameless acts with men and received in their own persons the due penalty for their error. And since they did not see fit to acknowledge God, God gave them up to a debased mind and of things that should not be done. (Before one focuses totally on homosexuality the following from Thessalonians needs noted.)

First Thessalonians 4:3-8 says, For this is the will of God, your sanctification (holiness): that you abstain from fornication; that each of you know how to control your own body in holiness and honor, not with lustful passion, like the Gentiles who know not God; that no one wrong or exploit a brother or sister in this matter, because the Lord is an avenger in all these things, just as we have already told you. For God did not call us to impurity but in holiness. Therefore whoever rejects this rejects not human authority but God, who also gives his Holy Spirit to you. (The issue is sex outside of marriage, both heterosexual and homosexual, or sex for pleasure and selfish interest.)

This writer finds it interesting that in modern times, according to reports about those sitting in church pews, the most prevalent sexual sins involving sex outside of marriage are fornication and adultery; it is not homosexuality or lesbianism. But what do preachers, priests, and many lay people preach about? It is not fornication and adultery. In fact this writer rarely misses Sunday worship and as far as can be remembered he has rarely heard a sermon or homily mention fornication or adultery, but he sure has heard about homosexuality.

Does the reader believe this chapter is saying anything about that hypocrisy? The above mentioned sins and the following verses mainly describe pleasure seeking and selfish behaviors that destroy meaningful relationships among friends and family and lead to turmoil in any society. In reference to the sexual sins these verses are referring to any sex outside of marriage. It is also interesting to note that the Old Testament practices of polygamy and concubines were accepted then and not mentioned in this list of sins. The writer continues with the following list of sins involving selfish behavior.

Verses 29-32 say, They were filled with every kind of wickedness, evil covetousness (greed), malice. Full of envy, murder, strife, deceit, craftiness, they are gossips, slanderers, God haters, insolent, haughty, boastful, inventors of evil, rebellious toward parents, foolish, faithless, heartless, ruthless. They know God's decrees, that those who practice such things deserve to die—yet they not only do them but even applaud others who practice them. (In their guilt they want to drag others to their arrogant, selfish, and socially destructive behaviors.)

All of these practices are a result of not worshiping the Creator as they make themselves and the things of the world more important. These are sins committed by those who reject God, but are they not also sins committed by those who do not reject God and sit in churches and synagogues? As we go through Romans we will learn that everyone sins and comes short of God's glory.

One way to respond to this partial list of sins, and it is a partial list, is by saying as Jesus did, he who is without sin cast the first stone (Jn 8:7). Are we not all sinners in need of repentance and deeper growth into holiness? Should any one of these sins cause one to be cast away or barred from the church? Which ones? Why? How should the modern day church react to this list of sins in Romans?

Chapter 2 is a continuation of the previous chapter. In verses 1-3 Paul says, Therefore you have no excuse, whoever you are when you judge others, for in passing judgment on another you condcmn yourself, because you, the judge, are doing the very same things. You say, "We know that God's judgment on those who do such things is in accordance with the truth." Do you imagine, whoever you are that when you judge those who do such things and yet do them yourself, you will escape the judgment of God? Or do you despise the riches of his kindness and forbearance and patience? Do you not realize God's kindness is meant to lead you to repentance?

These words are directed to religious people who judge the sins of others but do not see their own sins. Jesus in Mt 7:3 said, "Why do you see the speck in your neighbor's eye, but do not notice the log in your own eye? You hypocrite, first take the log out of your own eye, then you will see clearly to take the speck out of your neighbor's eye. " The message is to read God's word (Scripture) over against yourself, and then you will see your own sins and need for repentance, and then you will be less likely to judge others as not worthy of God. He is not saying that it is wrong to make a judgment, but there is a proper way to go about it and then convey it.

Another issue is that many Jews at the time believed that they were the righteous because God chose them, and Gentile sinners were not worthy of God and not accepted by God because God had not chosen them. They felt God would overlook their sins, which were nothing compared to the sins of the Gentiles. Meanwhile, the Jews isolated themselves from Gentiles and refused to socialize with them. They believed they would be made unclean if they came in contact with them. All this is contrary to the covenant God made with Abraham in Genesis 12 and 15 that through him a nation would come from him, and the world would be blessed.

Then Paul in verse 13 says, For it is not the hearers of the law who are righteous in God's sight, but the doers of the law who will be justified (Gen 22:15-17, Jas 2:18-24). (Here we will begin to see that justification has a beginning, a middle, and an end, and that one is not saved by works, but one is not saved without works. It begins by grace through faith, continues by grace through faith, and ends by grace through faith. Faith allows God's grace to transform hearts, and then work his works in and through those who are his people, Phil 2:12-13.)

Verses 14-16 say, When Gentiles, who do not possess the law, do instinctively what the law requires, these, though not having the law, are a law unto themselves. They show that what the law requires is written on their hearts, to which their own conscience also bears witness; and their conflicting thoughts will accuse or perhaps excuse them on the day when, according to the gospel, God, through Jesus Christ, will judge the secret thoughts of all.

God puts his light, natural law, within humans as he creates them. God rejects only those who reject him and his ways. If we have failed to present Christ and his message to others, and those others are following the light God gave them, they will be dealt with by God's grace, mercy, and compassion. It is not for humans to make judgments in such situations. All this is for God to deal with. Meanwhile the people of God are to make Jesus and his kingdom present wherever they may be.

Paul is trying to get the Jews to understand that Gentiles and Jews are both accepted by God according to God's standards and not their human standards. No one ritual or action, as important as it may be, determines who is in God's family and who is not. Even while the old covenant was in effect, God was more concerned with whether a person followed God's law and his natural law from the obedience of the heart. This was more important than following certain chosen rituals or actions while ignoring what is right. Humans need to be careful in their judgments. The primary issue has always been faith, and now it is the faith of the Son and faith in the Son that God sent. In this last age the faith of Jesus and faith in Jesus, not the law of Torah or any law, is what determines who is now a member of God's family.

Verses 17-24 say, But if you call yourself a Jew and rely on the law and boast of your relation to God and know his will and determine what is best because you are instructed in the law, and if you are sure that you are a guide to the blind, a light to those who are in darkness, a corrector of the foolish, a teacher of children, having in the law the embodiment of knowledge and truth, you, then that teach others, will you not teach yourself? While you preach against stealing, do you steal? You that forbid adultery, do you commit adultery? You that abhor idols, do you rob temples? You that boast in the law, do you dishonor God by breaking the law? (For these times this writer adds, you who condemn homosexuality, are you without sin?) For, as it is written, "The name of God is blasphemed among the Gentiles because of you."

His point is judge yourself and realize you also are a sinner in need of God's mercy and help. Work on your own sins before you even look at what others are doing. This may make you more merciful and compassionate toward what others are trying to deal with. This does not mean one can not call sin a sin, but be sure to look at your own struggle with sin.

The Jews boasted that God gave them his light and not the Gentiles. But they were not obedient to God. God gave them his light to take to the Gentiles, but they were disobedient and refused. They not only refused, but they kept God's light from the Gentiles by saying that God was not to go the Gentiles, for they were unclean sinners. Paul states that the real problem was their disobedience to God's commands and their hypocrisy. They dishonored God by living in sin blaspheming the name of God among the Gentiles. Paul's point is they are sinners also as are the Gentiles, and because of that both Jew and Gentile need Christ.

Verse 25 says, Circumcision indeed is of value if you obey the law; but if you break the law, your circumcision has become uncircumcision. (Obeying the commands from the heart is what is most important and here obeying the law is not primarily in reference to rituals such as circumcision, Sabbath laws, food laws, and purity laws, those laws that distinctly separate them from Gentiles. This was what too many of the Jews thought was most important, but Jesus says not so.)

Their first priority according to Jesus is to love God and neighbor as oneself, and to do to others what you want them to do to you, which is the essence of the law, Mk 12:33-34, Mt 22:37-40. Circumcision is of value only if it leads one also to obey from the heart the spirit of the whole law and represent God's light to the whole world. It must also be noted that the requirement of circumcision forced women into a situation where they could only be in the covenant by proxy.

Paul returns again to those not considered God's people. Verses 26-29 say, So, if those who are uncircumcised keep the requirements of the law, will not their uncircumcision be regarded as circumcision? Then those who are physically uncircumcised but keep the law will condemn you that have the written code and circumcision but break the law. For a person is not a Jew who is one outwardly, nor is true circumcision something external and physical. Rather, a person is a Jew who is one inwardly, and real circumcision is a matter of the heart—it is spiritual not literal. Such a person receives praise not from others but from God.

A person receives praise from God by doing from the heart what God desires. Paul's point is that Gentiles can do this as well as Jews. Following God's commands from the heart through the power of the Spirit demonstrates that one is a member of God's people not circumcision. As Paul goes on he will demonstrate that God's covenant faithfulness to Abraham is revealed through the faithfulness of Jesus for the benefit of all who have faith, Jew and Gentile alike. God's purpose to rescue the world from sin and death has been accomplished. The Messiah has done for the world what Israel was chosen to do but did not do. Now through faith in Jesus and repentance of sin, Jew and Gentile are one as God's people. God has fulfilled his promise to Abraham.

Chapter 3:1 asks the question, Then what advantage has the Jew? Or what is the value of circumcision? The answer in (2-8) states that the Jews were given the oracles of God (the Scriptures) and the promises contained within them. The Jews failed to take

them to the world as God called them to do. God's faithfulness in making the promise is not invalidated by their failure to keep their part of the covenant. God's faithfulness and truthfulness will prevail and will shine brightly as God acts for the good of all his created people. The justice of God will prevail meaning the righteousness of God. (This justice and righteousness of God is God's faithfulness to his covenant promise to Abraham that a nation and a land would be given through him and that the world will be blessed through Abraham's descendants.)

Even though God's people are unreliable, God will be reliable. He will keep his covenant promise, but in the process he must deal with everyone's major problem from the very beginning which is sin. As God promised he is taking care of the problem that began with the first humans, and then confirmed by every human. Through the life, death, and resurrection of Christ the world, both Jew and Gentile are now blessed. The person or group of people Paul is speaking with still does not want to be considered a sinner.

In verses 9-18 Paul informs that all are guilty; all are under the power of sin both Jew and Gentile. As it is written "There is no one who is righteous (perfectly righteous), not even one; there is no one who has understanding (perfect understanding), there is no one who seeks God (perfectly seeks God). All have turned aside, together they have become worthless; there is no one who shows kindness (perfect kindness), there is not even one." (Obviously this is a statement of hyperbole, an overstatement to express the truth that all are sinners and have lived in idolatry, for humans at one time or another have made other things more important to them than the things of God.)

He goes on to say that they use their tongues to deceive. Their lips are of venom. Their mouths are full of cursing and bitterness. Their feet are swift to shed blood; ruin and misery are in their paths, and the way of peace they have not known. There is no fear of God before their eyes. (Because humankind belongs to the species of humanity, all are guilty of sin, both Jew and Gentile.)

In verses 19-20 Paul tells them that one of the purposes of the law was to give knowledge of sin, and to learn that all have sinned, and to show the whole world is accountable to God. In verse 20 Paul informs them that no one will be justified by deeds prescribed by the law. The law or the Torah, nor anything in it, can justify anyone. Justification comes through the blood of Christ where sin is forgiven. (The law succeeds only in making humanity aware of their condition.)

Verses 21-26 say, But now apart from the law, the righteousness of God (meaning the justice or faithfulness of God) has been disclosed, and is attested by the law and the prophets, the righteousness of God through faith in Jesus Christ (or through the faith of Jesus Christ) for all who believe. (Faith in Jesus Christ is also translated the faith of Jesus Christ.) For there is no distinction, since all have sinned and fall short of the glory of God; they are now justified by his grace as a gift, through redemption that is in Christ Jesus, whom God put forward as a sacrifice of atonement by his blood effective through faith. He did this to show his righteousness (justice or faithfulness), because in his divine forbearance he had passed over the sins previously committed; it was to prove at the present time that he himself is righteous and that he justifies the one who has faith in Jesus (which also translated who has the faith of Jesus).

For Paul the cross is the climatic point in his definition of election. God has elected his Son Jesus, and through his grace those drawn to him are the elect. The cross is the ultimate point where the ancient problem of evil begun by Adam and Eve is addressed by the one God. The crucifixion and the resurrection reveal the faithfulness of the covenant God in his promise to Abraham.

NT Wright (2005, 119) says, God's faithfulness is revealed, through the faithfulness of the Messiah, for the benefit of all who believe, Jew and Gentile alike. That is the point of 3:21-26. Wright says that the context here is that God's promise to Abraham is fulfilled. Justification is not by faith in the Mosaic law; all are now one in Jesus Christ. In other words humanity is made right with God because of what Christ's faith did, not because of anything humanity did. That is the whole point of these verses.

Ephesians 2:13-16 says, But now in Christ Jesus you who once were far off have been brought near by the blood of Christ. For he is our peace; in his flesh he has made both groups (Jew and Gentile) into one and has broken down the dividing wall, that is, the hostility between us. He has abolished the law with its commandments and ordinances that he might create in himself one new humanity in place of the two, thus making peace, and might reconcile both groups to God in one body through the cross, thus putting to death that hostility through it.

This is what Paul is first referring to in his concept of justification. The justified, those now considered God's people, are called to do what Israel failed to do, which is to take God's light to the whole world to all of humanity and let Christ begin to reign through them. This is the beginning of the justification process. As Abraham became part of God's covenant through faith, now both Jew and Gentile become part of the new covenant through the faith of Jesus and what he did, not by circumcision or any works of the Old Testament law.

The issue is who belongs to the people of God and how can you tell, or how is it demonstrated. Like the old covenant, also in the new, God's people maintain their position in the covenant through God's grace by their obedience (2:6-8) and continued repentance. In the Old Testament sin was just covered, but under the New Testament sin is erased. God does not require perfection, but continual repentance keeps one cleansed of sin. Obedience expressed as following the ways of Christ is necessary to stay in the covenant but does not earn salvation. Salvation comes through the blood of Christ and the forgiveness of sin. Humanity can not do that for themselves; only Christ can do that for them. It is of the utmost of importance because as Rev 21:27 indicates, nothing unclean will enter into the eternal age. If uncleanness were to enter there would no longer be perfect joy, peace, and happiness.

This obedience is described by EP Sanders (1977, 75) as *covenantal nomism* indicating the inter-relationship between divine initiative (covenant) and human response (nomism). Dunn (2005, 4-6) gives an excellent description of the process. One confirms their part of the covenant by the obedience of faith and continual repentance. The inheritance is for the people of God as God's gift to them, but one can reject the inheritance by rejecting Jesus and his act on the cross, or by ignoring his teachings, or by dropping out of the family, thus eliminating one from receiving the inheritance gift.

Then the question Paul deals with in (27) is, Then what becomes of boasting? (The Jews boasted that only they are God's people; the Gentiles are excluded. And the works of the law, especially those that showed their distinction from Gentiles, enforced their thinking. Here the works of the law are primarily in reference to circumcision, the Sabbath, food laws, and their purity laws. These are the laws that separated them socially from the Gentiles and led to their boast of being the only people of God. But none of this was in the covenant with Abraham.) So verse 27 asks, By what law? (What law eliminates boasting and the belief that only the Jews are God's people?) The answer in (27) is the law of faith. The law of faith centers solely on Christ.

Verses 28-30 say, For we hold that a person is justified by faith (the faith of Christ) apart from works prescribed by the law (Torah). Or is God the God of Jews only? Is he not the God of Gentiles also? Yes, of Gentiles also, since God is one; and he will justify the circumcised on the ground of faith and the uncircumcised through the same faith. (This is first in reference to the faith of Christ and the cross and resurrection, and then in reference to the faith God makes available and gives as a gift to his people.) Verse 31 asks, Do we then overthrow the law by this faith? By no means! On the contrary we uphold the law. (The only way this makes sense is if Paul is saying, the law is upheld because love fulfills the law, Gal 5:6, 14. Jesus said he came to fulfill the law, Mt 5:17.)

Chapter 4:1-5 says, What then are we to say was gained by Abraham, our ancestor according to the flesh? For if Abraham was justified by works, he has something to boast about, but not before God. For what does the scripture say? "Abraham believed God, and it was reckoned to him as righteousness." Now to one who works, wages are not reckoned as a gift but as something due. But to one who without works trusts him who justifies the ungodly, such faith is reckoned as righteousness. (Paul's subject is initial justification. God accepts anyone as they are. No former merits or works are necessary for God to initially accept anyone.)

According to Paul Abraham's faith was credited to him as righteousness. As Augustine said (Epistle 194.5.19), "When God crowns your merits, he crowns nothing other than his own gifts." Humanity is never justified by their works, but they are not justified without works. Even faith is a gift of God encouraged by his grace. Even though it is a gift, Scripture calls faith a work (2 Thess 1:11), but it is a work of God's power.

Abraham trusted in the promise that God would do what he

said he would. God credits the attitude of Abraham that leads to his obedient faith. Justification in Scripture has three phases. There is initial justification and sanctification where one enters as God's chosen, then the process of justification where the Spirit continues to justify as well as transforms one more and more like Christ (also called sanctification), and then final justification and sanctification where one is finally purified, and then perfected by the Spirit into Christ. The whole process is the work of God's grace. In these verses Paul is thinking of initial justification or being accepted as an adopted child of God by grace through faith.

Verses 6-9 say, So also David (Ps 32) speaks of the blessedness of those to whom God reckons righteousness apart from works: "Blessed are those whose iniquities are forgiven, and whose sins are covered; blessed is the one against whom the Lord will not reckon sin." Is this blessedness, then, pronounced only on the circumcised, or also on the uncircumcised? We say, "Faith was reckoned to Abraham as righteousness."

The issue Paul is pressing is what justifies and determines who the people of God are in the present. Paul is dealing with Jewish Christians who say that in order for Gentiles to be considered God's people they have to first become Jews by accepting circumcision, the laws of Torah, along with being willing to be obedient to the food laws, purity laws, and Sabbath laws.

Paul's teaching is circumcision and those other Jewish laws are not necessary; justification is by faith in Jesus and what he has done. Sin is a major issue. In the new covenant sin is forgiven through the crucifixion and blood of Christ. God has fulfilled his promise to Abraham. Sin is reversed and the world is now being blessed through Abraham for all people not just the Jew. Both Jew and Gentile are God's people, and the laws of Torah are no longer necessary. That does not mean one can not follow them, but the issue is that justification comes through faith in Christ not the laws of Torah. One can continue to follow them for their cultural value but not for justification.

Verses 10-12 say, How then was it reckoned to him? Was it before or after he had been circumcised? It was not after but before he was circumcised. He received the sign of circumcision as a seal of the righteousness that he had by faith while he was still uncircumcised. The purpose was to make him the ancestor of all who believe without being circumcised and who thus have righteousness reckoned to them, and likewise the ancestor of the circumcised who are not only circumcised but who also follow the example of the faith that our ancestor Abraham had before he was circumcised.

Abraham's faith came before he was circumcised; therefore, he is the ancestor of those who have faith, both Jew and Gentile, not just the circumcised or Jew. Even so, it is important to see that Abraham obeyed God and was circumcised so God could seal him as a person of God, and it is important to see that Abraham continued to obey God's instructions, or else God would not have been able to carry through on his promise to Abraham. The key word is sealed. But circumcision is for the Jew not the follower of Christ; therefore Gentiles do not need to be circumcised.

Hebrews 11:8-12, 17-19 tells us that by faith Abraham obeyed by setting out for the land he was to receive as an inheritance not knowing where he was going. If he had not obeyed, the inheritance would not have been his. By faith he received the power of procreation, even though he was too old, and because of his sexual relations with Sarah descendants were born. But he had to use the power given to him. By faith Abraham, when put to the test, offered up Isaac, his only son of the promise, because of his trust in God. It is obvious that without the obedience of faith God's promise would not have come to fruition through Abraham. Faith includes obedience. It is the way of confirming one's part in the covenant. Being in the new covenant is following the teachings of Christ and being empowered by the Holy Spirit.

Rom 2:5-11 states at God's final, righteous judgment, he will repay according to one's deeds, and those who do not obey will receive God's wrath. Being made part of the righteous (God's people) does not demand perfection, but it does mean obedience and following his ways, and in the process receiving forgiveness of sins for imperfections. It is through the blood of Christ that sins are forgiven and not through the laws of Torah.

Paul is dealing with those who are saying that Gentiles need to first become Jews before they can be followers of Christ. Paul disagrees. Our inheritance is through Christ as an inheritance gift freely given. But again one can reject the free gift by adding other requirements such as the Mosaic law, or even by rejecting Christ, or by ignoring Christ, and by continual disobedience to him.

Verses 13-15 say, For the promise that he would inherit the world did not come to Abraham or to his descendants through the law but through the righteousness (meaning the relationship) of faith. If it is the adherents of the law who are to be the heirs, faith is null and the promise is void. For the law brings wrath; but where there is no law, neither is there violation. (The law brings wrath only because one of its primary purposes is to reveal sin, Gal 3:19. Righteousness of faith has to do with an ongoing relationship.)

Verses 16-18 say, For this reason it depends on faith (the faith of Christ that led to his crucifixion and one's faith in Christ), in order that the promise may rest on grace and be guaranteed to all his descendants, not only to adherents of the law but also to those who share the faith of Abraham . . . Hoping against hope, he believed that he would become, "the father of many nations," according to what was said, "So numerous shall your descendants be."

Verses 19-25 say, He did not weaken in faith when he considered his own body, which was already as good as dead (for he was about a hundred years old), or when he considered the barrenness of Sarah's womb. No distrust made him waver concerning the promise of God, but he grew strong in his faith as he gave glory to God, being fully convinced that God was able to do what he had promised. Therefore his faith "was reckoned to him as righteousness." Now the words, "it was reckoned to him," were written not for his sake alone, but for ours also. It will be reckoned to us who believe in him who raised Jesus our Lord from the dead, who was handed over to death for our trespasses and was raised for our justification.

God's grace encourages belief that leads to trust that leads to obedience. It is all through grace and it is all God's gift. Those now considered righteous are not those living a perfect life, but as Paul will soon elaborate those who are in the covenant at the present time, those who through faith are living life in Christ Jesus in the power of the Holy Spirit, and in the process are receiving continual forgiveness of sins through the blood of Christ. These righteous ones are both Jew and Gentile, and Paul considers them the new Israel of God.

Chapter 5:1-5 says, Therefore, since we are justified by faith, we have peace with God through our Lord Jesus Christ, through whom we have obtained access to this grace in which we stand; and we boast in our hope of sharing the glory of God. And not only that, but we also boast in our sufferings, knowing that suffering produces endurance, and endurance produces character, and character produces hope, and hope does not disappoint us, because God's love has been poured into our hearts through the Holy Spirit that has been given to us. (The value of suffering for Christ is stressed in

the New Testament. This is the joy the New Testament describes, a joy that is defined different from how the world understands joy.)

Peace with God and peace with each other comes through the grace of God. A vertical peace with God leads to a horizontal peace with each other. In the process of being at peace with God, one may suffer because of living life in Christ, but suffering for Christ produces character and hope. The hope is with the advent of the Holy Spirit, offered through the new covenant, hearts can be filled with God's love. But hearts need to be open to allow God's love to come through. This will never disappoint no matter how much suffering comes. It is Christ and the work of his Spirit that is our hope.

Verses 6-10 say, For while we were still weak, at the right time Christ died for the ungodly. Indeed, rarely will anyone die for a righteous person—though perhaps for a good person someone might actually dare to die. But God proves his love for us in that while we were still sinners Christ died for us. Much more surely then, now that we have been justified by his blood, will we be saved through him from the wrath of God. For if while we were enemies, we were reconciled to God through the death of his Son, much more surely, having been reconciled, will we be saved by his life. (We will be saved by his life as he lives his life in and through us by the power of the Holy Spirit.) Verse 11 says, But more than that, we even boast in God through our Lord Jesus Christ, through whom we have now received reconciliation. (Boasting is only through Christ, who is the hope of humankind.)

Sin has caused humankind to be separated from God, but through the death of Christ and his blood humankind is now reconciled and at peace with God. His blood is understood as an atoning sacrifice (Rom 3:25). These verses are saying that humankind is saved from God's wrath. Moderns do not like to hear about God's wrath, but it is what it is. Those yielding to the power of sin become enemies of God (Rom 3:9-18). But Christ's death reconciles sinful humanity to God (2 Cor 5:18-19, Col 1:21-22). The only boast left for anyone is in what Christ has done for all humans. Humankind's boast is not in the Mosaic law nor in themselves; it is only in Christ.

Verses 12-14 say, Therefore, just as sin came into the world through one man, and death came through sin, and so death spread to all because all have sinned—sin was indeed in the world before the law, but sin is not reckoned (recognized) when there is no law. Yet death exercised dominion from Adam to Moses, even over those whose sins were not like the transgression of Adam, who is the type of the one to come.

Tracing sin and death to one man, Adam, is based on Gen 3. Universal sin brings universal death (Rom 3:9). The Mosaic law makes sin and its consequences specific. With the law humankind can now understand that it is sin, which began with Adam but is confirmed by everyone, that causes death both spiritual and physical. Both Adam and Christ are considered types where the act of one brings consequences to others. The following verses bring further explanation. Adam's sin brought death and condemnation, whereas God's free gift of Christ brings life.

Verses 15-17 say, But the free gift is not like the trespass. For if the many died through the one man's trespass, much more surely have the grace of God and the free gift in the grace of the one man, Jesus Christ, abounded for the many. And the free gift is not like the effect of the one man's sin. For the judgment following one trespass brought condemnation, but the free gift following many trespasses brings justification. If, because of one man's trespass, death exercised dominion through that one, much more surely will those who receive the abundance of grace and the free gift of righteousness exercise dominion in life through the one man, Jesus

Christ. (The issue is sin, and only Christ can liberate humans from its consequences.)

Verses 18-19 say, Therefore just as one man's trespass led to condemnation for all, so one man's act of righteousness leads to justification and life for all. For just as by the one man's disobedience the many were made sinners, so by the one man's obedience the many will be made righteous.

If Adam's action leads to sin and death for all, then Christ's act on the cross leads to justification and life for all. If Adam's sin affects all, then Christ's resurrection affects all. If somehow original sin is passed to all, then Christ's cross and resurrection is passed to all. Therefore we carry within us the effects of both Adam and Christ. This act by Christ is then confirmed in baptism and a life of growing deeper into a life in Christ, or it is rejected by a life that ignores him.

Verses 20-21 say, But law came in, with the result that the trespass multiplied; but where sin increased, grace abounded all the more, so that, just as sin exercised dominion in death, so grace might also exercise dominion through justification leading to eternal life through Jesus Christ our Lord.

When the Mosaic law entered into the world, humans were able see more clearly how they are sinners and what the consequences are. That is even magnified by the teachings of Christ. Trespasses multiply because awareness of sin increases. The more that is understood the more one understands how great God's grace really is. The whole chapter is summed up in personal responsibility. The act of Adam, which is then confirmed by the actions of all who follow Adam, leads to death. All who confirm the act of Christ for their life will lead to eternal life. The message is that the hope of all humankind is only in Christ.

Through these first five chapters Paul's emphasis is that

justification for both Jew and Gentile is not the Mosaic law and especially not those laws that distinctly separate Jews from Gentiles. The Mosaic law could only lead to Christ. The faith of Christ and faith in Christ for both Jew and Gentile is the only hope for all humankind. Neither Jews nor Gentiles can boast that they are exclusively God's people. Jews can not require Gentiles to become a Jew before God accepts them or after God accepts them, nor can Gentiles teach that Jews are forbidden to remain obedient to the Mosaic law as part of their culture. They may continue in the Mosaic law as long as they understand the law can not save them. Because of Christ, Jew and Gentile can now live in unity and peace as God's people. The wall of hostility has been broken down (Eph 2).

Chapter 6:1 asks the question, What then are we to say? Should we continue in sin in order that grace may abound. The answer in verse 2 is, By no means! How can we who died to sin go on living it? (The discussion is not about being sinless, for such is not possible. The issue is living a sinful life and not being concerned with sin that immerses the world and those of us living within the world. Paul is talking to Jews who have become followers of Christ.)

Verses 3-4 say, Do you not know that all of us who have been baptized into Christ Jesus were baptized into his death? Therefore we have been buried with him by baptism into death, so that, just as Christ was raised from the dead by the glory of the Father, so we too might walk in newness of life. (Through baptism believers reenact Jesus' death and resurrection; it is putting to death sin and rising to new life (Col 3:1-25). This involves becoming a new creation in ways of thinking and acting. It is the experience of death to life. Baptism by immersion seems to be the symbol for this teaching.)

Verses 5-11 say, For if we have been united in him in a death like his, we will certainly be united with him in a resurrection like his. (How that happens is explained further.) We know that our old self was crucified with him so that the body of sin might be destroyed, and we might no longer be enslaved to sin. For whoever has died is free from sin. But if we have died with Christ, we believe that we will also live with him. We know that Christ, being raised from the dead, will never die again; death no longer has dominion over him. The death he died, he died to sin, once for all; but the life he lives, he lives to God. So you must consider yourselves dead to sin and alive to God in Christ Jesus. (This is the beginning of the new creation and transformation.)

Verses 12-14 say, Therefore, do not let sin exercise dominion in your mortal bodies, to make you obey their passions. No longer present your members to sin as instruments of wickedness, but present yourselves to God as those who have been brought from death to life, and present your members to God as instruments of righteousness. For sin will have no dominion over you, since you are not under law but under grace. (As Paul later says, For me to live is Christ, Phil 1:21.)

Verses 15-19 say, What then? Should we sin because we are not under law but under grace? By no means! Do you not know that if you present yourselves to anyone as obedient slaves, you are slaves of the one whom you obey, either of sin, which leads to death, or of obedience, which leads to righteousness? But thanks be to God that you, having once been slaves of sin, have become obedient from the heart, to the form of teaching to which you were entrusted, and that you, having been set free from sin, have become slaves of righteousness. I am speaking in human terms because of your natural limitations. For just as once you presented your members as slaves to impurity and to greater and greater iniquity, so now present your members as slaves to righteousness for sanctification (holiness).

Sanctification is the process of the Spirit leading one to deeper maturity into the ways of Christ. Humans are either a slave to sin and impurity or a slave to Christ and his righteousness. Obedient from the heart to the teaching of Jesus and his apostles is the way to sanctification. As the follower of Christ presents oneself to the obedience of Christ and his righteousness, one grows deeper into life in Christ as well as purity and holiness. This is a life long process not completed until Christ comes again perfecting all things. Obedience from the heart is key, for no one can perfectly do anything even if one desires.

Verses 20-23 say, When you were slaves of sin, you were free in regard to righteousness. So what advantage did you then get from the things of which you are now ashamed? The end of those things is death. But now that you have been freed from sin and enslaved to God, the advantage you get is sanctification (being made more holy). The end is eternal life. For the wages of sin is death, but the free gift of God is eternal life in Christ Jesus our Lord.

Sin earns death, but the free gift of God that leads to eternal life involves the process of sanctification which is the process of being made more and more like Christ. 1 Thess 4:3-8 says, For this is the will of God, your sanctification: that you abstain from fornication; that each of you know how to control your own body in holiness and honor, not with lustful passion, like the Gentiles who know not God; that no one wrong or exploit a brother or sister in this matter, because the Lord is an avenger in all these things, just as we have already told you. For God did not call us to impurity but in holiness. Therefore whoever rejects this rejects not human authority but God, who also gives his Holy Spirit to you.

Then Paul informs them of their call to love one another. Loving one another is doing for another what you would have one do for you if you were in their situation. First Corinthians 13:4-7 defines love as being patient, kind, not being envious, boastful, arrogant, or rude. It does not insist on its own way; it is not irritable or resentful; it does not rejoice in wrong doing, but rejoices in the truth. It bears all things, believes all things, hopes all things, endures all things. The cross of Christ, symbolizes the greatest act of love, giving oneself for the well being of another. Submitting oneself to Christ and his righteousness is growing toward the sanctification to which God calls his people.

Chapter 7:1-4 informs us that one belonged to the law of Moses only until Christ came. The law made God's people aware of sin until the one to deal with sin came into the world. Now that the one who eliminates sin has come, it is he that we now belong to. We have been set free from the law. An analogy from marriage is given that shows Christians who have died to sin and the law are no more bound to sin and the law than a woman is bound to her deceased husband. Verse 4 says, you have died to the law through the body of Christ, so that you may belong to another, to him who has been raised from the dead in order that we may bear fruit for God.

Verses 5-6 say, While we were living in the flesh, our sinful passions, aroused by the law, were at work in our members to bear fruit for death. But now we are discharged from the law, dead to that which held us captive, so that we are slaves not under the old written code but in the new life of the Spirit. (The call is to live by the spirit of the law by doing the most loving thing in all circumstances as one is led by the Holy Spirit.)

Life in the Spirit of Christ Jesus is Christ living in us and through us in the power of the Holy Spirit enabling faith to work through love. Following a written code in a slavish manner is not the way. The principle behind the law is what is most important so the spirit of the law can be put into operation in different situations and circumstances in a way that best expresses love for God and love for neighbor.

Verses 7-8 ask, What then should we say? That the law is sin? By no means! Yet, if it had not been for the law, I would not have known sin. I would not have known what it is to covet if the law had not said, "You shall not covet." But sin, seizing an opportunity in the commandment, produced in me all kinds of covetousness (envy and greed). He goes on to say in (9-11) that through the law sin seized him and brought death to him, but in (12) he says, So the law is holy, and the commandment is holy and just and good. (The law set forth God's norms, and from it we get themes, principles, values, virtues, and God's vision for humanity and his creation.)

The problem is not the law of Moses in itself; the problem is that it can not curb sin or eliminate it; it can not supply any power to overcome sin, and it can only produce a minimum ethic. Verse 13 says, Did what is good (the Mosaic law), then, bring death to me? By no means! It was sin, working death in me through what is good, in order that sin might be shown to be sin, and through the commandment might become sinful beyond measure. (The Mosaic law had its purpose, which was to make his people accountable and point out sin as well as lead and guide the people until the perfect comes.)

Verse 14 says, For we know that the law is spiritual; but I am of the flesh sold into slavery under sin. (This is humankind's dilemma, and all of us including Paul are strongly influenced by sin in daily life. He explains how this is even true for him now.) In verses 15-20 Paul says, I do not understand my own actions. For I do not do what I want, but I do the very thing I hate. Now if I do what I do not want, I agree that the law is good. But in fact it is no longer I that do it, but sin that dwells in me. For I know that nothing good dwells within me, that is, in my flesh. I can will what is right, but I cannot do it. For I do not do the good I want, but the evil I do not want is what I do. Now if I do what I do not want, it is no longer I that do it, but sin that dwells within me. (Paul is not relieving himself of his responsibility but is demonstrating the problem and power of sin.)

Paul is speaking of his own moral struggle, as well as the inner struggle or the war that goes on within all of us. He uses some hyperbole to overstate the case to get his point across. He goes on in (21-25) to say, I find it to be a law that when I want to do what is good, evil lies close at hand. For I delight in the law of God in my inmost self, but I see in my members another law at war with the law of my mind, making me captive to the law of sin that dwells in my members. Wretched man that I am! Who will rescue me from this body of death? Thanks be to God through Jesus Christ our Lord! (When we really examine ourselves in the light of Christ do we not all experience the same thing Paul is describing?)

This last verse is what Paul was leading toward. Threatened by total defeat in the battle with sin, the burdened sinner casts oneself upon God's mercy in Christ. Only then is freedom found from both the guilt and power of sin. Finally, in (25) Paul says, So then, with my mind I am a slave to the law of God (the law of life in Christ Jesus), but with my flesh I am a slave to the law of sin.

In other words, Paul says, I am a sinner in constant need of God's power and grace that comes from the Father, through Christ, in the power of the Holy Spirit. Paul will elaborate on that in the next chapter. The law made him aware of the problem of sin and everyone's need for Christ. Behind all this sound instruction is also his desire to counter those Jewish Christians who are teaching that Gentiles coming to Christ must first become a Jew and accept circumcision, the food laws, purity laws, and Sabbath day work laws before they can be accepted as a true follower of Christ. Paul's answer is absolutely not! One does not have to accept those laws to be justified in Christ.

We can transfer that into modern day test cases and include such boundary markers as one's position on inerrancy, what Bible translation is used, baptism, opposing abortion for all cases, contraception, opposing homosexuals marrying, the maleness of the clergy, speaking in tongues as the initial evidence for Spirit baptism, and other such teachings that people believe according to their conscience, but are sometimes difficult or impossible to find as plain teachings of Scripture. Even though important to different groups, they should not interfere with one becoming a follower of Christ and beginning the process of becoming more like Christ, unity in Christ, or the acceptance of each other as serious followers of Christ and his teachings.

Justification is not by certain doctrines, or certain ideological beliefs and interpretations deduced from Scripture or whatever by humans. Nor is justification by works of the Mosaic law, but by faith in Christ's life, crucifixion, and resurrection and by the work of the Holy Spirit in and through the believer. In the process as these Scriptures teach all have sinned and come short of the glory of God.

Chapter 8:1-2 says, There is therefore now no condemnation for those who are in Christ Jesus. For the law of the Spirit of life in Christ Jesus has set you free from the law of sin and death. (To be in Christ is to belong to this new order and to have the Spirit is to have the presence of God within our hearts working in and through us.

Being in Christ is a result of being baptized and sealed into Christ, 6:3-4.) Verses 3-4 say, For God has done what the law, weakened by the flesh, could not do: by sending his own Son in the likeness of sinful flesh, and to deal with sin, he condemned sin in the flesh, so that the just requirement of the law might be fulfilled in us, who walk not according to the flesh but according to the Spirit. (Only through the power of the Spirit can one walk by the Spirit.)

Verses 5-8 say, For those who live according to the flesh (dominated by selfish interests and the ways of the world) set their minds on the things of the flesh, but those who live according to the Spirit (dominated by living for Christ and his interests) set their minds on the things of the Spirit. To set the mind on the flesh is death, but to set the mind on the Spirit is life and peace. For this reason the mind that is set on the flesh is hostile to God; it does not submit to God's law—indeed it cannot, and those who are in the flesh cannot please God. (There are only two choices, and they are death or life. Our lives are either immersed in the things of God or the things of the world. Halfway in one and halfway in the other may be our choice, but it is not the choice God gives us. Only those who walk in the Spirit can please God.)

Verses 9-11 say, But you are not in the flesh; you are in the Spirit, since the Spirit of God dwells in you. Anyone who does not have the Spirit of Christ does not belong to him. But if Christ is in you, though the body is dead because of sin, the Spirit is life because of righteousness. If the Spirit of him who raised Jesus from the dead dwells in you, he who raised Christ from the dead will give life to your mortal bodies also through his Spirit that dwells in you. (This is the test for learning about one's particular condition. Having the Spirit, which is the Spirit of God and the Spirit of Christ, is the distinguishing mark of being a Christian. It is the Spirit that leads, guides, and enables his people as they live their life in Christ; it is the Spirit that produces the fruit that pleases God (Jn 15:1-11), and it is through his Spirit that God will raise them from the dead.)

Verses 12-17 say, So then, brothers and sisters, we are debtors not to the flesh—for if you live according to the flesh (the ways opposed to God), you will die; but if by the Spirit you put to death the deeds of the body, you will live. For all who are led by the Spirit of God are children of God. (Obviously, those that are not allowing the Spirit of God to lead them and bear God's fruit are not children of God, even though they may say they are.)

Verses 15-17 say, For you did not receive a spirit of slavery to fall back into fear, but you have received a spirit of adoption. When we cry, "Abba! Father!" it is that very Spirit bearing witness with our spirit that we are children of God, and if children, then heirs, heirs of God and joint heirs with Christ—if, in fact, we suffer with him so that we may also be glorified with him.

Paul does not say just believe, and then sit back and enjoy life. As they say, you can not just talk the talk without walking the walk. Just talking the talk will not get God's desired results for the one who believes. The idea is that the people of Christ must daily die and rise with Christ. They must daily put to death self and sin and live with him making his thoughts their thoughts and his priorities their priorities, and his actions their actions. If their desire is to seek his glory, this is to be done no matter what the consequences may be. Again, perfection is not required, but obedience from the heart is.

Paul in verses 18-25 says, I consider that the sufferings of this present time are not worth comparing with the glory about to be revealed to us. For the creation waits with eager longing for the revealing of the children of God; for the creation was subjected to futility, not of its own will but by the will of the one who subjected it, in hope that the creation itself will be set free from its bondage to decay and will obtain the freedom of the glory of the children of God. We know that the whole creation has been groaning in labor pains until now; and not only the creation, but we ourselves, who have the first fruits of the Spirit, groan inwardly while we wait for adoption, the redemption of our bodies. For in hope we were saved. Now hope that is seen is not hope. For who hopes for what is seen? But if we hope for what we do not see, we wait for it with patience.

This is saying that nature itself shares in the stress, pain, and anxiety that humans do, and both humans and nature will be restored to what God originally intended. It is not God's desire that humans and nature suffer as they do; the problem is sin. God's people are his stewards and have been given responsibility to care for his created people and his created earth as he would. The Spirit has been given to God's people to help as they wait for their adoption, meaning final adoption, the redemption of their bodies and the renewal of creation as it will become a new heaven and new earth.

Verses 26-27 say, Likewise the Spirit helps us in our weakness; for we do not know how to pray as we ought, but that very Spirit intercedes with sighs too deep for words. And God, who searches the heart, knows what is the mind of the Spirit, because the Spirit intercedes for the saints according to the will of God. (This is saying when you do not know how to pray, just be quiet and be in the presence of God, and the Spirit who knows how to pray for you will do the praying. Another positive way to pray when one is having difficulty praying is to read and meditate upon the Scriptures or hymns and let prayer rise from the readings.)

Paul assures us in verse 28 when he says, We know that all things work together for good for those who love God, who are called according to his purpose. (In some way God will work things out as we act as his stewards for his created beings and his created earth, for he is in control. In the meantime the Spirit will pray as we ought to pray even when we are not sure how to pray.)

Then in verse 29 Paul says, For those whom he foreknew he also predestined to be conformed to the image of his Son in order that he might be the firstborn within a large family. (God has predestined that his people be conformed to the image of his Son. God's created beings were created in the image of God in the beginning, but sin marred that image until humankind even forgot what that image was supposed to be. Therefore, the Father sent his Son to show us what being conformed in the image of God looks like and to call us to be conformed to that image.) Verse 30 says, And those whom he predestined he also called; and those whom he called he also justified; and those whom he justified he also glorified.

God sends his Son, and then by his grace calls humankind to his Son. Those who respond in the manner God laid out are justified and glorified by God's grace. Thus the will of God is that humankind be conformed to the image of the Father's Son, Jesus the Christ, the Messiah. Being conformed to the image of Jesus is a lifelong process, which is the sanctification (holiness) process. Justification and sanctification are all by God's grace and the work of the Holy Spirit.

Paul in Phil 2:12-13 adds, work out your own salvation with fear and trembling; for it is God who is at work in you, enabling you both to will and to work for his good pleasure. (God is doing the work in and through his people through the power of the Holy Spirit.) Paul in 1 Cor 1:30-31 says, He is the source of your life in Christ Jesus, who became for us wisdom from God, and righteousness, and sanctification and redemption, in order that, as it is written, "Let the one who boasts, boast in the Lord."

Verses 31-36 say, What then are we to say about these things? If God is for us, who can be against us? He who did not withhold his own Son, but gave him up for all of us, will he not give us everything else? (The reference is to giving his people justification, sanctification, redemption and glorification.) Who will bring any charge against God's elect? It is God who justifies. Who is it to condemn? It is Christ Jesus, who died, yes, who was raised, who is at the right hand of God, who indeed intercedes for us. Who will separate us from the love of Christ? Will hardship, or distress, or persecution, or famine, or nakedness, or peril, or sword? As it is written, "For your sake we are being killed all day long; we are accounted as sheep to be slaughtered." (This is a reference to the martyrs who were dying for Christ's cause. Paul's point is that nothing, not even death, will separate God from his loyal people who are in Christ through the Holy Spirit.)

Verses 37-39 say, No, in all these things we are more than conquerors through him who loved us. For I am convinced that neither death, nor life, nor angels, nor rulers, nor things present, nor things to come, nor powers, nor height, nor depth, nor anything else in creation, will be able to separate us from the love of God in Christ Jesus our Lord.

God offers to all his loyal followers the grace of final justification through Jesus Christ by the working of the Holy Spirit. The Holy Spirit is the initial down payment on this inheritance. It must be remembered that it is an inheritance. Whether the inheritance is accepted or rejected depends on individual free choice as individuals live out life confirming their part of the covenant and in the process receiving continual forgiveness with repentance when they fall short of God's will for them. Most important for Paul is that all this is because of Christ and not the Mosaic law. The inheritance is a gift, but if one drops out of the family, one can not expect to receive the inheritance.

In Chapter 9:1-5 Paul says, I am speaking the truth in Christ—I am not lying; my conscience confirms it by the Holy Spirit—I have great sorrow and anguish in my heart. For I could wish that I myself were accursed and cut off from Christ for the sake of my own people, my kindred according to the flesh. (Paul seems to be concerned that his people may be accursed for rejecting Christ. Is he saying he would be willing to be accursed if he could take their place and thus have his people no longer accursed?) Verse 4 says, They are Israelites, and to them belong the adoption, the glory, the covenants, the giving of the law, the worship, the promises; to them belong the patriarchs, and from them, according to the flesh, comes the Messiah, who is over all, God blessed forever. Amen.

Verses 6-8 say, It is not as though the word of God had failed. For not all Israelites truly belong to Israel, and not all of Abraham's children are his true descendants; but "It is through Isaac that descendants shall be named for you." This means that it is not the children of the flesh who are the children of God, but the children of the promise are counted as descendants. For this is what the promise said, "About this time I will return and Sarah shall have a son." (Abraham had a number of children but it was through the son with Sarah, Isaac, the promise to Abraham was carried on. The primary issue here is not about personal salvation; the issue is through whom God is going to carry his special promise.)

Verses 10-13 have the same idea with Isaac and his wife Rebecca. Twins, Esau and Jacob, were born to Rebecca, and the younger, Jacob, was chosen to carry the promise made to Abraham as opposed to the elder. In verse 13 God says, As it is written I have loved Jacob, but I have hated Esau. Therefore Jacob is chosen.

God did not hate Esau; God hated the actions of Esau because he sold his birthright for a bowl of soup. William Most (1994, 71) states that both Hebrew and Aramaic lack degrees of comparison of adjectives and adverbs, such as good, better, best. Because of that, translations into English sometimes come up with a strange arrangement of words that do not quite make sense, if the nature of the original languages is not understood.

Verses 14-29 are about God's right to choose. The issue in context is about who the promise would continue to go through. Verses 14-16 say, What then are we to say? Is there injustice on God's part? By no means! For he says to Moses, "I will have mercy on whom I will have mercy, and I will have compassion on whom I have compassion."

Again this is not in reference to personal salvation, but in reference to whom God chooses to carry the promise. God will choose who he wants for his special tasks. This is also Paul's response to Jews who do not accept the fact that God is now choosing the Gentiles and the church to work his promises.

Verses 17-18 say, For the scripture says to Pharaoh, "I have raised you up for the very purpose of showing my power in you, so that my name may be proclaimed in all the earth." So then he has mercy on whomever he chooses, and he hardens the heart on whomever he chooses. (God hardened Pharaoh's heart after Pharaoh hardened his own heart. In context, and if the reader looks at verse 25, it is obvious that God is referring to working his purposes through a group of people or a person who represents a group of people in order to bring about a special purpose of God.)

Verse 21 says, Has the potter no right over the clay, to make out of the same lump one object for special use and another for ordinary use? Paul quotes Hosea in 25-26 saying, "Those who were not my people I will call 'my people,' and her who was not beloved I will call 'beloved.' " "And in the very place where it was said to them, 'You are not my people,' there they shall be called children of the living God." (This is in reference to the Gentiles now being the people of God, something the Jews said is impossible.)

Verses 27-29 say, Isaiah cries out concerning Israel, "Though the number of the children of Israel were like the sand of the sea, only a remnant of them will be saved (to represent him); for the Lord will execute his sentence on the earth quickly." And as Isaiah predicted, "If the Lord of hosts had not left survivors to us, we would have fared like Sodom and been made like Gomorrah." (God's promises never included all Israelites but only a remnant (Isa 10:22). The nation he called came through Isaac then Jacob, and not the other children. Then from the nation only a remnant of them are called his special people.)

Verses 30-33 say, What then are we to say? Gentiles that did not strive for righteousness, have attained it, that is, righteousness through faith; but Israel, who did strive for the righteousness that is based on the law, did not succeed in fulfilling the law. Why not? Because they did not strive for it on the basis of faith (faith in Christ), but as if it were based on works. They have stumbled over the stumbling stone, as it is written, "See, I am laying in Zion a stone that will make people stumble, a rock that will make them fall, and whoever believes in him will not be put to shame."

Israel as a whole rejected Christ, who is the culmination of the promise, God's chosen one. God now chooses the church, the body of Christ, to which all people of all nations are invited, but it is primarily the Gentiles who will come because the Jews reject Christ. Then like Israel only a remnant of the individuals from the Gentile nations will come into the church to be called God's special people. God chooses the group that is responsible for bearing his light, but only a remnant within the group actually do so. God chooses as he will. Christ is the chosen one, and those from the whole world who choose Christ are now God's chosen people. In the Old Testament God chose a nation, but in the New Testament

God chose the church to which all people of all nations are invited. As Jesus said, many are called, but few are chosen. They are not chosen because they reject God's chosen one.

Chapter 10:1-4 says, Brothers and sisters, my heart's desire and prayer to God for them is that they may be saved. (This is in reference to his Jewish brothers and sisters. Salvation is now an issue.) I can testify that they have a zeal for God, but it is not enlightened. For being ignorant of the righteousness that comes from God, and seeking to establish their own, they have not submitted to God's righteousness. For Christ is the end of the law (its goal, its fulfillment) so that there may be righteousness for everyone who believes.

The righteousness that leads to salvation comes only from Christ not the Mosaic law. The goal of the law was to lead to Christ who takes away the sin of individuals and the world. He is the Righteous One, the promised one, who now gives both Jew and Gentile his righteousness through his grace to all who have the faith of Christ. The criteria for righteousness or understanding oneself in relationship to God is no longer the Mosaic law but the work of Christ and faith in Christ. And one's faith in Christ is also a work of God (Jn 6:29) to be accepted or rejected.

Verses 9-12 say, if you confess with your lips that Jesus is Lord and believe in your heart that God raised him from the dead, you will be saved. For one believes with the heart and so is justified, and one confesses with the mouth (acts) and so is saved. The scripture says, "No one who believes in him will be put to shame." For there is no distinction between Jew and Greek; the same Lord is Lord of all and is generous to all who call on him. (This is the point and main theme of the book of Romans. Jew and Gentile are one and are now united by and in Christ through justification.) Then verse 13 says, For everyone who calls upon the name of the Lord shall be saved.

Included here with belief is confession with the mouth. What about he who believes and is baptized shall be saved (Mk 16:16)? What about repent and be baptized and receive the gift of the Holy Spirit (Acts 2:38)? What about obedience (Rom 2:6, 13, Jas 2:14-26)? These are not works of the Mosaic law, but established by the grace of Christ through the new covenant. This is an example of the importance of being careful not to pick and chose from God's word what one wants while ignoring other parts of God's word. Yes, salvation is by grace through faith as a gift of God, but faith obviously involves more than just believing as the above Scriptures show, for even the devil believes. The answer is that belief is just the beginning of true faith; belief is the beginning of the justification process. As previously stated all are called just as they are, but they are not called just to stay as they are. God remakes his people in order to use them for his purposes.

Verses 14-17 say, But how are they to call on one in whom they have not believed? And how are they to believe in one of whom they have never heard? And how are they to hear without someone to proclaim him? And how are they to proclaim him unless they are sent? As it is written, "How beautiful are the feet of those who bring good news!" But not all have obeyed the good news; for Isaiah says, "Lord, who has believed our message?" So faith comes from what is heard, and what is heard comes through the word of Christ. (Notice how faith, belief, and obedience are all tied together, which takes us back to Rom 2:4-11.)

Verses 18-21 say, But I ask, have they (Jews) not heard? Indeed they have; for "Their voice has gone out to all the earth, and their words to the ends of the world." (The nation can not claim that they did not have the opportunity to hear.) In (20-21) God through Isaiah said "I have been found by those who did not seek me; I have shown myself to those who did not ask for me." But of Israel he says, "All day long I have held out my hands to a disobedient and contrary people." (This is a general statement about the group he originally chose to bear his light to the world. Israel as a nation can not claim that it could not understand God's message, for now even Gentiles have been able to understand.)

◦◦◦

In chapter 11:1-6 Paul says, I ask, then, has God rejected his people? By no means! I myself am an Israelite, a descendant of Abraham, a member of the tribe of Benjamin. God has not rejected his people whom he foreknew. Do you not know what the scripture says of Elijah, how he pleads with God against Israel? "Lord, they have killed your prophets, they have demolished your altars; I alone am left, and they are seeking my life." But what is the divine reply to him? "I have kept for myself seven thousand who have not bowed the knee to Baal." (Elijah was not alone as he thought, and neither is Paul.) Verses 5-6 say, So too at the present time there is a remnant, chosen by grace. But if it is by grace, it is no longer on the basis of works, otherwise grace would no longer be grace. (As in the time of Elijah a remnant was saved for God's work; it is the same now, but the chosen must respond to the one the Father chose, his only Son. One must respond to God's grace.)

Paul is talking to Jews so his reference to works is to works of the Mosaic law, especially the food laws, purity laws, Sabbath day work laws, and circumcision, those things that distinctly separate Jew from Gentile. Paul is saying the Israelites are not rejected, but the covenant has changed since Christ came. God has not withdrawn his call to the Israelites. All are chosen and called, but only a remnant is answering his call. It is no different from the time of Elijah.

Verses 7-10 say, What then? Israel failed to obtain what it was seeking. The elect obtained it (those elected by Christ because they responded to God's grace and chose God's elect, the Messiah, the Christ), but the rest were hardened, as it is written, "God gave them a sluggish spirit, eyes that would not see and ears that would not hear, down to this very day." And David says. "Let their table become a snare and a trap, a stumbling block and a retribution for them; let their eyes be darkened so that they cannot see, and keep their backs forever bent." (These are quotes from Isa 29:9-10 and Ps 69:22-23 which is explained by Isa 30: 9-14 to show that God allowed them to harden their hearts. Their hearts were hardened in blindness, deafness, and unbelief.)

In reading the Old Testament God is sovereign and in control. So when it says God gave them a sluggish spirit and let their eyes to be darkened, the writer is saying God allowed them to reject him and his ways. He could have blocked it, but he allows free choice. Because God is sovereign, the writers credit the wrong choice of people to God because he allowed it. In understanding Scripture it is important to understand the Hebrew culture and thinking of the Jews at that time.

Verses 11-12 say, So I ask, have they stumbled so as to fall? By no means! But through their stumbling salvation has come to the Gentiles, so as to make Israel jealous. Now if their stumbling means riches for the world, and if their defeat means riches for the Gentiles, how much more will the full inclusion mean!

He is primarily talking about the group (Gentiles) God is choosing to reveal his light and through which individuals will be reconciled to God. Because Israel refused to take God's light to the world, the Gentiles will take his light and salvation to the world, and so many more, both Jews and Gentiles, will be included. The reference is to Jeremiah 11:1-17. Because they break the covenant that God and the people agreed to on Mt Sinai, the promise and the land will be taken from them.

In verses 13-19 Paul tells the Gentiles he hopes his ministry to the Gentiles will make some of his fellow Jews jealous and thus cause them to come to Christ and be reconciled to Christ and find life from the dead. (This expression involves his own human thinking for the hope he has.) To express himself he uses the symbol of an olive tree. The root remains holy even as some of the branches are broken off (the Jews), and a wild olive shoot (the Gentiles) was grafted in their place to share the rich root of the olive tree. So he warns Gentiles not to boast because they do not support the root, the root supports them. He is reminding them that Israel has been humbled because of their boasting and arrogance, so Gentiles need to be careful.

Paul continues in verses 19-24 to say, You will say, "Branches were broken off so that I might be grafted in." That is true. They (Jews) were broken off because of their unbelief, but you (Gentiles) stand only through faith. So do not become proud, but stand in awe. For God did not spare the natural branches, perhaps he will not spare you. Note then the kindness and the severity of God (both are sides or aspects of God): severity toward those that have fallen, but God's kindness toward you, provided you continue in his kindness; otherwise you will also be cut off. And even those of Israel, if they do not persist in unbelief, will be grafted in, for God has the power to graft them. (Unbelief is refusal to recognize God's Messiah. It is important to notice how they are grafted in.) For if you have been cut off from what is by nature a wild olive tree and grafted, contrary to nature, into a cultivated olive tree, how much more will these natural branches be grafted back into their own olive tree.

God warns the Gentiles not to become boastful and proud over ethnic identity and thus becoming prejudicial toward others who are different just as the Jews did, or he will cut them off as he has done to the arrogant and proud Jews who claimed God was for them only.

Verses 25-27 say, So that you may not claim to be wiser than you are, brothers and sisters, I want you to understand this mystery; a hardening has come upon part of Israel, until the full number of the Gentiles come in. (Part implies the disobedience of some Jews and the obedience of other Jews.) And so (means in this manner) all Israel will be saved; as it is written, "Out of Zion will come the Deliverer; he will banish ungodliness from Jacob." "And this is my covenant with them, when I take away their sins." (This quote is a reference to Isa 59:20-21, Jer 31:31-34, and Ezek 36:26-28.)

There is nothing we have read in Romans that would even insinuate that anyone or any group of people as a whole will be brought into God's fold any other way than through Jesus Christ. God first chose Israel to bear his light to the world. Now he has chosen the church to bear his light to the world because Israel rejected his purpose. Both Jews and Gentiles are called to his church for this purpose. Individual salvation is now by entering the body of Christ through faith in Christ. All Israel and the whole Gentile world, meaning the elect of Gentiles or Jews, are brought into God's fold only through Christ's life, death, and resurrection and faith in him and his teachings and not by faith in the Mosaic law.

Verses 28-29 say, As regards the gospel they are enemies of God (by rejecting God's righteousness) for your sake; but as regards election they are beloved, for the sake of their ancestors; for the gifts and the calling of God are irrevocable. (The call is never taken away from them. The call is always there, but it is their choice to answer the call of Christ or reject it. The call is now through the new covenant (Isa 59:20-21, Jer 31:31-34, Ezek 36:26-28), and the call is for both Jew and Gentile to be reconciled and united to God and each other through Christ (see Ephesians chapter 2).

There are some who do not accept this analysis. Their interpretation is that irrevocable means Jews are God's people and do not have to accept Christ as the Messiah. Looking at the context of the last three chapters this writer has difficulty understanding that viewpoint. That does not mean that Jews will not have individual salvation. There are other places in Scripture such as Romans 2 that take care of that issue.

Since the Holocaust, many modern day scholars believe that verses 25-32 are saying in the end all of Israel will be saved because in the beginning they were God's special choice. But this writer does not see how in the context of the whole book of Romans, and especially chapters 9-11 they can reach that conclusion. Much depends on how one defines all Israel and what irrevocable means. It seems all Israel is not a reference to the nation of Israel but to all who are now God's special people called the new Israel of God. Also Scripture reminds us that God shows no partiality. And if all of Israel is to be saved referring to the nation, whether or not they rely on the righteousness of God through Jesus Christ, then should not everyone created be saved (universalism)?

Verses 30-32 say, Just as you were once disobedient to God but now have received mercy because of their disobedience, so they have now been disobedient in order that, by the mercy shown to you, they too may now receive mercy. For God has imprisoned all in disobedience so that he may be merciful to all.

All are sinners to be saved by God's gift of mercy through his Son, and the blood of his Son, Jesus, as the only way stated. In the end if God chooses to bring people who have not chosen Christ to him through Christ after their death, that is his choice. Or if he judges them on the basis of following from their heart what they understand as right (Rom 2:14-16) then again that is his choice. God wills as he will. But the norm as stated in the New Testament and the book of Romans is that justification and sanctification are through Christ in the power of the Holy Spirit. It begins with God's grace through faith, continues by God's grace through faith, and ends by God's grace through faith.

As Paul in Phil 2:12-14 says, Therefore, my beloved, just as you have always obeyed me, not only in my presence, but much more now in my absence, work out your own salvation in fear and trembling; for it is God who is at work in you, enabling you both to will and to work for his good pleasure. (We are not saved by works, but we are not saved without works, but it is God working his works through us by his grace. As St Augustine (Epistle 194.5.29) says, then God accounts or credits his works to us.)

Verses 33-36 say, O the depth of the riches and wisdom and knowledge of God! How unsearchable are his judgments, and how unsearchable are his ways! "For who has known the mind of the Lord? Or who has been his counselor?" For from him and through him and to him are all things. To him be the glory forever. Amen.

Chapter 12:1-2 says, I appeal to you therefore, brothers and sisters, by the mercies of God, to present your bodies as a living sacrifice, holy and acceptable to God, which is your spiritual worship. Do not be conformed to this world, but be transformed by the renewing of your mind, so that you may discern what is the will of God—what is good and acceptable and perfect.

Presenting your mind and body to Christ makes for a new and changed outlook that is no longer conformed to the ways and thinking of the world but one aligned with Christ. Paul says that this is your spiritual worship. It is the way to worship daily.

Verses 3-5 say, For by the grace given to me I say to everyone among you not to think of yourself more highly than you ought to think, but to think with sober judgment, each according to the measure of faith that God has assigned. For as in one body we have many members, and not all the members have the same function, so we, who are many, are one body in Christ, and individually we are members of one another. (Paul reminds them again about pride, arrogance, boasting, getting rid of inflated egos, and to recognize the mutual need of each other.)

In verses 6-8 Paul says, we have gifts that differ according to the grace given to us: prophecy, in proportion to faith; ministry, in ministering; the teacher, in teaching; the exhorter, in exhortation; the giver, in generosity; the leader, in diligence; the compassionate, in cheerfulness. (These are just some of the gifts God gives his people in order to edify each other. All the gifts are important; no one is more important than the other, and everyone in the church needs each other as they build up the body of Christ. Then the following are ways that help the church as well as everyone to get along with each other in harmony.)

Verses 9-18 say, Let love be genuine; hate what is evil, hold fast to what is good; love one another with mutual affection; outdo one another in showing honor. Do not lag in zeal, be ardent in Spirit, serve the Lord. Rejoice in hope, be patient in suffering, persevere in prayer. Contribute to the needs of the saints; extend hospitality to strangers. Bless those who persecute you; bless and do not curse them. Rejoice with those who rejoice, weep with those who weep. Live in harmony with one another; do not be haughty, but associate with the lowly; do not claim to be wiser than you are. Do not repay anyone evil for evil, but take thought for what is noble in the sight of all. If it is possible, so far as it depends on you, live peaceably with all.

Verses 19-21 say, Beloved, never avenge yourselves, but leave room for the wrath of God; for it is written, "Vengeance is mine, I will repay, says the Lord." No, "if your enemies are hungry, feed them; if they are thirsty, give them something to drink; for by doing this you will heap burning coals on their heads." Do not overcome by evil, but overcome evil with good. (These teachings on moral behavior are not only to encourage believers to respect each other and get along with each other, but they are a recipe for bringing peace and justice to the whole world.)

Chapter 13:1 says, Let every person be subject to the governing authorities; for there is no authority except from God, and those authorities that exist have been instituted by God. (Government is created and instituted by God; therefore, it is responsible to God. If it is in conflict with God, Peter in Acts 5:29 says, we must obey God rather than any human authority. This must be kept in mind as one reads the following instructions.)

Verses 2-3 say, Therefore whoever resists authority (when it is not opposed to God) resists what God has appointed, and those who resist will incur judgment. For rulers are not a terror to good conduct, but to bad. Do you wish to have no fear of authority? Then do what is good, and you will receive its approval; for it is God's servant for your good.

Government has been instituted by God for the good of humankind, and the common good for society, in order to promote and keep judicial and social justice. Those who reject this aspect of government will not be pleasing God when any form of justice is violated. But this is not about any individual's blind obedience to government. It is the individual's responsibility and the church's responsibility to challenge government with the virtues, values and vision of God. In the process the church is not to seek power but to challenge power when it ignores the justice for individuals and the common god that God demands.

Verse 4 continues, But if you do what is wrong, you should be afraid, for the authority does not bear the sword in vain! It is the servant of God to execute wrath on the wrongdoer. (One should be careful in using this as a proof text for capital punishment. It is simply saying that God has given government the authority to punish wrong doing.) Verses 5 says, Therefore one must be subject, not only because of wrath (punishment from governing authorities) but also because of conscience. (If one is aligned with God, one must not go against what God has instituted when it is doing the good God has designed it to do.)

Verses 6-7 say, For the same reason you also pay taxes, for the authorities are God's servants, busy with this very thing. Pay to all what is due them—taxes to whom taxes are due, revenue to whom revenue is due, respect to whom respect is due, honor to whom honor is due.

Taxes are approved by God to do the good God has designed it to do. What to do when taxes are used for the things God would oppose is another issue. This author believes protest would be in order. If one decides not to pay the taxes then one must accept the consequences that go with not paying them. Also read 1 Pet 2:13-17 about government. The Old Testament and the book of Revelation portray the evils of government, those things God's people must challenge.

Verses 8-10 say, Owe no one anything, except to love one another; for the one who loves another has fulfilled the law. (The way to true freedom is to repent of sin, and not be in debt to anyone except Christ, and to love one another.) The commandments, "You shall not commit adultery; You shall not murder; You shall not steal;

You shall not covet"; and any other commandment, are summed up in this word, "Love your neighbor as yourself." Love does no wrong to a neighbor; therefore, love is the fulfilling of the law.

Verses 11-14 say, Besides this, you know what time it is, how it is now the moment for you to wake from sleep. For salvation is nearer to us now than when we became believers; the night is far gone, the day is near. Let us then lay aside the works of darkness and put on the armor of light (Eph 6:13-17); let us live honorably as in the day, not in reveling and drunkenness, not in debauchery and licentiousness, not in quarreling and jealousy. Instead, put on the Lord Jesus Christ, and make no provisions for the flesh, to gratify its desires. (This is not only a reference to sexual things but to selfishness and greed. Also see Gal 5:13-26, Eph 5, and Col 3.)

Chapter 14:1-6 says, Welcome those who are weak in faith, but not for the purpose of quarreling over opinions. Some believe in eating anything, while the weak eat only vegetables. Those who eat must not despise those who abstain, and those who abstain must not pass judgment on those who eat; for God has welcomed them. Who are you to pass judgment on servants of another? It is before their own lord that they stand or fall. And they will be upheld, for the Lord is able to make them stand. Some judge one day to be better than another, while others judge all days to be alike. Let all be fully convinced in their own minds. Those who observe the day, observe it in honor of the Lord. Also those who eat, eat in honor of the Lord, since they give thanks to God; while those who abstain, abstain in honor of the Lord and give thanks to God.

Paul is attempting to promote harmony in a group where there are factions of people. It seems on one side are the Gentiles who have become Christians and are very serious about their freedom in

Christ. The other group seems to be mainly Jews who have grown up under the Old Testament Mosaic food laws, purity laws, Sabbath work day laws, circumcision, and observe other religious holy days such as Passover, Pentecost, Tabernacles, and the monthly new moon festival. Those who are vegetarians are probably a throwback to Daniel 1:1-17 where Daniel and his friends show their dedication to God by drinking no wine, and eating only vegetables and drinking water. Part of the issue may also be over Gentiles who believe it is acceptable to continue eating meat that has been sacrificed to the gods in the pagan temples, as long as they understand it simply as meat having nothing to do with pagan worship.

It seems as though the Gentile Christians are in the position of power and may have succumbed to an anti-Jewish sentiment toward believing and even unbelieving Jews. On the other hand, Paul may be trying to balance out what he is saying because he is answering charges of Jewish Christians that his gospel is *antinomian* (no need for rules) and anti Jewish, even though Paul is a Jewish Christian.

Verses 7-9 say, We do not live to ourselves, and we do not die to ourselves. If we live we live to the Lord, and if we die, we die to the Lord; so then, whether we live or whether we die, we are the Lord's. For to this end Christ died and lived again, so that he might be Lord of both the dead and the living. (Because God sent his Son out of love for the well being of humankind, the response needs to be to live for him and his purposes, living life for his glory is primary, and not getting bogged down in the things that are now considered *adiaphora*, meaning indifferent.)

Verses 10-12 say, Why do you pass judgment (on these things) on your brother or sister? Or you, why do you despise (because they do not agree with you) your brother or sister? For we will all stand before the judgment seat of God. For it is written, "As I live, says the Lord, every knee shall bow to me, and every tongue shall give praise to God." So then each of us will be accountable to God.

The issue is between what one group of Christians believe they are free to do as opposed to what another group of Christians feel is either necessary or at least their choice. If there are no distinct commands for or against, what one does or does not do is according to their conscience as Paul will soon explain. One is not to judge another in those areas; it is God who will judge, for each person is accountable to God. Does that not also apply to those modern day issues we squabble over?

Verses 13-14 say, Let us no longer pass judgment on one another, but to resolve instead never to put a stumbling block or hindrance in the way of another. I know that I am persuaded in the Lord Jesus that nothing is unclean in itself; but it is unclean for anyone who thinks it is unclean. (This is primarily in reference to the Jewish food laws and their purity laws based on the Mosaic law. Paul is saying that these practices are now adiaphora, neither harmful nor helpful. Following one's conscience is important.)

Verses 15-16 say, If your brother or sister is being injured by what you eat, you are no longer walking in love. Do not let what you eat cause the ruin of one for whom Christ died. (More important than one's right to eat or drink as one wants is the obligation not to destroy the work of God by causing a brother or sister to stumble (1Cor 10:23-24.) So do not let your good be spoken of as evil.

On the other hand it is important to educate so there is growth in the faith. Paul does call those who feel they must still follow the Mosaic law, the weak in the faith. This situation must be somewhat different from the one in Galatians (especially 5:1-13) where he strenuously opposes this thinking telling them that if they continue to believe that those things are necessary for salvation, their own salvation will be in danger. Paul quite often balances the things he says according to different situations or contexts.

Verses 17-21 say, For the kingdom of God is not food and drink but righteousness and peace and joy in the Holy Spirit. The one who thus serves Christ is acceptable to God and has human approval. Let us then pursue what makes for peace and for mutual upbuilding. Do not, for the sake of food, destroy the work of God. Everything is indeed clean, but it is wrong for you to make others fall by what you eat; it is good not to eat meat or drink wine or do anything that makes your brother or sister stumble. The faith that you have, have as your own conviction before God. Blessed are those who have no reason to condemn themselves because of what they approve. But those who have doubts are condemned if they eat, because they do not act from faith; for whatever does not proceed from faith is sin.

Whatever is done against conscience is sin, so that must be respected. On the other hand do the weak in faith have the right to restrict the freedom Christ has given whether it be over practices or understanding Scripture? This basically has been the root of disunity in churches and has brought many church splits. This is the Apostle Paul's attempt to deal with an issue that really has never been solved. In reading this chapter as all of the chapters, it is important to keep in mind that Paul is correcting local, situational issues in a certain era. Even so, there are sound principles within that can be timeless.

Chapter 15:1-4 says, We who are strong ought to put up with the failings of the weak, and not to please ourselves. Each of us must please our neighbor for the good purpose of building up the neighbor. For Christ did not please himself, but as it is written (Ps 69:9), "The insults of those who insult you have fallen on me." For whatever was written in former days was written for our instruction (1 Cor 9:8-10, 10:11), so that by steadfastness and by

the encouragement of the scriptures (meaning the Old Testament) we might have hope.

Verses 5-9 say, May the God of steadfastness and encouragement grant you to live in harmony with one another, in accordance with Christ Jesus, so that together you may with one voice glorify the God and Father of our Lord Jesus Christ. Welcome one another, therefore, just as Christ has welcomed you, for the glory of God. For I tell you that Christ has become a servant of the circumcised (the Jews) on behalf of the truth of God in order that he might confirm the promises given to the patriarchs, and in order that the Gentiles might glorify God for his mercy.

Paul then quotes Ps 18:49, Ps 117:1, Deut 32:43, and Isa 11:10 to show that the promises to Abraham were that both Jews and Gentiles will be blessed with God's hope. Verse 13 says, May the God of hope fill you with all joy and peace in believing, so that you may abound in hope by the power of the Holy Spirit.

Verses 14-16 say, I myself feel confident about you, my brothers and sisters, that you yourselves are full of goodness, filled with all knowledge, and able to instruct one another. Nevertheless on some points I have written to you rather boldly by way of reminder, because of the grace given me by God to be a minister of Christ Jesus to the Gentiles in the priestly service of the gospel of God, so that the offering of the Gentiles may be acceptable, sanctified by the Holy Spirit. (Filled with all knowledge and able to instruct one another is the call to all who are able to teach God's word.)

Verses 17-21 say, In Christ Jesus, then, I have reason to boast of my work for God. For I will not venture to speak of anything except what Christ has accomplished through me to win obedience from the Gentiles, by word and deed, by the power of signs and wonders (miracles), by the power of the Spirit of God, so that from Jerusalem and as far around as Illyricum (Albania) I have fully proclaimed the good news of Christ. (Paul never boasts in what he has done, only what Christ has done through him.) Verses 20-21 say, Thus I make it my ambition to proclaim the good news, not where Christ has already been named, so that I do not build on someone else's foundation, but as it is written (Isa 52:15), "Those who have never been told of him shall see, and those who have never heard of him shall understand."

That is his primary purpose. He plans to stop in Rome to smooth out a few problems, share his spiritual gifts with them, and to possibly even get some financial support from them for his future mission in Spain. Since the church in Antioch was the base for his three major missionary journeys east of Rome, he may be thinking of making Rome the base as he plans to expand his work mission west of Rome toward Spain.

Verses 22-26 say, This is the reason I have been so often hindered in coming to you. But now, with no further place for me in these regions, I desire, as I have for many years, to come to you when I go to Spain. For I do hope to see you on my journey and to be sent on by you, once I have enjoyed your company for a little while. At present however, I am going to Jerusalem in a ministry to the saints; for Macedonia and Achaia have been pleased to share their resources with the poor among the saints in Jerusalem.

In (27-29) he tells them that after he delivers this help to the Jerusalem poor, he plans to stop by to see them. In (30-32) he asks for their prayers that he be rescued from the unbelievers (probably the Jews) and that his ministry of charity be acceptable to the saints, so that by God's will he may come to them with joy and be refreshed by their company. Finally, in verse 33 he says, The God of peace be with all of you. Amen.

Chapter 16:1-2 says, I commend to you our sister Phoebe, a deacon of the church at Cenchreae (eastern port of Corinth), so that you may welcome her in the Lord as is fitting for the saints (believers), and help her in whatever she may require from you, for she has been a benefactor (probably financial) of many and of myself as well. (She may have been the one bringing the letter from Paul.) Then he mentions many names that are in the church at Rome.

Verses 3-5 say, Greet Prisca and Aquila who work with me in Christ Jesus, and who risked their necks for my life, to whom not only do I give thanks but also all the churches of the Gentiles. (They were back in Rome after they and many Christians had been expelled from Rome by Claudius, the Roman emperor from 41-54 AD. They worked with Paul in Corinth and Ephesus. See more about them in Acts 18, 1 Cor 16:19, 2 Tim 4:19.) Greet also the church in their house. (The early churches met in homes.) Greet my beloved Epaenetus who was the first convert in Asia for Christ. Greet Andronicus and Junia (7), my relatives who were in prison with me; they are prominent among the apostles, and they were in Christ before I was. Greet my relative Herodion (11). Verse 13 says, Greet Rufus and his mother—a mother to me also. (Rufus was the son of Simon of Cyrene, who carried the cross of Jesus. Others are listed, and overall at least nine are females.) Verse 16 says, Greet one another with a holy kiss. All the churches of Christ greet you. (The holy kiss became a symbol of love among Christians and a part of early Christian worship.)

Verses 17-18 say, I urge you, brothers and sisters, to keep an eye on those who cause dissensions and offenses, in opposition to the teaching that you have learned; avoid them. For such people do not serve our Lord Jesus Christ, but their own appetites (dietary laws?), and by smooth talk and flattery they deceive the hearts of the simple minded. (There is an apostolic teaching that all teachings and actions must be compared.) Verses 19-20 say, For while your obedience is known to all, so that I rejoice over you, I want you to be wise in what is good and guileless in what is evil. The God of peace will shortly crush Satan under your feet. The grace of our Lord Jesus Christ be with you.

Verse 21 says, Timothy, my co-worker, greets you; so do Lucius and Jason and Sosipater, my relatives. Verse 22 says, I Tertius, the writer of this letter, greet you in the Lord. (Tertius is acting as a secretary writing what Paul wants.) In (23) he says, Gaius (1 Cor 1:14), who is host to me and to the whole church, greets you. Erastus, the city treasurer, and our brother Quartus, greet you.

Paul ends the letter with a doxology. Verses 25-27 say, Now to God who is able to strengthen you according to my gospel and the proclamation of Jesus Christ, according to the revelation of the mystery that was kept secret for long ages but is now disclosed, and through the prophetic writings is made known to all the Gentiles, according to the command of the eternal God, to bring about the obedience of faith—to the only wise God, through Jesus Christ, to whom be the glory forever! Amen.

Paul, once again, emphasizes the obedience of faith taking us back to Rom 2:2-11. Righteousness is a major topic in the book of Romans. Being made righteous by the righteousness of Christ is the key to justification. The righteousness of God that leads to humankind's righteousness or justification begins by grace through faith, continues as long as one lives by grace through faith, as one matures in the ways of Christ, confirming one's part of God's covenant by being obedient to his teachings and receiving continual forgiveness for sins as one falls short, and then it ends by grace through faith. It is a righteousness that is all about relationship. The book of Romans, even though rather difficult, has been one of the most important books throughout the years in the study of Christian theology. As a way of review list some of the most important verses or thoughts the Apostle Paul is making in the letter to Romans.

THE FIRST LETTER
TO THE CORINTHIANS

The Apostle Paul established the church in Corinth, Greece (Acts 18:1-11). He writes this letter to the Corinthians from Ephesus. Ephesus is located in Asia Minor (Turkey) which is across the Aegean Sea exactly opposite Corinth (Acts 19:1-40). The date for writing is probably in the middle 50s. The letter in its present form may consist of a series of shorter letters written over a period of time, and then later placed together as one letter. Before writing the letter, Paul had received reports of strife among the members, and it is possible that he had even written to them previously.

The letter to the Corinthians is divided into issues or attempts to solve problems in the Corinthian church. We learn that problems in the church are nothing new. Some of the following are the issues: the problem of division in the church, an incestuous man, lawsuits among believers, and sexual immorality. Other problems are what to do about behavior in marriage, virgins, food sacrificed to idols, covering of women's heads in worship, women speaking in church, the abuse of the Eucharist, spiritual gifts, bodily resurrection of believers, and the collection for the poor in Jerusalem. The following is a brief summary of the chapters.

In chapter 1 Paul is in Ephesus and receives visitors telling him about the problems in the Corinthian church. Paul was the originator of the Corinthian church but later moved on to plant churches elsewhere. Factions had developed over who of the different early leaders was the best or the most proficient leader. Some were saying I belong to Paul, others Apollos, others Cephas (Peter), still others had developed a Christ faction, either rejecting his divinity (Ebionites), or his humanity (Docetic Gnostics), all of which was bringing about division in the church.

Paul responds by saying I or these others are not anyone's true leader. Jesus Christ, his cross, and the resurrection are the foundation of belief. Dividing over human leaders only divides the church. That message is still very relevant for today, for true unity is in Christ, and not the Pope, Martin Luther, John Calvin, John Wesley, or modern day popes in some of the independent churches, or any human leader God's people follow. There are basics we can all unite on. Outside of those basics, unity is in diversity, and not in conformity.

Paul says the message of the cross is foolishness to those who are perishing but to us who are being saved it is the power of God. The message of Christ and his cross is a stumbling block to the Jews and foolishness to non Jews (Gentiles). Christ is the power and wisdom of God, for the foolishness of God (so-called by the people of the world) is wiser than human wisdom, and the weakness of God (so-called by the people of the world) is stronger than human strength. Paul says that God chose Christ who is the wisdom of God as well as God's righteousness, sanctification, and redemption so that our boasting would not be in humans, or in the particular faith of humans but in Christ. Paul's point is our head is Christ not any human, so cease the division.

In chapter 2 Paul reminds them he did not come to them with smooth words (the world's rhetoric), for I resolved to know nothing but Christ and him crucified, so that your faith would rest not on human wisdom but on the power of God and his wisdom. Paul said that we received the Spirit of God so that we could understand the things of God, and we speak them not with words of human wisdom but with words taught by the Spirit, describing spiritual things in spiritual terms therefore, we have the mind of Christ.

Apparently, in chapter 3 some of these new Christians were making Christianity just another worldly philosophy and were carrying on their division over leaders and their opposition to Paul in the name of wisdom defined as philosophy. Thus they were defining their leaders in human terms like the many itinerant philosophers that traveled in Greece, Rome, and throughout the empire at the time. Then, again, he says Christ is the foundation not human workers not even us, for we are simply God's co-workers, and if our work is not built on Christ, it will be burned. He is saying that they belong to God's Son Jesus the Christ (Messiah), and all they do is for him. He reminds them that all who are adopted by Jesus the Christ are the temple of God and that God's Spirit lives in them. So he encourages them to become wise by the wisdom of God, not the wisdom of the world. He tells them to become a fool in the manner that the world describes a fool, and then they will gain real wisdom.

In chapter 4 Paul encourages them to become servants of Christ and stewards of the mystery of God. In the rest of the chapter Paul encourages them to stop listening to those who are not following after his teachings and the teachings of the apostles, for they are being misled.

In chapters 5-8 he discusses other problems in the Corinthian church among them are lawsuits among believers, a case of incest, and sexual immorality. He reminds them that their bodies are members of Christ, and anyone who joins their body with another in immorality becomes one with them, but whoever is joined to the Lord becomes one spirit with him. Again, he reminds them their bodies are the temple of the Holy Spirit, and God calls them to glorify God in their bodies.

In chapter 7 Paul gives advice to the married, virgins, and widows. He tells them sex is good and holy, if used properly. He teaches contrary to the world's wisdom that marriage is the only acceptable place for sexual activity. In Scripture sex outside of marriage is in most cases not accepted.

In chapter 8 he deals with idols and in chapter 9 he discusses his right as an apostle to receive pay for his work as an apostle, but explains why he does not take any payment. His purpose is simply to bring people to Christ and to discipline himself so that after preaching and teaching he will not lose his soul.

In chapter 10 he reminds them to remain strong in the faith in order to not lose their souls to Satan. He reminds them to pay heed to the Scriptures, which for them is the Old Testament, and the teachings of Christ, for they have been given to see who God is, and how he works and to be an example to God's people. He reminds them that the Eucharist the cup of blessing we bless is a participation in the blood of Christ, and the bread is a participation in the body of Christ. He tells them that they are one with Christ and each other because of their participation in that Holy Communion. Then he reminds them to do everything for the glory of God.

In chapter 11 Paul mentions the tradition of the Lord's Supper that he received. He says, "For I received from the Lord what I handed on that the Lord Jesus on the night he was handed over took bread, broke it, gave thanks, and said this is my body given for you. Do this in remembrance of me. In the same way also the cup saying, this cup is the new covenant in my blood. Do this, as often as you drink it, in remembrance of me. For as often as you eat this bread and drink this cup, you proclaim the death of the Lord until he comes. Therefore whoever eats the bread and drinks the cup of the Lord unworthily will have to answer for not using the body and blood of the Lord in the proper manner."

Eating in an unworthy matter is not discerning the body of Christ, not thinking about its real meaning and purpose, not thinking about how it applies to one's relationship to Christ and fellow believers. So Paul says to confess your sin. A person should first examine himself and then eat and drink. Some of the information in chapter 11 consists of liturgical items for a time that is no longer relevant. Some parts of the Liturgy can change and adapt to the times.

Chapter 12 tells us that there are many different spiritual gifts, and everyone has at least one for the common good and the glory of God, and like any body each part is necessary, but more important than any spiritual gift is love. He says that by one Spirit we have all been baptized into the one body, and now we are the body of Christ and individually members of it. The idea is that all members of Christ's body are necessary and important for the smooth function of the body of Christ, the church.

Chapter 13 is the great love chapter. Verses 4-7 especially define love as action, not feelings. It says love is patient, kind, not jealous, not arrogant, not inflated, not rude, does not seek its own way or interests, is not quick tempered, does not brood over injury or rejoice over wrongdoing but rejoices in the truth. It bears all things, believes, hopes, and endures all things. Love never fails. There is faith, hope, and love, and the greatest of these is love.

Chapter 14 is about one of the spiritual gifts which is speaking in tongues. The rules that guide it are stated, as well as why prophesy or teaching is greater than speaking in tongues. There are other rules for what went on in that particular church, many of which are outdated because times and customs change, but there are principles contained within them that could have timeless value.

Chapter 15 is the great resurrection chapter where numerous appearances of Christ after his resurrection are mentioned. One appearance is appearing to five hundred people at once, and Paul states that many of them are still alive. He mentions that when Christ returns, the kingdom of God instituted by Christ and now growing in the world like a mustard seed, will come into its fullest, its perfection, and death will be swallowed up in victory. The risen bodies are then described. The last chapter discusses Paul's travel plans and the collection he is taking from the different churches for the poor in Jerusalem who are suffering from a major drought. Let us now begin a verse by verse analysis.

Chapter 1:1-3 says, Paul called to be an apostle of Christ Jesus by the will of God, and our brother Sosthenes (Acts 18:12-17), To the church of God that is in Corinth, to those who are sanctified in Christ Jesus, called to be saints, together with all those who in every place call on the name of the Lord Jesus Christ, both their Lord and ours: Grace to you and peace from God our Father and the Lord Jesus Christ. (Sosthenes had succeeded Crispus as the ruler of the synagogue in Corinth when Crispus became a follower of Jesus. He also later converted to Christ.)

Paul is calling them to be holy as God is holy. Being sanctified in Christ means they are made holy by the work of Christ and because of that, they are called the saints of God. Their purpose is to grow in holiness by following his teachings and staying holy by the continual cleansing of their sins.

Corinth was a sailor's haven and a city of much immorality.

Temples of the goddess Aphrodite with her sacred prostitutes both male and female were throughout the city as were many other goddesses of the different pagan mystery cults. Most were involved in the fertility rites of the ancient agricultural societies often taking on an orgiastic nature. People would unite sexually with the temple prostitutes. People thought this would then cause the gods to do the same, and this would bring rain or sun to make the crops grow. This was basically the same concept found in ancient Canaan, which caused God to replace the Canaanites with the Hebrew people with the warning to the Israelites to never participate in such activity.

Throughout the empire there were also temples to the different Greek, Roman, and local gods, and to the Roman emperors who were declared gods by the Senate of Rome. In the process these temples had great economic and political clout. Most important economically were the many temples and monuments throughout the empire devoted to emperor worship. These were major expenditures by the people of wealth and power competing with each other to cement their relationship with the imperial court in an effort to secure their own political and economic dominance. Getting the resources to support these temples and monuments were gathered in the cities and towns in the form of taxes, tribute, and gifts from people wanting to share in the prosperity that comes from Roman favoritism. Great amounts of money were spent on putting on games to honor the emperor, and much of this money was gathered through taxes.

In verses 4-9 Paul continues his message on the call to holiness and is thankful to God that he has enriched them in speech and knowledge with spiritual gifts as they wait for the revealing of the Lord Jesus Christ. He tells them that God will be faithful to them because he has called them into fellowship with his Son Jesus Christ. Verse 8 says, He will also strengthen you to the end, so that you may be blameless on the day of our Lord Jesus Christ. (This call to holiness is the grace of perseverance God grants to those who grow in grace and continue to receive his forgiveness through the blood of Christ.)

Verses 10-13 say, Now I appeal to you, brothers and sisters, by the name of our Lord Jesus Christ, that all of you be in agreement and that there be no divisions among you, but that you be united in the same mind and same purpose. For it has been reported to me by Chloe's people that there are quarrels among you, my brothers and sisters. What I mean is that each of you says, "I belong to Paul," or "I belong to Apollos," or "I belong to Cephas," or "I belong to Christ." Has Christ been divided? Was Paul crucified for you? Or were you baptized in the name of Paul? Even though Paul mentions a few he did baptize in (14-16), verse 17 says, Christ did not send me to baptize but to proclaim the gospel, and not with eloquent wisdom, so that the cross of Christ not be emptied of its power. (Paul teaches Christ is the basis of unity, not humans no matter how eloquent.)

Too many in Corinth took pride in their ability to speak in a Greek, sophisticated, philosophical way, and it was influencing in a negative way what Paul had taught them about being one in Christ and trusting only in the wisdom of Christ and the power of the cross. Polished speakers were taught the finer forms of Greek rhetoric. For the people of that era Greek rhetoric was a determining factor to decide who the better speakers were. In the process it also gave a false impression about who the wise were.

Paul disagrees and in verses 18-25 says, For the message about the cross is foolish to those who are perishing, but to us who are being saved it is the power of God. For it is written, "I will destroy the wisdom of the wise (the world's wisdom), and the discernment of the discerning I will thwart." Where is the one who is wise? Where is the scribe? Where is the debater of this age? Has God not made foolish the wisdom of the world? For since, in the wisdom of God, the world did not know God through wisdom (the world's wisdom), God decided, through the foolishness of our proclamation (what the world claims is foolish), to save those who believe. For Jews demand signs (more miracles), and Greeks desire wisdom (from the Greek philosophical point of view), but we proclaim Christ crucified, a stumbling block to the Jews and foolishness to the Gentiles, but to those who are called, both Jews and Greeks, Christ the power of God and the wisdom of God. For God's (so-called) foolishness is wiser than human wisdom, and God's (so-called) weakness is stronger than human strength.

The true wise ones are not the wise and powerful of this world who spend their time impressing the world with their speaking ability and worldly wisdom but those who believe and trust in the Christ who was crucified and risen and now living his life in and through his people. Real wisdom is Christ.

Verses 26-31 say, Consider your own call, brothers and sisters, not many of you were wise by human standards, not many were powerful, not many were of noble birth. But God chose what is foolish in the world to shame the (so-called) wise; God chose what is weak in the world to shame the (so-called) strong; God chose what is low and despised in the world, things that are not, to reduce to nothing things that are, so that no one might boast in the presence of God. He (God) is the source of your life in Christ Jesus, who became for us wisdom from God, and righteousness and sanctification and redemption in order that as it is written, "Let the one who boasts, boast in the Lord."

The believer finds his wisdom in Christ and the teachings of Scripture, primarily the teachings of Christ. The believer is made righteous and sanctified by the righteousness of Christ by being put right with God and made holy through the blood of Christ, and then sanctification (holiness) continues as Christ lives in and through his follower who in the end is given final justification, sanctification, and redemption. It is all by the working of grace through the working of the Father, Son, and Holy Spirit. According to Paul this is the real wisdom and Paul's primary message.

～ つ つ ～

In chapter 2:1-2 Paul says, When I came to you, brothers and sisters, I did not come proclaiming the mystery of God to you in lofty words of wisdom. For I decided to know nothing among you except Jesus Christ and him crucified.

What a difference that is from some of the most popular preachers today, many of whom are more like psychotherapists, or preachers that attempt to fit America's positive thinking philosophy into their preaching where nothing is wrong, all is well, and if we just think good thoughts, it is going to get better. Obviously that thinking was even around in Paul's day, for in (3-5) he says, And I came to you in weakness and in fear and in much trembling. My speech and my proclamation were not with plausible words of (earthly) wisdom, but with a demonstration of the Spirit and of power, so that your faith might rest not on human wisdom but on the power of God.

The power of God through his word and working through the Spirit imparts a deeper wisdom that only those mature in Christ or open to the leading of the Spirit can understand. Mixing human wisdom with God's wisdom may fool the people for awhile, but in the long run it is counterproductive. The church becomes no different from the local Kiwanis, Lions, or Rotary clubs that serve good purposes. But that is not the only purpose of Christ's church.

Verses 6-8 say, Yet among the mature we do speak wisdom,

though it is not a wisdom of this age or of the rulers of this age, who are doomed to perish. But we speak God's wisdom, secret and hidden (because the world is not open to it), which God decreed before the ages for our glory. None of the rulers of this age understood this; for if they had, they would not have crucified the Lord of glory. (This is probably a reference to both political rulers and the cosmic, demonic rulers behind them, Acts 4:26, Eph 1:20-21, 3:10, 6:12).

In verses 10-12 Paul says, these things God has revealed to us through the Spirit (the Spirit received at baptism); for the Spirit searches everything, even the depths of God. For what human being knows what is truly human except the human spirit that is within? So also no one comprehends what is truly God's except the Spirit of God. Now we have received not the Spirit of the world, but the Spirit that is from God. And we speak of these things in words not taught by human wisdom but taught by the Spirit, interpreting spiritual things to those who are spiritual.

The Spirit received is God's own Spirit, who knows what is in God as our human spirit knows what is in us; therefore his people are able to understand spiritual things meaning the wisdom of God. If one is not open to learning from God's Spirit, one can not understand God's wisdom.

Verse 14 says, Those who are unspiritual do not receive the gifts of God's Spirit, for they are foolishness to them, and they are unable to understand them because they are spiritually discerned. (They do not have God's Spirit because they are not open to being taught by it. This is why the people who are immersed in the wisdom of the world do not understand the things of God.) Verses 15-16 say, Those who are spiritual discern all things, and they are themselves subject to no one's scrutiny. (They are only responsible to the scrutiny of Christ.) For who has known the mind of the Lord so as to instruct him? (No human is in a position to instruct Christ.) But Paul says, we have the mind of Christ.

Paul is saying the people of the world with their worldly wisdom are not able to judge correctly the people of God and what they are trying to accomplish in the world, but those with God's wisdom can very easily see why the world is the way it is. With the mind of Christ one can now think like Christ and understand like Christ. As St Anselm said centuries ago, "I believe in order to understand." Paul will now return to the issue of disunity and rivalries within the church, which is a major issue throughout the book applying what he has just been discussing.

Chapter 3:1-3 says, And so, brothers and sisters, I could not speak to you as spiritual people (who are mature in Christ), but rather as people of the flesh as infants in Christ (who are still immersed in worldly wisdom and values). I fed you with milk (baby food), not solid food, for you were not ready for solid food. (They have barely reached the point that they can even be called babes in Christ. They certainly are not ready to move on to deeper things.) Paul continues, Even now you are still not ready, for you are still of the flesh. (He is saying that they are still being led by their broken, sin filled natures instead of their grace filled Spirit nature. Then he tells them why.) Verse 4 says, For as long as there is jealousy and quarreling among you, are you not of the flesh, and behaving according to human inclinations? For when one says, "I belong to Paul," and another, "I belong to Apollos," are you not merely human (behaving with your broken nature)?

Verses 5-9 say, What then is Apollos? What is Paul? Servants through whom you came to believe, as the Lord assigned to each. I planted, Apollos watered, but God gave the growth. (God uses his people for his purposes in his own way.) So neither the one who plants nor the one who waters is anything, but only God who gives the growth. The one who plants and the one who waters have a common purpose, and each will receive wages according to the labor of each. For we are God's servants, working together; you are God's field, God's building. (God's body, and God's field are the church).

Verses 10-12 say, According to the grace of God given to me, like a skilled master builder I laid a foundation (planted), and someone else is building on it (watering). Each builder must choose with care how to build on it. For no one can lay any foundation other than the one that has been laid; that foundation is Jesus Christ. (The teaching and unity that Paul is talking about have their foundation only in Jesus Christ and him crucified and resurrected.)

Verses 12-15 say, Now if anyone builds on the foundation with gold, silver, precious stones, wood, hay, straw—the work of each builder will become visible, for the Day will disclose it, because it will be revealed with fire, and the fire will test what sort of work each has done. (Fire is the means of judgment in determining the value of what is taught and practiced in the church.) If what has been built on the foundation survives, the builder will receive a reward. If the work is burned up, the builder will suffer loss; the builder will be saved, but only as through fire. (Fire is a symbol of both judgment and purification. The builders will be saved based upon the intentions of their teachings; they will be judged. The one who built with false teaching, teaching contrary to Christ will be rejected.)

Verse 16 says, Do you not know that you are God's temple and that God's Spirit dwells in you? (The followers of Christ filled with the Spirit are the church of the living God, especially when gathered together, and each has the Spirit of God within them. When they depart the assembly, they are the Spirit of Christ going out into the world to make the Spirit of Christ present to the world.) Verse 17 says, If anyone destroys God's temple, God will destroy that person.

If evil people martyr the follower of Christ or the church, they will be eventually judged. Those who divide and destroy God's body through false teachings and actions, those contrary to the teachings of Christ, will be condemned. Most divisive and harmful is the wisdom of this age that seeps into the church, a wisdom that is in opposition to the wisdom that comes from God. Karl Barth, the great Reformed theologian in *Church Dogmatics*, 1, 1, 36, warned that the great problem of the church is heresy, the corruption of its message, not paganism and doubt.

Verses 18-23 say, Do not deceive yourselves. If you think you are wise in this age (in the way of worldly wisdom), you should become fools (in the eyes of the world) so that you may become wise. For the wisdom of this world is foolishness with God. For it is written, "He catches the wise in their craftiness," and again, "The Lord knows the thoughts of the wise (those of worldly wisdom), that they are futile." So let no one boast about human leaders. (They are evaluating their favorite leaders by human wisdom and exaggerating their importance.) For all things are yours, whether Paul or Apollos or Cephas or the world or life or death or the present or the future—all belong to you, and you belong to Christ, and Christ belongs to God. (The only boast is in Christ and his wisdom, and that they belong to him.)

❦

Chapter 4:1-5 says, Think of us in this way, as servants of Christ and stewards of God's mysteries. Moreover it is required of stewards that they be found trustworthy. But with me it is a very small thing that I should be judged by you or by any human court . . . It is the Lord who judges me . . . who will bring to light the things now hidden in darkness and will disclose the purposes of the heart. Then each one will receive commendation from God. (The only judgment that really counts is the judgment of God. Only the Lord knows the heart; he alone will be the final judge.)

In verses 6-7 Paul says, I have applied all this to Apollos and myself for your benefit, brothers and sisters, so that you may learn through us the meaning of the saying, "Nothing beyond what is written," so that none of you will be puffed up in favor of one against the other. (Only what is from Jesus is to judge, not humankind's speculative reasoning.) For who sees anything different in you? What do you have that you did not receive? And if you received it, why do you boast as if it were not a gift?

Paul is saying that all is a gift from God, and all we do for God comes from him working in and through us. If the above is true for teachers such as Paul and Apollos, then it is also true for them and their church factions. So no one should be getting puffed up over themselves, their speculation or their wisdom.

In verses 8-13 Paul contrasts his life in Christ with the laxity and judgmental tone of the Corinthians who apparently are doing very little for the cause of Christ as they sit in comfort and boast in applying their different worldly wisdoms in judgment of Paul, who has originally taught them. Paul reminds them in (9) contrary to them sitting around in comfort as kings, we have become a spectacle to the world . . . We are fools for the sake of Christ, but you are wise in Christ. (At least they think they are wise.) We are weak, but you are strong. (At least in their arrogance they think so.) You are held in honor (in their comfort), but we in disrepute. To the present hour we are hungry and thirsty, we are poorly clothed and beaten and homeless, and we grow weary from the work of our own hands. When reviled, we bless; when persecuted, we endure;

when slandered, we speak kindly. We have become like the rubbish of the world, the dregs of all things, to this very day.

Verses 14-16 say, I am not writing this to make you ashamed, but to admonish you as my beloved children. (Because Paul founded this church, he stakes a claim to be their spiritual father.) Verse 15 says, For though you might have ten thousand guardians in Christ, you do not have many fathers. Indeed, in Christ Jesus I became your father through the gospel. I appeal to you, then, be imitators of me. (As an apostle of Christ his teachings and actions are to be imitated.)

Verses 17 says, For this reason I sent you Timothy, who is my beloved and faithful child in the Lord, to remind you of my ways in Christ Jesus, as I teach them everywhere in every church. (The young Timothy is one of Paul's most faithful helpers, Acts 16:1-3, 1 Thess 3:2, and had helped found the Corinthian church, 2 Cor 1:19.) Verses 18-20 say, But some of you, thinking that I am not coming to you, have become arrogant. But I will come to you soon, if the Lord wills, and I will find out not the talk of these arrogant people but their power. For the kingdom of God depends not on talk but on power. (It comes not from their arm-chair babble but from what their actions are accomplishing for Christ and his purposes.) Then in verse 21 Paul asks, What would you prefer? Am I to come to you with a stick (with discipline), or with love in a spirit of gentleness? (Paul has reached it with their attitude.)

Chapter 5 begins to deal with some other issues in this problem filled church. Verses 1-2 say, It is actually reported that there is sexual immorality among you, and of a kind that is not found even among pagans; for a man is living with his father's wife. And you are arrogant! Should you not rather have mourned, so that he who has done this would have been removed from among you? (Sexual immorality is translated from the Greek word *porneia,* which is sometimes translated as fornication. Others include as porneia the twelve immoralities listed in Leviticus 18.)

In verses 3-8 Paul pronounces judgment on the man and tells the assembly in (5) to hand the man over to Satan, so that his spirit may be saved in the day of the Lord. (Paul is saying that they are to excommunicate him in order to encourage him to repent of his sin, and to make sure others do not feel that sinning is no real problem, for that would only leaven the church in a negative manner. The church is not to celebrate malice and evil but sincerity and truth.)

In verses 9-13 Paul says, I wrote to you in my letter not to associate with sexually immoral persons—not at all meaning the immoral of the world, or the greedy and robbers, or idolaters, since you would then need to go out of the world. But now I am writing to you not to associate with anyone who bears the name of brother and sister who is sexually immoral or greedy, or is an idolater, reviler, drunkard, or robber. Do not even eat with such a one. For what have I to do with judging those outside? Is it not those who are inside that you are to judge? God will judge those outside. "Drive out the wicked person from among you."

Today, when evil is spotted in a congregation how quick someone usually yells do not judge, so that you may not be judged using Mt 7:1. Taking all Scripture in context we know there is a time not to judge but also a time to judge. The context of Scripture tells us when it is proper and when it is not proper. There is a proper time to judge evil outside the church as well as inside the church (Mt 7:15-20, Heb 5:14, 1 Thess 5:22). We will see the sexually immoral man repents and is brought back in.

Chapter 6:1-3 says, When any of you have a grievance against another, do you dare to take it to court before the unrighteous (the government with its pagan judges), instead of taking it before the saints (the church)? Do you not know the saints (believers) will judge the world? And if the world is to be judged by you, are you incompetent to try trivial cases? Do you not know that we are to judge angels—to say nothing of ordinary matters (Dan 7:22, 27). (This writer does not know how believers will judge angels and the world.)

Verses 4-6 say, If you have ordinary cases, then, do you appoint as judges those who have no standing in the church? I say this to your shame . . . (Paul expected serious and honest Christians to be able to settle their differences among themselves or have believers judge between them rather than have their case settled by an unbeliever. Possibly the law has become too complicated for that today, even though the principle still has some validity.)

In verse 7 Paul says, In fact, to have law suits at all with one another is already a defeat for you. Why not rather be wronged? Why not rather be defrauded? (Instead of making the wrong witness Paul suggests suffering wrong.) Verses 8-11 say, But you yourselves wrong and defraud—and believers at that. Do you not know that wrongdoers will not inherit the kingdom of God? Do not be deceived! Fornicators (porneia, which probably include the sexual prohibitions of Leviticus 18), idolaters, adulterers, male prostitutes (those at the pagan temples), sodomites (usually young men hiring themselves out to older men), thieves, the greedy, drunkards, revilers, robbers—none of these will inherit the kingdom of God. And this is what some of you used to be. But you were washed (baptized), you were sanctified (made holy), you were justified (entered into the kingdom) in the name of the Lord Jesus Christ and in the Spirit of our God. (They were transformed and supposedly no longer participating in those things. Notice greed is ranked with the worst sexual sins. The modern day church should pay heed.)

Verse 12 says, "All things are lawful for me," but not all things are beneficial. "All things are lawful for me," but I will not be dominated by anything. (The libertine quoted, "All things are lawful." But Paul's response is that not all things are beneficial, and one is not to be dominated by anything opposed by God. The libertines argued that satisfying sexual desire is like taking food to satisfy hunger. In other words it is the natural thing to do. Paul rejects that thinking. The libertine today also argues like Adam Smith, one of the early promoters of pure capitalism that making as much money for myself for my own selfish interests is the way of capitalism; therefore, it is good for the economy and all involved. This is the thinking behind today's theory of "trickle down" economics.)

Verses 13-14 say, "Food is meant for the stomach and the stomach for food," and God will destroy both one and the other. The body is meant not for fornication (porneia) but for the Lord, and the Lord for the body. And God raised the Lord and will also raise us by his power. (God will decide who will inherit the kingdom and who will not, and the body will not be destroyed but be raised.)

Verses 15-20 say, Do you not know that your bodies are members of Christ? Should I therefore take the members of Christ and make them members of a prostitute? Never! Do you not know that whoever is united to a prostitute becomes one body with her? For it is said, "The two shall become one flesh." But anyone united to the Lord becomes one spirit with him. Shun fornication (porneia)! Every sin that a person commits is outside the body; but the fornicator sins against the body itself. Or do you not know that your body is a temple of the Holy Spirit within you, which you have from God, and that you are not your own? For you were bought with a price; therefore glorify God in your body.

Your body is not really your body. God has given it to you on loan for the purpose of glorifying God in all you do, and any act of porneia has the opposite effect as does participating in any of the sins listed in verses 9 and 10. The body is meant for holiness, for it is the body of Christ in which the Spirit resides. Scripture does not put its mark of approval on any sex outside of marriage.

❧❧

Chapter 7:1 says, Now concerning the matters about which you wrote: "It is well for a man not to touch a woman."

This statement was not made by Paul but by some ascetics in the church, who believe the highest form of spirituality was never to have sexual relations, even if married. Throughout history, every once in awhile, a small group promotes this thinking. There were others who believed Christ was coming soon, so they were just going to sit and wait. Others were even rejecting their marriage. They were questioning whether sexual intimacy was possible for anyone in Christ. Others were saying the opposite. They believed because they were in Christ, the flesh did not matter. They could be sexually intimate with anyone as much as they desired.

These are the arguments two different groups of Gnostics have made throughout history in many religions, especially those religions in the Far East, but also found in Israel. Gnostics believed people including Christ were just spirits. The flesh was not real; it was simply a mirage. They did not believe anyone including Jesus had a physical body nor did he rise bodily from the dead. Paul reacts to this Gnostic statement by stating the opposite and by responding that sexual immorality is real.

To the libertines verse 2 says, But because of cases of sexual immorality (plural in the Greek), each man should have his own wife and each woman her own husband. (It is interesting to note that in the Old Testament one finds polygamy and concubines, but somewhere along the line it began to become less acceptable. Possibly God was allowing humanity to learn by experience that in developing solid family life multiple partners are not a good thing. With Christ each person is to be married to one partner only, and sex outside of marriage is not acceptable.)

Verses 3-5 say, The husband should give to his wife her conjugal rights, and likewise the wife to her husband. (This is directed to those married individuals who have embraced asceticism.) For the wife does not have authority over her own body, but the husband does; likewise the husband does not have authority over his own body, but the wife does. Do not deprive one another except perhaps by agreement for a set time, to devote yourself to prayer, and then come together again, so that Satan may not tempt you because of your lack of self control. (Paul makes very strong statements to both male and female in regards to equality, sex within marriage, and sex outside of marriage, which is a big difference between the Old and New Testaments.)

Verses 6-9 say, This I say by way of concession, not command. I wish that all were as I myself am. But each has a particular gift from God, one having one kind and another a different kind. To the unmarried and widows I say that it is well for them to remain unmarried as I am. But if they are not practicing self-control they should marry. For it is better to marry than be aflame with passion. (Paul's reasons for favoring celibacy are given in verses 26, 32-34 and will be discussed there.)

Verses 10-11 say, To the married I give this command—not I but the Lord—that the wife should not separate from her husband (but if she does separate, let her remain unmarried or else be reconciled to her husband), and that the husband should not divorce his wife. Verses 12-14 say, To the rest I say—I and not the Lord—that if any believer has a wife who is an unbeliever, and she consents to live with him, he should not divorce her. And if any woman has a husband who is an unbeliever, and he consents to live with her, she should not divorce him. For the unbelieving husband is made holy through his wife, and the unbelieving wife is made holy through her husband. Otherwise your children would be unclean, but as it is they are holy. (In some sense it seems they are brought within the sphere of holiness as long as they respect each other and do what is right. Otherwise the separated partner is left for the world to gobble up.)

Verses 15-16 say, But if the unbelieving partner separates, let it be so; in such a case the brother or sister is not bound. It is to peace that God has called you. Wife, for all you know, you might save your husband. Husband, for all you know, you might save your wife. (The key is to have peace with each other. If that is not possible, separation is acceptable. It does not seem that a provision for remarriage is given. It is interesting to note that those obsessed with taking the homosexual Scriptures literally for some reason ignore the literalness of these Scriptures.)

In verses 17-20 Paul tells them to remain in the condition in which they were called; lead the life that the Lord has assigned them wherever they were when they received the Lord's call. Also, circumcision or uncircumcision is not the issue, but obeying the commands of God is everything. (He is saying wherever you are obey God's commands; one does not have to drastically change the situation one is in at the time.)

Verses 21-24 say, Were you a slave when called? Do not be concerned about it. Even if you can gain your freedom, make use of your present condition now more than ever. For whoever was called in the Lord as a slave is a freed person belonging to the Lord, just as whoever was free when called is a slave of Christ. You were bought with a price; do not become slaves of human masters. In whatever condition you were called, brothers and sisters, there remain with God.

He is not telling slaves they must remain as slaves to a human, but he is saying whether you are slave or free, the key is you are free because you are a slave to Christ. He is saying as far as possible, whatever your situation, give glory to God by being as Christ would be if he were in your place. Minority Christians living in an aristocracy had to be careful not to advocate or even suggest any form of revolution, for it could lead to ending their existence. They were content to just plant seeds and let them patiently develop.

Verses 25-28 say, Now concerning virgins, I have no command of the Lord, but I give my opinion as one who by the Lord's mercy is trustworthy. I think that in view of the impending crisis, it is well for you to remain as you are. Are you bound to a wife? Do not seek to be free. Are you free from a wife? Do not seek a wife. But if you marry, you do not sin, and if a virgin marries, she does not sin. Yet those who marry will experience distress in this life, and I would spare you that. (It was a time that many Christians were being made martyrs and he is warning them of the extra stress with a family.)

Verses 29-31 say, I mean brothers and sisters the time has grown short; from now on, let even those who have wives be as though they had none, and those who mourn as though they were not mourning, and those who rejoice as though they were not rejoicing, and those who buy as though they had no possessions, and those who deal with the world as though they had no dealings with it. For the present form of this world is passing away.

This is a form of rhetorical metaphor to stress the danger of the current situation. The seeds of life in Christ and the kingdom of God are being planted, and they are growing like a mustard seed. The ways of the world are being challenged and in the process of change, Paul is telling his listeners to be prepared for the people of the world to make life difficult for you. It is the time of martyrs, a time when all must decide just how serious one is about their belief and stand for Christ.

So Paul is saying for the time being this is my recommendation until the crisis is over. Not everyone agrees with this writer's interpretation of the matter. Scholars do not agree on what the impending crisis is. Some believe Paul thinks the end of the world and judgment is near. Other's think Paul discourages marriage for anyone so they can give full attention to ministry. No one knows for sure, but we do know his letter to the Corinthians, and all his letters are mainly to deal with situational issues for those particular churches in that particular time.

In verses 36-40 Paul continues, If anyone thinks he is not behaving properly toward his fiancée, if his passions are strong, and so it has to be, let him marry as he wishes; it is no sin. Let him marry. But if someone stands firm in his resolve, being under no necessity but having his own desire under control, and has determined in his own mind to keep her as his fiancée, he will do well; and he who refrains from marriage will do better. (In other words the one who refrains from marriage under the current circumstances will have an easier time.)

Those who use this to show that Paul believes not marrying is a higher spirituality forget that the issue is directions for an impending crisis. Later in Ephesians 5:21-23 Paul gives a deeper and more in depth view of marriage where the message is primarily to the husband. Temple Bristow (1988, 35) says that in Ephesians the Greek has 47 words directed at wives while 143 words are directed to husbands. Husbands are to be an example, responsive, supportive, and not lord it over his wife but be a servant showing the same love Christ expressed in loving the church.

Verses 39-40 say, A wife is bound as long as her husband lives.

But if the husband dies, she is free to marry anyone she wishes, only in the Lord. But in my judgment she is more blessed if she remains as she is. And I think that I too have the Spirit of God. (Keep in mind that the impending crisis may bring forth the death of many martyrs in a time where the situation and the church were quite different from our time in America today.)

Temple Bristow (1988, 108) believes that Paul's plea for sexual purity and equality whether single or married expresses two ideas that were absolutely new to the ancient world. No other religion nor any philosophy had affirmed sexuality as a gift of God that must be exercised within specific moral boundaries, and no other religion nor any philosophy had so outspokenly declared the equality of men and women before God.

Chapter 8:1-3 says, Now concerning food sacrificed to idols: we know that "all of us possess knowledge." Knowledge puffs up, but love builds up. Anyone who claims to know something does not yet have the necessary knowledge; but anyone who loves God is known by him. (Paul is not impressed with the "know it alls" of religion. Later he will say, Now I know only in part; then I will know fully, even as I have been fully known, 1 Cor 13:12.)

Knowledge inflates the ego, but love is humble and serves others. Among the issues that threatened to divide the church was the issue of meat or food offered to pagan idols. One of the main places to buy meat was from the priests at the pagan temples. After the person offered the food up to the idol, the priest would sell it. It became a meat shop. The issue for the new Christian was should a believer eat it or not. The more knowledgeable believer who understands that an idol is nothing more than a piece of wood or bronze understands there is no real god behind it, so it does not matter if one eats the food. But pagans just converted to Christianity are not so sure.

Paul in verses 4-6 says, Hence, as to the food offered to idols, we know that "no idol in the world really exists," and that "there is no God but one." Indeed, even though there may be so-called gods in heaven or on earth—as in fact there are many gods and many lords—yet for us there is one God, the Father, from whom are all things and for whom we exist, and one Lord, Jesus Christ, through whom are all things and through whom we exist. (Paul is saying that knowledge teaches there is only one God so there are no gods behind these idols, but people make things their lord and god, and demons and evil spirits are at work, and they are behind what people worship.) So verse 7 says, It is not everyone who has this knowledge. Since some have become so accustomed to idols until now, they still think of the food they eat as food offered to an idol (and in eating it they become one with the god); and their conscience being weak is defiled.

Those who claim superior knowledge in (8) say, "Food will not bring us close to God." But Paul in (9) says, We are no worse off if we do not eat, and no better off if we do. But take care that this liberty of yours does not somehow become a stumbling block to the weak. (In seeing others eating the food that was offered to idols, the convert from a former religion may think it is acceptable to worship both that god and the one God as did many throughout the Old Testament.)

Verses 10-13 say, For if others see you, who possess knowledge, eating in the temple of an idol might they not, since their conscience is weak be encouraged to the point of eating food sacrificed to idols? So by your knowledge those weak believers for whom Christ died are destroyed. But when you thus sin against members of your family, and wound their conscience when it is weak, you sin against

Christ. Therefore, if food is a cause of their falling, I will never eat meat, so that I may not cause one of them to fall.

Paul's point is that nothing should be judged from the point of view of knowledge only. Love for another trumps knowledge as does wounding another's conscience. Even though one's freedom permits an activity, if it causes harm to another, or wounds a soul's conscience, it should be rejected, at least for the time being. One is never to do anything that may cause a brother or sister to fall from Christ. Again, keep in mind that Paul is writing to situational issues in his time era. The principles behind his writing can be adapted to modern times but only through careful thought.

Chapter 9:1 says, Am I not free? Am I not an apostle? Have I not seen Jesus the Lord? Are you not my work in the Lord? Paul goes on in (2-19) to interject his example of being free but putting constraints on his freedom for the well-being of others so that Christ may be honored and glorified. Paul freely forfeited the apostolic privilege of financial support, providing his own, as well as the right to a wife like Peter and the other apostles, in order to better advance the cause of Christ. Verse 16 says, If I proclaim the gospel, this gives me no ground for boasting, for an obligation is laid on me, and woe to me if I do not proclaim the gospel!

Verses 19-23 say, For though I am free with respect to all, I have made myself a slave to all, so that I might win more of them. To the Jews I became as a Jew, in order to win Jews. To those under the law I became as one under the law (though I myself am not under the law) so that I might win those under the law. To those outside the law I became as one outside the law (though I am not free from God's law but am under Christ's law) so that I might win those outside the law. To the weak I became weak, so that I might win the weak. I have become all things to all people, so that I might by all means save some. I do all for the sake of the gospel, so I may share in its blessings. (Paul believes he is free except for his obligation to not do anything that opposes who Christ is and what he teaches, and he is free to act from love to serve the common good and to serve others and their well-being, as well as serve God and his word just as Christ did.)

Verses 24-27 say, Do you not know in a race the runners all compete, but only one receives the prize? Run in such a way that you may win it. Athletes exercise self-control in all things; they do it to receive a perishable wreath (trophy), but we an imperishable one (eternal life). So I do not run aimlessly, nor do I box as though beating the air; but I punish (discipline) my body and enslave it, so that after proclaiming to others I myself should not be disqualified.

Today we live in a world which encourages individual freedom without constraints, and the pursuit of worldly happiness at any expense. Serving self in all areas, political, economic, and social has become the god of too many. In the process concern for others and the common good of all has basically been lost. Paul's view, which is the way of Christ, is a corrective approach. It involves self-denial in the pursuit of serving others in the hope of serving God for the well-being of others and the community (the common good). In this way God is glorified and the kingdom of God advances. This is what real freedom means, free to be what Christ wants his people to be. Being a slave to Christ sets one free from the things of the world that enslave and enable one to serve as Christ served.

In the following Paul continues to reflect on the principles of behavior which help to reconcile the weak with the strong. Having reflected on his own experience as an apostle, he will now reflect upon the lesson of Israel. Paul will warn his fellow Christians about the danger of pride.

Chapter 10:1-5 says, I do not want you to be unaware, brothers and sisters, that our ancestors were all under the cloud, and all passed through the sea, and all were baptized into Moses in the cloud and in the sea, and all ate the same spiritual food, and all drank the same spiritual drink. For they drank from the spiritual rock that followed them, and the rock was Christ. Nevertheless, God was not pleased with most of them, and they were struck down in the wilderness.

Paul reminds the Corinthians that all the Israelites were under the cloud representing the presence of God, and all of them passed through the sea, representing God's mighty deeds (the Exodus, the liberation from Pharoah in Egypt). Passing through the cloud and the sea also represents them being baptized into Moses. Baptized means immersed and signifies belonging to the one in whom they were baptized. They all ate the same spiritual food and drink given to them by the Father. In some way Paul is saying the presence of Christ (the rock) was with them and feeding them. Even so, these signs did not insure the Israelites against God's wrath. They were disobedient and they reaped the consequences, their rebellion was punished. Paul is indicating to the Corinthians to not think that because they are baptized and eat and drink the bread and wine of the Lord's Supper (Eucharist) that they can not fall from God's grace. Just like the people of old, falling from God's grace is possible. God never take away one's freedom of choice.

Verse 6 says, Now these things occurred as examples for us, so that we might not desire evil as they did. (Providing examples is one of the main purposes the Old Testament serves for Christians. From it we learn the nature of God, who God is, who we are as his people, how he wants us to relate to him, ourselves, and all he created, including people, things, and his created order.)

Verses 7-11 say, Do not become idolaters as some of them did; as it is written, "The people sat down to eat and drink, and rose up to play." We must not indulge in sexual immorality as some of them did, and twenty-three thousand fell in a single day. We must not put Christ to the test as some of them did, and were destroyed by serpents. And do not complain as some of them did, and were destroyed by the destroyer. These things happened to them to serve as an example, and they were written down to instruct us on whom the end of the ages have come.

Paul is saying with the crucifixion and resurrection of Christ and the sending of the Spirit we are in the last age, the church age. We have a new covenant, but the writings of the old covenant are still very valuable, for the new brings the old all it was intended to be. It fulfills completes and perfects all the old was intended to be.

Verses 12-13 say, So if you think you are standing, watch out that you do not fall. No testing has overtaken you that is not common to everyone. God is faithful, and he will not let you be tested beyond your strength, but with testing he will also provide the way out so that you may be able to endure it. (Through God's testing one grows in the faith and is able to give witness to one's faith.)

Verses 14-17 say, Therefore my dear friends, flee from the worship of idols. I speak as to sensible people; judge for yourself what I say. The cup of blessing that we bless, is it not a sharing in the blood of Christ? The bread that we break, is it not a sharing in the body of Christ? (He is saying that we share or participate in the blood and body of Christ when we drink the wine and eat the bread of Holy Communion.) Because there is one bread, we who are many are one body, for we all partake of the one bread.

Paul is saying our unity, one with each other and the holy Trinity, is what the Eucharist portrays. Through the forgiveness of sins each of us relates to and participates in the Father, Son, and Holy Spirit.

As they are one, we are one. In Jn 17:20-23 Jesus prays that we all be one as you Father are in me and I am in you, may they also be in us, so that the world may believe that you have sent me.

He emphasizes this concept because in verses 18-22 he compares eating meat sacrificed to the pagan gods with what Christians believe about what happens at Holy Communion. Pagans believe they are participating in their gods. Paul tells them in (20) that they are sacrificing to demons and not to God. In (21) he says, You can not drink the cup of the Lord and the cup of demons. In reference to eating the meat outside the pagan temples in (23-24), Paul says all things are lawful, but all things are not beneficial, nor do all things build up people. Do not seek your own advantage, but that of the other. (Again, the principle is act out of love and what is best for another as the other grows in Christ. Do not act from your knowledge and what you deem best for you. Be careful not to wound another's conscience or do what is harmful to another.)

Verses 25-26 say, Eat whatever is sold in the meat market without raising any question on the grounds of conscience, for "the earth and its fullness are the Lord's." But in (27-28) he says, if an unbeliever invites you to a meal and you are disposed to go, eat whatever is set before you without raising any question on the ground of conscience. But if someone says to you, "This has been offered in sacrifice," then do not eat it, out of consideration for the one who informed you, and for the sake of conscience—I mean the other's conscience, not your own. In verses 29-30 Paul says, For why should my liberty be subject to the judgment of someone else's conscience. If I partake with thankfulness, why should I be denounced because of that for which I give thanks? (This last verse does not logically follow Paul's instructions to how the more mature believer is to act when among the new converts. But they would make sense when the stronger Christian asks this defending his right to eat.)

Paul does say that when he is not among new converts he is free to eat meat that had been offered to idols. Paul does not allow others to make their conscience the standard of God's truth. They need to be more educated and grow deeper in understanding God's truth and the meaning of real freedom. But in the meantime they need to be given room to grow. Patience is necessary. This principle can be applied to many modern day issues. This writer encourages those maturing in the faith to decide what those issues are.

Verses 31-33 say, So, whether you eat or drink, or whatever you do, do everything for the glory of God. (That is the key.) Give no offense to Jews or to Greeks, or to the church of God, just as I try to please everyone in everything I do, not seeking my own advantage, but that of many, so that they may be saved. (His pleasing everyone in everything means only for everyone and everything that involves their salvation and growth in the faith. He is not to hinder their growth in the faith by forcing them into beliefs and actions they are not ready to understand. On the other hand the new convert needs to be gently led forward to a deeper maturity and understanding of the faith.)

Chapter 11:1-2 says, Be imitators of me as I am of Christ. (Paul stresses the importance of Christian example in attitude, love, and obedience.) I commend you because you remember me in everything and maintain the traditions just as I handed them on to you. (The traditions were handed down orally, but now they are beginning to be put in writing. They may have remembered the traditions, but as we read Corinthians, they certainly are not putting them into operation very well. There is much disorganization, lack of love, selfishness, and disunity. Modern day churches are not the only ones with problems, but these human imperfections should not hinder personal faith.)

Verse 3 says, But I want you to understand that Christ is the head of every man, and the husband is the head of his wife, and God is head of Christ.

The Greek word for head can be also translated as *source*, and does not mean an absolute ruler. It also indicates that what follows is grounded in God. We know that the source of the Son is the Father, and Father and Son are equal, so one thing Paul is saying is that even though Eve was created from Adam, man and woman are created equal, even though created different. In the beginning (Gen 2:18) God created woman as an *ezer* (the Hebrew word). According to John Temple Bristow (1988, 16) the word can also be translated as "partner." If the word translated head or source has any inclination toward leadership it is a leadership that leads by example, and one that is responsive, supportive and does not lord it over the other, but is a servant of the other, as Christ is a servant.

Before moving on it is important to understand that in the culture at that time women were not allowed to be taught, let alone teach in a group. They were not even permitted to speak to a man in public, and if a man were seen speaking to a woman in public, it was believed he was seeking sexual favors. This was also true for women in Greek society. In the synagogue recent changes had begun to allow women to attend, but they had to sit behind a screen, or be separated by a wall and be neither seen nor heard. At the other extreme in some pagan temples there were women priestesses leading pagan worship defying convention and appearing as prostitutes, which many of them were as they participated in the agricultural fertility rites with their hair hanging down. A woman with her hair hanging down was a sign that one was unmarried and available. That basic background is needed to help understand this difficult chapter. When this is understood, we can not escape the fact that Christianity laid the seeds for a revolution about how women are treated.

Then in verses 4-5 Paul says, Any man who prays or prophesies with something on his head disgraces his head, but any woman who prays or prophesies with her head unveiled (or uncovered) disgraces her head—it is one and the same thing as having her head shaved (society's punishment for prostitution). For if a woman will not veil herself (cover herself or her head), then she should cut off her hair; but if it is a disgrace for a woman to have her hair cut off or to be shaved, she should wear a veil (or a cover on her head). The great stride forward in Hebrew culture is that now not only can women participate in worship, but they can even pray, even though there are some conditions.

Women wearing a head covering outside of the home was the custom at the time to show that the woman is spoken for and that she is under the jurisdiction of her husband. This part of the chapter is about proper liturgical dress in worship at a certain time in history for both men and women, and the issue for them is not so much the dress as what one is saying theologically when one worships. It is important to note that both men and women have leadership roles, both are permitted to teach, which is what prophesying is. The issue is about their appearance in that role. This is not about who is in charge; it is about what impression one is giving by how one appears in worship at the liturgy at a time when woman are just beginning to be able to participate in worship. It is mainly about respecting proper custom so as not to promote scandal at a time the church was a minority and needed to maintain a certain respect and balance in the society in which they lived in order to get people to listen to the primary message.

Unbound, flowing hair was regarded as sensual, and if in public, a woman was seen as tempting men to sin. Jewish tradition (the

Mishna, the oral law) declared that a man can divorce his wife if seen in public with unbound hair, or if seen talking to a man in public. The man would not even have to return the dowry in this situation. Therefore many Jewish women even wore a head covering in the home. Again, Paul's concern is to not upset social convention too much, for his primary goal is to first get people to understand who Jesus is and what he did; then later to understand better what he taught about those things contrary to conventional society.

A woman shaved or with short hair in those days signified a prostitute. A woman with her hair uncovered or let loose and not braided on top of her head showed that she was unmarried, responsible to no man, and should not be appearing with men in public. A woman with her hair down in public was seen as tempting men to sin. Appearing in such manner was like the women priests who led the orgiastic worship of the pagan gods.

Some of the married woman in the Corinthian church by not having their heads covered may be appearing that way because of a desire to return to celibacy as a part of their asceticism, which was an issue in early Christianity. For not having their heads covered showed that they were virgin like and not responsible to any man. It was thought to be like a wedding ring today. Paul is saying that these women are dishonoring both Christ and their husbands. It is causing turmoil, and there is a confusion of gender involved. Hairstyles are no longer relevant to modern day Christians, but the principle behind these instructions, of being sensitive to what message our dress codes and styles convey to others, still has some value.

Verses 7-10 say, For a man ought not to have his head veiled (covered), since he is the image and reflection of God; but woman is the reflection of man. (He is not saying that she is not a reflection of Christ, but it is saying she is also a reflection of her husband. Gen 1:27 states that God created both male and female in his image.)

Indeed (in the beginning) man was not made from woman, but woman from man. Neither was man created for the sake of woman, but woman for man. For this reason a woman ought to have a symbol of authority on her head, because of the angels.

Temple Bristow (1988, 58-60) states Paul is saying that woman is the glory of man. She is not the distraction of man, as the Essenes claimed, nor an object to be owned and used as the Greeks and traditional Jews believed, but the very glory of man. This is a gigantic upgrade in an attitude about women in ancient society. Second, in (1 Cor 11:9), Paul reminds his readers that woman was created a partner because man needs woman. Third, Paul adds in 1 Cor 11:11 that each needs the other. Fourth, as 11:12 says, For just as woman came from man, so man comes from woman; but all things come from God. The implication is that if Eve was inferior to Adam by virtue of being made out of his body, then every man is inferior to his mother for the same reason. The source of all is God. As God designed man, therefore God also designed woman. Therefore, we humans are not inferior to each other, only to God.

What he means by "because of the angels" in verse 10 is anyone's guess. The reference to the angels may have reference to the worship on earth being taken by the angels to be joined to the worship that is in going on in the heavenly liturgy, so it needs to be done in an orderly manner. It may be that Paul is using the order of creation to show the argument used by the people at that time to temporarily support the social custom of attire, for in the following he is going to say the order of creation is not a good argument, but nevertheless it is acceptable, and the one used in that period of time.

As verses 11-12 say, Nevertheless, in the Lord woman is not independent of man or man of woman. For just as woman came from man, so man comes through woman; but all things from God. (He seems to now be rejecting the order from creation in Genesis because Christ has come making all things new. He is saying in the Lord (Jesus) they are equal and dependent on each other; therefore, the issue is not subordination.)

No one said this is an easy chapter to interpret and understand. If everything is to be taken literally for today, then many changes need to be made including all women wearing veils or head coverings (prayer shawl) at worship, greeting each other with a holy kiss, which Paul will command in 16:20, and to follow the order of worship Paul presents in 14:26-33 among other things. Obviously this writer rejects that type of thinking.

Then in verses 13-16 Paul says, Judge for yourselves: is it proper for a woman to pray to God with her hair unveiled? Does not nature itself teach you that if a man wears long hair, it is degrading to him, but if a woman wears long hair, it is her glory? For her hair is given to her for a covering. But if anyone is disposed to be contentious— we have no such custom, nor do the churches of God.

Again he uses the order of nature argument, but then states under the new covenant it is only temporary and not a timeless law. Paul goes along with social custom for the moment because the church is a minority, and he does not want too much social upheaval because it will keep the masses of people from coming to the church to hear the basis message of Christ and his teachings. He is content to plant the seeds of faith and then progress patiently.

This writer is not exactly sure what Paul is saying about the order of creation and angels, but he does seem to be saying the issue is custom (social convention) not God's law. It seems to be nature or natural for those people at the time, but is it really the nature of God to wear hair a certain way? Sometimes humans confuse nature or what is natural for the time with natural law thus confusing nature with the social mores of a certain area.

Paul is trying to give scriptural and authoritative reinforcement for customs that prescribe differences between the sexes while also maintaining a woman's equality with man and the right to pray and prophesy in worship. Paul wants social custom to be respected as much as possible while protecting equality and a new role for women.

Another point of view often expressed by the fundamentalists is that this whole section is about the order of nature, and thus it is timeless. A woman is to be subjected to a man as man is subjected to Christ and as Christ is subjected to the Father. But the question is: Is the Son subordinated to the Father, or are they mutually equal, partners, and interdependent with each other?

Verses 17-19 say, Now in the following instructions I do not commend you, because when you come together it is not for the better but for the worse. For, to begin with, when you come together as a church, I hear that there are divisions among you; and to some extent I believe it. Indeed, there have to be factions (cliques) among you, for only so will it become clear who among you are genuine. (They think the factions are necessary to prove who is superior, or who is speaking the truth. Paul rejects this thinking. In the following incident the factions seem to be socio-economic.)

Verses 20-22 say, When you come together, it is not really to eat the Lord's Supper. For when the time comes to eat, each of you goes ahead with your own supper, and one goes hungry and another becomes drunk. (Paul is saying that their only interest in coming together is to make it a social occasion. They certainly are not displaying any love or concern for the poor, nor is there much dignity in their actions.) In (22) he says, Do you not have homes to eat and drink in? Or do you show contempt for the church of God and humiliate those who have nothing? What should I say to you? Should I commend you? In this matter I do not commend you!

Verses 23-29 say, For I received from the Lord what I also handed on to you, that the Lord Jesus on the night when he was betrayed took a loaf of bread, and when he had given thanks, he broke it and said, "This is my body that is for you. Do this in remembrance of me." In the same way he took the cup also, after supper, saying, "This cup is the new covenant in my blood. Do this, as often as you drink it, in remembrance of me." For as often as you eat this bread and drink this cup, you proclaim the Lord's death until he comes. Whoever, therefore, eats the bread or drinks the cup of the Lord in an unworthy manner will be answerable for the body and blood of the Lord. Examine yourselves, and only then eat of the bread and drink of the cup. For all who eat and drink without discerning the body, eat and drink judgment on themselves.

The believer is to understand the blood of Christ was shed for sin. Thus humiliating one's brother and sister by ignoring them and not sharing your food and material blessings with them, and then eating and drinking Christ's body and blood is not acceptable. It is a grievous sin.

Verses 30 says, For this reason many of you are weak and ill, and some have died. (This writer can not explain what that means other than the possibility that in the early church this occurred, as did many miracles, in order to teach the idea that taking the Lord's body and blood without seeking forgiveness of sins is not acceptable to God the Father. Possibly, the same thing does not continue today because we now have the written Scriptures.)

Verses 31-34 say, But if we judged ourselves, we would not be judged. But when we are judged by the Lord, we are disciplined so that we may not be condemned along with the world. So then, my brothers and sisters, when you come together to eat, wait for one another. If you are hungry, eat at home, so that when you come together, it will not be for your condemnation. About the other things I will give instructions when I come. (A key message is that when you come to participate in Holy Communion make sure you respect the sacrament, do not socially distinguish yourself from others, examine your heart, and make a confession of your sins.)

∾∾

Chapter 12:1-3 says, Now concerning spiritual gifts, brothers and sisters, . . . I want you to understand that no one speaking by the Spirit of God ever says, "Let Jesus be cursed!" and no one can say, "Jesus is Lord except by the Holy Spirit." (This chapter stresses the work of the Holy Spirit and its source being from the Father and the Son who desire that all be one and united to God and each other.)

Verses 4-11 say, Now there are varieties of gifts (*chrismata*), but the same Spirit; and there are varieties of services, but the same Lord; and there are varieties of activities, but it is the same God that activates all of them in everyone. (Notice the Father, Son, and Holy Spirit.) To each is given the manifestation of the Spirit for the *commom good*. To one is given through the Spirit the utterance of wisdom, and to another the utterance of knowledge according to the same Spirit, to another faith by the same Spirit, to another gifts of healing by the one Spirit, to another the working of miracles, to another prophecy, to another the discernment of spirits, to another various kinds of tongues, to another the interpretation of tongues. All these are activated by one and the same Spirit, who allots to each one individually just as the Spirit chooses.

The real test of God's special gifts is whether they contribute to the common good and benefit the development and purpose of the community of Christ. The early church was given these special gifts, especially the miraculous, in order to get it established. That is not to say these gifts can not break out at different times perhaps even in our time, but it is not the norm.

Verses 12-13 say, For just as the body is one and has many members, and all the members of the body, though many, are one body, so it is with Christ. For in the one Spirit we were all baptized into one body—Jews or Greeks, slaves or free—and we are all made to drink of the one Spirit. (There is one Spirit who baptized into one body, the church, and it is the same Spirit that gives spiritual gifts to all, not on the basis of works but grace.)

Verses 14-20 say, Indeed, the body does not consist of one member but of many. If the foot would say, "Because I am not a hand I do not belong to the body," that would not make it any less a part of the body. And if the ear would say, "Because I am not an eye I do not belong to the body," that would not make it any less a part of the body. If the body were an eye where would the hearing be? If the whole body were hearing, where would the sense of smell be? But as it is, God arranged the members in the body, each one of them as he chose. If all were a single member where would the body be? As it is, there are many members, yet one body.

Verses 21-26 say, The eye cannot say to the hand, "I have no need of you." On the contrary, the members of the body that seem to be weaker are indispensable, and those members of the body that we think less honorable we clothe with greater honor, and our less respectable members are treated with greater respect; whereas our more respectable members do not need this. But God has so arranged the body, giving the greater honor to the inferior member, that there may be no dissension within the body, but the members may have the same care for one another. If one member suffers, all suffer together with it; if one member is honored, all rejoice together with it. (Is that the way most churches actually practice spiritual gifts?)

Verses 27-31 say, Now you are the body of Christ and individually members of it. And God has appointed in the church first apostles, second prophets, third teachers; then deeds of power, then gifts of healing, forms of assistance, forms of leadership, various kinds of tongues. Are all apostles? Are all prophets? Are all teachers? Do all work miracles? Do all possess gifts of healing? Do all speak in tongues? Do all interpret? But strive for the greater gifts. And I will show you a still more excellent way.

Paul is teaching the importance of each member and the necessity of humility as well as the dignity of each member in the body represented as the church. But there is something higher and better than the gifts. The following chapter explains what that is.

Chapter 13:1-3 says, If I speak in the tongues of mortals and of angels, but do not have love, I am a noisy gong or a clanging cymbal. And if I have prophetic powers, and understand all mysteries and all knowledge, and if I have all faith, so as to remove mountains, but do not have love, I am nothing. If I give away all my possessions, and if I hand over my body so that I may boast, but do not have love, I gain nothing. (The more excellent way is love. Buddhists call it compassion, and compassion is a very important aspect of love, even though compassion is not the whole of love. Without love one is not of God no matter what is achieved, 1 Jn 4:7-21.)

Verses 4-7 define love as action. Love is patient; love is kind; love is not envious or boastful or arrogant or rude. It does not insist on its own way; it is not irritable or resentful; it does not rejoice in wrongdoing, but rejoices in the truth. It bears all things, believes all things, hopes all things, endures all things.

Love is primarily defined as actions or ways to act. One can love without having the feeling of love, and this is not being a hypocrite, especially when it is done for the glory of God. In this way it is possible to love enemies as Jesus called his people to do.

Verses 8-12 say, Love never ends. But as for prophecies, they will come to an end; as for tongues, they will cease; as for knowledge, it will come to an end. For we know only in part, and we prophesy only in part; but when the complete comes, the partial will come to an end. (With the new heaven and new earth all these things will no longer be needed, but love is the basis of eternity.) When I was a child, I spoke like a child, I thought like a child; when I became an adult, I put an end to childish ways. For now we see in a mirror, dimly, but then we will see face to face. Now I know only in part; then I will know fully, even as I have been fully known.

We do not know everything we would like to know about God and his ways. We do not even have a full meaning of Scripture and all its implications. That will come with the new heaven and new earth. While on earth our knowledge and understanding will always be in part, even though we are able to know what is needed to know.

Verse 13 says, And now faith, hope, and love abide, these three; and the greatest of these is love. (While on earth we must remain in faith, hope, and love, if we are to mature in Christ. Love is the greatest because it expresses one's faith and hope, and it is eternal, for when one is with Christ forever, there will no longer be a need for faith and hope.)

Chapter 14:1-5 says, Pursue love and strive for the spiritual gifts, and especially that they may prophesy. For those who speak in a tongue do not speak to other people but to God; for nobody understands them, since they are speaking mysteries in the Spirit. On the other hand, those who prophesy speak to other people for their upbuilding, and encouragement and consolation. Those who speak in a tongue build up themselves, but those who prophesy

build up the church. Now I would like all of you to speak in tongues, but even more to prophesy. One who prophesies is greater than one who speaks in tongues, unless someone interprets, so that the church may be built up.

Besides love Paul stresses order and for God's gifts to upbuild the church. Even though all members are equal some gifts have more value than others. Notice how prophecy is defined. It is not to tell the future as most use it today. Prophecy is taking God's word and applying it to life in the times. It is for teaching, encouraging, and consoling.

Verses 6-12 say, Now, brothers and sisters, if I come to you speaking in tongues, how will I benefit you unless I speak to you in some revelation or knowledge or prophesy or teaching? It is the same with lifeless instruments that produce sound, such as the flute or the harp. If they do not give distinct notes, how will anyone know what is played? And if the bugle gives an indistinct sound, who will get ready for battle? So with yourselves; if in a tongue you utter speech that is not intelligible, how will anyone know what is being said? For you will be speaking into the air. There are doubtless many different kinds of sounds in the world, and nothing is without sound. If then I do not know the meaning of a sound, I will be a foreigner to the speaker and the speaker a foreigner to me. So with yourselves; since you are eager for spiritual gifts, strive to excel in them for building up the church.

Verses 13-19 say, Therefore, one who speaks in a tongue should pray for the power to interpret. For if I pray in a tongue, my spirit prays but my mind is unproductive. What should I do then? I will pray with the Spirit, but I will pray with the mind also. Otherwise, if you say a blessing with the Spirit, how can anyone in the position of an outsider say the "Amen" to your thanksgiving, since the outsider does not know what you are saying? For you may give thanks well enough, but the other person is not built up. I thank God that I speak in tongues more than all of you; nevertheless, in church I would rather speak five words with my mind, in order to instruct others also, than ten thousand words with a tongue. In verse 20 he urges them to think as adults.

Verses 21-25 say, In the law it is written, "By people of strange tongues and by the lips of foreigners I will speak to the people; yet even then they will not listen to me," says the Lord. Tongues, then, are a sign not for believers but for unbelievers, while prophesy is not for unbelievers but for believers. If, therefore, the whole church comes together and all speak in tongues, and outsiders or unbelievers enter, will they not say that you are out of your mind? But if all prophesy, an unbeliever or outsider who enters is reproved by all and called to account by all. After the secrets of the unbeliever's heart are disclosed, that person will bow down before God and worship him, declaring, "God is really among you."

Apparently, the issue of tongue speaking is also causing division in the church. Paul was not opposed to tongue speaking, for it is one of his gifts, but in the assembly for worship, it is only to be used, if there is someone who can interpret what is being said. If not it is to be used for private use only, or possibly outside the church for evangelizing, but again an interpreter is necessary.

Verses 26-33 say, What should be done then my friends? When you come together, each one has a hymn, a lesson, a revelation, a tongue, or an interpretation. Let all be done for building up. If anyone speaks in a tongue, let there be only two or at most three, and each in turn; and let one interpret. But if there is no one to interpret, let them be silent in church and speak to themselves and God. Let two or three prophets speak, and let the others weigh what is said. If the revelation is made to someone else sitting nearby, let the first person be silent. For you can all prophesy one by one, so that all may learn and all be encouraged. And the spirits of prophets are subject to the prophets, for God is a God not of disorder but of peace.

This is the closest representation of a worship session in the early church. If as some churches contend that everything done in churches today must only be from the Bible, why is their worship not done in this manner?

Verses 33b-36 are put in parentheses by the NRSV to indicate that a later scribe may have added the verses. The subject before and after the paragraph is prophecy. Other versions do not add the parentheses. The Greek manuscripts have it as a paragraph. Some of the earliest versions place it after verse 40. It says, As in all the churches of the saints, women should be silent in the churches. For they are not permitted to speak, but should be subordinate, as the law also says. If there is anything they desire to know, let them ask their husbands at home. For it is shameful for a woman to speak in church. Or did the word of God originate with you? Or are you the only ones it has reached?

One reason some think a later scribe added this paragraph is because in chapter 11 women are prophesying, while in Gal 3:28 Paul says in Christ all are equal. Paul using the law to support the submission of women is contrary to everything he has said on the subject of women. If Paul did say it, then one must look for the special situation that brought it on. Titus 2:5 says they are not to teach so that the word of God not be discredited. Such a reason could be valid for that era but certainly not in modern times.

As stated previously, in the Corinthian culture women and men were not to be seen talking together in public. Apparently with their new found freedom some of the women were openly confronting the men or even competing with them in the worship service. This was another cause of division and strife within the church. Up to this point women were not even permitted to be educated in most things including religion, and some of them fell prey to heretical teaching about sexuality and marriage. Paul was asking the women who were not prophesying to volunteer (volunteer is the nuance of the Greek word) to be quiet, and to ask their questions to their husbands at home instead of interjecting them into the liturgy.

The purpose of Paul's words is to promote unity, not to teach about women's role in the church. Again as in some of the other items Paul has mentioned in Corinthians, one needs to keep in mind the situational nature of his teachings for those in that specific time. How could Paul approve of women praying and prophesying during public worship (chapter 11), and then a few pages later write that women must remain silent during worship? If he did write those words, the answer can be found in the Greek words used. The word used for silence means voluntary silence. The word used is the one used in the midst of disorder. It is that kind of silence Paul must be referring to.

The Greek language also has different words for "speak." The word used by Paul means talk. Since Paul's instructions were given to a church troubled by tumult and discord during the worship services, he told the women not to talk—that is not to converse. Paul is saying that it is shameful to keep talking during the worship period. The law that Paul appeals to is the law of love. The principle that carries over is not that women can never teach in the church but that all things must be done with respect, decency and with order.

It is also necessary to keep in mind what was going on in the pagan temples in Corinth. Women were letting their hair down, leading worship in ecstatic language, and participating in sexual orgies. Paul does not want the women in Christ's church to even resemble the women in the pagan temples, especially the temples of Aphrodite. (Much of the information about women presented here was taken from *What Paul Really Said About Women* by John Temple Bristow.)

Verse 37 returns to the issue of prophecy and speaking in tongues. One must remember that the numbered verses, as well as the punctuation, were added hundreds of years later in the Middle Ages. Verses 37-40 say, Anyone who claims to be a prophet, or to have spiritual powers, must acknowledge that what I am writing to you is a command of the Lord. Anyone who does not recognize this is not to be recognized. So my friends, be eager to prophesy, and do not forbid speaking in tongues; but all things should be done decently and in order.

Chapter 15:1-2 says, Now I would remind you, brothers and sisters, of the good news that I proclaimed to you, which you in turn received, in which also you stand, through which also you are being saved, if you hold firmly to the message that I proclaimed to you—unless you have come to believe in vain. (Paul says, they are in the process of being saved, if they hold firmly to the message. Otherwise their belief is in vain.)

Verses 3-8 say, For I handed on to you as of first importance what I in turn had received; that Christ died for our sins in accordance with the scriptures, and that he was buried, and that he was raised on the third day in accordance with the scriptures, and that he appeared to Cephas, then to the twelve. Then he appeared to more than five hundred brothers and sisters at one time, most of them are still alive, though some have died. Then he appeared to James, then to all the apostles. Last of all, as to one untimely born, he appeared also to me. (This is part of the good news. Christ has died; Christ has risen; and then Christ has appeared to many including more than five hundred people many who are still alive. So he is saying if you do not believe me, there are many others still alive that are available for you to ask.)

Then Paul in (9-11) says, For I am the least of the apostles, unfit to be called an apostle, because I persecuted the church of God. But by the grace of God I am what I am, and his grace toward me has not been in vain. On the contrary, I worked harder than any of them—though it was not I, but the grace of God that is with me. Whether then it was I or they, so we proclaim and so you have come to believe.

Verse 12 says, Now if Christ is proclaimed as raised from the dead, how can some of you say there is no resurrection of the dead. (The issue is the resurrection of the body. There were many who believed the spirit would be resurrected but not the body. Many of the Sadducees, the high priests in charge of the temple and its finances, did not believe in any form of resurrection.)

Verses 13-19 say, If there is no resurrection of the dead, then Christ has not been raised; and if Christ has not been raised, then our proclamation has been in vain and your faith has been in vain. We are even found to be misrepresenting God, because we testified of God that he raised Christ—whom he did not raise if it is true that the dead are not raised. For if the dead are not raised then Christ has not been raised. If Christ has not been raised, then your faith is futile and you still are in your sins. Then those also who have died in Christ have perished. If for this life only we have hoped in Christ, we are of all people most to be pitied. (The logic Paul is using needs to be reflected upon by everyone examining the claims of the New Testament.)

Verse 20 says, But in fact Christ has been raised from the dead, the first fruits of those who have died. (In the Old Testament the first fruits of the ground were consecrated to God, which then consecrated the rest of the produce. So as Christ has risen to be with the Father as the first fruits of rising again, the rest of his followers are also set aside to rise to the Father.)

Verses 21-25 say, For since death came through a human being, the resurrection of the dead has also come through a human being; for as all die in Adam, so all will be made alive in Christ. But each in his own order: Christ the first fruits, then at his coming those who belong to Christ. Then comes the end, when he hands over the kingdom to God the Father, after he has destroyed every ruler and every authority and power. For he must reign until he has put all his enemies under his feet. (That is what is now in progress as the kingdom is growing like a mustard seed as his people become his eyes, ears, mouth, hands, and feet until he comes again to complete the process.)

Verses 26-28 say, The last enemy destroyed is death. For "God has put all things in subjection under his feet." But when he says, "All things are put in subjection," it is plain that this does not include the one who put all things in subjection under him. When all things are subjected to him, then the Son himself will be subjected to the one who put all things in subjection under him, so that God may be all in all.

In plain words what happens at the end is written. When Christ comes again, he will present his kingdom along with those who have worked to expand it on earth, and Christ will present all to the Father so God may be all in all. At this point everything opposed to God will be destroyed including death. Notice there is no rapture where some are taken and some are left, which is then followed by a thousand year reign before he comes again to judge the living and the dead. This is a theory rejected by all Roman Catholic, Orthodox, and mainline Protestant scholars. It is a theory developed only by twisting Scripture to fit a preconceived notion; it has no biblical basis.

Then verse (29) is inserted which says, Otherwise, what will those people do who receive baptism on behalf of the dead? If the dead are not raised at all, why are people baptized on their behalf? (Nothing else is said about this anywhere in the Bible. We do not know if Paul approves this or not, although if it is something approved, there would be more instructions. Without advocating the practice Paul uses it for the sake of his argument. In other words, if the dead are not raised, why are you baptizing the dead?)

Verses 30-34 say, And why are we putting ourselves in danger every hour? I die every day! That is as certain, brothers and sisters, as my boasting of you—a boast that I make in Christ Jesus our Lord. If with merely human hopes I fought with wild animals in Ephesus, what would I have gained by it? (There is no other information on that.) If the dead are not raised, "Let us eat and drink, for tomorrow we die." Do not be deceived: "Bad company ruins good morals." Come to a sober and right mind, and sin no more; for some people have no knowledge of God. I say this to your shame.

Paul's logic is why should I be facing death daily for the cause of Christ if the dead are not raised? I would be a fool. I would be better off living for my own selfish interests and pleasures if Christ was not raised. Only a fool would sacrifice his life as I am doing daily.

Verses 35-41 say, But someone will ask, "How are the dead raised? With what kind of body do they come?" Fool! What you sow does not come to life unless it dies. And as for what you sow, you do not sow the body that is to be, but a bare seed, perhaps of wheat or of some other grain. But God gives it a body as he has chosen, and to each kind of seed its own body. Not all flesh is alike, but there is one flesh for human beings, another for animals, another for birds, another for fish. There are both heavenly bodies and earthly bodies, but the glory of the heavenly is one thing, and that of the earthly is another. There is one glory of the sun, and another glory of the moon, and another glory of the stars; indeed, star differs from star in glory.

Verses 42-49 say, So it is with the resurrection of the dead. What is sown is perishable, what is raised is imperishable. It is sown in dishonor, it is raised in glory. It is sown in weakness, it is raised in power. It is sown a physical body, it is raised a spiritual body. If there is a physical body, there is a spiritual body. Thus it is written, "The first man, Adam, became a living being"; the last Adam became a life-giving spirit. But it is not the spiritual that is first, but the physical, and then the spiritual. The first man was from the earth, a man of dust; the second man is from heaven. As was the man of dust, so are those who are of the dust; and as the man of heaven, so are those who are of heaven. Just as we have borne the image of the man of dust, we will also bear the image of the man of heaven (Phil 3:21).

Verses 50-58 say, What I am saying, brothers and sisters, is this: flesh and blood cannot inherit the kingdom of God, nor does the perishable inherit the imperishable. Listen, I will tell you a mystery! (The mystery is the secret made known in Christ.) We will not all die, but we will all be changed, in a moment, in the twinkling of an eye, at the last trumpet (1 Thess 4:13-17). For the trumpet will sound, and the dead will be raised imperishable, and we will be changed. For this perishable body must put on the imperishability, and this mortal body must put on immortality. When this perishable body puts on imperishability, and this mortal body put on immortality, then the saying that is written will be fulfilled: "Death has been swallowed up in victory." "Where, O death is your victory? Where, O death is your sting?" The sting of death is sin, and the power of sin is the law (which exposes our sin). But thanks be to God who gives us the victory through our Lord Jesus Christ. (God gives us the victory over sin now, Rom 8:1-2, and later over death, Rom 8:11.) Therefore my beloved be steadfast, immovable (not shaken by false teachings like there is no bodily resurrection), always excelling in the work of the Lord, because you know that in the Lord your labor is not in vain.

ᴄᴏ🙙ᴏᴡ

Chapter 16:1-4 says, Now concerning the collection for the saints: you should follow the directions I gave to the churches of Galatia. On the first day of every week, each of you is to put aside and save whatever extra you earn, so that collections need not be taken when I come. And when I arrive, I will send any whom you approve with letters to take your gift to Jerusalem. If it seems advisable that I should go also, they will accompany me.

Verses 5-9 say, I will visit you after passing through Macedonia—for I intend to pass through Macedonia—and perhaps I will stay with you or even spend the winter, so that you may send me on my way, wherever I go. (Thessalonica was the capital of Macedonia.) I do not want to see you now just in passing, for I hope to spend some time with you, if the Lord permits. But I will stay in Ephesus until Pentecost, for a wide door for effective work has opened to me, and there are many adversaries.

Ephesus was the capital of Asia, and Paul is writing to the Corinthians from there. Pentecost was the Jewish holy day to celebrate the giving of the law of Moses and the Ten Commandments. It is a Christian holy day to celebrate the official beginning of the church with the sending of the Holy Spirit.

Verses 10-14 say, If Timothy comes, see that he has nothing to fear among you, for he is doing the work of the Lord just as I am; therefore let no one despise him. Send him on his way in peace, so that he may come to me; for I am expecting him with the brothers.

Now concerning our brother Apollos, I strongly urge him to visit you with the other brothers, but he was not at all willing to come now. He will come when he has the opportunity. Keep alert, stand firm in your faith, be courageous, be strong. Let all that you do be done in love.

Verses 15-18 say, Now, brothers and sisters, you know that members of the household of Stephanas were the first converts in Achaia, and they have devoted themselves to the service of the saints; I urge you to put yourselves at the service of such people and of everyone who works and toils with them. I rejoice at the coming of Stephanas and Fortunatus and Achaicus, because they have made up for your absence; for they refresh my spirit as well as yours. So give recognition to such persons.

Verses 19-24 say, The churches of Asia send greetings. Aquila and Prisca, together with the church in their house, greet you warmly in the Lord. All the brothers and sisters send greetings. Greet one another with a holy kiss. I, Paul, write this greeting with my own hand. Let everyone be accursed who has no love for the Lord. Our Lord come! (*Maranatha* is the word for Our Lord come.) The grace of the Lord Jesus be with you. My love be with all of you in Christ Jesus.

In 1 Corinthians Paul has combined instruction with the intent to correct and encourage. The church had been started by Paul only a few years before this letter. Much of the letter deals with situational problems that developed within the local church. He deals with questions in the church as the people attempt to live out their lives in Christ in a city with the reputation as a sailor's town. But the letter does more than provide additional information from the founding apostle. It also encourages the church to become united as one and to put its leaders in proper perspective. They are asked to recognize Paul's unique authority and his right to instruct them in the faith, but also to see others as co-workers in whom Christ is the foundation.

As a way of review list some of the most important verses and thoughts Paul is making in the letter of 1 Corinthians.

THE SECOND LETTER
TO THE CORINTHIANS

After Paul sent the first letter to the Corinthians the situation in Ephesus got worse, and his plans to visit Corinth changed. The situation in Corinth also changed. New religious teachers arrived teaching a different message. Paul saw them as a hindrance to the work he had begun there, and he decided to get to Corinth and confront them. After going to Corinth, Paul then returned to Ephesus believing the trip had been a disaster. He sent Titus, his co-worker to Corinth and learned that his trip to some extent had been a success.

It is obvious that what is called 2 Corinthians was not written as one coherent letter. It is broken into numerous parts, and it is uneven in literary form. It could be a combination of shorter letters written over a period of time just as 1 Corinthians, and then placed together. One needs to be alerted to this when reading through the letters. Still for the Christian it is God's inspired word.

Some high lights in 2 Corinthians are as follows. Paul is having problems with some of the members who seem to be susceptible to being led astray by false teachers who are not only leading some away from the apostolic teachings, but are very critical of Paul. In chapters 1-7 Paul reviews his relationship with them and defends his actions, his conduct, and his apostolic authority. Again, he has some success but the church has become very challenging to him. In chapters 10-13 he launches into a very aggressive attack against his accusers and calls them false apostles led by Satan. Even though the chronological order is not easily determined, the content can still be easily discerned.

In chapter 1 Paul mentions how he and his followers have suffered for Christ but have received comfort from God, which has taught them how to console others in their affliction. God will give his grace when it is needed.

In chapter 2 Paul tells them that God's people are the aroma of Christ leaving the odor of Christ wherever they go among those who are being saved and those who are perishing. One odor leads to life because they judge themselves, receive forgiveness, and then follow Christ; the other leads to death because it judges them guilty of sin when they refuse to judge themselves. Paul is saying when we represent Christ by our words and actions, we are the aroma of Christ.

In chapter 3 he has much to say about the new covenant and the transformation of the believers. He says they are a letter of Christ written on hearts and read by all, a letter of Christ administered by us written not in ink but by the Spirit of the living God, not on tablets of stone but on hearts. So in addition to being an aroma of Christ by representing Christ through one's words and actions, they are also Christ's letter to the world.

Paul says Christ has qualified him to be a minister of the new covenant, not of the letter but of the Spirit, for the letter brings death, but the Spirit brings life. He says the non-believers can not understand this, for a veil lies over their hearts when they read the old covenant, and the veil can not be taken away until they receive Christ and his teachings. Whenever the person turns to the Lord, the veil is taken away, and they can see and understand the meaning of the Scriptures. Because some people do not see Christ as the fulfillment of the Old Testament law, the one who reveals the deeper implications of that law, they can not understand its deeper meaning. In chapter 4 Paul states that they are ministers ministering under God's light, even though their message may be hard to understand. The treasure is in clay jars, but the Holy Spirit will make it clear.

Paul says in chapter 5 we aspire to please the Lord and walk by faith in Christ and not by sight even as we suffer in the body for doing so. For we will all appear before the judgment seat of Christ, so that each one may receive recompense, according to what he has done in the body, whether good or evil. He says the love of Christ impels us, for he died for all so that those who live might no longer live for themselves but for him who for their sake died and was raised. Paul is saying what we do is important. It is important to note that salvation is not by works, but we are not saved without works. That will be further explained.

Paul then says whoever is in Christ is a new creation, the old has passed away, the new has come. All this is from God who has reconciled us to himself through Christ and given us the ministry of reconciliation, namely God is reconciling the world to himself in Christ not counting our trespasses against us and entrusting to us the ministry of reconciliation. So we are ambassadors for Christ. For our sake he made him to be sin who did not know sin, so that we might become the righteousness of God in him.

In chapter 6 Paul says we appeal to you not to receive the grace of God in vain, for now is the acceptable time. Now is the day of salvation. He tells them to open wide their hearts. He then calls them to holiness and not to be mismatched with unbelievers, especially those teaching a message contrary to and opposing Christ. He asks them, what fellowship light has with darkness or righteousness with lawlessness. He reminds them that they are God's temple with God living in them. He is their God, and they are his people.

In chapter 7 he says since we have these promises, let us cleanse ourselves from every defilement of flesh and spirit, making holiness perfect in the fear of God. Then Paul expresses joy over what seems to be the restoration of good relations between him and the Corinthians, at least most of them.

In chapters 8 and 9 he encourages the Corinthians to give to his collection for the poor, the suffering, and the hungry in Jerusalem. He tells them whoever sows bountifully will reap bountifully, and whoever sows sparingly will reap sparingly. His theory on giving also is grounded in the fact that Jesus became poor although he was rich so that by his poverty we might become rich. One's giving is acceptable according to what one has, not according to what one does not have. Then he says that it is a matter of equality. Your surplus at the present time should supply their needs, so that later their surplus may also supply your needs, that there may be equality. As it is written whoever had much did not have more, and whoever had little did not have less. His concern is the teaching on economic balance within the Mosaic law so that all have their basic needs met. Today, the political extremists in America call that socialism and reject that biblical teaching, even as they call themselves followers of Christ.

In chapters 10-13 Paul aggressively defends his apostleship and challenges the false teachers for teaching a different Jesus and a different way than the apostles. He calls them false apostles, deceitful workers, who masquerade as apostles of Christ, then he says no wonder for even Satan masquerades as an angel of light. So it is not strange that his ministers masquerade as ministers of righteousness. In the rest of the chapter Paul shows the different ways he has suffered physically for Christ. A prevalent theme is boasting. Boasting is not to be who we are and what we have done triumphantly for our personal glory, but who Christ has made us to be for his glory, and what he is doing through us as we suffer for his name.

Then in chapter 13 he says examine yourselves to see whether you are living in faith. Test yourselves to see if Christ is living in you. Then he says I hope you discover that you have not failed. Paul tells them that he will pray for their maturity in Christ.

It is obvious that what is called 2 Corinthians was not written as one coherent letter. It is broken into numerous parts, is uneven in literary form, and is a combination of letters formed into one. Still for the Christian it is God's inspired word. Let us now examine this letter verse by verse.

⸙⸙⸙

Chapter 1:1-7 says, Paul an apostle of Jesus Christ by the will of God, and Timothy our brother, to the church of God that is in Corinth, including all the saints throughout Achaia: Grace to you and peace from God our Father and our Lord Jesus Christ. Blessed be the God and Father of our Lord Jesus Christ, the Father of mercies and the God of all consolation, who consoles us in all our affliction, so that we may be able to console those who are in any affliction with the consolation with which we ourselves are consoled by God. For just as the sufferings of Christ are abundant for us, so also our consolation is abundant through Christ. If we are being afflicted, it is for your consolation and salvation; if we are being consoled, it is for your consolation, which you experience when you patiently endure the same sufferings that we also are suffering. Our hope for you is unshaken; for we know that as you share in our sufferings, so also you share in our consolation.

Paul had recently experienced great affliction and suffering on behalf of Christ, but he found his comfort in Christ who suffered to the point of death in his crucifixion, and then rose from the dead with the promise that all who undergo suffering for him and the advancement of his kingdom will rise as he rose. According to Paul at this particular time in the development of Christianity, serious followers of Christ will suffer, for its teaching will not resonate with what normally is accepted by the people immersed in the world and its ways. Why does the reader believe that is not the case in America?

Verses 8-11 say, We do not want you to be unaware, brothers and sisters, of the affliction we experienced in Asia (probably Ephesus); for we were so utterly, unbearably crushed that we despaired of life itself. Indeed, we felt that we had received the sentence of death so that we could rely not on ourselves but God who raises the dead. He who rescued us from so deadly a peril will continue to rescue us; on him we have set our hope that he will rescue us again, as you also join in helping us by your prayers, so that many will give thanks on our behalf for the blessings granted us through the prayers of many.

Paul talks about a fellowship of comfort in the midst of suffering. He also indicates the Corinthians are adding to his current suffering. Paul expresses his total dependence on God for his ministry. Notice how many times he mentions suffering and comfort. A major issue in 2 Corinthians is suffering and who the true apostles are and who the false apostles are. According to Paul being willing to suffer for the purposes of Christ as opposed to the things that the world labels as important is a key identifying marker of a true apostle. Part of his problem in Corinth is coming from the false apostles, who are living in comfort and are dressing up Christ with the world's wisdom. In the process these false apostles are drawing some who accepted the gospel of Christ away from him.

Paul will propose that there are two ways to represent Christ; one is through human wisdom, human success, and worldly triumphalism represented by boasting in what humans see as success. The other is through the wisdom of God represented by suffering related to the cross of Christ. Paul will show that his words and actions represent the latter while the words and wisdom of his rivals in Corinth represent the former. This will be a major thesis in this book. This writer wonders what he would say about many churches in America who identify so closely with the American culture of prosperity, comfort, and success and wave their flags as a sign of dominance in all of America's military adventures. Does the reader think the non-violent Jesus would be rejoicing with them?

Paul in verse 12 says, Indeed, this is our boast, the testimony of our conscience: we have behaved in the world with frankness and godly sincerity, not by earthly wisdom but by the grace of God—and all the more toward you.

Paul boasts only in what the grace of God has done through those suffering for Christ and his teachings. In (13-17) Paul tells them he has always been straight with them writing only what is true and what they understand, that his boast is in them as God's people, and that he had planned to come to them earlier but decided to spare them because he was upset with the behavior of some of them. Throughout the book Paul is upset because he feels he has to defend his integrity.

In verses 18-20 Paul says, As surely as God is faithful, our word to you has not been "Yes and No." For the Son of God, Jesus Christ, whom we proclaimed among you, Silvanus and Timothy and I, was not "Yes and No"; but in him it is always "Yes." For in him (Christ) every one of God's promises is a "Yes." For this reason it is through him that we say the "Amen," to the glory of God. (Yes and No means maybe it is true and maybe it is not. The old covenant is the promise, and the new covenant is the fulfillment of the promise, and the fulfillment is in and through Christ. In other words the promises and fulfillment are true beyond doubt. They are a Yes.)

Verses 21-22 say, it is God who establishes us with you in Christ and has anointed us, by putting his seal on us and giving us his Spirit in our hearts as a first installment. (Having the Spirit, the presence of God within the church and within the followers of Christ is part of the fulfilled promise. God has called them through the Spirit by Paul's preaching which produced faith. Upon their baptism (Acts 2:38) the gift of the Holy Spirit is the first installment of their promised inheritance indicating the balance will follow as they continue to be led by the Spirit and not the flesh, Rom 8:1-8.)

Then Paul in verses 23-24 says, But I call on God as witness against me; it was to spare you that I did not come again to Corinth. I do not mean to imply that we lord it over your faith rather we are workers with you for your joy, because you stand firm in the faith. (His reason for not coming at that time when he had wanted to come and at the time they were expecting him was to spare them from his wrath. He was upset with them for their lack of being rooted in the faith. So he gave them time to begin to come to their senses. Even though there are numerous problems in the church, here he speaks to those who are standing firm in the faith encouraging them to stay with him and not the false teachers who are distorting God's truth.)

∽∂∾

Chapter 2:1-5 is a deeper explanation on why he did not come to visit them when he said he would. Paul was in a painful confrontation with someone in the church, but it was not just with that one person but his confrontation was with a group of people within the Corinthian church. (With the certain individual no one is sure what this particular issue is about or who the person is, but it may have been over the person involved in *porneia* that Paul had requested expulsion from the church for the person's own good and the good of the church; see 1 Cor 5:1-2.)

By the time Paul is writing the person has now repented, so Paul in (6-8) says, This punishment by the majority is enough for such a person; so now instead you should forgive and console him, so that he may not be overwhelmed by excessive sorrow. So I urge you to reaffirm your love for him. I wrote for this reason: to test you and to know whether you are obedient in everything. Anyone whom you forgive, I forgive also. What I have forgiven, if I have forgiven anything, has been for your sake in the presence of Christ. And we do this so that we may not be outwitted by Satan; for we are not ignorant of his designs.

So Paul is saying the issue is now over, but this is one of the reasons why he delayed coming. It is also important to note that excessive sorrow is not good. Simply being sorrowful and repenting is all that is necessary. One does not need to continually beat oneself over and over. Repent, change what is necessary and move on.

Verses 14-17 say, But thanks be to God, who in Christ always leads us in triumphal procession (enables us to overcome), and through us spreads in every place the fragrance that comes from knowing him. (That is if we follow his teachings.) For we are the aroma of Christ to God among those who are being saved and among those who are perishing; to the one a fragrance from death to death, to the other a fragrance of life to life. Who is sufficient for these things? (The aroma signifies life to those being saved but death, separation from God, for the rest.) For we are not peddlers of God's word like so many; but in Christ we speak as persons of sincerity, as persons sent from God and standing in his presence. (He uses the term peddlers of God's word to apply to those false teachers who have come to Corinth using Christ and his teaching to serve themselves and in the process receive pay from the Corinthians.)

To Paul this smells of greed, deceit, and self service. So Paul gives a powerful figure of speech when he states that those living their life in Christ for the benefit of Christ are an aroma of Christ. In other words when they are near there is the smell of Christ not the smell of greed, selfishness and deceit as with the false teachers. Paul is upset because some in Corinth are following these false teachers and opposing Paul, the one who had initially preached to them about the death and resurrection of Christ, and the coming of the Holy Spirit who is at work among them.

Chapter 3 continues with the issue of leadership and the challenge to Paul's authority. In verses 1-3 Paul says, Surely we do not need, as some do, letters of recommendation to you or from you, do we? You yourselves are our letter, written on our hearts, to be known and read by all; and you show that you are a letter of Christ, prepared by us, written not with ink but with the Spirit of the living God, not on tablets of stone but on tablets of human hearts.

Apparently Paul's credentials were being questioned. Others had come to Corinth with credentials, possibly from some strong opposition movement, and Paul's authority, credentials, and teaching are being questioned. Paul is responding to the church by questioning why they are asking him for his credentials. He points to them and tells the church their very existence is his letter of recommendation. Since Paul's preaching is the gospel of Christ, they are letters from Christ. Through Paul's preaching the Spirit of Christ (through the grace of God) came to live in their hearts transforming them. Christ in them is Paul's letter of recommendation. Paul's credentials are not like those who come with letters of ink, or even like the commandments that God wrote on stone but his credentials are written by the Spirit.

Verses 4-6 say, such is the confidence that we have through Christ Jesus toward God. Not that we are competent of ourselves to claim anything as coming from us, our competence is from God, who has made us competent to be ministers of a new covenant, not of the letter but of spirit; for the letter kills but the Spirit gives life.

Paul claims his competence is not of himself; he is simply an instrument used by God to send the presence of God in Christ through the Holy Spirit to live within those who hear the good news about the death and resurrection of Christ and the coming kingdom of God that is now breaking in upon the world.

Both Jeremiah (31:31-34) and Ezekiel (36:26-29) had talked about the coming of a new covenant with God sending the Spirit to work within hearts. Paul is indicating that by the Spirit transforming hearts and working new attitudes, dispositions, and actions in the hearts of God's people, they all become letters of Christ. Instead of God writing on stone as he did when he gave Moses the law, he now writes on hearts by the Spirit who now works inwardly changing attitudes, dispositions and character, which in the process begins to transform the world and its structures. In the Old Testament the Spirit is primarily involved in the works of God, but now he gives it personally to all his people.

This process begins as an interior law, a law of perfection, a law of freedom, the law of the Spirit of life in Christ Jesus. Through the Spirit one is no longer bound by a written code, for the person is now free to do the most loving thing in all situations as the whole law is summed up in loving God with all your new found God-given power and your neighbor as yourself. Of course, this freedom does not mean the elimination of the commandments and themes of the law as some have attempted to say. But by the spirit of the law, the law of life in Christ Jesus, ethics rise to a higher level. But it is only through the law of the Spirit of life in Christ Jesus that one is freed from the things of the world that bind and destroy whoever is controlled by them.

Paul then begins to show the difference between the old law and the new law. First the written law of the letter kills or brings death while the law of the Spirit brings life. The old law gave a minimum ethic to protect individuals and society and move things in the direction God desired. The new law goes beyond a minimum ethic in order to do the most loving thing in all circumstances. The old law pointed out why Christ is needed, but the old law could not bring salvation.

Verses 7-11 tell us the glory of the new is higher. He calls the old law the ministry of condemnation, for in it humankind saw clearly their sin and how it brings death. But the new law is called the ministry of justification or the ministry of reconciliation and salvation, and this is a greater glory. Verses 10-11 say, Indeed, what once had glory has lost its glory because of the greater glory; for if what was set aside came through glory, much more has the permanent come in glory! (The old part of God's covenant was temporary until it led to the new and permanent covenant of the Spirit and a higher glory.)

Verses 12-16 say, Since, then, we have such a hope, we act with great boldness, not like Moses, who put a veil over his face to keep the people of Israel from gazing at the end of the glory that was being set aside. But their minds were hardened. Indeed to this very day whenever Moses (the Torah) is read, a veil lies over their minds;

but when one turns to the Lord the veil is removed. (When one reads the Old Testament through the words and actions of Christ the fullness of the old law is understood. Paul is saying that because the people of the old law do not read in such manner, they miss where the old law was intended to go; they miss its fulfillment.)

Verses 17-18 say, Now the Lord is the Spirit, and where the Spirit of the Lord is, there is freedom. And all of us, with unveiled faces, seeing the glory of the Lord as though reflected in a mirror, are being transformed into the same image from one degree of glory to another; for this comes from the Lord, the Spirit. (God's people are being remade into the image of God in which they were originally created.)

Turning to Christ brings transformation that goes on in hearts which produces life and freedom in the Spirit of Christ Jesus. It all comes from the Father through Christ in the power of the Holy Spirit. In these times, in this last age, the church age, God in Christ through the Spirit is at work, speaking and acting in his people primarily through the Spirit and the word. It is in this way that the kingdom of God makes its impact in the world.

Under the old law one could not see God or be in his presence without being put to death, but under the new law the presence of God lives in hearts. By the power of the Holy Spirit Christ lives within and through his people. God's people are now the temple of his presence. First Corinthians 3:16-17 says, Do you not know that you are God's temple and that God's Spirit dwells in you? If anyone destroys God's temple, God will destroy that person. For God's temple is holy, and you are that temple. (In other words if and when you are being attacked by the world, and even if you become one of the martyrs, it is not you alone that is being attacked, God is also being attacked.)

Chapter 4:1-2 says, Therefore, since it is by God's mercy that we are engaged in this ministry, we do not lose heart. We have renounced the shameful things that one hides; we refuse to practice cunning or to falsify God's word; but by the open statement of the truth we commend ourselves to the conscience of everyone in the sight of God. (Paul was apparently accused by the false apostles in Corinth of being cunning, falsifying God's word, and veiling it or keeping the real truth hidden.)

Verses 3-6 say, And even if our gospel is veiled, it is veiled to those who are perishing (the false apostles). In their case the god of this world has blinded the minds of the unbelievers, to keep them from seeing the light of the gospel of the glory of Christ, who is the image of God. For we do not proclaim ourselves; we proclaim Jesus Christ as Lord and ourselves as your slaves for Jesus' sake. For it is the God who said, "Let light shine out of darkness," who has shone in our hearts to give the light of the knowledge of the glory of God in the face of Jesus Christ.

The glory of God is now seen in Jesus and when seen in the hearts of his people, God is glorified. By the power of the Holy Spirit God's people are called to reflect the glory of God as they let Christ live in and through them. Through the power of the Holy Spirit the character traits, attitudes, virtues, values, and vision of Christ will live in and through them as they become instruments of God. In this way they reflect his image and serve his purposes.

Verse 7 says, But we have this treasure (glory of God) in clay jars (meaning our frail, weak bodies), so that it may be made clear that this extraordinary power belongs to God and does not come from us. (According to Paul, the true gospel of Christ, the glory of God, is not about wealth, health, and prosperity. It is carried by broken, frail people who are of no account according to the people of the world.)

Verses 8-12 say, We are afflicted in every way, but not crushed; perplexed, but not driven to despair; persecuted, but not forsaken; struck down, but not destroyed; always carrying in the body the death of Jesus (our crucified self), so that the life of Jesus may also be made visible in our bodies. For while we live, we are always being given up to death for Jesus' sake, so that the life of Jesus may be made visible in our mortal flesh. So death is at work in us, but life in you.

Paul is saying when one dies to self, one finds the true meaning of life, and this is how the kingdom of God advances. The treasure is the life of Christ living in and through his people for the glory of God and the advancement of the kingdom. The clay jars are we humans and anything used to convey God's word including the Bible. The Bible is not god. It is a clay jar also, for, even though inspired of God, it is just made of worldly material. It witnesses to God who speaks the living word to his people through it, which then lives in the hearts of his people.

As Christ suffered for God's plan and the well-being of others, Paul is willing to do the same (2 Cor 1:5-8, Acts 5:41, Rom 8:15-17). Paul lives by daily dying and rising with Christ (Rom 6:8). Daily he puts self to death so Christ can live in and through him, and he does this as a model for all to follow.

Verses 13-18 say, But just as we have the same Spirit of faith that is in accordance with scripture—"I believed and so I spoke"—we also believe, and so we speak, because we know that the one who raised the Lord Jesus will raise us also with Jesus, and will bring us with you into his presence. Yes, everything is for your sake, so that grace, as it extends to more and more people, may increase thanksgiving, to the glory of God. So we do not lose heart. Even though our outer nature is wasting away (physical body), our inner nature (soul) is being renewed day by day. For this slight momentary affliction (suffering for Christ) is preparing us for an eternal weight of glory beyond all measure, because we look not at what can be seen but at what cannot be seen; for what can be seen (life in this world) is temporary, but what cannot be seen is eternal.

The world and Paul's outer self, the physical body, are in the process of deteriorating or dying, but the world through the advancement of the kingdom and Paul's inner self are being renewed in Christ daily as preparation for what is eternal. At the coming of Christ all will be made new and perfected (Rom 8:18-25). This eschatological interpretation of the inner-outer man is confirmed by the common Jewish conception that in the age to come the lost glory of Adam and Eve will be restored to the righteous who suffer for God and his plan. So as Paul said, I consider that the sufferings of this present time are not worth comparing with the glory about to be revealed to us in Christ Jesus (Rom 8:18).

Paul's argument throughout 2 Corinthians is best understood within a history of salvation perspective focused on the restoration of God's people in Christ under a new covenant. This means that reconciliation with God through Christ is the beginning of the eschatological redemption of the world, the new covenant, the new creation, the new exile or second exodus. The glory of God is now manifested to his people permanently by the Holy Spirit. Isaiah 49:8 says, In a time of favor I have answered you, on a day of salvation I have helped you; I have kept you and given you as a covenant to the people, to establish the land, to apportion the desolate heritages; saying to the prisoners, "Come out," to those who are in darkness, "Show yourselves."

It has been said that reconciliation in Christ is Paul's way of explaining that Isaiah's promise of restoration from the alienation of exile has begun to be fulfilled by the forgiveness of sins through

Christ and through the new covenant foretold by Jeremiah (31:31) and Ezekiel (36:26-27). The presence of God, his glory, is now manifested to all who come to him, both Jew and Gentile. God has fulfilled his promise to Abraham.

∞∞

Chapter 5:1-5 is about having an eternal building from God, a resurrected body not made with earthly hands, when the earthly tent we live in dies. Paul says he groans in his earthly tent as he yearns for his heavenly body so that what is mortal is swallowed up by (eternal) life. Verse 5 says, He who has prepared us for this very thing is God, who has given us the Spirit as a guarantee (Rom 8:11, 1 Jn 3:24). In verses 6-9 Paul says, So we are always confident; . . . for we walk by faith and not by sight. Yes, we do have confidence, and we would rather be away from the body (physical death) and at home with the Lord (eternally in his presence). So whether we are at home or away, we make it our aim to please him. (Purpose in life is pleasing God by words, actions, and standing with those he stood with and for the things he said are important.) Verse 10 says, For all of us must appear before the judgment seat of Christ, so that each of us may receive recompense for what has been done in the body, whether good or evil.

Too many churches and their theologians ignore or want to eliminate verses such as verse 10, but it can not be done without distorting Scripture. There will be a judgment and the life lived will be part of that judgment. Humans are saved by grace, and it is God's free gift (Rom 3:24, Gal 2:15-16, Eph 2:8-10) so how does that match up with verse 10 and other verses like Rom 2:16, Phil 2:16-18, Jas 2:18-26 and others? The partial answer is that we are not saved by our good works, but we are not saved without good works either. But the good works are God's grace working in us and through us. Phil 2:16-18 says, Work out your own salvation with fear and trembling; for it is God who is at work in you, enabling you both to will and to work for his good pleasure. (One works out their salvation by letting God and his grace work in and through them.)

In verse 11 Paul says, Therefore, knowing the fear of the Lord, we try to persuade others; . . . Then in verse 13 he tells them if he and those with him appear a little crazy, it is for their benefit. Verses 14-15 say, For the love of Christ urges us on, because we are convinced that one has died for all; therefore all have died. (He explains that verse with the following verse.) And he died for all so that those who live might live no longer for themselves, but for him who died and was raised for them. In Gal 2:19-20 Paul says, For through the law I died to the law, so that I might live to God. I have been crucified with Christ; and it is no longer I who live, but it is Christ who lives in me. And the life I now live in the flesh I live by faith in the Son of God, who loved me and gave himself for me.

This is further explained by Jesus in Mt 16:24-27 who told his disciples, If any want to become my followers, let them deny themselves and take up their cross and follow me. For those who want to save their life will lose it, and those who lose their life for my sake will find it. For what will it profit them if they gain the whole world and forfeit their life? Or what will they give in return for their life? For the Son of Man is to come with his angels in the glory of his Father, and then he will repay everyone for what has been done. (The issue is dying to self by turning one's life over to God, so that by the power of the Holy Spirit Christ can live in and through his people.)

Paul states in verse 16 that at one time he regarded Christ as another human only but no longer, and because of that he no longer views anyone from the point of view of the world but as

Christ views them. Verses 17-21 say, So if anyone is in Christ, there is a new creation: everything old has passed away; see everything has become new! All this is from God, who reconciled us to himself through Christ, and has given us the ministry of reconciliation; that is, in Christ God was reconciling the world to himself, not counting their tresses against them, and entrusting the message of reconciliation to us.

In the cross Christ took all the sins of the world, past, present, and future, upon himself thus making each one a new creation, canceling what stood between him and his created humans. He reconciled humanity to himself making them fit to be in relationship with him and fit to enter eternity where no sin can enter (Rev 21:27). With this he gave to those making up the church, the ministry of reconciliation. This ministry involves the renewal of not only humans but the world and its structures. This is the idea behind the kingdom of God now breaking into the world, which Christ said was one of the main reasons he entered into the world (Lk 4:43).

Colossians 1:13-20 says, He has rescued us from the power of darkness and transferred us into the kingdom of his beloved Son, in whom we have redemption, the forgiveness of sins. He is the image of the invisible God, . . . for in him all things in heaven and on earth were created, things visible and invisible, . . . all things have been created through him and for him. . . and through him God was pleased to reconcile to himself all things, whether on earth or heaven, by making peace through the blood of the cross. (All things are to be reconciled to God, not just individuals.)

First Corinthians 15:25 says, For he must reign until he has put all enemies under his feet. Verse 28 continues, When all things are subjected to him, then the Son himself will also be subjected to the one who put all things in subjection under him, so that God may be all in all. Eph 1:8-10 says, With all wisdom and insight he has made known to us the mystery of his will, according to his good pleasure that he set forth in Christ, as a plan for the fullness of time, to gather up all things in him, things in heaven and things on earth. (Again the emphasis is on all things, which is what the advancement of the kingdom is about and why it was so important.)

This is God's plan and while on earth the people of Jesus are to be his eyes, ears, hands, feet and mouth as they continue the mission of the in-breaking of his kingdom reconciling all things to him until all things become subject to him. All things mean all things. It is not just all people. God wants all things which include governments, institutions, systems, and whatever to be united to him for the advancement of the kingdom. The image is Christ as the head and his people as his body (the church) continuing his mission until he comes again.

Verses 20-21 say, So we are ambassadors for Christ, since God is making his appeal through us; we entreat you on behalf of Christ, be reconciled to God. For our sake he made him to be sin who knew no sin, so that in him we might become the righteousness of God. (It is through the righteousness of Christ that his people are made the righteousness of God, declared and made righteous through the blood of Christ and identified as the people of God.)

Chapter 6:1-2 says, As we work together with him (God) we urge you also not to accept the grace of God in vain. For he says, "At an acceptable time I have listened to you, and on a day of salvation I have helped you." See, now is the acceptable time; see, now is the day of salvation!

The eschatological day of salvation promised by the prophet Isaiah has arrived. Paul is saying at this very moment God is working his grace and salvation. Do not be like Adam and Eve and fall back into a false gospel losing the grace God has given you and continues to maintain in you. The fall of humanity and Israel has been reversed. Now is the day of salvation. The presence of the Spirit bringing about transformation is the evidence that one is a new creation in Christ.

Verse 3 says, We are putting no obstacle in anyone's way, so that no fault may be found with our ministry, but as servants of God we have commended ourselves in every way (not by words only but by actions): through great endurance, in afflictions, hardships, calamities, beatings, imprisonments, riots, labors, sleepless nights, hunger, by purity, knowledge, patience, kindness, holiness of spirit, genuine love, truthful speech, and the power of God; with the weapons of righteousness for the right hand and the left; in honor and dishonor, in ill repute, and good repute. We are treated as imposters, and yet are true; as unknown, and yet as well known; as dying, and see—we are alive; as punished, and yet not killed; as sorrowful, yet always rejoicing; as poor, yet making many rich; as having nothing, and yet possessing everything.

Paul states all this to show the difference between true apostles and the false apostles in their midst who are critical of him and in the process living more for the glory of themselves than the glory of God.

Verses 11-13 say, We have spoken frankly to you Corinthians; our heart is wide open to you. There is no restriction in our affections, but only in yours. (Paul says this to those who have been led by the others to doubt and question him.) In return—I speak as to children—open wide your hearts also. (Paul's appeal for affection and acceptance is emotionally charged.)

Verses 14-15 say, Do not be matched with unbelievers. For what partnership is there between righteousness and lawlessness? (Do not attach your belief in God's truth with a system that has a false message as many of God's people did in the past. They worshiped both the one God and the pagan gods.) Or what fellowship is there between light and darkness? What agreement does Christ have with Beliar? Or what does a believer share with an unbeliever? What agreement has the temple of God with idols? (His point is that Christianity is not compatible with the distortion and rejection of the apostles' teachings exemplified by his opponents.)

Then he explains why as (16) continues, For we are the temple of the living God; as God said, "I will live in them and walk among them, and I will be their God, and they shall be my people. Verses 17-18 say, Therefore come out from them, and be separate from them, says the Lord, and touch nothing unclean; then I will welcome you, and I will be your Father, and you shall be my sons and daughters, says the Lord Almighty."

One can not totally be separate from unbelievers in living life, but one can reject what is false and always stand for the ways of God in any situation. It seems the context here has reference to making sure the apostolic teachings are not compromised.

Chapter 7:1 says, Since we have these promises, beloved, let us cleanse ourselves from every defilement of body and of spirit, making holiness perfect in the fear of God. (Since God lives in and through his people, keep cleansed of sin, keeping oneself holy before God.) Verse 2 says, Make room in your hearts for us; we have wronged no one, we have corrupted no one, we have taken advantage of no one. (These are charges his opponents in Corinth are making against him.) Verses 3-4 say, I do not say this to condemn you, for I said before that you are in our hearts . . . I often boast about you; I have great pride in you; I am filled with consolation; I am overjoyed in all our affliction.

The rest of the chapter verses 5-16 are Paul expressing his joy over Titus coming to him in Macedonia informing him that all is well with their relationship and that Paul's call for repentance produced a godly grief that led to repentance. Paul is overjoyed at the re-establishment of good relations. Paul says in verse 10 that godly grief produces a repentance that leads to salvation and brings no regret, but worldly grief produces death. In verse 16 Paul says, I rejoice, because I have complete confidence in you. (It appears the majority of Corinthians responded positively to Paul and that it was a minority group following these false apostles.)

Chapter 8 is about the collection for the poor in Jerusalem that Paul had initiated with the churches in Macedonia, which were probably the churches at Philippi, Thessalonica, and Beroea. It was an effort by Paul to help promote unity among the churches with alms for the poor to help bring relief from a severe famine. Paul in (1-2) says, We want you to know, brothers and sisters, about the grace of God that has been granted to the churches of Macedonia; for during a severe ordeal of affliction, their abundant joy and their extreme poverty have overflowed in a wealth of generosity on their part. (Paul presents this collection for the poor as a great opportunity for overflowing and sharing the grace that God has given to them. In chapters 8 and 9 the theme of abundant grace is stressed.)

Verses 3-7 say, I can testify, they voluntarily gave according to their means, and even beyond their means, begging us earnestly for the privilege of sharing in this ministry to the saints—and this, not merely as we expected; they gave themselves first to the Lord and, by the will of God, to us, so that we might urge Titus that, as he had already made a beginning, so he should also complete this generous undertaking among you. Now as you excel in everything . . . we want you to excel also in this generous undertaking.

The year before Corinth had agreed to give generously to the collection that Paul was organizing for the poor in Jerusalem. Paul is planning to come back through on his way to Jerusalem, so he is reminding them to have their donation ready. He reminds them that if they have given themselves to the Lord, they will give generously. Throughout the Old Testament and then in the Gospels, God calls on his people to take care of the poor, and the church throughout the centuries has been a beacon of light to the needy.

In parts of today's world and especially the United States the church has become quite prosperous. This author wonders how much of the budget of today's churches, made up of very prosperous people, goes to helping those who are struggling to survive. We do know that too many comfortable people outside the church show very little compassion for the poor and tend to blame them for their situation, something Jesus never did. It seems the wealthier we are the less compassionate we are toward the poor.

Verses 8-9 say, I do not say this as a command, but I am testing the genuineness of your love against the earnestness of others. For you know the generous act of our Lord Jesus Christ, that though he was rich (in heaven with the Father), yet for your sakes he became poor (entered into this world and was crucified), so that by his poverty (death) you might become rich. And in this matter I am giving my advice. (His advice in 10-11 is to give generously to the collection and become spiritually rich. This is the kind of riches that counts in the eyes of God, Mt 25:31-46. The values of God are not the values of the world.)

Verses 12-15 say, For if the eagerness is there, the gift is acceptable for according to what one has—not according to what one does not have. I do not mean that there should be relief for others and pressure on you, but it is a question of a fair balance between your present abundance and their need, in order that there may be a fair balance. As it is written, "The one who had much did not have too much, and the one who had little did not have too little."

Some thoughts on this for discussion are the following. A fair balance is something Christian capitalists need to promote. Capitalism certainly has its strong points, but there is no special economic system described in the Bible, even though one can find principles and values that any complete economic system should pay attention to if they want to please God. The selfish greed and survival of the fittest attitude as well as the growing gap between the rich and the poor apparent in the United States today is partly because of an unjust wage system (Jas 5:1-6), the destruction of unions that had much to do with the development of a middle class, and Congress favoring the wealthy and big corporations with most favored legislation, grants, and tax breaks at the expense of the middle class and those struggling. Then the tax breaks to the wealthy have to be made up by those not getting the tax breaks. This spreading the wealth upward, which is factually and statistically proven, is in reality welfare for the wealthy. This is not what Scripture calls a fair balance.

These things need to be addressed in today's American economic system, for it is not the way of Christ. The idea advocated by some Americans that the Bible promotes what has become American capitalism, which many question if it still is capitalism, has no biblical warrant. The concept of capitalism was not even known in those times.

The idea that we bail out Wall Street and banks, and big corporations with corporate welfare because they are too big to fail has never been a capitalist idea, which says to let the market work, and if something fails, so be it. This has led some to say that we now have a system of socialism for the rich and capitalism for the rest of the people. Tax money and tax breaks given to anyone are government welfare, for someone has to pay for it. And welfare for the rich is astronomical compared to welfare for the poor and needy. America does not have a pure capitalist system and never did. We have a mixed economic system that was designed to let entrepreneurs make a fair profit for their efforts, but also to use government for the creation of what is necessary for the common good.

God is a God of justice. The word justice is used over one thousand times in the Bible, and the reference is primarily to what is known today as social justice or distributive justice to help the struggling get on their feet. In the Bible God never governs to benefit the wealthy, and he never takes their side. He constantly warns the wealthy that their eternal life is in danger, and they need to repent and think like he thinks and act like he acts. Because God is a God of justice, in any situation in which power is misused and the powerful take advantage of the non-powerful, God takes the side of those who do not have power and wealth. God calls his people to correct inequity in all forms of power relationships for the benefit of the common good and the dignity of those struggling to support their families.

This is the aspect of family values that needs added to the mix in today's American society. God's justice applies to every form of abuse of power, unjust economic distribution such as an unjust wage system, power legislating for its own benefit at the expense of the poor, violations of human rights, etc. Justice in Scripture is not restricted to the retributive justice of the courtroom. In fact that form of justice is rarely the form of justice that Scripture mentions. Government is instituted by God and responsible to God, and God's people need to challenge their government and its leaders, whatever the form of government may be in order to both balance personal initiative and care for those in need. Some will counter what is being said here by saying the Scriptures are talking about a free will offering, but the principle carries over. God created government for his purposes, and like all earthy systems created by humans, they are also accountable to God (Rom 13:1, Col 1:15-20).

God's purpose in Jesus' mission is to establish his kingdom of justice and peace. That means God is for the oppressed not the oppressor. He is on the side of the exploited not the exploiter. He is for the victim and not the victimizer. Micah 6:8 states that the Lord requires you to do justice, love kindness, and to walk humbly before your God. The people of the Old Testament were told that without justice their worship would not be accepted, and it was the ruler's responsibility to make justice happen. The ruler (government) was to be the protector of those without power and wealth.

Jeremiah 22:13-17 is just one of many examples. "Woe to him who builds his house by unrighteousness, and his upper rooms by injustice; who makes his neighbors work for nothing; and does not give them their (just) wages; who says, "I will build myself a spacious house with large upper rooms," and cuts out windows for it, paneling it with cedar, and painting it with vermillion. Are you a king (political leader) because you compete in cedar? Did not your father eat and drink and do justice and righteousness? Then it was well with him. He judged the cause of the poor and needy; then it was well.

Is not this to know me? says the Lord. But your eyes and heart are only on dishonest gain, for shedding innocent blood, and for practicing oppression and violence. Jesus added, Blessed are those who hunger and thirst for righteousness, for they will be filled (Mt 5:6). (The root word of righteousness is justice.)

If God's people believe this is God's inspired word, then what was true then is also true today. Should the people today think God is not aware of the injustice in today's world when the wealthy and powerful control and regulate politics and the market for their own benefit at the expense of those without power and wealth? Today the comfortable say politics and economics are to be separated from things religious, but that comes from the powerful and the comfortable not Jesus and the prophets.

In verse 19 Paul returns to the collection and says that this generous undertaking of the giving for those in need is for the glory of the Lord and to show goodwill. Verses 20-21 say, We intend that no one should blame us about this generous gift that we are administering, for we intend to do what is right not only in the Lord's sight but also in the sight of others. Verse 24 says, Therefore openly before the churches, show them the proof of your love and of our reason for boasting about you.

Paul's attitude toward possessions is positive. Wealth is a gift, a financial blessing from God to be used not just for oneself but for others in a generous manner, especially for the common good. God graces his people so they may grace others and be a blessing to them. Profit is a good thing, but a fine line must be found between selfish greed, which the Bible calls an idol (Col 3:5) and a fair and healthy profit that distinguishes one for effort and risk of capital.

Chapter 9:1-4 begins with Paul telling them that he sent others ahead to prepare them for the collection so that his boasting about their generosity would not embarrass him or them. So he says in (5) I thought it necessary to urge the brothers to go on ahead to you, and arrange in advance for this bountiful gift that you have promised, so that it may be ready as a voluntary gift and not as an extortion.

Verses 6-9 say, the point is this: the one who sows sparingly will also reap sparingly, and the one who sows bountifully will also reap bountifully. Each of you must give as you have made up your mind, not reluctantly or under compulsion, for God loves a cheerful giver. And God is able to provide you with every blessing in abundance, so that by always having enough of everything, you may share abundantly in every good work. As it is written (Ps 112:9), "He scatters abroad, he gives to the poor; his righteousness endures forever." (So just as the righteous one in the Psalm gives to the poor out of delight in God's commandments, the Corinthians willingness to give to the needs of the saints expresses their righteousness in obedience to their confession of the gospel of Christ.)

It must also be stated that even though God loves a giver who gives willingly, the Jews at that time, under the Jewish law, whether living in Israel or not, were required to give to support the temple in Jerusalem, which helped run the government theocracy in Israel. In fact those who lived in Israel were required by the government to give in addition 1/10 of all they had. Paul is not invoking that in this situation. This giving in the collection of Paul is beyond what government required of them.

Verses 10-12 say, He who supplies seed to the sower and bread for food will supply and multiply your seed for sowing and increase the harvest of your righteousness. You will be enriched in every way for your great generosity, which will produce thanksgiving to God through us; for the rendering of this ministry not only supplies the needs of the saints but also overflows with many thanksgivings to God.

As the people of God give abundantly from their hearts to those in need, God will keep blessing them abundantly in order for them to keep giving. In this way God will continue to be glorified and righteousness will keep increasing. God's glory and righteousness are always together.

Verses 13-15 say, Through the testing of this ministry you glorify God by your obedience to the confession of the gospel of

Christ and by the generosity of your sharing with them and with all others, while they long for you and pray for you because of the surpassing grace of God that he has given you. Thanks be to God for his indescribable gift!

God's grace is to overflow through his people to touch all that his people come in contact with in order to produce righteousness to the glory of God. What matters to Paul is not the approval of humans including the Corinthians, but the approval of God. Willing to give to those in need is seen as a test of one's faith and a means of glorifying the God of abundant grace. This graciousness centered in the indescribable gift of his Son Jesus, who emptied himself taking the form of a slave being born in human likeness and dying on a cross for the benefit of humankind is the ultimate reason for God's people to be instruments of grace not only to God's people in need but to a world badly in need of experiencing God's light.

In chapter 10 some scholars believe these last three chapters are misplaced and are a fragment of a letter written to Corinth at some other time or at least should be placed elsewhere in the letter. In verses 1-2 Paul says that he is appealing to them by the meekness and gentleness of Christ, which gives us two characteristics of Jesus. Meekness is a reference to a form of humbleness and quietness that does not railroad its way through people. Paul wants to remain gentle but is having a problem with those who have come to Corinth and are accusing him with acting by human standards. Paul admits he is a human only, but he has been chosen by Christ and empowered by the Holy Spirit to perform his apostolic work.

Verses 3-5 say, Indeed, we live as human beings, but we do not wage war according to human standards; for the weapons of our warfare are not merely human, but they have divine power to destroy strongholds. We destroy arguments and every proud obstacle raised up against the knowledge of God, and we take every thought captive to obey Christ. (Every thought is put under the teaching and actions of Christ.)

Verse 6 says, We are ready to punish every disobedience when your obedience is complete. (As an apostle, Paul's purpose is to preach and teach in order to bring everyone to the obedience of Christ, but he has the authority to declare those who are not obedient to Christ as rejected or castoffs from God.) Verses 7-8 say, Look at what is before your eyes. If you are confident that you belong to Christ, remind yourself of this, that just as you belong to Christ, so also do we. Now even if we boast a little too much of our authority, which the Lord gave for building you up and not for tearing you down, I will not be ashamed of it. (Paul is saying this to those in Corinth being influenced by the false apostles who have come to Corinth to destroy his apostolic authority. He does not want to use his apostolic power, but he will if he must.)

Verses 9-11 say, I do not want to seem as though I am trying to frighten you with my letters. For they (the false apostles) say, "His letters are weighty and strong, but his bodily presence is weak, and his speech contemptible." Let such people understand that what we say by letter when absent, we will also do when present. Verse 12 says, We do not dare to classify or compare ourselves with some of those who commend themselves. But when they measure themselves by one another, and compare themselves with one another, they do not show good sense.

Paul is saying do not fool yourselves, the gospel will be proclaimed and defended. It is to be noted that his opponents are saying he has courage when not around us. They are saying he writes boldly enough, but he does not back it when around people, and he is not an impressive speaker. They are probably saying that by the standards of Greek rhetoric, which was what measured a speaker in those times. Paul does not pass the test. Paul is not impressed with their arrogant attitude and the way they compare themselves to human standards and ignore the standards of Christ by which Paul measures himself.

In verses 13-16 Paul's hope is that as the faith of the Corinthians increases, the sphere of action among them will be greatly enlarged so that the good news can be proclaimed in lands beyond them to the glory of God. Verses 17-18 say, "Let the one who boasts, boast in the Lord." For it is not those who commend themselves that are approved, but those whom the Lord commends. (Paul's boasting about his apostolic authority is, in reality, a boast in the Lord who established Paul's apostleship.)

Chapter 11:1 says, I wish you would bear with me in a little foolishness. (The foolishness he is referring to is that he is going to boast in his credentials, something he should not have to do.) Verse 2 says, I feel a divine jealously for you, for I promised you in marriage to one husband, to present you as a chaste virgin to Christ. (Paul is saying that he has a divine jealousy for them when they follow after false apostles since he is the one who married them to Christ.)

Verses 3-4 say, But I am afraid that as the serpent deceived Eve by its cunning, your thoughts will be led astray from a sincere and pure devotion to Christ. (His point is that Satan is leading them from him and from Christ.) For if someone comes and proclaims another Jesus than the one we proclaimed, or if you receive a different spirit from the one we received, or a different gospel from the one you accepted, you submit to it readily enough (Gal 1:6-9).

That is what some were doing by running after these false

teachers. Who they were is difficult to know. They were probably Hellenistic Jews trained in Greek rhetoric, which was very important for debaters and speakers of that time. They may also have been Jews influenced by the Ebionites, who did not accept Jesus as divine, or perhaps they were influenced by the Gnostics who did not believe Jesus was human. They believed he was some super divine spirit only.

It appears that whoever they were, they were taking money from the Corinthians and characterizing themselves with spectacular displays, and intense emotion, trying to impress worldly people with worldly power, worldly strength, self-importance, and tinsel, and glitter as they were peddling the gospel for financial gain (2 Cor 2:17). Do we not see the same in today's world? In contrast Paul boasts in his weakness. He has put off self and put on Christ so the power of God is able to live in and through him giving glory to God in place of self. In the eyes of the world, this is weakness.

Verses 5-6 say, I (Paul) think that I am not in the least inferior to these (so-called) super apostles. I may be untrained in speech (Greek rhetoric), but not in knowledge (Godly wisdom and knowledge); certainly in every way and in all things we have made this evident to you. In 7-12 these so-called super apostles even twisted Paul's determination not to be a financial burden on them while he preached and taught them into a charge against him. Paul lets them know how foolish their charge against him is as they boast in their worldly wisdom, and in (13-15) he says, For such boasters are false apostles, deceitful workers, disguising themselves as apostles of Christ. And no wonder! Even Satan disguises himself as an angel of light. So it is not strange if his ministers also disguise themselves as ministers of righteousness. Their end will match their deeds.

Those disguising themselves as apostles of Christ are in reality ministers of Satan. This writer wonders how many smooth tongued preachers in America today Paul would identify not as ministers of Christ but as false teachers and ministers of Satan. How many out there on television and radio and in the churches are really preaching for money and preaching themselves and their interests instead of Christ, as they use God's word for their own selfish ends? Does the reader think that is a valid thought or not?

Obviously, there is a faction in Corinth being led astray. They believe these false teachers are legitimate and in the process are defending them. Another question for today is how literate in God's word are the people today? Do people today really want to hear what God has to say, or do they have itching ears and hire people who will tell them what they want to hear (2 Tim 4:3-4)? Another question related to being literate in God's word: Are people today able to distinguish between God's word and current culture's teachings dressed up as God's word that in reality actually oppose the teachings of God? Can the reader think of any modern day examples?

In verses 16-21 Paul asks the Corinthians to bear with him as he boasts like the fools who are opposing him. His point is that some of the people are falling for the boasting of the so-called super apostles and in the process they are being made slaves to them and their false teaching. These false teachers have put on airs, and in the process are taking advantage of them. Thus Paul sarcastically asks them to put up with his foolish boasting so he can assert his claims to the truth he teaches (see 10:12-18).

So in verses 22-28 he says, Are they Hebrews? So am I. Are they Israelites? So am I. Are they descendants of Christ? So am I. Are they ministers of Christ? I am talking like a madman—I am a better one: with far greater labors, far more imprisonments, with countless floggings, and often near death. Five times I have received from the Jews the forty lashes minus one. Three times I was beaten with rods. Once I received a stoning. Three times I was shipwrecked; for a night and a day I was adrift at sea; on frequent journeys, in danger from rivers, danger from bandits, danger from my own people, danger from Gentiles, danger in the city, danger in the wilderness, danger at sea, danger from false brothers and sisters; in toil and hardship, through many a sleepless night, hungry and thirsty, often without food, cold and naked. And, besides, other things, I am under daily pressure because of my anxiety for all the churches.

Paul states all this in contrast to the so-called super apostles who have suffered nothing for the false Christ they believe in and preach. Paul's boasting is about what God is doing through him for the glory of God not himself. Then in (28) Paul says, Who is weak, and I am not weak? Who is made to stumble, and I am not indignant?

Paul expresses sympathy with those Corinthians not yet strong in the faith and indignation at those who distort God's truth. Like Jesus Paul felt indignation when he saw stumbling blocks placed in the way of those not yet mature in the faith. When Paul saw such charlatans diverting the unwary in his churches from the pathway of true religion, or when he heard of moral wrongs committed by the Christians, he was angered and hurt.

Then in verses 30-33 Paul says, If I must boast, I will boast of the things that show my weakness. The God and Father of the Lord Jesus (blessed be he forever!) knows that I do not lie. (According to the thinking of worldly people Paul's weakness is that he no longer asserts self but has diminished self. But Paul does this in order to let Christ live through him. Paul boasts only in those things that according to human standards are not worthy of human glory, but he does this to let Christ work through him for God's glory.)

Chapter 12:1-6 tells about Paul being caught up in the third heaven in paradise fourteen years ago and in exceptional revelations from God heard things not to be repeated. The time of the revelations would be shortly after his conversion. In verses 7-12 he says, to keep me from being too elated, a thorn was given me in the flesh, a messenger of Satan to torment me, too keep me from being too elated. (What this thorn was has conjured up many guesses, but nobody knows what it really was.) Three times I appealed to the Lord about this, that it would leave me, but he said to me, "My grace is sufficient for you, for power is made perfect in weakness." So I will boast all the more gladly in my weakness, so that the power of Christ may dwell in me. Therefore I am content with weaknesses, insults, hardships, persecutions, and calamities for the sake of Christ; for whenever I am weak, then I am strong.

Weakness in the eyes of the world is losing self and not promoting self and ego. In the eyes of the world's wisdom not living and doing everything for self and self-glorification is a sign of weakness. Paul believes otherwise, for he sees himself as an instrument to be used by Christ for his purposes, glory, and honor, and Paul is willing to suffer as Christ suffered for the glory of God. For example, even a religious experience and revelations can not legitimatize apostleship, but only weakness and suffering. Paul will only boast in the latter.

Paul had stated in Rom 8:17 that we are children of God and joint heirs with Christ, if we suffer with him so that we also may be glorified with him. Paul knows the pain that comes from a voluntary witness to the gospel. Paul knows well the death and resurrection of Christ, and the call of Christ to his disciples to lose self and to walk in his footsteps. The super apostles did not buy into this. Paul is calling his people to be an icon for Christ, to offer a life that is a replacement for the former temple sacrifice. As he said in 2:15 we are called to be the aroma of Christ. Paul is saying that the goal of ministry for disciples of Christ and the church is not to turn a profit, or help people find what is personally fulfilling, or to feel good about themselves, or even have a big membership, but is to embody the cross in loss of self for the well-being of others to the glory of God. In this way God's grace is transformed into a vehicle of God's power. Boasting in the Lord and not self becomes the boast that marks one as legitimate before God and others. In this way God's people become his ambassadors (5:20) and even feel the pain Christ felt.

Verses 11-13 say, I have been a fool! You forced me to it (defending himself). Indeed you should have been the ones commending me, for I am not at all inferior to these super-apostles, even though I am nothing (in the eyes of the world). The signs of a true apostle were performed among you with utmost patience, signs and wonders and mighty works. Verses 14-15 say, Here I am ready to come to you this third time. And I will not be a burden, because I do not want what is yours but you, for children ought not to lay up for their parents, but parents for their children. (Paul wants them personally as people of Christ, and he does not want any pay from them. He will work in his skill as a tent maker to support himself.) I will most gladly spend and be spent for you. If I love you more, am I to be loved less?

In 16-18 he tells them that neither he nor those with him took advantage of them, nor acted toward them with any deceit or even took money from them for themselves. (Paul is saying he is not like the so-called super apostles.) Verse 19 says, Have you been thinking all along that we have been defending ourselves before you? We are speaking in Christ before God. Everything we do, beloved, is for the sake of building you up. For I fear that when I come, I may find you not as I wish; I fear that there may perhaps be quarreling, jealously, anger, selfishness, slander, gossip, conceit, and disorder. I fear that when I come again, my God may humble me before you, and that I may have to mourn over many who previously sinned and have not repented of impurity, sexual immorality, and licentiousness that they have practiced. (This is Paul's call for self-examination and repentance so that when he comes it will be a happy and mutually rewarding time.)

Chapter 13:1-4 says, This is the third time I am coming to you. "Any charge must be sustained by the evidence of two or three witnesses." I warned those who sinned previously and all the others, and I warn them now while absent, as I did when present on my second visit that if I come again, I will not be lenient—since you desire proof that Christ is speaking in me. He is not weak in dealing with you, but is powerful in you. For he was crucified in weakness, but lives by the power of God. For we are weak in him, but in dealing with you we live with him by the power of God. (Paul will assert his apostolic authority in dealing with sinners at Corinth, but it will be with the authority of Christ.)

Verse 5 says, Examine yourselves to see whether you are living in the faith. Test yourselves. (One examines and tests by comparing oneself to Christ and his words and actions.) Do you not realize that Jesus Christ is in you?—unless, indeed, you fail to meet the test! (Paul is asking them if they are letting the gospel of Christ, dying to self and rising to new life, work in them and through them.)

Verses 6-7 say, I hope you will find out we have not failed. But we pray to God that you may not do anything wrong—not that we may appear to have met the test, but that you may do what is right, though we may have seemed to have failed. (It seems like some have not responded to the apostolic message.)

Verses 8-10 say, For we cannot do anything against the truth, but only for the truth. For we rejoice when we are weak and you are strong. This is what we pray for, that you may become perfect (mature in the faith). So I write these things while I am away from you, so that when I come, I may not have to be severe in using the authority that the Lord has given me for building up and not tearing down. (Paul hopes that he will not need to exert his apostolic authority. His desire is that he will not have to exert the strength of his power but that the church will discipline itself and take care of the problems.)

Verses 11-13 say, Finally, brothers and sisters, farewell. Put things in order, listen to my appeal. Agree with one another, live in peace; and the God of love and peace will be with you. Greet one another with a holy kiss. All the saints greet you. The grace of the Lord Jesus Christ, the love of God, and the communion of the Holy Spirit be with you.

This ends the book of Corinthians, two books filled with problems in the church. Is this any different from today? The New Testament letters are all basically dealing with problems in the early church. The problems in today's churches may be somewhat different, even though the essence behind them at times will be the same. The Bible is not written to always give us exact answers to all the problems in the modern day church, for times are different. But Scripture does give us principles, guidelines, and ways to think and work through the problems. All the problems were not solved instantaneously then, and all the problems will not be solved instantaneously today. But God promises as his people work together, the Spirit will be sent to lead them. As a way of review list some of the most important verses or thoughts the Apostle Paul is making in the letter of 2 Corinthians.

THE LETTER
TO THE GALATIANS

Often called the Magna Charta of Christian liberty, the letter deals with the question whether Gentiles must become Jews before they can become Christians. Paul writes to the Galatians who are located in Asia Minor which is modern day Turkey. He writes probably around 53-55 AD during his first missionary journey. This is one of his earliest writings. In chapter one he writes that he is surprised they are so quickly chasing after a different gospel and following those who are perverting the gospel of Christ. Paul, then, tells them that even if we or an angel from heaven should preach to you a gospel other than the one we preached to you, let that one be accursed.

Paul tells them his gospel did not come from humans but from a revelation of Jesus Christ, and by the grace of God. Christ called Paul to proclaim Jesus as Lord and Savior primarily to the Gentiles. After 3 years of being in Damascus and Arabia, he goes to Jerusalem where he meets with Peter and James, then goes to Antioch of Syria and Cilicia (Turkey) his home area. Even though he confers with no one else in Judea, the word spread that the one who had previously persecuted them is now preaching the very faith that he had once tried to destroy.

Chapter two says that fourteen years later he along with Barnabus and Titus go to the first church council in Jerusalem to certify that Paul will be in charge to preach to the Gentiles (the uncircumcised) and Peter will be in charge to preach to the circumcised (the Jews). Apparently, Paul stayed in his home area of Cilicia until the time was ripe for him. The primary discussion at the meeting centers on the concept of justification. The question is: Under the new covenant instituted by Jesus, who are the new people of God, and how are they to be identified?

One group of Jewish Christians said that before one becomes a Christian, they should be circumcised and follow the works of the OT law, certainly the Jewish food laws, the purity laws, and the whole system of the Sabbath laws. Paul disagreed saying they are no longer factors determining who the people of God are. Initial justification (being accepted by God) and sanctification (maturing and being made holy) is only through Christ Jesus (what he did and what he taught).

Paul says that the Old Testament law can only lead one to Christ. Now Christ has fulfilled the Mosaic law. Paul said through the law, I died to those laws, that I might live for God. I have been crucified with Christ; yet I no longer live, but Christ lives in me, and I live by faith in the Son of God who has loved me and given himself up for me. I do not nullify the grace of God, for if justification comes through the (Mosaic) law, then Christ died for nothing. In other words if the law of Moses was complete, why did Christ have to come into the world and institute a new covenant, a new law, then die on the cross? Christ and faith in him is what initially determines who God's people are. Then the Holy Spirit yields fruit for God in and through the justified.

In chapter three he calls the Galatians stupid for running after a different gospel. He asks them if they received the Spirit from the Mosaic law or from Christ. Of course the answer is Christ, for under the old law the Spirit only fell on a very select few, those God called for a very select purpose. But under the new law, the Holy Spirit is sent by Christ to those who become believers in Christ. Then Paul reminds them again that Abraham, their father, who was given God's promise (Gen 12:1-3) was justified by faith not by the works of the Mosaic law. The Mosaic law came long after Abraham had died. So it is those with faith in Christ who are God's children. That no one is justified by the law is clear, for the one who is made righteous, or justified, is the one who by faith trusts in what Jesus has done. Christ ransomed us from the curse of the law by becoming a curse for us on the tree (cross). Thus the blessing of Abraham is extended to the Gentiles through Christ Jesus, so that all, both Jew and Gentile may receive the promise of the Spirit by their obedience to the faith of Christ (Acts 2:38, Rom 2:4-14, Jas 2:14-26).

This is the fulfillment of prophecy that foretold the good news to Abraham that through him all the nations would be blessed, not just the Jews and their particular laws. Consequently, those with faith are blessed along with Abraham who had faith. For all who depend on the works of the Mosaic law are under a curse, for it is written cursed be everyone who does not persevere in doing all the things written in the law. The idea is that no one can save themselves because no human can perfectly do all of the law. They will miss the mark, which is the definition of sin. The purpose of the Mosaic law was to reveal sin. The law could not forgive sin, only reveal it. Paul says that the Mosaic law is our disciplinarian to lead us to Christ.

Now all who are baptized into Christ have been clothed in or put on Christ. All are now one in Christ. No longer are people free or slave, Jew or Gentile, male or female but one in Christ and Abraham's descendants, heirs according to the promise. Being justified in Christ determines who a Christian is and not the Old Testament laws. The dividing line or distinction between all people, both Jew and Gentile, as far as who his people are is ended. This is what had to be hashed out in the first church council in Jerusalem.

Chapter four tells us we are now free. God sent the Spirit of God into our hearts, so we are no longer slaves (to the Mosaic laws) but adopted children of God. Therefore no longer ruled by the elemental spirits or powers of the world, for you have been set free to be ruled by Christ. Paul tells them that he will remain in pain until Christ is formed in them. This chapter informs us that in the fullness of time the promise was made to Abraham and his descendant. Notice it does not say descendants but descendant, and that descendant is Christ. The promise made to Abraham is fulfilled in and through Christ.

In the rest of this chapter he compares the freedom of the Christian with Sarah and Hagar the women of Abraham. The child of Sarah, Abraham's wife called the free woman, had the child of the promise who was Isaac. It is through Isaac's descendants that Christ will come. The child of Hagar, Abraham's concubine, who was Sarah's slave woman, was driven out. Paul tells us like Isaac we are the children of promise who are born free.

In chapter five Paul says for freedom Christ has set us free, so stand firm, and no longer submit to the yoke of slavery and do not be misled by the false teachers who are preaching that circumcision and the Mosaic laws are necessary in order to he considered a child of God. In fact Paul says I wish they would castrate themselves.

Then he says do not use your freedom to serve the sinful flesh rather serve one another through love, for the whole law is fulfilled in loving your neighbor as yourself. Freedom is not doing what one wants, for that is serving the sinful flesh and results in slavery. Real freedom is submitting to Christ and serving him only and his law of love. Live by the Spirit and not by your flesh. Paul then lists the works of the flesh that some live by: fornication, impurity, licentiousness, idolatry, sorcery, enmities, strife, jealousy, anger, quarrels, dissensions, factions, envy, drunkenness, carousing, and things like these where no one will enter the kingdom of God. He tells his people to live by the fruit of the Spirit: love, joy, peace, patience, kindness, generosity, faithfulness, gentleness, and self control. Live by the virtues produced by the Holy Spirit that is sent by the Father through his Son in the power of the Holy Spirit, and not by the vices of the sinful flesh.

In chapter six he gives some parting instructions such as to bear one another's burdens and fulfill the law of Christ, which is the law of love, and to never tire of doing good, for we will reap what we sow. If we reap to the flesh, we will reap corruption of the flesh, but if we sow to the Spirit, we reap eternal life from the Spirit. It is within these bounds that real freedom is found. Let us look in detail beginning with chapter one.

Chapter1:1-5 says, Paul an apostle—sent neither by human commission nor from human authorities, but through Jesus Christ and God the Father, who raised him from the dead—and all the members of God's family who are with me, To the churches of Galatia:

Grace to you and peace from God our Father and the Lord Jesus Christ, who gave himself for our sins to set us free from the present evil age, according to the will of our God and Father, to whom be the glory forever and ever. Amen. (The age we live in is always said to be evil because Satan is roaming the earth, 6:11, 16.)

In Paul's greeting to the Galatians he reminds them that he has been commissioned and sent by God the Father and his Son Jesus the Christ (Messiah) who gave (sacrificed, Eph 5:2, Lev 4-5) himself for our sins, and then was resurrected. He reminds them that this was part of God's plan for humankind. He reminds them that included in God's plan is to grant them grace by setting them free from the world and its ways, which he calls this present evil age, and to make them part of the kingdom of God. This kingdom has already broken into the world with Jesus. It is through the kingdom of God and making it present in their lives, as they become the eyes, ears, mouth, hands, and feet of Christ until he comes again that gives meaning to their lives and glorifies God.

As Paul writes in Col 1:13, He has rescued us from the power of darkness and transferred us into the kingdom of his beloved Son, in whom we have redemption, the forgiveness of sins, and Rev 1:5b-6 adds, To him who loves us and freed us from our sins by his blood, and made us to be a kingdom, priests serving his God and Father, to him be glory and dominion forever and ever. Amen.

In verses 6-9 Paul says, I am astonished that you are so quickly deserting the one who called you in the grace of Christ and turning to a different gospel—not that there is another gospel, but there are some who are confusing you and want to pervert the gospel of Christ. But even if we or an angel from heaven should proclaim to you a gospel contrary to what we proclaimed to you, let that one be accursed! As we have said before, so now I repeat, if anyone proclaims to you a gospel contrary to what you received, let that one be accursed!

A group of people calling themselves followers of Christ were telling the Galatians that Gentiles wanting to become children of God had to first become a convert to the Mosaic law and become a Jew before they could become a follower of Christ. This was perverting the freedom and grace of the gospel (good news) of Christ.

Apparently, whoever these people were, they were accusing Paul of making entry into Christ and his kingdom too easy, for in (10) he says, Am I now seeking human approval? Or am I trying to please people? If I were still pleasing people, I would not be a servant of Christ. (That is an interesting verse for today's preachers and followers of Christ to contemplate.) Then verse 11 says, For I want you to know, brothers and sisters, that the gospel that was proclaimed by me is not of human origin; for I did not receive it from a human source, nor was I taught it, but I received it through a revelation of Jesus Christ. (Paul makes it clear that his message is from God, and not from humans.)

Verses 13-24 say, You have heard, no doubt of my earlier life in Judaism. I was violently persecuting the church of God and was trying to destroy it. I advanced in Judaism beyond many among my people of the same age, for I was far more zealous for the traditions of my ancestors. But when God, who set me apart before I was born and called me through his grace, was pleased to reveal his Son to me, so that I might proclaim him among the Gentiles. I did not confer with any human being, nor did I go up to Jerusalem to those who were already apostles before me, but I went away at once into Arabia, and afterwards I returned to Damascus.

It is difficult to discern how many years are involved in these verses. The main ideas are that God had a plan for him even before he was born, and before his Christ (Messiah) experience with Jesus, and he was a violent persecutor of Christians, rejecting Jesus as the Messiah. But then Jesus appeared to him on the road to Damascus, and this experience changed his life. Sometime after this, he went to Arabia, and then returned to Damascus.

Verses 18-24 say, Then after three years I did go up to Jerusalem to visit Cephas (Aramaic for Peter) and stayed with him fifteen days; but I did not see any other apostle except James the Lord's brother. (James was not one of the original twelve apostles.) In what I am writing to you, before God, I do not lie! Then I went into the regions of Syria and Cilicia, and I was still unknown by sight to the churches of Judea that are in Christ; they only heard it said, "The one who was formerly persecuting us is now proclaiming the faith he once tried to destroy." And they glorified God because of me. (Again it is very difficult to determine how many years are involved.)

The reader can go back to Acts chapters 9, 22, and 26 for more information about Jesus appearing to Paul. It may be difficult comparing the details because of the differences, but that is no surprise in a society where the narrative is passed on to different communities orally before it was written. What is important is that the main ideas and the message God wants his people to hear are preserved even though the exact details may not always coincide.

Again, the Bible was never meant to be a detailed history book, even though the core of history is in it. The Bible is primarily a book of theology, spiritual direction, a form of catechism to enable all to remember the core of history and God's teachings on who he is, who we are as his people, how we are to relate to God, ourselves, others he created, and to his created earth.

Chapter 2: 1-3 says, Then after fourteen years (after what fourteen years, beginning with what and ending with what is difficult to discern) I went up again with Barnabas (Acts 11:25, 13:1-3, 15:2, I Cor 9:6) taking Titus (2 Cor 7:6, 8:6, 16-17) along with me. I went up in response to a revelation. Then I laid before them . . . the gospel that I proclaim among the Gentiles, in order to make sure that I was not running, or had not run, in vain. But

even Titus, who was with me, was not compelled to be circumcised, though he was a Greek.

Circumcision goes back to those who are teaching that one has to accept the Mosaic law and become a Jew before one could become a Christian. Paul is saying the Jerusalem leaders agreed that Titus did not need to be circumcised to become a member of God's family. (That should have settled the issue.)

Verses 4-5 say, But because of false believers secretly brought in, who slipped in to spy on the freedom we have in Christ Jesus, so that they might enslave us—we did not submit to them even for a moment, so that the truth of the gospel might always remain with you. (This is a reference to what happened while he was in Jerusalem, false believers appeared saying circumcision and following the whole Old Testament law was necessary to be saved. From the very beginning this was a major issue, Acts 15:5.)

In verses 6-8 Paul explains that in Jerusalem key apostles approved him to be primarily an apostle to the Gentiles, while Peter is to be the primary apostle to the Jews. Verses 9-10 say, when James (probably the brother of Jesus, who became the leader of the Jerusalem church) and Cephas (Peter) and John (the apostle?), who were acknowledged pillars, recognized the grace that had been given me, they gave to Barnabas and me the right hand of fellowship, agreeing that we should go to the Gentiles and they to the circumcised (Jews). They asked only one thing, that we remember the poor, which was exactly what I was eager to do. (What a good suggestion to all of us, including our politicians, as they wrangle over what they believe are the more important political, economic, social, and ethical issues.)

Verses 11-13 say, But when Cephas came to Antioch, I opposed him to his face, because he stood self-condemned; for until certain people came from James (from the Jerusalem church), he used to eat with the Gentiles. But after they came, he drew back and kept himself separate for fear of the circumcision faction. And the other Jews (Jewish Christians) joined him in this hypocrisy, so that even Barnabas was led astray by their hypocrisy.

Serious religious Jews, mainly from the group of Pharisees, would not eat at the same table with those who were not circumcised, and who did not obey all the OT food laws. If they would eat at the same table, it would symbolize full acceptance of them as brothers. To not eat with them implied they were unclean before God and not accepted by him. In Paul's mind Peter refusing to eat with Gentile Christians is hypocrisy. He is denying the freedom of the gospel (the good news) and is distorting its intention.

Verses 14-16 say, But when I saw that they were not acting consistently with the truth of the gospel, I said to Cephas before them all, "If you, like a Jew, live like a Gentile and not like a Jew (he no longer abided by the food laws because of his special vision from God, Acts 10:9-16), how can you compel the Gentiles to live like Jews?" We ourselves are Jews by birth and not Gentile sinners (Jews called Gentiles sinners because they did not obey the Mosaic law); yet we know that a person is justified not by the works of the law (Old Testament law) but through faith in Jesus Christ. (This can also be translated the faith of Christ, which this writer believes is the better translation. It is what Christ does that justifies, and the faith we have is a gift from God.)

Verse 16 continues, And we have come to believe in Christ Jesus, so that we might be justified by faith in Christ, and not by doing the works of the law, because no one will be justified by the works of the law (also Rom 3:21-26). (The works of the law are a reference to the works of the Mosaic law such as circumcision, obeying all the food laws, the purity laws, and the sabbath laws.)

The issue of justification in this context of Paul and Peter is over who is considered a child of God in the present, and how you can tell. The issue here is not about final salvation. NT Wright (2005, 112) believes the word justified is not a statement about how someone becomes a Christian, but is a statement about who belongs to the people of God, and how you can tell that in the present. That is the subject under discussion. It is not by the works of the Mosaic law but by the faith of Christ who obeyed the Father accepting the cross, and then by one who has the faith of Christ. (The Mosaic law is exempted from the issue of justification; it is not an issue.)

Verses 17-21 say, But in our effort to be justified in Christ, we ourselves have been found to be sinners, is Christ then a servant of sin? (Does Christ serve sin's purpose by exposing us as sinners?) Certainly not! . . . For through the law I died to the law, so that I might live to God. For I have been crucified with Christ; and it is no longer I who live, but it is Christ who lives in me. I do not nullify the grace of God; for if justification comes through the law, then Christ died for nothing. (The law does not justify anyone; it is only Christ who justifies and forgives sin.)

The Mosaic law led Paul to Christ, and through grace Paul is justified as Christ lives in and through him. As Christ died to the world, Paul died to the law and to self letting Christ work his works in and through him. Paul in Phil 2:12-13 says, work out your own salvation in fear and trembling; for it is God who is at work in you, enabling you both to will and to work for his good pleasure. (In this way the people of Christ become the eyes, ears, mouth, hands, and feet of Jesus continuing his mission of the kingdom until he comes again.)

❧

In Chapter 3:1-5 says, You foolish Galatians! Who has bewitched you? It was before your eyes that Jesus Christ was publically exhibited as crucified! The only thing I want to learn from you is this: Did you receive the Spirit by doing the works of the law or by believing what you heard? Are you so foolish? Having started with the Spirit, are you now ending with the flesh (the Mosaic law)? Did you experience so much for nothing?—if it really was for nothing. Well then, does God supply you with the Spirit and work miracles among you by your doing the works of the law, or by your believing what you heard? (The issue is the choice between Christ, and what he does for you; and the Mosaic law, and what it does for you.)

Verses 6-9 say, Just as Abraham "believed God, and it was reckoned to him as righteousness," so, you see, those who believe are the descendants of Abraham. And the scripture, foreseeing that God would justify the Gentiles by faith, declared the gospel beforehand to Abraham saying, "All the Gentiles shall be blessed in you." For this reason, those who believe are blessed with Abraham who believed.

The issue is: God called Abraham and told him that the world would be blessed through him and his descendants, and Abraham believed God would do what he said he would. God has now done that, not through the Mosaic law, which came hundreds of years after Abraham's death, but through Jesus. Therefore Abraham could not have been justified by the Mosaic law; it was by faith. God has fulfilled his promise through Christ. The question Paul is proposing is: Do you believe that or not? Jews and Gentiles are now brought together as one, justified by Christ and made one. God has fulfilled his promise. Abraham's true descendants are not the circumcised but those who believe God has fulfilled his promise through Christ. Paul is saying, therefore the debate over circumcision, food laws, and the purity laws are adiaphora, meaning no issue, for we are all one in Christ.

Verses 10-12 say, For all who rely on the works of the law (for justification) are under a curse; for it is written, "Cursed is everyone who does not observe and obey all things written in the book of the law." (The point is no one can obey all of the Mosaic law perfectly.) Now it is evident that no one is justified before God by the law; for "The one who is righteous will live by faith." (Only those in a relationship with Christ are in a righteous relationship, for then they live by the same faith Christ lived, and now Christ lives in and through them doing his works.) But the law does not rest on faith; on the contrary, "Whoever does the works of the law will live by them." (One either lives by the faith of Christ or lives by the works of the Mosaic law.)

Verses 13-14 say, Christ redeemed us from the curse of the law by becoming a curse (on the cross) for us—for it is written, "Cursed is everyone who hangs on a tree"—in order that in Christ Jesus the blessing of Abraham might come to the Gentiles, so that we might receive the promise of the Spirit through faith. (The faith is that the Father sent Christ to fulfill the promise that the world would be blessed by Abraham and his descendants).

Verses 15-18 say, Brothers and sisters, I give an example from daily life: once a person's will has been ratified, no one adds to it or annuls it. Now the promises were made to Abraham and to his offspring; it does not say, "And to offsprings," as of many; but it says, "And to your offspring," that is, to one person, who is Christ. My point is this: the law, which came four hundred thirty years later, does not annul a covenant previously ratified by God, so as to nullify the promise. For if the inheritance comes from the law, it no longer comes from the promise; but God granted it to Abraham through the promise. (The promise bypassed the law.)

Verses 19-22 say, Why then the law? It was added because of transgressions (as a way of pointing out sin), until the offspring would come to whom the promise had been made; and it was ordained through the angels by a mediator. Now a mediator involves more than one party; but God is one. Is the law then opposed to the promises of God? Certainly not! For if a law had been given that could make alive, then righteousness would indeed come through the law. But the scripture has imprisoned all things under the power of sin, so that what was promised through faith in Christ might be given to those who believe.

The law can not make anyone alive; it can only point out sin. Only Christ can forgive sin and make one alive. The righteousness that comes through Christ is about a relationship that puts a person into the family of God and keeps them there as the person continually allows God to do his works in them and through them, while the Father through the Son with the power of the Holy Spirit continually purifies them of sin.

Verses 23-26 say, Now before faith (in Christ) came, we were imprisoned and guarded under the law until faith would be revealed. Therefore the law was our disciplinarian until Christ came, so that we might be justified by faith. But now that faith has come, we are no longer subject to a disciplinarian, for in Christ Jesus you are all children of God through faith. (Justification comes through the faith and obedience of Christ, not the Mosaic law. Paul is saying to make sure you are putting your faith in the right place.)

Paul now states that a person's faith in Christ leads to being baptized into Christ. Verses 27-29 say, As many of you as were baptized into Christ have clothed yourselves with Christ. (You have undressed yourself of your selfish desires and interests and clothed yourself with Christ and his desires and interests.) There is no longer Jew or Greek, there is no longer slave or free, there is no longer male or female; for all of you are one in Christ Jesus. And if you belong to Christ, then you are Abraham's offspring, heirs according to the promise. (Faith followed by baptism clothes one in Christ and fulfills the promise to Abraham. The world has been blessed and all, both Jew and Gentile are justified in Christ and made one as God planned and promised Abraham. The Mosaic law has been bypassed.)

❦

Chapter 4:1-7 says, My point is this: heirs, as long as they are minors, are no better than slaves, though they are the owners of the property; but they remain under guardians and trustees until the date set by the father. So with us; while we were minors, we were enslaved to the elemental spirits of the world. But when the fullness of time had come, God sent his Son, born of a woman, born under the law, in order to redeem those who were under the law, so that we might receive adoption as children. And because you are children, God has sent the Spirit of his Son into our hearts crying, "Abba! Father!" So you are no longer a slave but a child, and if a child then also an heir, through God.

Being enslaved to the elemental spirits is a reference to either the cosmic powers that rule the universe, the powers that pagan people believed ruled the world, or to the rules and regulations of the works of the Mosaic law. Paul is saying that we are no longer controlled by either. We are now controlled by God the Father, the Creator and covenant God, who initiated a new creation and a new covenant and sends the Spirit of his Son into our hearts to redeem us and make us God's adopted children.

Verses 8-10 say, Formerly, when you did not know God, you were enslaved to beings (elemental spirits) that by nature are not gods. Now, however, that you have come to know God, or rather to be known by God (The grace of God comes first.) how can you turn back again to the weak and beggarly elemental spirits? How can you want to be enslaved to them again? You are observing special days, and months, and seasons, and years. (Probably a reference to making these required Jewish holy days a requirement for those desiring to be a part of God's people. It is possible that this group is trying to blend Christianity with both Judaism and their former pagan religion.) Paul in verse 11 says, I am afraid that my work for you may have been wasted.

In verses 12-20 Paul reminds them of the good will they showed him in the beginning, and how they respected him even with his physical problem (eye disease? see 6:11). In verse 16 he asks, Have I now become your enemy by telling you the truth? Paul tells them in (19) that he will be in pain until Christ is formed in them. (Christ is formed in God's people through the Spirit.)

In verses 21-27 he compares being a slave to Christ with being a slave to the law. He compares the two covenants by using an allegory. He uses Abraham's two wives as examples. Hagar is the slave woman corresponding to Jerusalem in slavery with her children. Sarah, Abraham's wife, corresponds to Jerusalem, who is free and is our mother. She is the mother of Isaac, the child of God's promise. It was through Isaac that God's promise was fulfilled and not through Ishmael who was the child of Hagar, (see Gen 21.) Verses 28-31 say, Now you, my friends, are children of the promise, like Isaac. But just as at that time the child who was born according to the flesh persecuted the child who was born according to the Spirit, so it is now also. But what does the scripture say? "Drive out the slave and her child; for the child of the slave will not share the inheritance with the child of the free woman." So then, friends, we are children not of the slave but the free woman.

This is all an allegory to show that the Mosaic law and the law of the pagans enslaves their followers while the faith of Christ sets his followers free from the things of the world that enslaves them, and that includes the different forms of religion humans developed that are outside God's promise to Abraham. Since Christ is Abraham's offspring according to the promise, he is the link to freedom symbolized by Sarah. To revert to the Mosaic law is to return to slavery.

Chapter 5:1-3 says, For freedom Christ has set us free. Stand firm, therefore, and do not submit again to a yoke of slavery. Listen! I, Paul, am telling you that if you let yourself be circumcised (as the way for justification and fellowship with God and each other), Christ will be of no benefit to you. Once again I testify to every man who lets himself be circumcised that he is obliged to obey the entire law. (Circumcision indicated the willingness to live by the law and receive forgiveness through the sacrificial worship system by the offering of bulls and goats, Heb 10:4-18, and not Christ.)

Verses 4-6 say, You who want to be justified by the law have cut yourself off from Christ; you have fallen away from grace. For through the Spirit, by faith, we eagerly wait for the hope of righteousness. For in Christ Jesus neither circumcision nor uncircumcision counts for anything; the only thing that counts is faith working through love. (Faith in Christ works through loving Christ, receiving the Holy Spirit he sends, and allowing the power of the Holy Spirit to live in and through you. To choose the law is to abandon Christ, the one who fulfills the law, reinterprets it, redefines ethnic identity, and sends the Holy Spirit.)

Verses 7-11 say, You were running well; who prevented you from obeying the truth? Such persuasion does not come from the one who called you. A little yeast leavens the whole batch of dough. I am confident about you in the Lord that you will not think otherwise. But whoever it is that is confusing you will pay the penalty. But my friends, why am I still being persecuted if I am still preaching circumcision? In that case the offense of the cross has been removed.

Apparently, his opponents were saying that Paul is still preaching the necessity of circumcision. They probably misunderstood Paul when he said it did not matter if one is circumcised, but he did not teach that one must be circumcised to have fellowship with God and each other; that teaching would eliminate the necessity of Christ and the cross. Then in (11) Paul shockingly says, I wish those who unsettle you would castrate themselves!

Paul now expounds on the opposite of slavery which is freedom. Verses 13-14 say, For you were called to freedom, brother and sisters; only do not use your freedom for self indulgence, but through love become slaves to one another. For the whole law is summed up in a single commandment, "You shall love your neighbor as yourself." (Another way to look at that is to do to others what you would want them to do to you.) Verse 15 says, If, however, you bite and devour one other, take care that you are not consumed by one another. (This is what has happened to many including Christians.)

Verses 16-18 say, Live by the Spirit, (the Spirit of life in Christ Jesus letting the Spirit work in and through you), and do not gratify the works of the flesh. (Spirit and flesh represent opposing ways of life, loyalties, and thought.) For what the flesh desires is opposed to the Spirit, and what the Spirit desires is opposed to the flesh; for these are opposed to each other, to prevent you from doing what you want. But if you are led by the Spirit, you are not subject to the law. (At the most the Mosaic law or any law can only produce a minimum ethic, and it can not bring salvation. In Romans 7 Paul associates the law with the flesh and boasting in self.)

Verses 19-21 say, Now the works of the flesh are obvious: fornication impurity, licentiousness, idolatry, sorcery, enmities, strife, jealousy, anger, quarrels, dissensions, carousing, and things like these (see also Rom 1:29-31,1 Cor 6:9-10, Eph 5:3-4, Col 3:5-11). I am warning you, as I warned you before; those who do such things will not inherit the kingdom of God. (Those who continue to live in the vices the flesh produces will not inherit the kingdom.)

Verses 22-26 say, By contrast, the fruit of the Spirit is love, joy, peace, patience, kindness, generosity, faithfulness, gentleness, and self control (see also 2 Cor 6:6-7, Col 3:12-17). There is no law against such things. And those who belong to Christ Jesus have crucified the flesh with its passion and desires. If we live by the Spirit, let us also be guided by the Spirit. Let us not become conceited, competing against one another, envying one another. (These are the virtues the Spirit desires to produce.)

Chapter 6:1 says, My friends, if anyone is detected in a transgression, you who have received the Spirit should restore such a one in a spirit of gentleness. Take care that you yourselves are not tempted. (Pride and arrogance are the culprits.) Verse 2 says, Bear one another's burdens, and in this way you will fulfill the law of Christ. (The law of Christ is a metaphor for life in the Spirit and being what Christ wants his people to be and do.) Verse 3 says, For if those who are nothing think they are something, they deceive themselves. (Again the problem is pride and arrogance which thrives on self-illusion.)

Verses 4-5 say, All must test their own work; then that work, rather than their neighbor's work, will become a cause for pride. For all must carry their own loads. (All are responsible to God for the fruit they bear. Pride in this sense can be a humble and positive thing, the other side of responsible behavior.) Verse 6 says, Those who are taught the word must share in all good things with their teacher. (Teachers are entitled to financial support from their students.)

Verses 7-9 say, Do not be deceived; God is not mocked, for you reap whatever you sow. If you sow to your own flesh, you will reap corruption from the flesh; but if you sow to the Spirit, you will reap eternal life from the Spirit. So let us not grow weary in doing what is right, for we will reap at harvest time (judgment), if we do not give up.

Paul teaches that justification has a beginning and an end and sandwiched between is sanctification where God makes his people more holy. Both justification and sanctification are accomplished by God's grace through Christ in the power of the Holy Spirit. Verse 10 says, So then, whenever we have an opportunity, let us work for the good of all, and especially for those of the family of faith. (Harvest time reaping is based on whether or not they allow the Spirit do the works of God in them and through them.)

Verses 11-13 say, See what large letters I make when I am writing with my own hand! (This may be an indication that he did have a problem with his eyesight.) Verse 2 says, It is those who want to make a good showing in the flesh that try to compel you to be circumcised—only that they may not be persecuted for the cross of Christ. Even the circumcised do not themselves obey the law, but they want you to be circumcised so that they may boast about your flesh. (It sounds like those today who love to boast about how many converts they get and how huge their assembly has become.)

Paul in (14-16) says, May I never boast of anything except the cross of our Lord Jesus Christ, by which the world has been crucified to me, and I to the world. For neither circumcision nor uncircumcision is anything; but a new creation is everything! As for those who follow this rule—peace be upon them, and mercy, and upon the Israel of God.

Verses 17-18 say, From now on, let no one make trouble for me; for I carry the marks of Jesus branded on my body. (This is Paul's proof for whom and what he stands for.) May the grace of our Lord Jesus Christ be with your spirit, brothers and sisters. Amen. This ends Paul's letter to the Galatians.

As a way of review list some of the most important verses or thoughts the Apostle Paul is making in the letter to the Galatians.

THE LETTER
TO THE EPHESIANS

Ephesians, Philippians, Colossians, and Philemon are called the prison epistles because Paul writes them while in prison. He was imprisoned in Rome, Ephesus, Philippi, Jerusalem, and who knows where else. Exactly what prison he is in while writing the different letters is not really known. He is in prison because of his preaching Christ and the kingdom of God, and this upsets the people of the status quo, the people of power and wealth, who always reject change.

The Apostle Paul writes to the Ephesians who were located in Asia Minor (Turkey). Ephesus was the most important city in Asia Minor and was a great seaport and export center. It was sacred to the worship of the fertility goddess, later identified with the Greek Artemis, and a center of the emperor cult. From Ephesus churches were established in Colossae and other areas in the Lycus valley.

Acts 19 tells the story of the church being established in Ephesus. Much later tradition has it that Ephesus becomes the center for the Apostle John. Tradition also has it that John took care of Jesus' mother Mary in Ephesus. Even though Jesus did entrust Mary to his care this author wonders why Mary is not with James the brother of Jesus who is in charge of the church in Jerusalem.

In chapter 1 he tells them that before the world even began God predestined them by his grace in and through Christ to be chosen as his people, his adopted children. It is Christ who is predestined, and it is through Christ that they have redemption by his blood, which brings the forgiveness of sin. God has made known the mystery of his will, as a plan for the fullness of time to sum up all things in heaven and earth in Christ and bring them to unity.

Paul tells then that they are chosen (predestined) in Christ to live for the praise of his glory as they are sealed with the promise of the Holy Spirit, which is the first installment of their inheritance toward redemption as God's possession. Then he says may the eyes of your hearts be enlightened that you may know your hope.

In chapter 2 Paul says that previously they were dead in their sins following the desires of their flesh and its impulses, following the ways of the world and Satan, the ruler of this world. But Christ brought them to life and saved them by his grace and raised them up to live and reign with him. This is all the work of Christ, given to them as a gift, so that their only boast is in him and never themselves.

They are the work of Christ, for they have been created for the good works of Christ. In this way they learn their reason for being. For all people, Jew and Gentile, Christ is our peace. He has made Jew and Gentile to be one. The dividing line of hostility, the old law (Mosaic) with its legal claims, is now eliminated by his blood on the cross. Now everyone has access in one Spirit to the Father. All are now fellow citizens built into the household of God, the church, built upon the foundation of the apostles and prophets with Christ Jesus the cornerstone. (This is the basis of God's promise to Abraham.)

In chapter 3 Paul says this mystery was made known to him

that the Gentiles are co-heirs, members of the same body, and co-partners in the promise in Christ Jesus through the good news. He prays that all will be strengthened with power through his Spirit in the inner self, and that Christ may dwell in their hearts through faith, and that they be rooted and grounded in love so that all may be filled with the fullness of God. He states that the purpose of the church is to make known the wisdom of God. Then he closes this particular speech by saying, "Now to him who is able to accomplish far more than all we ask or imagine, by the power at work within us, to him be the glory in the church and in Christ Jesus to all generations. (This is an especially good verse for followers of Christ to meditate upon.)

In chapter 4 Paul urges them to live in a manner worthy of God's call. He says in all gentleness, patience, humility, and love strive to preserve the unity of the Spirit in the bond of peace, for there is one body, one Spirit, one hope, one Lord, one faith, one baptism, one God and Father of all who is over all through all, and in all. The church leaders are to equip God's holy ones for the work of ministry to build up the body of Christ until all attain the unity of the faith and knowledge of the Son of God to maturity. He tells them that they are to live the truth in love as they grow in every way into him who is the head of the church, Christ, who holds all things together bringing about the body's growth that builds itself up in love. Paul then calls them to put away their old self that is corrupted through deceitful desires, and be renewed in the Spirit of their minds, and put on the new self, created in God's way in righteousness and holiness of truth.

Then he tells them what righteousness and holiness entails. They are to speak the truth in love and, when angry, not to let the anger become sin. They are told not to let the sun set on their anger and leave room for the devil. They are told not to steal, and to labor at honest work, not to use foul language, to use only language that edifies, to remove all bitterness, fury, anger, shouting, reviling, and malice, and they are told to be kind to one another, compassionate, and to forgive one another as God forgives them.

In chapter 5 Paul tells them to be imitators of God and live in love, and to put away immorality and greed. He tells them that no immoral, impure, or greedy person, which is idolatry, will enter into heaven, and that they are not to take part in the fruitless works of darkness rather they are to expose them, and live as children of the light, for the wrath of God is coming on the disobedient. He tells them that the days are evil so they are to make the best of their days, and to give thanks for everything in the name of the Lord Jesus. In the process they are to sing psalms, hymns, and spiritual songs, and not to get drunk on wine in which lies debauchery. Instead they are to be filled with the Spirit.

Then he gives advice to wives and husbands to be subordinate to each other. These guidelines for ways to treat each other were household rules at the time, and because churches were house churches at the time the guidelines were carried over to the church. They are not meant to be timeless laws, but there are timeless principles contained within them. Paul compares submission to each other with Christ's love for the church. He tells them that this is a great mystery. Here he speaks in reference to Christ and the church, for a man should love his wife as himself and as Christ loved the church giving himself up for it, and the wife should respect her husband.

In chapter 6 Paul gives directions on how children and parents are to respect each other. Directions are given for slaves and masters, and these principles can possibly be transferred to employer-employee relations. Finally, he describes the armor of God they are to put on in order to stand firm against the tactics of the devil. He says that the struggle is not with flesh and blood but with the evil spirits of the spirit world leading the world's rulers of this present darkness. Therefore, he tells them to put on the armor of God to resist these evil days, to gird their loins with the truth, to clothe themselves with the breastplate of righteousness, and to put on their feet the gospel of peace, making faith their shield in order to quench the flaming arrows of the evil one (the devil). They are to take the helmet of salvation, and the sword of the Spirit which is the word of God. Finally, he tells them to pray at every opportunity in the Spirit.

Chapter 1:1-2 begins with Paul, an apostle of Christ Jesus by the will of God, To the saints who are in Ephesus and are faithful in Christ Jesus: Grace to you and peace from God our Father and the Lord Jesus Christ.

Verses 3-4 say, Blessed be the God and Father of our Lord Jesus Christ, who has blessed us in Christ with every spiritual blessing in heavenly places, just as he chose us in Christ before the foundation of the world to be holy and blameless before him in love. (Even before the world and humans were created God decided that humans would be blessed to become God's adopted sons and daughters through his Son Jesus, and it would be through Jesus that humankind could be made holy and blameless.)

Verses 5-8a say, He destined us for adoption as his children through Jesus Christ, according to the good pleasure of his will, to the praise of his glorious grace that he freely bestowed on us in the Beloved. In him we have redemption through his blood, the forgiveness of our trespasses, according to the riches of his grace that he lavished on us. (It is through the gift of his blood that we are made blameless, and it is through his grace that we are made holy, meaning sanctified.)

Verses 8b-10 say, With all wisdom and insight he has made known to us the mystery of his will, according to his good pleasure that he set forth in Christ, as a plan for the fullness of time, to gather up all things in him, things in heaven and things on earth. (The mystery is that when the time was ripe, he sent his Son Jesus to unite all things to him and to make them all into one. All things mean all people and all things in creation in order to bring unity, peace, and justice.)

Verses 11-14 say, In Christ we have also obtained an inheritance, having been destined according to the purpose of him who accomplishes all things according to his counsel and will, so that we, who were the first to set our hope on Christ, might live for the praise of his glory. (This is the human's purpose for being: to live for the praise of his glory.) In him you also, when you had heard the word of truth, the gospel of your salvation, and had believed in him, were marked with the seal of the promised Holy Spirit; this is the pledge of our inheritance toward redemption as God's own people, to the praise of his glory.

The pledge of our inheritance, our redemption, is being sealed with the Holy Spirit, by baptism, Acts 2:38, Gal 3:27, 1 Peter 3:20-22, and then God calls his people to live for the glory of Christ. Using the word inheritance makes it a gift, but like any inheritance if one drops out of the family, there will be no inheritance.

Verses 15-19 say, I have heard of your faith in the Lord Jesus and your love toward all the saints, and for this reason I do not cease to give thanks for you as I remember you in my prayers. I pray that the God of our Lord Jesus Christ, the Father of glory, may give you a spirit of wisdom and revelation as you come to know him, so that with the eyes of your heart enlightened, you may know what is the hope to which he has called you, what are the riches of his glorious inheritance among the saints, and what is the immeasurable greatness of his power for us who believe, according to the working of his great power. (He had heard of their faith and love and the power it had in their area of life. He prays that their hearts continue to be enlightened by God's revelation and wisdom and that the power of God may be seen by all who come in contact with them.)

Verses 20-23 say, God put this power to work in Christ when he raised him from the dead and seated him at his right hand in the heavenly places, far above all rule and authority and power and dominion, and above every name that is named, not only in this age but also in the age to come. And he has put all things under his feet and has made him the head over all things for the church, which is his body, the fullness of him who fills all in all. (Paul reminds them that Christ has defeated the hostile powers at the cross, and then established the church to advance the kingdom of God and begin to defeat evil.)

God's power is seen in the resurrected Christ, who is now at the right hand of God. God's plan is now to unite all things in Christ. His plan to do this is through Christ and the church of which Christ is the head and his followers his body. Christ the head and his followers the body is a metaphor for the mystery of the unity God desires. The victory of Christ has already been achieved cosmically, but is in the process of being worked out in this world until Christ comes again to complete the victory (see 1 Cor 15:20-28).

⚘

Chapter 2:1-2 says, You were dead through the trespasses and sins in which you once lived, following the course of this world, following the ruler of the power of the air (Satan), the spirit that is now at work among those who are disobedient. (The spirit at work in this world is the spirit of Satan, and he represents the spirit of the world.)

Verses 3-7 say, All of us once lived among them (trespasses/sins) in the passion of our flesh, following the desires of flesh and senses, and we were by nature children of wrath, like everyone else. (God is a God of love and a God of wrath.) But God who is rich in mercy, out of the great love in which he loved us even when we were dead (spiritually dead) through our trespasses, made us alive (spiritually) together with Christ (by being born of God)—by grace you have been saved—and raised us up with him and seated us with him in the heavenly places in Christ Jesus, so that in the ages to come he might show the immeasurable riches of his grace in kindness toward us in Christ Jesus.

We are raised up to reign with Christ and let him work in and through us by being his ears, his eyes, his mouth, his hands, and his feet to bring in more fully the kingdom of God that Christ initiated. His followers are to continue his mission until he comes again to perfect all things.

Verses 8-10 say, For by grace you have been saved through faith, and this is not your own doing; it is the gift of God—not the result of works, so that no one may boast. For we are what he has made us, created in Christ Jesus for good works, which God prepared beforehand to be our way of life. (The good works are what he works in and through us.)

All this is by God's grace, his free gift of mercy. Faith is the channel. Paul does not really say one is saved because of one's faith; it is the faith of Christ that causes all things. God calls his people to be his instrument to work his works, to be what he called them to be and do, as we become his eyes, ears, mouth, hands, and feet in advancing his kingdom until he comes again. This working of God's grace is explained in Phil 2:12-13. It says, work out your salvation with fear and trembling; for it is God who is in you, enabling you both to will and to work for his good pleasure. (It is God who uses his people as his instrument as he works in them and through them.)

Verses 11-14 say, So then, remember that at one time you Gentiles by birth, called "the uncircumcision" by those who are called "the circumcision"—a physical circumcision made in the flesh by human hands—remember that you were at that time without Christ, being aliens from the commonwealth of Israel, and strangers to the covenants of promise, having no hope and without God in the world. But now in Christ Jesus you who once were far off have been brought near by the blood of Christ. For he is our peace; in his flesh he has made both groups (Jew and Gentile) into one and has broken down the dividing wall, that is, the hostility between us. (With the new covenant Christ has made peace between Jew and Gentile. Both are made one through the blood of the cross. God has fulfilled his promise to Abraham.)

Verses 15-18 say, He has abolished the law with its commandments and ordinances (the Mosaic law with its circumcision, food laws, purity laws, and Sabbath work laws), that he might create in himself one new humanity in place of two, thus making peace, and might reconcile both groups to God in one body through the cross, thus putting to death that hostility through it. So he came and proclaimed peace to you who were far off and peace to those who were near; for through him both of us have access in one Spirit to the Father.

The cross of Christ is what reconciles all people to God, making them one with God and one with each other. The issue is that which makes for peace, the cross. As Christ gave of himself, loses self, to reconcile all to the Father, his people are now to give of themselves (metaphorically lose self) to be reconciled to God and to each other.

Verses 19-22 say, So then you are no longer strangers and aliens, but you are citizens with the saints and also members of the household of God, built upon the foundation of the apostles and prophets, with Christ Jesus himself as the cornerstone (a messianic term, see Isa 28:16, Ps 118:21-25, Mt 21:42). In him the whole structure is joined together and grows into a holy temple in the Lord; in whom you also are built together spiritually into a dwelling place for God.

Those who are one in Christ are the household of God, the church. Christ is the cornerstone, the head, the foundation of which the apostles, prophets, and those reconciled to the Father through the Son, are built spiritually into the household of God, (see 1 Cor 3:16-17, 1 Pet 2:4-10). This was God's purpose in his promise to Abraham. The metaphor is one new man, Christ as head, and the church as his body advancing the kingdom of God into this world. The world in Scripture is called this present evil age.

Chapter 3:1-4 says, This is the reason that I Paul am a prisoner for Christ Jesus for the sake of you Gentiles—for surely you have already heard of the commission of God's grace that was given me for you, and how the mystery was made known to me by revelation, as I wrote above in a few words, a reading of which will enable you to perceive my understanding of the mystery of Christ. (The Jerusalem council designated him as the apostle to the Gentiles and Peter the apostle to the Jews.)

Verses 5-6 say, In former generations this mystery was not made known to humankind, as it has now been revealed to his holy apostles and prophets by the Spirit; that is, the Gentiles have become fellow heirs, members of the same body, and sharers in the promise in Christ Jesus through the gospel. (This is the good news, the mystery. God is blessing the Gentiles through the Messiah. God has fulfilled his promise to Abraham. Now both Jew and Gentile are blessed by God and are the one people of God.)

Verses 7-13 say, Of the gospel (the good news) I have become a servant according to the gift of God's grace that was given me by the working of his power. Although I am the very least of all the saints, this grace was given to me to bring to the Gentiles the news of the boundless riches of Christ, and to make everyone see what is the plan of the mystery hidden for ages in God who created all things; so that through the church the wisdom of God in its rich variety might now be made known to the rulers and authorities in the heavenly places. This was in accordance with the eternal purpose that he has carried out in Christ Jesus our Lord, in whom we have access to God in boldness and confidence through faith in him. I pray therefore that you may not lose heart over my sufferings for you; they are your glory.

The Church is to reveal the wisdom of God, the mystery of God not only to Jews and Gentiles but to the cosmic powers. Paul is in prison for revealing this wisdom. Most Jews did not approve of Paul's message, for they did not accept Jesus as the Messiah, risen from the dead, nor did they accept him as the one who forgives sin. Because Paul believes Jesus is Lord and not the emperor, Jews that oppose him alert the Roman authorities that Paul is advocating revolution by proclaiming Jesus and his kingdom as opposing the Roman emperor (Acts 17:6-7).

Because the Roman authorities are not interested in a regime change, they are hostile to Paul. It is difficult to say why it is to be revealed to the cosmic powers. Possibly the gods or spiritual beings who control the masses are the cosmic powers, and by the action of the church, they are put on notice that their days are numbered because of the death and resurrection of Christ. The message is probably more to the people that the days of the spiritual powers are numbered than it is to the cosmic powers, who probably already know.

Verses 14-19 say, For this reason (Paul's revealing the mystery of God's love) I bow my knees before the Father, from whom every family on heaven and earth takes its name. I pray that, according to the riches of his glory, he may grant that you may be strengthened in your inner being with power through his Spirit, and that Christ may dwell in your hearts through faith, as you are being rooted and grounded in love. I pray that you may have the power to comprehend, with all the saints, what is the breadth and length and height and depth, and to know the love of Christ that surpasses knowledge, so that you may be filled with all the fullness of God.

It is the Spirit that strengthens our inner being, if we submit to the Spirit by allowing Christ to dwell in our hearts through faith. In this way we root ourselves in God's love. Paul then prays that God's people will understand the vastness of this love and thus be filled with the fullness of God's wisdom and love.

Verses 20-21 say, Now to him who by the power at work within us (the fullness of God in his Spirit) is able to accomplish abundantly far more than all we can ask or imagine, to him be glory in the church and in Christ Jesus to all generations, forever and ever. Amen. (All of God's people will find it beneficial to meditate on these two verses.)

Chapter 4:1-3 says, I therefore, the prisoner in the Lord, beg you to lead a life worthy of the calling to which you have been called, with all humility and gentleness, with patience, bearing with one another in love, making every effort to maintain the unity of

the Spirit in the bond of peace. (Because of what Christ has done, God calls his people to lead a life worthy of his call, to live humbly with gentleness, patience, love for each other, and in peace and unity under Christ. These are guideline for living in social harmony and glorifying God who created them.)

Verses 4-5 describe the structural unity. There is one body and one Spirit, just as you were called to the one hope of your calling (Jesus), one Lord (Jesus), one faith (in what Christ has done), one baptism (into Christ Jesus), one God and Father of all (monotheism), who is above all and through all and in all. (Unity is in the Father, through the Son, and by the power of the Holy Spirit, who is above all of us and lives in and through us.)

Verses 7-8 say, But each of us was given grace according to the measure of Christ's gift. Therefore it is said, "When he ascended on high . . . he gave gifts to his people." Verse 10 says, He who descended (Christ) is the same one who ascended far above all the heavens, so he might fill all things. (It is God's desire that all things be filled and brought to unity by and through the gift and the gifts of the Spirit that he sends.) Verses 11-13 say, The gifts he gave (for the organization of structural unity) were that some would be apostles, some prophets, some evangelists, some pastors and teachers, to equip the saints for the work of ministry, for building up the body of Christ, until all of us come to the unity of the faith and of the knowledge of the Son of God, to maturity, to the measure of the full stature of Christ.

The purpose of the gifts is to build up the body of Christ, the church until all come to the knowledge and maturity of Christ and the unity of the faith. It is God's wise plan to unite all people and all social groups in union with Christ and build up the church to bring to fullness the kingdom of God. Remember the church is called to advance the kingdom of God, thus it is the channel for

God's wisdom, and God's wisdom and God's power is Christ (1 Cor 1:24), the very one who instituted the kingdom of God on earth.

Verses 14-16 say, We must no longer be children, tossed to and fro and blown about by every wind of doctrine, by people's trickery, by their craftiness in deceitful scheming. (To protect against such actions writers begin to put the faith in writing, which eventually becomes the New Testament, and begin to put more organization and structure into the faith as we see taking place here.)

Verses 15-16 say, But speaking the truth in love, we must grow up in every way into him who is the head, into Christ, from whom the whole body, joined and knit together by every ligament with which it is equipped, as each part is working properly, promotes the body's growth in building itself up in love. (This is the metaphor for mature growth for both individuals and the church. The picture is of Christ who is the head and his followers as his body the church, working together in love through the gifts of the Spirit, leavening the world with the kingdom of God, the kingdom that Christ initiated at his incarnation, his coming into the world.)

Verses 17-24 say, Now this I affirm and insist on in the Lord: you must no longer live as the Gentiles (pagans) live in the futility of their minds. They are darkened in their understanding, alienated from the life of God because of their ignorance and hardness of heart. They have lost all sensitivity and have abandoned themselves to licentiousness, greedy to practice every kind of impurity. That is not the way you learned Christ! For surely you have heard about him and were taught in him, as truth is in Jesus. You were taught to put away your former way of life, your old self, corrupt and deluded by lusts. And be renewed in the spirit of your minds, and to clothe yourself with the new self, created according to the likeness of God in true righteousness and holiness (see Rom 12:1-2, 8:1-17).

Many are alienated from the life of God because of ignorance of God's word and/or hard hearts against his truth even when exposed to it. Many are no longer sensitive to the needs of others, but are concerned with their own greedy lusts of the flesh such as lust for sex, money, material things, and power. This is not the way of Christ and his truth. God calls his people to be renewed in their minds, to put away the old self, and to put on the new self according to holiness and righteousness (see Rom 12, Col 3).

Verses 25-32 add more examples of holiness and righteousness. So then, putting away falsehood, let all of us speak the truth to our neighbors, for we are members of one another. Be angry but do not sin; do not let the sun go down on your anger (learn to deal with your anger), and do not make room for the devil. Thieves must give up stealing; rather let them labor and work honestly with their own hands, so as to have something to share with the needy. (The reason to give up stealing and to work is interesting.) Let no evil talk come out of your mouths, but only what is useful for building up, as there is need, so that your words may give grace to those who hear. And do not grieve the Holy Spirit of God, with which you were marked with a seal for the day of redemption. Put away from you all bitterness and wrath and anger and wrangling and slander, together with all malice, and be kind to one another, tenderhearted, forgiving one another, as God in Christ has forgiven you.

Chapters 5 and 6 continue the examples of holiness and righteousness. Chapter 5:1-9 says, Therefore be imitators of God, as beloved children, and live in love, as Christ loved us and gave himself up for us, a fragrant offering and sacrifice to God. But fornication and impurity of any kind, or greed, must not even be mentioned among you, as is proper among saints. Entirely out of place is obscene, silly, and vulgar talk; but instead, let there be thanksgiving. Be sure of this, that no fornicator or impure person, or one who is greedy, that is an idolater, has any inheritance in the kingdom of Christ and of God. (Note the new definition of idolatry.) Let no one deceive you with empty words, for because of these things the wrath of God comes on those who are disobedient. Therefore do not be associated with them. For once you were in darkness, but now in the Lord you are light. Live as children of light—for the fruit of the light is found in all that is good and right and true.

Verses 10-20 continue the ways of righteousness and holiness. Paul says, Try to find out what is pleasing to the Lord. Take no part in the unfruitful works of darkness, but instead expose them. For it is shameful even to mention what such people do secretly; but everything exposed by the light becomes visible, for everything that becomes visible is light. Therefore it says, "Sleeper, awake! Rise from the dead (the spiritually dead), and Christ will shine on you." Be careful then how you live, not as unwise people but as wise, making the most of the time, because the days are evil. So do not be foolish, but understand what the will of the Lord is. Do not get drunk with wine, for that is debauchery; but be filled with the Spirit, as you sing psalms and hymns and spiritual songs among yourselves, singing and making melody to the Lord in your hearts, giving thanks to God the Father at all times and for everything in the name of our Lord Jesus Christ. Much of this letter is showing what being filled with the Spirit looks like.

The following are household codes given for all those living as an extended family, which was a normal pattern of living in those particular times. The following are to be looked at more as virtues to be worked upon and developed by all people throughout time, and not to be seen as legalist rules and regulations that are timeless. The message is given in order to help guide those new Christians that are living in a stable situation to give a positive Christian witness to a people living in a certain type of culture.

Paul sets the theme for relationships between husband and wife, slaves and masters, and parents and children. It is important to be aware of the nuances of the Greek vocabulary. In all relationships verse 21 says, Be subject to one another out of reverence for Christ. (In other words give of oneself to each other; be supportive of each other. This is key to understanding the following.) Verses 22-24 say, Wives, be subject to (supportive of) your husbands as you are to the Lord. For the husband is the head of (the servant of) the wife just as Christ is the head (servant of) of the church, the body of which he is the Savior. Just as the church is subject to (supportive of) Christ, so also wives ought to be (supportive of), in everything, to their husbands. (In that society in that time, this is how the wife showed her respect for Christ and her husband. We must remember that being the head or leader to Christ meant to serve and be responsive to one's needs, not to "lord it over others.")

Verses 25-31 says, Husbands, love (be responsive to) your wives, just as Christ loved the church and gave himself up for her, in order to make her holy by cleansing her with the washing of water by the word, so as to present the church to himself in splendor, without spot or wrinkle or anything of the kind—yes, so that she may be holy and without blemish. (There can be no love greater than this.) In the same way, husbands should love their wives (respond to their needs) as they do their own bodies. He who loves his wife loves himself. For no one ever hates his own body, but he nourishes it and tenderly cares for it, just as Christ does for the church, because we are members of his body. "For this reason a man will leave his father and mother and be joined to his wife, and the two will become one flesh." This is a great mystery, and I am applying it to Christ and the church. Each of you, however, should love his wife as himself, and a wife should respect her husband. (The above words in parentheses are the translation of the Greek words by John Temple Bristow in his book titled, *What Paul Really Said About Women*, 45-47.)

The last verse is one of the two key verses in understanding this message to wife and husband. The other verse is verse 21 that says to be subject to one another out of reverence for Christ. The instructions to the wife and the husband that are located between verses 21 and 33 are how in that culture it was put into practice. For modern day people to take these verses out of context that a wife is to be subject to her husband and have it mean that she is to be in blind obedience to every whim of her husband is a distortion of these Scriptures. The respect shown between husband and wife, especially that by the husband for the wife is not like anything taught in the ancient world. Modern people after 2000 years are just beginning to understand all of its ramifications.

Chapter 6:1-3 says, Children, obey your parents in the Lord, for this is right. "Honor your father and mother"—this is the first commandment with a promise: "so that it may be well with you and you may live long on the earth." (This writer is not sure how that promise works. Experience shows that it was not meant to be understood legalistically. Parents are to be obeyed in the Lord. Not all things that parents demand from their children fit under godly instructions.) Verse 4 says, And fathers, do not provoke your children to anger, but bring them up in the discipline and instruction of the Lord. (This writer sees nowhere that children are to be pounded into submission as a form of discipline. They are to learn discipline, but how that is done varies. The one who disciplines is to do so with love as Christ does, Heb 12:5-11.)

Verses 5-8 say, slaves, obey your earthly masters with fear and trembling, in singleness of heart, as you obey Christ; not only while being watched, and in order to please them, but as slaves of Christ, doing the will of God from the heart. Render service with enthusiasm, as to the Lord and not to men and women, knowing that whatever good we do, we will receive the same again from the Lord, whether we are slaves or free.

This was good advice at a time when Christianity was a small minority, and slaves could be beaten to death for the most minor reason. So the message is whatever situation one is in at the time do what has to be done in a manner that gives glory to God. To encourage them to run away would only cause them harm. At this time slavery was a normal way of life. Later the seeds to end slavery will be planted.

Verse 9 says, And, masters, do the same to them. Stop threatening them, for you know that both of you have the same master in heaven, and with him there is no partiality. (To this author, this short verse on slavery is saying to treat your slave as you would want your master in heaven to treat you. This will eventually lead to the freedom of slaves, but it will not be for a long time. Even Christians are slow to be obedient to God's word when they are benefiting economically, politically, and socially.)

Verses 10-12 say, Finally, be strong in the Lord and in the strength of his power. Put on the whole armor of God, so that you may be able to stand against the wiles of the devil. For our struggle is not against enemies of blood and flesh, but against the rulers, against the authorities, against the cosmic powers of this present darkness, against the spiritual forces of evil in the heavenly places.

The message is that there is a cosmic battle going on in the spiritual world, and it spills over into this world. It is a battle being waged between the forces of good and the forces of evil. The forces of evil, led by the devil, are trying to draw the people of the earth into the battle by tempting then to yield to their evil ways. The only way the people of the earth can defend themselves is by putting on the armor of God. What is the armor of God and how can it be used against the devil and those under his authority?

Verses 14-17 say, Stand therefore, and fasten the belt of truth around your waist (Christ is the way, the truth, and the light), and put on the breastplate of righteousness. (Righteousness comes only in and through Christ as he lives in and through his people.) As shoes for your feet put on whatever will make you ready to proclaim the gospel of peace. (Christ is our peace.) With all these take the shield of faith (faith in Christ or Christ's faith), with which you will be able to quench all the flaming arrows of the evil one. Take the helmet of salvation, and the sword of the Spirit, which is the word of God. (In this way Satan is defeated, and one is protected from his darts and his temptation to do evil.)

Verses 18-20 say, Pray in the Spirit at all times in every prayer and supplication. To that end keep alert and always persevere in supplication for the saints. Pray also for me, so that when I speak, a message may be given to me to make known with boldness the mystery of the gospel, for which I am an ambassador in chains. Pray that I may declare it boldly, as I must speak.

Paul was in prison for his message about Christ and the kingdom Christ initiated. Paul proclaimed Christ as King, not the emperor. All the major cities had temples of emperor worship as well as temples to the Roman and local gods, and these were very closely tied into the economic success of the area. The preaching of Paul was a threat to the people of power and wealth, so they wanted him shut down (Acts 17:1-15, 19:14-40). (Instead of Paul being depressed, he prayed that he would proclaim the gospel of the kingdom more boldly.)

Verses 21-23 say, So that you also may know how I am and what

I am doing, Tychicus will tell you everything. He is a dear brother and a faithful minister in the Lord. I am sending him to you for this very purpose, to let you know how we are, and to encourage your hearts. Peace be to the whole community, and love with faith, from God the Father and the Lord Jesus Christ. Grace be with all who have an undying love for our Lord Jesus Christ. This ends the book of Ephesians.

As a way of review list some of the most important verses or thoughts the Apostle Paul is making in the letter to the Ephesians.

THE LETTER
TO THE PHILIPPIANS

The story of Paul establishing the church in Philippi is told in Acts 16:11-40. The city was located on the coast of northern Greece (Macedonia) on the Egnatian Way, the main east-west road in the Roman Empire. There were many gold, silver, and copper mines in the area. It was a Roman colony heavily populated by war veterans with a long historical background of characters like Brutus, Cassius, Mark Antony, and Caesar Augustus. Like most Roman cities there were temples to worship the Roman emperor, the Roman gods, and the local pagan gods, and they were closely tied to the economics of the area.

The Christian community established there was the first church planted in Europe, and Lydia, a woman, was the first convert. The establishment of the church in Philippi is in Acts 16. The immediate occasion of Paul's writing was the return of Epaphroditis, who had been sent by the Philippian church with aid for Paul, and who had been seriously ill while staying with Paul. So he thanks them for their gifts, and then sends them this letter.

Chapter 1 says, Paul and Timothy, who are slaves of Christ,

write this letter to the holy ones in Christ who are at Philippi in Greece. He prays that their love and knowledge will increase, and that they may discern what is of true value, so that on the day of Christ they may be pure and blameless and filled with the fruit of righteousness that comes through Christ for the glory and praise of God.

At this point Paul is in prison for his preaching. We are not sure where he is imprisoned but it is probably either in Rome or Ephesus. He tells them that even though he is in prison he is able to preach the word of God, and others are being emboldened to do the same because of his example. He tells his people not to worry about him because Christ will be magnified in his body either by life or death for, as he tells them, for him to live is Christ, and to die is gain, and he is torn between the two. He longs to depart and be with Christ, but he knows he needs to stay on earth for the benefit of the believers.

Therefore, they are to conduct themselves in a way that is worthy of Christ. They are to stand firm in the Spirit with one mind struggling together for the faith of the gospel. They have been granted, for the sake of Christ, not only to believe in him but also to suffer for him, so rejoice in the opportunity that he deems you worthy to be of service to God. This concept of suffering for Christ is an enigma to us comfortable modern Americans. History teaches that the more comfortable people become the less likely they are to be willing to suffer, and the less likely they are to make Jesus and his teachings their priority.

In chapter 2 he tells them to have the same attitude as Christ, who though he was in the form of God, emptied himself taking the form of a slave, coming in human likeness, and humbled himself, becoming obedient to death on a cross. Because of this, God exalted him and bestowed on him the honor that at the name of Jesus all should worship him. Paul then tells God's people to be of the same mind, heart, and love, and to do nothing out of selfishness, and to humbly regard others as more important than themselves, looking out for each other's interests, even more than their own. He tells them as they live in this crooked generation to work out their own salvation in fear and trembling, for God is at work in them for his good purpose. Paul tells them to shine as lights in this dark, broken world, and to do it without grumbling and complaining.

In chapter 3 Paul tells them to beware of the evil workers, and not to put their confidence in the things of the flesh. He reminds them that if anyone could be confident in the flesh, it is him, but whatever gain he had, he considered it loss for the sake of Christ. He considers it all rubbish, so that he may be found in Christ, not having any righteousness of his own based on the Mosaic law but the righteousness that comes through the faith of Christ. Paul desires most of all the righteousness that comes from God and knowing Christ and the power of his resurrection.

Paul again challenges those teaching the necessity of circumcision and following the Old Testament Mosaic food laws, purity laws, and Sabbath day work laws before Gentiles, non-Jews, can become a follower of Christ. He calls them enemies of the cross. Again he demonstrates his willingness to suffer for this belief rather than live in comfort like those false teachers that seem to follow him wherever he goes, and he will not shy away from even being conformed to a death like Christ's death.

Paul tells them that he has yet to attain perfect maturity. He has not yet obtained the goal but that he is pressing on toward the goal, the prize of God's upward calling in Christ Jesus. Then he encourages them to adopt his same attitude and not get too comfortable in their thinking and actions and to reject a boastful attitude that expresses too much confidence in their eternal destiny.

He reminds them that the final end of enemies of the cross of Christ will be destruction. Their glory is in their shame, for their minds are focused on earthly things. But for him and the followers of Christ their citizenship is in heaven, and they await a Savior who will bring all things in subjection to himself, and glorify their bodies to conform to his body. Paul's primary citizenship is not in the country of his earthly citizenship but in heaven.

In chapter 4 he urges a couple of women to end their feuding and encourages others to help them to get along with each other. Then he tells them to rejoice in the Lord and be kind to everyone, to eliminate anxiety, and be thankful, and in prayer let their requests be known to God, then the peace of God that passes all understanding will come to them. Finally he teaches them how to control their thinking. He encourages them to purify their thoughts by whatever is true, whatever is honorable, whatever is just, whatever is pure, whatever is pleasing, whatever is commendable, and if there is any excellence, or if there be any praise, think about these things. Paul says he has learned that no matter what situation he is in he can survive, for he knows how to find strength, for as he says, I can do all things through him who strengthens me. Finally, he tells them that the God they worship and represent will supply their every need (not want) through his Son, Jesus Christ.

Chapter 1 begins by stating who the letter is from and to whom it is addressed, which was the style in those times. Verses 1-2 say, Paul and Timothy, servants (literally slaves) of Christ Jesus, To all the saints in Christ Jesus who are in Philippi with the bishops and deacons: Grace to you and peace from God our Father and the Lord Jesus Christ. (Because of God's grace, his people are at peace with God and all of God's creation.)

Verses 3-6 say, I thank my God every time I remember you, constantly praying with joy in every one of my prayers for all of you, because of your sharing in the gospel from the first day until now. I am confident of this, that the one who began a good work among you will bring it to completion by the day of Jesus Christ.

Paul is encouraging them by making sure they understand that the God who began the work of Christ in and through them will also bring it to maturity and complete it. This is their hope, their confidence of faith.

Verse 7 says, It is right for me to think this way about all of you, because you hold me in your heart, for all of you share in God's grace with me, both in my imprisonment and in the defense and confirmation of the gospel. (The two major works of the church for God's people are to confirm the message of the gospel, the good news, and to defend it.) Verses 8-10 say, For God is my witness, how I long for all of you with the compassion of Jesus Christ. And this is my prayer, that your love may overflow more and more with knowledge and full insight to help you determine what is best, so that in the day of Christ you may be pure and blameless, having produced the harvest of righteousness that comes from Jesus Christ for the glory and praise of God.

Paul prays that they keep open to insight into God's knowledge so that they will continue to allow Christ to produce a harvest of righteousness in them and through them making them pure and blameless as they prepare for the day of their judgment. The Bible does not talk about love being an emotion. It is action based on knowledge and insight into Christ and his word.

Verses 12-14 say, I want you to know, beloved, that what has happened to me has actually helped to spread the gospel, that it has become known throughout the whole imperial guard and to everyone else that my imprisonment is for Christ; and most of the brothers and sisters, having been made confident in the Lord by my imprisonment, dare to speak the word with greater boldness and without fear. (A good example of a leader is overcoming adversity and encouraging others to do what they are called to do.)

Then he states in (15-19) that some proclaim Christ from envy and rivalry, but others from goodwill. These proclaim Christ out of love, knowing that I have been put here for the defense of the gospel; the others proclaim Christ out of selfish ambition, not sincerely but intending to increase my suffering in my imprisonment. What does it matter? Just this, that Christ is proclaimed in every way, whether out of false motives or true; and in that I rejoice. Yes, and I will continue to rejoice, for I know that through your prayers and the help of the Spirit of Jesus Christ that this will turn out for my deliverance.

Verse 20 says, It is my eager expectation and hope that I will not be put to shame in any way, but that by my speaking with all boldness, Christ will be exalted now as always in my body, whether by life or by death. (Paul is in prison somewhere and under Roman military guard, but his only concern is that Christ is being made known.)

Verses 21-24 say, For to me, living is Christ and dying is gain. If I am to live in the flesh, that means fruitful labor for me; and I do not know which I prefer. I am hard pressed between the two; my desire is to depart and be with Christ, for that is far better; but to remain in the flesh is more necessary for you. Since I am convinced of this, I know that I will remain and continue with all of you for your progress and joy in the faith, so that I may share abundantly in your boasting in Christ Jesus when I come to you again.

Paul's only concern in life is to live for Christ and to share with others who Christ is, what he did, and what he expects of those who call themselves followers of Christ. He prefers death so he can go to be with Christ, but he knows before that time comes, there is more work for Christ that he needs to do. His defense of the gospel is his effort to convince others of what Christ has done for them and to teach others the values of the kingdom. Christ came to establish the kingdom that is now in the process of making its impact upon the world.

So in verses 27-30 he tells them to live their life in a manner worthy of the gospel of Jesus Christ (as a citizen of the kingdom of heaven), so that, whether I come and see you or am absent and hear about you, I will know that you are standing firm in one spirit, striving side by side with one mind for the sake of the gospel (the good news of Christ and the kingdom) and are in no way intimidated by your opponents. For them this is evidence of their destruction, but of your salvation. And this is God's doing. For he has graciously granted you the privilege not only of believing in Christ, but of suffering for him as well—since you have the same struggle that you saw I had and now hear that I still have.

How many Christians does the reader know who would consider it a privilege to suffer for Christ and his teachings? Paul's constant theme in his letters involves the privilege of suffering for him. It is no wonder that so many in these modern times do not think the message of Christ and the in-breaking kingdom into the world is relevant to them. Suffering for Christ and the values of the kingdom are not something most comfortable people in America are interested in hearing or dealing with. The attitude of too many seems to be how can Christ benefit me, what can Christ do for me rather than what can I do for him and his cause.

Paul sees salvation as not only believing in Christ but as having the privilege or grace of suffering for Christ. As Christ suffered, Paul is suffering, and he offers this as encouragement for those to whom he writes who are also suffering as they stand for and with

Christ and the values of God's kingdom for its advancement into the world. The message of Christ is not just about personal salvation and one's private spirituality as many seem to think. We are missing the primary message if we stop there. This first chapter could be titled the joy of suffering for Christ. Is this the message that we hear from those who preach today?

Chapter 2:1-3 says, If then there is any encouragement in Christ, any consolation from love, any sharing in the Spirit, any compassion and sympathy, make my joy complete: be of the same mind, having the same love, being in full accord (agreement) and of one mind. Do nothing from selfish ambition or conceit, but in humility regard others better than yourselves. (He is warning them not to let their egos get in the way of their witness to Christ and to remember that following Christ means to be a servant to him and others.) Verse 4 says, Let each of you look not to your own interests, but to the interest of others. (Paul knows they are somewhat divided by petty jealousies, so he shows them the way to overcome it. The answer is to imitate Christ. Be humble, lose self and live for the well-being of others.)

Verses 5-11 say, Let the same mind be in you that was in Christ Jesus, who though he was in the form of God, did not regard equality with God as something to be exploited, but emptied himself, taking the form of a slave, being born in human likeness. And being found in human form, he humbled himself and became obedient to the point of death—even death on a cross. Therefore God highly exalted him and gave him the name that is above every name, so that at the name of Jesus every knee should bend, in heaven and on earth and under the earth, and every tongue should confess that Jesus Christ is Lord, to the glory of God the Father.

Paul calls the people of God to become slaves of Christ and imitate Christ for the glory of God. The call is to be a sacrificial offering for the love of Christ and the love of one's fellow humans. Most scholars believe Paul is quoting a hymn.

Verses 12-13 say, Therefore, my beloved, just as you have always obeyed me, not only in my presence, but in my absence, work out (demonstrate) your own salvation in fear and trembling, for it is God who is at work in you, enabling you both to will and to work for his good pleasure.

It is God who does his works in and through his people. The Father through the Son in the power of the Holy Spirit lives in and through his people as the mission of Christ continues until Christ comes to complete it. St Augustine stated in his Epistle (194.5.29) and replicated in William Most (1994, 62) "When God crowns your merits, he crowns nothing other than his own gifts." This is the idea behind working out your salvation.

Verses 14-15 say, Do all things without murmuring and arguing, so that you may be blameless and innocent children of God without blemish in the midst of a crooked and perverse generation, in which you shine like stars in the world. (In the midst of whatever perverse and crooked generation one lives, God calls his people to be shining lights.) Paul in (16-18) says, It is by holding fast to the word of life that I can boast on the day of Christ that I did not run in vain or labor in vain. But even if I am being poured out as a libation over the sacrifice and the offering of your faith (his present suffering for Christ), I am glad and rejoice with all joy—and in the same way you also must be glad and rejoice with me.

Verses 19-24 say, I hope in the Lord Jesus to send Timothy to you soon, so that I may be cheered by news of you. I have no one like him who will be genuinely concerned for your welfare. All of them are seeking their own interests, not those of Christ. But

Timothy's worth you know, how like a son with a father he has served with me in the work of the gospel. I hope therefore to send him as soon as I see how things go with me; and I trust in the Lord that I will also come soon.

Verses 25-30 say, Still, I think it necessary to send to you Epaphroditus—my brother and co-worker and fellow soldier, your messenger and minister to my need; for he has been longing for all of you, and has been distressed because you heard that he was ill. He was indeed so ill that he almost died. But God had mercy on him, and not only on him but on me also, so that I would not have one sorrow after another. I am the more eager to send him, therefore, in order that you may rejoice on seeing him again, and that I may be less anxious. Welcome him then in the Lord with all joy, and honor such people, because he came close to death for the work of Christ, risking his life to make up for those services that you could not give me.

Chapter 3:1-2 says, Finally, my brothers and sisters, rejoice in the Lord. To write the same things to you is not troublesome to me, and for you it is a safeguard. Beware of the dogs, beware of the evil workers, beware of those who mutilate the flesh. (This is a reference to those who are teaching that to become an adopted son of God, one has to be first circumcised and then obey the purity laws, food laws and Sabbath day work laws contained in the Mosaic law.)

In verses 3-6 Paul says, For it is we who are the circumcision (the people of God), who worship in the Spirit of God (or worship God through the Holy Spirit sent by the Father through Christ) and boast in Christ Jesus and have no confidence of the flesh— even though I, too, have reason for confidence in the flesh (if that were the criteria). If anyone has reason to be confident in the flesh, I have more: circumcised on the eighth day, a member of the people of Israel, of the tribe of Benjamin, a Hebrew born of Hebrews; as to the law, a Pharisee; as to zeal, a persecutor of the church; as to righteousness under the law, blameless. (Here he states his credentials as a Jew, but his point is they really do not mean anything as far as being part of the new covenant of Christ, for one is justified through Christ.)

Verses 7-9 say, Yet whatever gains I had, these I have come to regard as loss because of Christ. More than that I regard everything as loss because of the surpassing value of knowing Christ Jesus my Lord. For his sake I have suffered the loss of all things, and I regard them as rubbish, in order that I may gain Christ and be found in him, not having a righteousness of my own that comes from the (Mosaic) law, but one that comes through faith in Christ, the righteousness of God based on faith. (Faith in Christ can also be translated from the Greek as the faith of Christ, for it is the faith of Christ that led him to the cross, and it is he who brings the righteousness of God.)

Paul counts all he had in the past through the Mosaic law as nothing. All that counts now is the righteousness that comes from Christ. One is made righteous and initially added to the body of Christ because of the righteousness of Christ, because Christ has fulfilled God's promise to Abraham, not because of the Mosaic law. The Mosaic law came a long time after Abraham. Also in the past there was no absolute promise of a resurrection from the dead, but now there is a promise. Because of Christ, that promise has been made, and it begins with one being justified through Christ. It has nothing to do with the Mosaic law.

In verses 10-12 Paul says, I want to know Christ and the power of his resurrection and the sharing of his sufferings by becoming like him in his death, if somehow I may attain the resurrection of the dead. Not that I already have obtained this or have already reached the goal; but I press on to make it my own, because Christ Jesus has made me his own. (Even the Apostle Paul had not arrived to the point that he knows he will be raised. He knows he must allow God to complete his work in and through him.)

Verses 13-15 say, Beloved, I do not consider that I have made it my own; but this one thing I do: forgetting what lies behind and straining forward to what lies ahead, I press on toward the goal for the prize of the heavenly call of God in Christ Jesus. (Paul knows that he must stay steadfast in the faith until the end. He realizes that he must continue to allow Christ to work in and through him for God's grace to have its final perfection, and to reach his goal.) Then in (16) he says, Let those of us then who are mature be of the same mind; and if you think differently about anything, this too God will reveal to you. Only let us hold fast to what we have attained.

Verses 17-19 say, Brothers and sisters, join in imitating me, and observe those who live according to the example you have in us. (Paul is their mentor, their human example to follow.) For many live as enemies of the cross of Christ; I have often told you of them, and now I tell you even with tears. Their end is destruction; their god is their belly; and their glory is in their shame; their minds are set on earthly things. (The path to destruction is living for self and the things of the world, the things that Christ opposes. Their god being their belly probably has reference to the Old Testament food laws.)

Verses 20-21 say, But our citizenship is in heaven, and it is from here that we are expecting a Savior, the Lord Jesus Christ. He will transform the body of our humiliation that it may be conformed to the body of his glory, by the power that also enables him to make all things subject to himself.

The primary citizenship for the Philippians is with Rome. Secondarily, it is in Macedonia. Paul is saying that the primary citizenship with the follower of Christ is in the kingdom of God. Second, their citizenship is in the country in which they live. The choice in values the people have is between the two, but the promise of being resurrected comes from living the values of the kingdom of God. By doing this they confirm their place in God's covenant. Does the reader think most Christians in America today think as Paul thought on this issue?

Chapter 4:1 says, Therefore, my brothers and sisters, whom I love and long for, my joy and crown, stand firm in the Lord in this way, my beloved. (This actually belongs to the ending of the last chapter. The chapters, verses, and punctuation in Scripture did not come until the Middle Ages.)

Verses 2-3 say, urge Euodia and Syntyche to be of the same mind in the Lord. Yes, and I ask you also, my loyal companion, help these women, for they have struggled beside me in the work of the gospel, together with Clement and the rest of my co-workers, whose names are written in the book of life (see Ex 32:32, Ps 69:28, Dan 12:1). (No one is sure if this Clement is the one who later became a pope.)

Verses 4-7 say, Rejoice in the Lord always; again I will say, Rejoice. Let your gentleness be known to everyone. The Lord is near. Do not worry about anything, but in everything by prayer and supplication with thanksgiving let your requests be known to God. And the peace of God, which surpasses all understanding, will guard your hearts and your minds in Christ Jesus. (Paul teaches to rejoice in all circumstances, for God is working, often in ways we do not understand. Be steadfast in prayer, trust that God is working his will, eliminate worry now that prayer is made, and then accept the peace God promises he will give.)

Verses 8-9 say, Finally, beloved, whatever is true, whatever is honorable, whatever is just, whatever is pure, whatever is pleasing, whatever is commendable, if there is any excellence and if there is anything worthy of praise, think about these things. (This is teaching thought control.) Keep on doing the things that you have learned and received and heard and seen in me, and the God of peace will be with you. (Paul is their mentor and model.)

Verses 10-14 say, I rejoice in the Lord greatly that now at last you have revived your concern for me; indeed, you were concerned for me, but had no opportunity to show it. Not that I am referring to being in need; for I have learned to be content with whatever I have. I know what it is to have too little, and I know what it is to have plenty. In any and all circumstances I have learned the secret of being well-fed and of going hungry, of having plenty and of being in need. I can do all things through him who strengthens me. In any case it was kind of you to share my distress. (This is Paul's secret for survival.)

Verses 15-17 say, You Philippians indeed know that in the early days of the gospel, when I left Macedonia, no church shared with me in the matter of giving and receiving, except you alone. For even when I was in Thessalonica, you sent me help for my needs more than once. Not that I seek the gift, but I seek the profit that accumulates to your account. (His point is that God knows and sees what they have done.)

Verses 18-19 say, I have been paid in full and have more than enough; I am fully satisfied, now that I have received from Epahroditus the gifts you sent, a fragrant offering, a sacrifice acceptable and pleasing to God. And my God will fully satisfy every need of yours according to his riches in glory in Christ Jesus. (Paul assures them that God will take care of their needs. Of course, this goes without saying that needs and wants can be quite different.)

Finally verse 20 says, To our God and Father be glory forever and ever. Amen. (Paul's reason for being is to live for the glory of God.)

This ends the letter to the Philippians. As a way of review list some of the most important verses or thoughts Paul is making in this letter.

THE LETTER
TO THE COLOSSIANS

Paul wrote this letter while in prison somewhere, but we do not know where. He writes to the church in Colossae which was located in the Lycus Valley, in southwest Asia Minor (Turkey), the land of many hot springs and earthquakes. Little is known about the city. Colossians and Ephesians are similar. Seventy-three verses of Colossians are found within the one hundred-fifty five verses of Ephesians

In chapter 1 Paul and his faithful worker Timothy write to the holy ones in Colossae. He prays that they be filled with the knowledge of Christ's will through all spiritual understanding and to live a life worthy of the Lord. He says that Christ has delivered us from the power of darkness and transferred us to the kingdom of his beloved Son in whom we have redemption, the forgiveness of sins. He explains that Christ is the image of the invisible God, and in him were created all things in heaven and earth, visible and invisible. Christ is before all things and in him all things hold together. He is the head of the body the church. He is the beginning, the first born from the dead that in all things he might be preeminent, for in him all fullness was pleased to dwell, and through him to reconcile all things for him, making peace by the blood of the cross whether on earth or in heaven.

Paul states that he is now suffering afflictions for the body of Christ and he identifies his sufferings with Christ's suffering in order to continue the call to others for their redemption. There was nothing lacking in Christ's sufferings but the call to lose self for Christ must continue throughout history, and this continues the suffering of Christ. As the believer suffers for the mission of Christ, Christ suffers with the sufferer. Then he mentions the mystery which has been hidden for ages but now manifested and that mystery is Christ in you, the hope of glory. As the follower of Christ loses self for Christ, Christ lives in and through the person continuing his mission until he comes again making all things new. This is described as a mystery.

In chapter 2 he says as you received Christ Jesus the Lord, so walk in him and be rooted in him, and see that no one captivates you with an empty seductive philosophy according to human tradition according to the elemental powers of the world and not Christ, for it is in Christ that dwells the fullness of the deity. You were buried with him in baptism in which you were also raised with him bringing you to life, so do not submit again to religious rules and regulations which are not of the Lord. While they seem to have the appearance of wisdom, they are not of value.

In chapter 3 Paul says, if then you were raised with Christ, seek what is above where Christ is seated at the right hand of God. Think of what is above, not what is on earth. You have died to self, and your life is hidden with Christ in God. Put to death those parts of you that are earthly: immorality, impurity, passion, evil desire, and the greed that is idolatry. Because of these the wrath of God is coming upon the disobedient. Put away anger, fury, malice, slander, and obscene language out of your mouths. Stop lying to one another. Then he says put on, as God's chosen ones, holy and beloved heartfelt compassion, kindness, humility, gentleness, patience, bearing one another and forgiving one another. Over all these put on love, the bond of perfection, and let the peace of Christ control your hearts. Let the word of Christ dwell in you richly. Teach and admonish each other singing psalms, hymns, and spiritual songs with gratitude in your hearts to God. And whatever you do in word and deed, do everything in the name of the Lord Jesus. Then he goes over basically the same information that is in Ephesians giving wisdom for wives and husbands, children and parents, and slaves and masters.

In chapter 4 Paul says to devote yourself to prayer, and pray that God may open a door that we may speak the mystery of Christ for which I am in prison, the mystery of Christ working in and through you for the glory of God. Paul reminds them to conduct themselves wisely toward outsiders that they may make the most of their opportunity and to let their speech be gracious.

Chapter 1:1-2 says Paul, an apostle of Christ Jesus by the will of God, and Timothy our brother, To the saints and faithful brothers and sisters in Christ in Colossae: Grace to you and peace from God our Father.

Verses 3-8 say, In our prayers for you we always thank God, the Father of our Lord Jesus Christ, for we have heard of your faith in Christ Jesus and the love you have for all the saints because of the hope laid up for you in heaven. You have heard of this hope before in the word of the truth, the gospel that has come to you. Just as it is bearing fruit and growing in the whole world, so it has been bearing fruit among yourselves from the day you heard it and truly comprehended the grace of God. This you learned from Epaphras, our beloved fellow servant. He is a faithful minister on your behalf (probably established the church), and he has made known to us your love in the Spirit (the Spirit of Christ). (The idea of bearing fruit comes from John 15. The faith and love of the church at Colossae were so vibrant that people in the region were talking about it.)

Verses 9-10 say, For this reason, since the day we learned it, we have not ceased praying for you and asking that you may be filled with the knowledge of God's will in all spiritual wisdom and understanding, so that you may lead lives worthy of the Lord, fully pleasing to him, as you bear fruit in every good work and as you grow in the knowledge of God. (Growth in the knowledge of God leads to spiritual wisdom, leads to a deeper understanding of God's will, and leads to bearing fruit for God, which leads to living a life worthy of God.)

Verses 11-12 say, May you be made strong with all the strength that comes from his glorious power, and may you be prepared to endure everything with patience, while joyfully giving thanks to the Father, who has enabled you to share in the inheritance of the saints in the light. (It is God who gives his people the strength needed in order to withstand the attacks against them as they bear fruit for God and share in the inheritance of the saints, the believers. Keep in mind an inheritance is a gift as long as one remains in the family.)

Verses 13-14 say, He has rescued us from the power of darkness and transferred us into the kingdom of his beloved Son, in whom we have redemption the forgiveness of sins. (The bearing of fruit is for the advancement of the kingdom. With Jesus the kingdom has broken into the world. His followers are called to advance the kingdom. They are called to be his eyes, ears, voice, hands, and feet carrying on the mission of the kingdom, which is to transform both individuals and the world until he comes again. The metaphor is the image of Christ as the head, and the church of his followers as his body advancing the values of the kingdom in a broken, evil world.)

Matthew 13:24-52 has the good growing together with the bad, and both making an impact upon the world until the harvest (judgment). Rev 1:5-6 says, To him who loves us and freed us from our sins by his blood, and made us to be a kingdom, priests serving his God and Father, to him be glory and dominion forever and ever. Rev 5:10 says, you have made them to be a kingdom and priests serving our God and they will reign on earth. (God's people reign with Christ by allowing him to live in and through them for the advancement of the kingdom that will only be made perfect at his second coming.)

Verses 15-16 say, He (Jesus) is the image of the invisible God, the firstborn of all creation; for in him all things in heaven and on earth were created, things visible and invisible, whether thrones or dominions or powers—all things have been created through him and for him. (That means all things, seen and unseen, including people, governments and its institutions as well as the spiritual world. All are to be brought to unity under Christ and the values of the kingdom.) Verses 17-18 say, He himself is before all things, and in him all things hold together. He is the head of the body, the church; he is the beginning, the first born from the dead, so that he might come to have first place in everything.

Paul is reminding them that they are to make Christ first in their lives. This is God's purpose for them, to bring all things under subjection to Christ. The good news is not just about one's personal salvation.

Verses 19-20 sum up the reason for making Christ first in their lives. For in him (Christ) all the fullness of God was pleased to dwell, and through him God was pleased to reconcile to himself all things, whether on earth or in heaven, by making peace through the blood of the cross.

Christ is the firstborn of all creation, a symbol that he has priority in all things. God is known through Jesus Christ, and first born of the dead in Hebrew means that because of the resurrection of Jesus his followers will be resurrected. In the Hebrew culture the firstborn get the major inheritance. Thus because Christ is the firstborn Son, with firstborn being a metaphor, he gives an inheritance to us through the resurrection. The Creator God is also the Redeemer God.

Verses 21- 23 say, And you who were once estranged and hostile in mind, doing evil deeds, he has now reconciled in his fleshly body through death, so as to present you holy and blameless and irreproachable before him—provided that you continue securely established and steadfast in the faith, without shifting from the hope promised by the gospel that you heard, which has been proclaimed to every creature under heaven. (The followers of Christ stay holy and blameless provided that they remain steadfast in the faith and stay in relationship to him. By staying in relationship to Christ one continues to receive forgiveness of sins and his Spirit continues to bear fruit for God.)

Verse 24 says, I am now rejoicing in my sufferings for your sake, and in my flesh I am completing what is lacking in Christ's afflictions for the sake of the body, that is, the church. (There is nothing lacking in Christ's sufferings, but as the followers of Christ are called to continue the mission of Christ, they will suffer for his cause because the world opposes his values. This suffering continues the work that Christ began and unites the suffering of his followers to his suffering. Paul's point seems to be the kingdom and its values will not continue to transform individuals and the world and its systems if his people are not willing to stand strong for them and even suffer for them.)

Verses 25-27 say, I (Paul) became its (the church) servant according to God's commission that was given to me for you, to make the word of God fully known, the mystery that has been hidden throughout the ages and generations but has now been revealed to his saints. To them God chose to make known how great among the Gentiles are the riches of the glory of this mystery, which is Christ in you, the hope of glory.

The mystery consists of two things. First, God has chosen Christ to reconcile both Jew and Gentile, to him and to each other. Christ is the unity of all things, for all things were created through him and for him and will be brought together by him. Second, Christ lives in and through his people by the Holy Spirit making them holy and keeping them blameless as they confess their sins and continue his mission of advancing the kingdom of God in this broken world. This is a mystery according to the Apostle Paul.

Verse 28 says, It is he (Christ) whom we proclaim, warning everyone and teaching everyone in all wisdom, so that we may present everyone mature in Christ. (This is the goal and purpose of hearing God's word and having a relationship with Christ for both individuals and the church.) Paul then in (29) says, For this I toil and struggle with all the energy that he powerfully inspires within me.

In chapter 2:1-5 Paul tells them that he wants their hearts to be encouraged and united in love and to have the knowledge of God's mystery that is Christ himself in whom is hidden all the treasures of wisdom and knowledge. (According to Paul the knowledge or wisdom that is of real value is found only in Christ, who is working in and through his people.) Paul wants them to be assured of this understanding so they are not deceived by those attempting to make plausible (reasonable) arguments against them using the world's reasoning. He reminds them that he (Paul) continues struggling for them, even though he is not with them; yet he is with them in spirit, and rejoices in their steadfast faith.

Verses 6-7 say, As you therefore have received Christ Jesus the Lord, continue to live your lives in him, rooted and built up in him and established in the faith, just as you were taught, abounding in thanksgiving. See to it that no one takes you captive through philosophy and empty deceit, according to human tradition, according to the elemental spirits of the universe (the powers worldly people believed controlled the spirit world, and consequently them), and not according to Christ. For in him the whole fullness of deity dwells bodily, and you have come to fullness in him, who is the head of every ruler and authority.

He reminds them not to get caught up in the plausible arguments against them that are based on the world's thinking and to stay rooted in Christ, who is the fullness of God. It is Christ who conquered all things through the cross, and it is Christ who is in charge of all things and all authorities whether seen or unseen.

Verses 11-12 say, In him also you were circumcised with a spiritual circumcision, by putting off the body of the flesh in the circumcision of Christ; when you were buried with him in baptism, you were also raised with him through faith in the power of God, who raised him from the dead.

The same power of God that raised the Son also raises to new life those who are buried with him in baptism. Paul calls this a spiritual circumcision because the old heart is cut away and replaced with a new heart filled with the Spirit of Christ, the Holy Spirit.

Verses 13-15 say, And when you were dead in trespasses . . .

God made you alive together with him, when he forgave all our trespasses, erasing the record that stood against us with its legal demands (the need for physical circumcision and following the food, purity, and Sabbath laws). He set this aside, nailing it to the cross. He disarmed the rulers and authorities (those powers, spiritual beings that the people of the world thought controlled all things) and made a public example of them, triumphing over them in it (the cross).

Verses 16-19 say, Therefore do not let anyone condemn you in matters of food and drink or of observing festivals, new moons, or sabbaths. (This refers to the Mosaic law or any law associated with a calendar set by heavenly bodies as established by pagan religions to control the spiritual beings.) These are only a shadow of what is to come, but the substance belongs to Christ. (The purpose of the old law was to lead to Christ.) Do not let anyone disqualify you, insisting on self-abasement and worship of angels, dwelling on visions puffed up without cause by a human way of thinking, and not holding fast to the head (Christ) from whom the whole body (church), nourished and held together by its ligaments and sinews (spiritual gifts), grows with a growth that is from God. (It seems that the religion Paul is opposing is using visions of angels and spiritual beings, asceticism, and the worship of spiritual beings on Jewish holy days to placate the evil spirits that they think control their lives.)

These false teachers in the area are combining aspects of the Mosaic law with Gnosticism and the pagan religions of the area and probably mixing with it some Greek philosophy. This is the age old problem of people combining all aspects of religion into one religion in order to make it acceptable to all. Paul is teaching that all this does is to corrupt the one true religion that centers on God the Father, the Son, and the Holy Spirit. He tells them to hold fast to

Christ, who is the very image of God, and the head of the church, for it is within the church that God is at work destroying evil.

Verses 20-22 say, If with Christ you died to the elemental spirits of the universe, why do you live as if you still belonged to the world? (Since these people believed that the spirits controlled the affairs of the world, Paul is saying, if you died to these spirits, or no longer believe they control the affairs of the world, why are you acting as though they do?) Why do you submit to regulations, "Do not handle, Do not taste, Do not touch"? All these regulations refer to things that perish with use; they are simply human commands and teachings. (This is a reference to the asceticism that was made a requirement in a religion that apparently some in the church at Colossae were accepting. Ascetics live a rigorous life of do nots.)

Verse 23 says, These have indeed an appearance of wisdom in promoting self-imposed piety, humility, and severe treatment of the body, but they are of no value in checking self-indulgence. (Paul seems to be saying that when asceticism is forced upon a person as a condition of salvation, it will only produce a form of spiritual pride.)

Chapter 3:1-4 says, So if you have been raised with Christ (born of God and called to reign with Christ), seek the things that are above, where Christ is, seated at the right hand of God. Set your minds on things that are above (the values of the kingdom), not on things that are on earth (values of the world), for you have died (to self and selfish interests), and your life is hidden with Christ in God (to live for Christ and the values of the kingdom). When Christ who is your life is revealed, then you also will be revealed with him in glory.

Verse 5 says, Put to death, therefore, whatever in you is earthly:

fornication, impurity, passion, evil desire, and greed, which is idolatry. (Since greed is called idolatry it amazes this writer that the modern day church basically ignores how greed affects people today.) Verses 6-7 say, On account of these (all these things in verse 5) the wrath of God is coming on those who are disobedient. These are the ways you also once followed, when you were living that life.

Again, it is interesting that many Christians as well as our so-called Christian politicians seem to think that God's wrath is only going to come upon those with sexual sins and ignore their greed and the rampant greed of others. This writer has rarely, maybe never, heard any of these politicians or any church leader bring up the idea that God's wrath is going to fall upon those immersed in the modern day idol of greed. This writer does not remember hearing a sermon or homily on greed, which to this writer seems to be a major problem the world and America have to deal with.

Verses 8-11 continue with those things of the world that the new self no longer permits. Some more vices that also are to be eliminated are: anger, wrath, malice, slander, and abusive language from your mouth. Do not lie to one another, seeing that you have stripped off the old self with its practices and have clothed yourselves with the new self, which is being renewed in knowledge according to the image of its creator. In that renewal there is no longer Greek and Jew, circumcised and uncircumcised, barbarian, Scythian, slave and free; but Christ is all and in all. (Because the followers of Christ are born of God, Christ is in them, and all of them are made one, equal with one another. Therefore all are called to exchange their vices for the virtues of the kingdom.)

Verses 12-17 say, As God's chosen ones, holy and beloved, cloth yourselves with compassion, kindness, humility, meekness (gentleness), and patience. Bear with one another and, if anyone has a complaint against another, forgive each other; just as the Lord has forgiven you, so you also must forgive. Above all, clothe yourself with love, which binds everything together in perfect harmony. And let the peace of Christ rule in your hearts, to which indeed you were called in the one body. And be thankful. Let the word of Christ dwell in you richly; teach and admonish one another in all wisdom; and with gratitude in your hearts sing psalms, hymns, and spiritual songs to God. And whatever you do, in word and deed, do everything in the name of the Lord Jesus, giving thanks to God the Father through him. (All the above virtues and values are the result of Christ dwelling in the hearts of his people.)

The following are household codes given for all those living as an extended family, which was a normal pattern of living in those particular times. The following are to be looked at more as virtues to be worked upon and developed by all people throughout time, but not to be seen as legalist rules and regulations that are timeless. The message is given in order to help guide those new Christians that are living in a stable situation to give a positive Christian witness to a people living in a certain type of culture.

Verses 18-19 say, Wives be subject to your husbands, as is fitting in the Lord. Husbands, love your wives and never treat them harshly. (See Eph 5:21-33 for a more thorough discussion of the subject.) Verses 20-21 say, Children, obey your parents in everything, for this is your acceptable duty in the Lord. Fathers, do not provoke your children, or they may lose heart. (See Eph 6:1-4 for a more thorough discussion.)

Verses 22-25 say, Slaves, obey your earthly masters in everything, not only while being watched and in order to please them, but wholeheartedly fearing the Lord. Whatever your task, put yourself into it, as done for the Lord and not your masters, since you know that from the Lord you will receive the inheritance as your reward; you serve the Lord Jesus Christ. For the wrong doer will be paid back for whatever wrong has been done, and there is no partiality.

As stated in Ephesians, because Christians are a small minority at this time, the Christians are encouraged to not upset the stability of society in such a way that the majority within that particular society will be turned off from hearing the basic message of who Christ is, what he did, and the message of the kingdom.

Chapter 4:1 says, Masters, treat your slaves justly and fairly, for you know that you also have a master in heaven. (Those in charge of other people are to treat them as they would want God to treat them. This will eventually lead people in a different time to see the need to abolish slavery. See also the book of Philemon. Verse 1 should be included with the last chapter, for it all fits together; the following verses start a new subject. We must remember that there were no chapter and verse divisions or punctuation in Scripture until the Middle Ages.)

Verses 2-6 say, Devote yourself to prayer, keeping alert in it with thanksgiving. At the same time pray for us as well that God will open to us a door for the word, that we may declare the mystery of Christ, for which I am in prison, so that I may reveal it clearly, as I should. Conduct yourself wisely toward outsiders making the most of the time. Let your speech always be gracious, seasoned with salt, so that you may know how you ought to answer everyone.

For Paul these instructions are important. Always be in prayer about the way to get the word to others concerning the mystery of Christ. Pray that you reveal the mystery and the word clearly and answer people in a way that they will understand. In the process conduct yourself wisely to those you are trying to reach using some common sense as to the way you use your words.

In verses 7-14 he tells them he is sending Tychicus and Onesimus to them to inform them of what is happening, and so they may give encouragement to them. Paul lists those who are with him and who send greetings to them. They are Aristarchus, Mark, the cousin of Barnabas, Jesus who is called Justus, Epaphrus, who probably established the church in Colossae, Laodicea, and Hierapolis; Luke the beloved physician, and Demas. Verses 15-16 say, Give my greetings to the brothers and sisters in Laodicea, and to Nympha (not sure why a mother would give that name to her daughter) and the church in her house. And when this letter has been read among you, have it read also to the church of the Laodiceans; and see that you read also the letter from Laodicea. (Is this a lost letter that would have been included as Scripture, and if so, should it really matter? Why or why not?) Verses 17-18 say, And say to Archippus, "See that you complete the task that you have received from the Lord." I, Paul, write this greeting with my own hand. Remember my chains. Grace be with you.

This ends Paul's letter to the church at Colossae. As a way of review list some of the most important verses or thoughts Paul makes in this letter to the Colossians.

THE FIRST LETTER
TO THE THESSALONIANS

First Thessalonians written approximately in AD 51 is the first book written in the New Testament. Thessalonica was the capitol and an important commercial center located on the Egnatian Way, the main east-west Roman road, and on the best natural harbor in Macedonia. Thessalonica was very closely tied to Rome. There were temples there for the worship of the Roman emperor, the worship of Roman gods and goddesses as well as the local gods. All of these were closely tied to the economics of the land. One can read about the establishment of the church in Thessalonica in Acts 17:1-9. Paul's stay in Thessalonica was difficult, and now he writes to them from Corinth.

Chapter 1 begins with the letter by Paul, Silvanus (Silas), and Timothy to the Thessalonians located in Greece. Thanks are given to the Thessalonians for their faith, hope, and love. They had become a model for the whole area as these Gentiles had turned from idols to serving the living God, and as Paul said to await his Son from heaven whom he raised from the dead, Jesus, who delivers his people from the coming wrath.

In chapter 2 Paul said in speaking to you we were not trying to please human beings but God, who judges our hearts. We did not use flattering speech as a pretext for greed nor did we seek praise from human beings (as the wandering pseudo philosophers). We were gentle even though we imposed our weight as apostles of Christ. We were determined to share not only the good news of God but also our very selves. You are now our witnesses. We encouraged you then and now to conduct yourselves as worthy of the God who calls you into his kingdom and glory.

Paul emphasizes that we give thanks that in your receiving the word of God from us, you received it not as a human word but the word of God as it truly is, which is now at work in those of you who believe. Then he encourages them by telling them that they are suffering for the word of God just as Jesus and the prophets did.

In chapter 3 Paul encourages their love for each other to increase and abound and to strengthen their hearts and be blameless in holiness before God the Father in order to prepare for when Jesus and all the holy ones come in final glory.

In chapter 4 he tells them that God's will for them is holiness, that they refrain from immorality, and to acquire a wife in honor not in lustful passion. He tells them that God did not call any of them to live in impurity but to live in holiness, and whoever disregards this disregards God. He encourages them to progress more and more in love for one another and to aspire to live a tranquil life, to mind their own affairs, and to look for respectable work so they may conduct themselves properly toward outsiders. This way they will not have to depend on any one to live.

He tells them not to worry about those who have died, for as Jesus rose from the dead so will they. When Christ returns, the dead in Christ will rise or be with him, and then all will be caught up with them to meet the Lord in the air, and Jesus will escort them to his new creation, the new heaven and new earth. Thus we will always be with the Lord, so console each other with these words.

In chapter 5 he says we do not know when that coming will be. We just know he will come like a thief in the night, at a time when everyone is saying all is peace and security, then suddenly disaster for them will come. But Paul tells them they are not in darkness like those to whom disaster will come, for they are children of the light. So, he encourages them to stay alert and sober and to put on the breastplate of faith and love and the helmet that is the hope for salvation, for God has not destined them for wrath but to gain salvation through the Lord Jesus Christ who died that we may live with him.

Therefore, Paul says, encourage one another and build one another up. Then, he reminds them to respect those who are laboring among them in the Lord, those who are over you in the Lord and who admonish you. Show them special esteem. Finally, he says admonish the idle, cheer the fainthearted, support the weak, and be patient with all. Rejoice always and pray without ceasing. In all circumstances give thanks, and do not quench (stifle) the Spirit. He tells them to refrain from every sort of evil, and to test everything to see if it is of God.

Chapter 1:1-5 says, Paul, Silvanus, and Timothy, To the church of the Thessalonians in God the Father and the Lord Jesus Christ: Grace to you and peace. We always give thanks to God for all of you and mention you in our prayers, constantly remembering before our God and Father your work of faith and labor of love and steadfastness of hope in our Lord Jesus Christ. For we know, brothers and sisters beloved by God, that he has chosen you, because our message of the gospel (good news) came to you not in

word only, but also in the power of the Holy Spirit and with full conviction; just as you know what kind of persons we proved to be among you for your sake.

Faith, hope, and love are the three theological virtues, and all three of them are works of God's grace worked in and through God's people. If one has faith, one will have hope and if one has both faith and hope, one will have love. When this happens, the word of God is working its power in union with the Holy Spirit.

Verses 6-8 say, And you became imitators of us and of the Lord, for in spite of persecution you received the word with joy inspired by the Holy Spirit, so that you became an example to all the believers in Macedonia and Achaia. For the word of the Lord has sounded forth from you not only in Macedonia and Achaia, but in every place your faith in God has become known, so that we have no need to speak about it. For the people of those regions report about us what kind of welcome we had among you, and how you turned to God from idols, to serve a living and true God, and wait for his Son from heaven, whom he raised from the dead—Jesus, who rescues us from the wrath to come.

The key is the working of God's word by the power of the Holy Spirit. The Thessalonians were transformed from the worship of dead idols to the living God by the Holy Spirit working through the word of God, and then they became the examples God called them to be.

The persecution and suffering they are experiencing is from various areas. Most of the Jews in the synagogue rejected Jesus as the Messiah and rejected the teaching that he rose from the dead. They were also upset that the Gentiles (the God fearers) in the synagogue were leaving to form a church. Some of these Jews went to the market place and rounded up those who believed that these new Christians were acting contrary to the emperor, saying there is another king named Jesus who is advocating his overthrow by establishing another kingdom.

The message of Paul and the early Christians is that Jesus is the Lord and Savior who is bringing peace to the world. The emperor is not the lord and savior and he is not to be worshiped as he claims. Furthermore, the emperor's peace is established and maintained by violence, while Christ's peace is brought and maintained by love and non-violence. Not only that, the emperor's kingdom will end, but the kingdom of God's Son will never end. This challenges the Pax Roma (Roman Peace) and upsets the politicians in power as well as the merchants, for their power and wealth are tied in to the activity of the emperor cult and worship as well as the local worship of the Roman and pagan gods.

Chapter 2:1-4 says, You yourselves know, brothers and sisters, that our coming to you was not in vain, but though we had already suffered and been shamefully mistreated at Philippi, as you know, we had courage in our God in spite of great opposition. For our appeal does not spring from deceit or impure motives or trickery, but just as we have been approved by God to be entrusted with the message of the gospel, even so we speak, not to please mortals, but to please God who tests our hearts. (Paul reminds them of the persecution he, Timothy, and Silvanus suffered for them, and that God had approved them after testing their hearts and seeing that they sought to please God instead of humans.)

Verses 5-8 say, As you know and as God is our witness, we never came with words of flattery or with a pretext for greed; nor did we seek praise from mortals, whether from you or from others, though we might have made demands as apostles of Christ. But we were gentle among you, like a nurse tenderly caring for her own children.

So deeply do we care for you that we are determined to share with you not only the gospel of God but also our own selves, because you have become very dear to us.

Verses 9-12 say, You remember our labor and toil, brothers and sisters; we worked night and day, so that we might not burden any of you while we proclaimed to you the gospel of God. You are witnesses, and God also, how pure, upright, and blameless our conduct was toward you believers. As you know we dealt with each one of you like a father with his children, urging and encouraging you and pleading that you lead a life worthy of God, who calls you into his own kingdom and glory.

Paul's goal was always to help people understand that God is calling them to be a part of his kingdom that is now making its mark upon the world, and they are to lead a life worthy of that call in order to play their part in advancing the kingdom.

Verse 13 says, We also constantly give thanks to God for this, that when you received the word of God that you heard from us you accepted it not as a human word but as what it really is, God's word, which is also at work in you believers. (There is no doubt in Paul's mind that what he taught them was God's word, and that God's word bears fruit through the Holy Spirit within those who accept it as such. Peter agreed in 2 Peter 3:16 that Paul spoke God's word, even though some were twisting it to their own destruction.)

Verses 14-16 say, For you, brothers and sisters, became imitators of the churches of God in Christ Jesus that are in Judea. For you suffered the same things from your own compatriots as they did from the Jews, who killed both the Lord Jesus and the prophets (the leaders of the Jews, not all Jews killed Jesus and the prophets), and drove us out; they displease God and oppose everyone by hindering us from speaking to the Gentiles so that they may be saved. Thus they have been constantly filling up the measure of their sins; but

God's wrath has overtaken them at last. (Some Jews in the area were causing much suffering among the Christians. The background is in Acts 17:1-9. God's wrath overtaking them probably has reference to the idea that the Jews causing the problem were not succeeding.)

Verses 17-18 say, As for us, brothers and sisters, when, for a short time, we were made orphans by being separated from you—in person not in heart—we longed with great eagerness to see you face to face. For we wanted to come to you—certainly I, Paul, wanted to again and again—but Satan blocked our way. (Paul believes a real Satan is at work in the world.) Verses 19-20 say, For what is our hope or joy or crown of boasting before our Lord Jesus at his coming? Is it not you? Yes, you are our glory and joy! (Because the church has survived, Paul will present them at the coming of the Lord as his joyful reward.)

Chapter 3:1-5 says, Therefore when we could bear it no longer (the persecution), we decided to be left alone in Athens; and we sent Timothy, our brother and co-worker for God in proclaiming the gospel of Christ, to strengthen and encourage you for the sake of your faith, so that no one would be shaken by these persecutions. (The persecutions are obviously very intense, and Paul is concerned that they might lose their faith.) Indeed, you yourselves know that this is what we are destined for (suffering). In fact, when we were with you, we told you beforehand that we were to suffer persecution; so it turned out as you know. For this reason when I could bear it no longer, I sent to find out about your faith; I was afraid that somehow the tempter had tempted you and that our labor had been in vain. (As in 2:18 Paul is concerned with the damage Satan is capable of doing.)

Verses 6-10 say, But Timothy has just now come to us from you, and has brought us the good news of your faith and love. He has told us also that you always remember us kindly and long to see us—just as we long to see you. For this reason, brothers and sisters, during all our distress and persecution we have been encouraged about you through your faith. For we now live (abundantly and eternally), if you continue to stand firm in the Lord. How can we thank God enough for you in return for all the joy that we feel before our God because of you? Night and day we pray most earnestly that we may see you face to face and restore whatever is lacking in your faith. (Paul is encouraged that through all the persecutions their faith has remained steadfast but wants to come to strengthen them all the more.)

Verses 11-13 say, Now may our God and Father himself and our Lord Jesus direct our way to you. And may the Lord make you increase and abound in love for one another and for all, just as we abound in love for you. And may he so strengthen your hearts in holiness that you may be blameless before our God and Father at the coming of our Lord Jesus with all the saints. (Through all the persecutions led by Satan, the faith and love of the Thessalonians has remained fairly strong.)

Chapter 4:1-2 says, Finally, brothers and sisters, we ask and urge you in the Lord Jesus that, as you learned from us how you ought to live and to please God . . . you should do so more and more. For you know what instructions we gave you through the Lord Jesus. (Learning to live to please God is a most important teaching from Paul.)

Verses 3-8 say, For this is the will of God, your sanctification (growing in holiness): that you abstain from fornication (sex outside of marriage); that each one of you know how to control your own body in holiness and honor, not with lustful passion, like the Gentiles who do not know God; that no one wrong or exploit a brother or sister in this matter, because the Lord is an avenger in all these things, just as we already told you before hand and solemnly warned you. For God did not call us to impurity but to holiness. Therefore whoever rejects this rejects not human authority but God, who also gives his Holy Spirit to you.

Apparently sexual promiscuity was rampant in the area. The worship of Dionysius was especially popular, and the Phallus was the primary symbol. Dionysius was the god of wine and fertility. The pseudo-philosophers who earned their wages by gathering people and teaching their ideas were often very promiscuous in private. Also the Romans were known for their wild parties and orgies involving drunkenness and sex in the open.

Verses 9-12 say, Now concerning love of the brothers and sisters, you do not need to have anyone write to you, for you yourselves have been taught by God to love one another; and indeed you do love all the brothers and sisters throughout Macedonia. But we urge you beloved to do so more and more, to aspire to live quietly, to mind your own affairs, and to work with your hands, as we directed you, so that you may behave properly toward outsiders, and be dependant on no one.

They are not to live in a way that brings unnecessary censure on them from society. As a small minority their goal is to attract people so they can hear and be open to God's word. So Paul encourages them to be industrious, control their sex lives, and be known for their love, and not live like the people in their culture who are bound for the wrath of God. Paul's letter constantly encourages them in their persecutions and sufferings to be steadfast in their faith, hope, and love so that the planting of God's kingdom in Thessalonica does not fade away and die.

Verses 13-18 say, But we do not want you to be uninformed, brothers and sisters, about those who have died, so that you may not grieve as others do who have no hope. For since we believe that Jesus died and rose again, even so, through Jesus, God will bring with him those who have died. For this we declare to you by the word of the Lord, that we who are alive, who are left until the coming of the Lord, will by no means precede those who have died. For the Lord himself, with a cry of command, with the archangel's call and with the sound of God's trumpet, will descend from heaven, and the dead in Christ will rise first. Then we who are alive, who are left, will be caught up in the clouds together with them to meet the Lord in the air; and so we will be with the Lord forever. Therefore encourage one another with these words.

This is all apocalyptic language to give comfort to those in Christ that the living and the dead will be together with Christ, so it is wise to be careful in trying to exactly describe how things will be. He is also saying it is Christ's arrival that will bring justice and peace to the world not the emperor's arrival.

This whole section is for the encouragement of the Thessalonians. Paul uses the apocalyptic literature of eschatology (end times) to describe this event. The Thessalonians, as all the followers of Jesus, are the eschatological people of God, the people of the kingdom that has already broken into the earth but has not yet come in its final perfection. In these verses in order to encourage the Thessalonians to persevere in their suffering, Paul talks about a time of judgment.

The time involving Christ coming is called the *parousia*. The word is not an OT word, but is borrowed from the court of Roman princes and emperors. According to Wright (2005, 55, 142) it was used when the Roman emperor returned to Rome after a victory in battle. He is making his parousia, his presence as opposed to his absence. Paul is saying what counts is the parousia (presence) of

Jesus, and not the Roman emperor. The idea in his return to Zion is not that his followers go to heaven but that they meet him in the air where he escorts them back to earth where he is establishing something new.

Paul's concern in AD 51 with the Thessalonians was not that he thought Jesus was coming in that time, as he will soon say no one knows when that will be. There is no literature of those times that talks about the world ending in those times. Jesus told them to take the message into all the world baptizing in the name of the Father, the Son, and the Holy Spirit, and the apostles and disciples are following his command. So Paul's primary concern is that he plant stable Jewish-Gentile churches on Gentile soil before the Day of the Lord (wrath of God) comes upon Jerusalem and the temple, which happens in AD 70, and is a coming of Jesus in that a judgment of God is made that confirms Jesus' fulfillment concerning what would happen to Jerusalem and the temple.

Anytime in Scripture when God comes in clouds it is a metaphor for God making an announcement or judgment. Paul is saying that when that occurs, there will be turmoil, so Paul wants churches planted to take advantage of the situation. Remember the Day of the Lord, a time of judgment and renewal, happens numerous times according to Scripture. The fall of Jerusalem and the temple is a Day of the Lord just as his end time coming will be a Day of the Lord. So this metaphor that Paul is using can be applied to both times. Often times metaphors are used to express theology or principles that have multiple applications.

Chapter 5:1-3 says, Now concerning the times and the seasons, brothers and sisters, you do not need to have anything written to you. For you yourselves know very well that the day of the Lord will

come like a thief in the night. When they say, "There is peace and security," then sudden destruction will come upon them, as labor pains come upon a pregnant woman, and there will be no escape. (In Paul's mind he is first referring to what is going to happen in Jerusalem, but it will also be at the final coming of Jesus.)

Verses 4-10 say, But you, beloved, are not in darkness, for that day to surprise you like a thief; for you are all children of light and children of the day; we are not of the night or of darkness. So then let us not fall asleep as others do, but let us keep awake and be sober; for those who sleep sleep at night, and those who are drunk get drunk at night. But since we belong to the day, let us be sober, and put on the breastplate of faith and love, and for a helmet the hope of salvation. For God has destined us not for wrath (such as what will occur in Jerusalem as Jesus constantly foretold) but for obtaining our salvation through our Lord Jesus Christ, who died for us, so that whether we are awake or asleep (the word Paul uses for those who die in Christ) we may live with him (Christ).

Verses 11-15 say, Therefore encourage one another and build up each other, as indeed you are doing. But we appeal to you, brothers and sisters, to respect those who labor among you, and have charge of you in the Lord and admonish you; esteem them very highly in love because of their work. Be at peace among yourselves. And we urge you beloved, to admonish the idlers, encourage the fainthearted, help the weak, be patient with all of them. See that none of you repays evil for evil, but always seek to do good to one another and to all.

Verses 16-22 say, Rejoice always, pray without ceasing, give thanks in all circumstances; for this is the will of God in Christ Jesus for you. (This is a very difficult task.) Do not quench the Spirit. (The Holy Spirit wants to bear fruit for God, but because of our other interests we can stifle it.) Do not despise the words of prophets, but test everything (to see if it is of the faith of the apostles); hold fast to what is good; abstain from every form of evil.

The prophets both old and new apply the virtues, values and vision of the kingdom to individuals and society and call both to repentance. That is how everything is tested and how one holds fast to what is good and abstains and challenges the evil that is working in society through the working of Satan and his demons. This is how God's word works in and through his people.

Verses 23-24 say, May the God of peace himself sanctify you entirely (not partly but entirely); and may your spirit and soul and body (the whole person) be kept sound and blameless at the coming of our Lord Jesus Christ. The one who calls you is faithful, and he will do this.

This sanctification is done by God's people continually allowing Christ to live the virtues, values, and vision of God in and through them through the working of the Holy Spirit and when they fall short, receiving God's forgiveness through confession of sin and receiving the body and blood of Christ in Holy Communion.

Finally verses 25-28 say, Beloved, pray for us. Greet all the brothers and sisters with a holy kiss (a type of warm greeting). I solemnly command you by the Lord that this letter be read to all of them (churches). The grace of the Lord Jesus Christ be with you.

This ends the letter of 1 Thessalonians. As a way of review list some of the most important verses or thoughts Paul makes in this letter.

THE SECOND LETTER
TO THE THESSALONIANS

Again it is Paul, Silvanus, and Timothy who write to the church in Thessalonica located in Greece. They thank God because the faith of the Thessalonians is flourishing and their love for one another is growing more and more. Paul says they boast about the Thessalonians regarding their endurance in all the afflictions and persecutions they are enduring because of Christ. Their faith and love are evidence that they are worthy of the kingdom of God for which they are suffering. At the coming of Christ Paul tells them that God will judge those who are persecuting them. They will pay the penalty of eternal ruin, separated from the presence of the Lord for not obeying the good news of God. Paul prays that God will continue to make the Thessalonian church worthy of his calling and bring to fulfillment their every effort of faith and good purpose.

In chapter 2 he says with regard to the coming of the Lord do not be alarmed by any statement that the Day of the Lord is already here. This tells us that they thought the Day of the Lord Paul was talking about was to occur within history and not to end history. Paul tells them it has not occurred yet. He says, Do not be deceived in any way, for the apostasy must come first, then the lawless one, the one doomed to perdition, who opposes and exalts himself above every so called god and object of worship and sits himself in the temple, claiming he is God. For the time being he is restrained but will be revealed in his time.

Paul says that the mystery of lawlessness is now at work, but the one who restrains him is only doing so for the present until he is removed from the scene. Then the lawless one, who is empowered and led by Satan and the deceit of his miracles, will be revealed whom the Lord Jesus will kill with his breath rendering him powerless, but not before many are led astray and believe his lies.

Is Paul talking literally, cosmically, or metaphorically? In apocalyptic literature it is always difficult to know. This lawless one is obviously some political power with religious authority. People of power often attempt to have some form of religious authority backing them in order to convince the masses of people to follow them. Paul tells the Thessalonians to stand firm and hold fast the traditions that you were taught by him either by oral statement or written letter. This letter and 1 Thessalonians are the first writings of the New Testament. The threat against the early Christian teachings is one of the major reasons the Christians decided it was important to put in writing what they believe and hope to accomplish.

In chapter 3 Paul requests that they pray for him, so that the word of the Lord may spread. He tells them that the Lord is faithful and will strengthen them, and guard them against the evil one. He tells them to shun anyone who conducts himself in a disorderly way and not according to the tradition received from us. He reminds them Paul, Silvanus, and Timothy work at earning their living with their hands so they would not have to depend on the church as they taught them the gospel (good news) and the apostolic tradition. He encourages them to use his work ethic as their model. Some must have been taking advantage of the compassion of the church by trying to live off the church's charity, so Paul tells them, if anyone was unwilling to work, neither should that person eat. Everyone has a responsibility to contribute as long as they are able and as long as there are jobs to be had. Then he reminds them to do what is right and good.

∽∂∾

Chapter 1:1-5 says, Paul, Silvanus, and Timothy, To the church of the Thessalonians in God our Father and the Lord Jesus Christ: Grace to you and peace from God our Father and the Lord Jesus Christ. We must always give thanks to God for you, brothers and sisters, as is right because your faith is growing abundantly, and the love of everyone of you for one another is increasing. Therefore we ourselves boast of you among the churches of God for your steadfastness and faith during all your persecutions and the afflictions that you are enduring. This is evidence of the righteous judgment of God, and intended to make you worthy of the kingdom of God, for which you are also suffering. (Paul believes people must be worthy of the kingdom of God, and being willing to suffer for the values of the kingdom is a primary way of being made worthy. Does the reader think most American Christians are able to resonate with this as they live in and for their comfort?)

Paul in verses 6-8 says, For it is indeed just of God to repay with affliction those who afflict you, and to give relief to the afflicted as well as to us, when the Lord Jesus is revealed from heaven with his mighty angels in flaming fire, inflicting vengeance on those who do not know God and on those who do not obey the gospel of our Lord Jesus. (A day is coming when God will make all things right, and God will bring suffering and affliction on those who made others suffer because of their rejection and disobedience to God's call. God comforts the afflicted and afflicts the comfortable.)

Verses 9-12 say, These will suffer the punishment of eternal destruction, separated from the presence of the Lord and from the glory of his might, when he comes to be glorified by his saints (believers) and to be marveled at on that day among all who have believed, because our testimony to you was believed. To this end we always pray for you, asking that our God will make you worthy of his call and will fulfill by his power every good resolve and work of faith, so that the name of our Lord Jesus may be glorified in you, and you (may be glorified) in him, according to the grace of our God and the Lord Jesus Christ.

For those made worthy of God's call by glorifying him in all things, God will glorify them. God made them worthy through his power by fulfilling their good resolve and faith. This goes back to Paul's statement in Phil 2:12-13 that says, work out your own salvation in fear and trembling; for it is God who is at work in you, enabling you both to will and to work for his good pleasure. God's people are to be a channel to continue the work of Christ. What does the reader think about the statement by Paul about God repaying and afflicting with vengeance the enemies of Christ?

Chapter 2:1-4 says, As to the coming of our Lord Jesus Christ and our being gathered together to him, we beg, you, brothers and sisters, not to be quickly shaken in mind or alarmed, either by spirit or by word or by letter, as though from us, to the effect that the day of the Lord is already here. Let no one deceive you in any way; for that day will not come unless the rebellion comes first and the lawless one is revealed, the one destined for destruction. He opposes and exalts himself above every so-called god or object of worship, so that he takes his seat in the temple of God, declaring himself to

be God. Wright (2005, 140-145) says that all of this is leading up to and fulfilled in AD 70 with the destruction of Jerusalem and the temple just as Jesus foretold. As stated parousia is not an Old Testament word. It was used for the Roman emperors when their presence was made known. Jesus' presence is made known in AD 70 when what he foretold comes true.

From Paul's day to our day people spread the rumor that the Day of the Lord is happening now or is soon to happen. Paul tells them in AD 51 that the Day of the Lord is not yet, for the rebellion and appearance of the lawless one has yet to take place. Who that is and what it is about is not specified by Paul, but as usual it is subject to many theories. This writer believes Paul is thinking that this Day of the Lord is first about the destruction of the temple and Jerusalem, which then can be linked analogically with the last judgment and the renewal of creation, which is also called the Day of the Lord. In this situation Paul is probably referring to the Roman emperor as the lawless one who declares himself as God. He is the lawless one because he believes he is a law unto himself and believes himself to be a god; his titles include the lord and savior who has brought peace to the earth. He with his Roman army will then destroy the city of Jerusalem and the temple, the religious center for the Jews.

The Day of the Lord (2 Peter 3:10) will be preceded by false prophets, persecutions, and a "desolating sacrilege" (see 1 Mac 1, Dan 9:20-27,11:31, 12:11, Mt 24, Lk 21:5-36). The symbols of the many days of the Lord are all interrelated, which is a major reason they are difficult to put in a chronological time line. But these all occurred before and at the destruction of the temple and Jerusalem in 70 AD.

Verses 5-8 say, Do you not remember I told you these things when I was still with you? And you know what is now restraining him, so that he may be revealed when his time comes. (They knew what was restraining him, but we do not know.) For the mystery of lawlessness is already at work, but only until the one who restrains it is removed. And then the lawless one will be revealed, whom the Lord Jesus will destroy with the breath of his mouth, annihilating him by the manifestation of his coming.

Again keep in mind the metaphorical nature of apocalyptic literature, which is primarily to express theology. This can also mean God's people will overcome and defeat the lawless one and his work through the presence of Christ working in them. If Paul meant Christ would literally come in that time and defeat the lawless one and Satan's work, then Paul was wrong. If Paul was talking about the end time only, then he was misleading the Thessalonians about what was to happen soon to ease their persecution (see v 7), and he is ignoring what Christ foretold about Jerusalem and the temple. The fact is there is practically no literature at the time that was predicting the literal end of the world.

Verses 9-12 say, The coming of the lawless one is apparent in the working of Satan, who uses all power, signs, and wonders, and every kind of wicked deception for those who are perishing, because they refused to love the truth and so be saved. For this reason God sends them a powerful delusion, leading them to believe what is false. So that all who have not believed the truth but took pleasure in unrighteousness will be condemned.

We can not logically put this all together because it is apocalyptic literature. But the themes and symbolism are there for the Day of the Lord in reference to both the end time and the "desolating sacrilege" of the temple and destruction of Jerusalem, which will occur in less than twenty years in Paul's time period. The themes and symbols for either Day of the Lord can easily be understood while actual historical events are very difficult to pinpoint. Beware of those who apply all of this to the end of the known world, those who think they know the exact chronological history and exact historical events of what Paul is in reference to. These people have been wrong time after time throughout history because they ignore the nature of the literature. These people are easily identified on radio, television, and their best selling books. Their manipulation of the Scriptures to their interest attracts those not educated in the methods of biblical interpretation and consequently they are easily misled.

Verses 13 says, But we must always give thanks to God for you, brothers and sisters beloved by the Lord, because God chose you as the first fruits for salvation through sanctification by the Spirit and through belief in the truth. (Salvation begins by belief in God's truth, but then sanctification by the Spirit must take place where the Spirit bears fruit within those who believe for the advancement of the kingdom. Paul talks about this in all his letters, so for those who say Paul believes the world was going to end soon does not make sense.)

Verses 14-15 say, For this purpose he called you through our proclamation of the good news, so that you may obtain the glory of our Lord Jesus Christ. So then, brothers and sisters, stand firm and hold fast to the traditions that you were taught by us, either by word of mouth or by letter. (The traditions came by letter and word of mouth.)

Verses 16-17 say, Now may our Lord Jesus Christ himself and God our Father, who loved us and through grace gave us eternal comfort and good hope, comfort your hearts and strengthen them in every good work and word.

Chapter 3:1-5 says, Finally, brothers and sisters, pray for us, so that the word of the Lord may spread rapidly and be glorified

everywhere, just as it is among you, and that we may be rescued from wicked and evil people; for not all have faith. But the Lord is faithful; he will strengthen you and guard you from the evil one. And we have confidence in the Lord concerning you, that you are doing and will go on doing the things that we command. May the Lord direct your hearts to the love of God and to the steadfastness of Christ.

Verses 6-9 say, Now we command you, beloved, in the name of our Lord Jesus Christ to keep away from believers who are living in idleness and not according to the tradition that they received from us. For you yourselves know how you ought to imitate us; we were not idle when we were with you, and we did not eat anyone's bread without paying for it; but with toil and labor we worked night and day, so that we might not burden any of you. (Paul was a tentmaker.) This was not because we do not have the right, but in order to give you an example to imitate. (The teacher had a right to be paid, but because Paul did not want to take money from them, he worked at his trade.)

Verses 10-12 say, For even when we were with you, we gave you this command: Anyone unwilling to work should not eat. For we hear that some of you are living in idleness, mere busybodies, not doing any work. Now such persons we command and exhort in the Lord Jesus Christ to do their work quietly and to earn their own living.

What that meant then and what it means today must take into consideration the different environments. It assumes there are jobs that pay a living wage that can support a family. It is not to be used as it is by the comfortable in our times to denigrate the welfare system and those needing government assistance to survive.

Verses 13-17 say, Brothers and sisters, do not be weary in doing what is right. Take note of those who do not obey what we say in this letter; have nothing to do with them, so that they may be ashamed. Do not regard them as enemies, but warn them as believers. Now may the Lord of peace himself give you peace at all times in all ways. The Lord be with all of you. I, Paul, write this greeting with my own hand. This is the mark in every letter of mine; it is the way I write. The grace of the Lord Jesus Christ be with all of you.

As a way of review list some of the most important verses or thoughts in 2 Thessalonians.

THE FIRST LETTER TO TIMOTHY

Timothy, Titus, and Philemon are called the Pastoral Epistles. The church now has a definite organized leadership that is trying to preserve the traditions of the past. Paul is the voice of apostolic authority in what is fast becoming a post apostolic age. As usual authorship is not easy to discern. Many think the author may have been a later disciple of Paul. Others believe the author is Paul as he writes to Timothy, his child in the faith, who is leading the church in Ephesus located in Asia Minor (Turkey). He tells him to instruct certain people not to teach false doctrine. Some were deviating from the apostolic faith promoting myths, endless genealogies, and endless speculations turning to meaningless talk and wanting to be teachers of the law but without understanding what they were saying. He said we know the law is good, but it is not meant for the righteous person in Christ but is for the unholy to realize their ungodliness and through that realize their need for Christ.

Paul states that Christ Jesus came into the world to save sinners and Paul says he was foremost in sin, but he saw his need for Christ and was led to him. Paul states some are rejecting conscience and making a shipwreck of the faith. Paul is telling Timothy to make sure that sound teaching prevails. The old law of the Old Testament is be used in the proper manner and not to be used for fanciful and speculative theories but to lead people to Christ who is the promise and fulfillment of the law.

In chapter 2 Paul asks for prayers, supplications, petitions, and thanksgivings for everyone such as government leaders and all in authority that we may lead a quiet and tranquil life in all devotion and dignity. He says this is good and pleasing to God our Savior who wills everyone to be saved and come to knowledge of the truth, for there is one God and one mediator between God and the human race, Christ Jesus, who gave himself as a ransom for all. His prayer is that men should pray lifting up holy hands without anger and argument.

Paul says that women should adorn themselves with proper conduct, dressing modestly not wanting to attract attention with their dress, and be in self control. Women who have reverence for God are to impress with their good deeds not their physical qualities. Then, he says women are to be silent in the church. They are not to have authority over or teach men because of original sin beginning with Eve. He says they can be saved by honoring and worshiping God by doing their God-given responsibility of motherhood, being fruitful and having children, provided they persevere in faith, love, holiness, and in self control.

The Roman Catholics are still holding on to this teaching of Paul to some extent as are fundamentalist Protestants. Most mainline Protestant churches believe this was valid for the culture of the time when in the Old Testament and the Jewish religion, women were the property of men and were not permitted any education including religious teachings. In public they were not even to be seen talking to anyone but their husband. Since this is no longer the case, this teaching is no longer valid. Most mainline churches do not see this as well as many of the regulations of the New Testament as timeless rules.

More often they look for the virtues, values, and the principles behind the teachings for what may be timeless. It is their belief that because Christianity at this time was a small minority, it would often go along with many cultural customs until the time was ripe for change. They did this in order to not conflict too much with the culture of the time. Their primary goal was to attract people to Christ so his message could be heard, and then as time went on, the seed of his deeper message could take root. The idea behind much mainline Protestant thinking is that church customs can change as culture changes, but who Christ is and his teachings in the proper context do not change. The biblical problem throughout history has been trying to discern what was a church custom and what was not.

Chapter 3 gives qualifications for ministers such as bishops and deacons, and interestingly enough for women. To some the qualifications for women come in the deacon orders. The controversy is: Does that mean women could be deacons? Or was this for wives of deacons? For those who believe that women should be silent in the church as stated in the first chapter, this chapter now states bishops are to have one wife. Should one be ignored and the other followed? How should this list of rules be understood?

If it is all culturally bound, then all of it is subject to the changing times, or can we pick and choose the ones we want? Are these to be timeless rules? Others say that Paul did not really write this about women and the qualifications for Holy Orders. It was added by a scribe much later in Christian history. The problem with that is it was accepted into the canon as inspired Scripture. Read it and see what you think.

The problem for Roman Catholics, the Orthodox, and Fundamentalists is binding one as church law but not the other. Another interesting point for Catholics is they teach that church law can change. So the question is why is one changed and the other not? Their teaching that none of the apostles were women is challenged even by some of their own scholars. Of course these issues are for those within those churches to wrestle with and not for those outside those churches to use to condemn them. No church has reached perfection, even though within every church one may find some members who think their church is the one that has reached perfection.

Chapter 4 talks about the last time and a false use of asceticism. According to Scripture the last time is the last age and it began with the shedding of Christ's blood, his resurrection, and his sending the Holy Spirit as a deposit in the church on the day of Pentecost (Acts 2:17). In the last time some will turn away from the faith by paying attention to deceitful spirits and demonic instructions. They deny marriage and teach abstinence from foods that God created to be received with thanksgiving for those who know and believe the truth. The writer says that everything created by God is good and nothing is to be rejected if received in thanksgiving, for it is made holy by the invocation of God in prayer. This teaching of asceticism was coming from those who said salvation depended on Jewish food laws and being celibate. This was a form of Christian Gnosticism later declared a false teaching.

The writer tells Timothy to give sound teaching to these people that is nourished from the word of faith. Command and teach these things, and let no one have contempt for your youth. Set an example in speech, conduct, faith, love, and purity. Attend to the reading, the public reading of scripture, exhortation and teaching, and do not neglect the gift conferred on you in Holy Orders. Be absorbed in them so that your progress may be evident to everyone. He encourages them to attend to themselves and their teaching, persevere in both tasks, for by doing so you will save both yourself and others. Christian Gnosticism was primarily developed from speculation about myths and genealogy.

Chapter 5 says not to rebuke an older man. Treat him as your father, older women as mothers, younger men and women as brothers and sisters with complete purity. Then he has rules for widows who are to be treated with respect, and to remarry, if they are young. Elders, who are also called presbyters, from which comes the word priest, are to be paid. Those who preside well, and especially those who preach and teach, are worthy of double honor.

In chapter 6 there are rules for slaves and masters, both are called to be Christ like in their dealings with each other, so that Christianity will not have a bad reputation in their particular culture. In the rest of chapter 6 he urges Timothy to teach the things of Christ and the apostles, for those who do not are morbid and conceited and nothing but trouble will come from these false teachings. He reminds them that we brought nothing into the world and will take nothing out of it, so if we have food and clothing, be content with that. They are not to be greedy for material gain.

Paul reminds them that those who want to be rich are falling into temptation and the trap that will plunge them into ruin and destruction. He says the love of money is the root of all evil, and some in their desire for it have strayed from the faith. He tells Timothy to avoid all of this. Instead pursue righteousness, devotion, faith, love, patience, and gentleness. Compete well for the faith and lay hold of eternal life, and wait for the King of kings and Lord of lords who alone has immortality.

Paul tells Timothy to tell the rich in the present age not to be proud and not to rely on such an uncertain thing as wealth, but rather on God. Tell them to do good, to be rich in good works, to be generous, ready to share, thus accumulating as treasure a good foundation for the future, so as to win the life that is true life. Finally he says to Timothy guard that which has been entrusted to you and avoid the absurdities of so-called knowledge by which some have deviated from the faith.

⁓ᗡᘉ⁓

Chapter1:1-2 says, Paul, an apostle of Christ Jesus by the command of God our Savior and of Christ Jesus our hope, To Timothy, my loyal child in the faith: Grace, mercy, and peace from God the Father and Christ Jesus our Lord. (The key words are Savior, hope, grace, mercy, peace, which are all related to who Christ is and what he stands for and calls his people to be. They are to be people of hope, grace, mercy, and peace.)

Verses 3-4 say, I urge you, as I did when I was on my way to Macedonia, to remain in Ephesus so that you may instruct certain people not to teach any different doctrine, and not to occupy themselves with myths and endless genealogies that promote speculations rather than the divine training that is known by faith. (This was an issue with Gnostic Christianity.)

They are not to teach a doctrine different from the apostles whose foundation is Jesus Christ and what he teaches. They are to stay away from making speculative theology and a morality contrary to the teachings of Jesus a requirement for becoming a follower of Christ and important in their teaching. This is also a modern day issue with some teachers of religion. Laws of food and drink are not the teaching of Christ as the laws of asceticism are not. The kingdom of God is not about food and drink but righteousness and peace and joy in the Holy Spirit (Rom 14:17).

Verse 5 says, But the aim of such instruction (apostolic faith instruction) is love that comes from a pure heart, a good conscience, and sincere faith. (These are two items that are to be the core of spiritual direction: love that comes from a sincere heart, and a good conscience coming from a sincere heart.) Verses 6-7 say, Some people have deviated from these and turned to meaningless talk, desiring to be teachers of the law, without understanding either what they are saying or the things about which they make assertions. (There is also much meaningless talk and speculative theology from modern day teachers of Christianity.)

Verses 8-11 say, Now we know that the law is good, if one uses it legitimately. This means understanding that the law is laid down not for the innocent but for the lawless and disobedient, for the godless and sinful, for the unholy and profane, for those who kill their father and mother, for murderers, fornicators, sodomites, slave traders, liars, perjurers, and whatever is contrary to the sound teaching that conforms to the glorious gospel of the blessed God, which he entrusted to me.

Notice he includes slave traders, which eventually sets in motion that slavery is not acceptable. The value of basic law is to protect society. Law can only produce a minimum ethic, which is to try to protect society from evil people and those who care only for themselves and have no concern for others. Sound teaching and doctrine in the context of the letter to Timothy is defined by who Christ is and morality.

Verses 12-17 say, I am grateful to Christ Jesus our Lord, who has strengthened me, because he judged me faithful and appointed me to his service, even though I was formerly a blasphemer, a persecutor, a man of violence (see Acts 26:9-11). But I received mercy because I had acted ignorantly in unbelief, and the grace of our Lord overflowed for me with the faith and love that are in

Christ Jesus. The saying is sure and worthy of full acceptance, that Christ Jesus came into the world to save sinners—of whom I am foremost. But for that very reason I received mercy, so that in me, as the foremost, Jesus Christ might display the utmost patience, making me an example to those who would come to believe in him for eternal life. To the King of the ages, immortal, invisible, the only God, be honor and glory forever and ever. Amen.

Paul sings God's praises for the grace, mercy, and compassion showered upon him. If God looked into Paul's heart, and saw he was acting ignorantly in unbelief, and acted with grace toward him, can he do the same with those today who act ignorantly in unbelief? What does the reader think? Does Rom 2:14-16 have any bearing on the question?

Verses 18-20 say, I am giving you these instructions, Timothy, my child, in accordance with the prophecies made earlier about you, so that by following them you might fight the good fight, having faith and good conscience. By rejecting conscience, certain persons have suffered shipwreck in the faith; among them are Hymenaeus and Alexander, whom I have turned over to Satan, so that they may learn not to blaspheme. (Paul is saying he warned Hymenaeus and Alexander that rejecting the lead of their conscience, and their turning from the faith leads to evil, and if they do not repent, it will lead to dire consequences.)

Chapter 2:1-7 says, First of all, then, I urge that supplications, prayers, intercessions, and thanksgivings be made for everyone, for kings and all who are in high positions, so that we may lead a quiet and peaceable life in all godliness and dignity. This is right and is acceptable in the sight of God our Savior, who desires everyone (not just some) to be saved and come to the knowledge of the truth.

For there is one God; there is also one mediator between God and humankind, Christ Jesus, himself human, who gave himself a ransom for all—this was attested at the right time. For this I was appointed a herald and an apostle . . . a teacher of the Gentiles in faith and truth. (Teaching that there is only one mediator is to correct the Gnostics and their teaching that it is necessity to go through many mediators in order to reach God and be liberated from the physical and material.)

The reason given for praying for government leaders and people in high positions is that they may have peace and dignity as they lead a godly life, and so that others may have the opportunity to come to the knowledge of the truth and learn about the one mediator between God and humankind, the one who gave of himself on the cross in order to bring salvation to all.

This verse has been used against the Roman Catholic and Orthodox use of Mary and the saints, but Roman Catholics and the Orthodox do not replace Jesus as the one mediator. They simply teach that Mary and the saints can pray for you just as people on earth can pray for you. They do not teach that their people should worship Mary and the saints; they simply venerate them or have a deep respect for them. Of course many people of faith, both Catholic and Protestant do not understand their church's teachings very well.

Verses 8-10 say, I desire, then, that in every place the men should pray, lifting up holy hands without anger or argument; also that the women should dress themselves modestly and decently in suitable clothing, not with hair braided, or with gold, pearls, or expensive clothes, but with good works, as is proper for the women who profess reverence for God.

Are we not praying properly if we do not lift up our hands, and are women never to wear expensive clothes to worship, nor wear anything made of gold or pearls, or braid their hair? The message is for men to pray and be at peace with each other, and women to be known for their good works, and not the way they dress. Since gold and pearls were the most expensive gems at the time, they are being told not to show off their riches in the assembly. This is not a timeless law about how to dress and that men can only pray when they lift up their hands.

This letter is written to Timothy who was the leader in the church at Ephesus. Someone was teaching a different doctrine and the church was suffering from angry arguments and women competing with each other. Women prostitutes were into the fine art of cosmetics, fashion, and adornment and were required to peroxide their hair, and these things were catching on with other women. John Temple Bristow discusses all these things in his book *What Paul Really Said About Women,* which has been discussed in 1 Corinthians. There is nothing here about timeless laws, but there may be some important principles such as how one dresses may have a positive or negative influence on how some may view your religion.

Verses 11-12 say, Let a woman learn in silence with full submission. I permit no woman (probably means wife) to teach or have authority over man (probably means her husband); she is to keep silent. (The principle is the way one acts shows the respect one has for the spouse. Keep in mind a respected woman in that time was not to be taught let alone teach, and they were not to be seen talking to a man in public. Again the reader is referred to 1 Corinthians.) Verses 13-14 say, For Adam was formed first, then Eve; and Adam was not deceived, but the woman was deceived and became a transgressor.

This appears to uphold the traditional interpretation of the rabbis, which states that Adam was superior to Eve because he was created first and created more powerful in strength, and she was the first to fall into temptation. Elsewhere this teaching is balanced by saying that Eve was created because Adam needed her, and that all men are born from women (1 Cor 11:8-12). Also, elsewhere it is stated that the fall of humankind was Adam's sin, not Eve's sin, and that death came through man (Rom 5:12-19, 1 Cor 15:21-22). Context is important, even though it is not always an explanation of differences. Another difficult verse is verse (15) which says, Yet she will be saved through childbearing, provided they continue in faith and love and holiness, with modesty.

Another reason the context of the time is so important in understanding these verses is that in this context certain false teachers were rejecting marriage, such as those who created the Dead Sea Scrolls and other Gnostics in the area. The writer is saying that under the circumstances women are to concentrate on being a good wife and raising your children. Salvation is not bound to a rigid formula even though there are norms. The idea is while the church is a small minority do not be labeled as upstarts upsetting the stability of society too much. First let Christianity take root, and then give it time to develop.

Because the churches were located in houses, the church was to be like the households of the surrounding society. Church etiquette was not to be too much different from household etiquette. At this point in society women were not permitted to be educated; if they received any education, it was from their husbands, and most wives were much younger than their husbands. All this must be considered when trying to understand verses such as this, and it must be understood that these are not timeless laws.

The kingdom of God is breaking in at different rates in different places. Another issue was that at that time two salaries were not necessary to survive, which is necessary for those today in the middle class, working poor, and the poor. These verses are not to be used as timeless laws, but they are appropriate for the culture of that time, and for a new church struggling to survive. The church wanted to emphasize its main message (Christ) without being labeled as a group trying to upset the acceptable standards of society.

A major reason for this message to women was that some of the women in the church were acting like the prostitutes in the famous temple of Diana located in Ephesus. The writer of the letter to Timothy is trying to disassociate itself from the women of that temple. Titus gives a major reason for these instructions to women at this time: chapter 2 verse 5 says, so that the word of God not be discredited. (When that was no longer the case these rules were mainly disbanded, even though some churches have carried some of them over to modern times.)

Later because Jesus taught women, some churches would gradually do the same and it became more and more acceptable. God's good future, the kingdom of God, was breaking into the world in different ways, at different rates, in different places, so it was being careful not to upset the stability of society too quickly. Titus 2:3 and 1 Cor 12 have women teaching in the church as the beginning of the change.

Chapter 3:1-7 says, The saying is sure: whoever aspires to the office of bishop (overseer) desires a noble task. Now a bishop must be above reproach, married only once (since polygamy was accepted in the Old Testament, this probably means the husband of one wife), temperate, sensible, respectable, hospitable, an apt teacher, not a drunkard, not violent but gentle, not quarrelsome, and not a lover of money. He must manage his own household well, keeping his children submissive and respectful in every way—for if someone does not know how to manage his own household, how can he take

care of God's church? (Down through history this has caused some church groups to not ordain or hire someone who is not married.) He must not be a recent convert, or he may be puffed up by conceit and fall into condemnation by the devil. Moreover, he must be well thought of by outsiders, so that he may not fall into disgrace and the snare of the devil. (This does not mean that one must be one hundred percent perfect in all these areas. This is not to be a legalistic list of laws. These are guidelines to be taken in the spirit of the law, and not in the letter of the law.)

Verses 8-13 say, Deacons likewise must be serious, not double-tongued, nor indulging in much wine, nor greedy for money; they must hold fast to the mystery of the faith with a clear conscience. And let them first be tested; then, if they prove themselves blameless, let them serve as deacons. Women (either the wives of deacons, or women deacons; no one is absolutely positive of the intended meaning) likewise must be serious, not slanderers, but temperate, faithful in all things. Let deacons be married only once (be husband of one wife, or possible wife of one husband), and let them manage their children and their households well; for those who serve well as deacons gain a good standing for themselves and great boldness in the faith that is in Christ Jesus.

Verses 14-16 say, I hope to come to you soon, but I am writing these instructions to you so that, if I am delayed, you may know how one ought to behave in the household of God, which is the church of the living God, the pillar and bulwark of the truth. Without any doubt, the mystery of our religion is great: He was revealed in flesh, vindicated in spirit, seen by angels, proclaimed among Gentiles, believed in throughout the world, taken up in glory. (For the church to be the pillar and ground of the truth, it must be well ordered, its officers must live exemplary lives, and its members must be good people living in submission to Christ and its leaders.)

Chapter 4:1-2 says, Now the Spirit expressly says that in later times some will renounce the faith by paying attention to deceitful spirits and teachings of demons (Eph 6:12, Jas 3:15, Rev 6:13-14), through the hypocrisy of liars whose consciences are seared with a hot iron. ("Later times" appears to be used by the writer to say this prophecy is being fulfilled now.) Verses 3-5 say, They forbid marriage and demand abstinence from foods, which God created to be received with thanksgiving by those who believe and know the truth. For everything created by God is good, and nothing is to be rejected, provided it is received with thanksgiving; for it is sanctified by God's word and by prayer.

The false teachers were teaching that marriage was forbidden along with certain foods (Col 2:6). This teaching is rejected because everything God created is good, but it can be misused, so sanctify it (make it holy) by God's word and prayer. Verse 6 says, If you put these instructions before the brothers and sisters, you will be a good servant of Christ Jesus, nourished on the words of the faith and of the sound teaching you have followed.

Verses 7-10 say, Have nothing to do with profane myths and old wives' tales (as told by these false teachers). Train yourself in godliness, for, while physical training is of some value, godliness is valuable in every way, holding promise for both the present life and the life to come. The saying is sure and worthy of full acceptance. For to this end we toil and struggle, because we have our hope set on the living God, who is the Savior of all people, especially of those who believe. (Spiritual training in godliness is even more valuable than physical training. One may choose voluntarily to not eat or drink certain items as a part of spiritual training, but to make them mandatory for all is not acceptable.)

Verses 11-13 say, These are the things you must insist on and teach. Let no one despise your youth, but set the believers an example in speech and conduct, in love, in faith, in purity. Until I arrive, give attention to the public reading of scripture, to exhorting, to teaching.

This is the acceptable approach to spiritual training. The church adopted this practice from the synagogue. Reading and teaching the meaning of Scripture is to be a key purpose of the church, and when the church neglects it or gives it a minor position, the church brings ruin and loss of purpose upon itself. The church will then lose its influence on its people and the world around it. This writer sees that happening in many churches in our times.

Verses 14-16 say, Do not neglect the gift that is in you, which was given to you through prophecy with the laying on of hands (ordination) by the council of elders (presbyters). Put these things into practice, devote yourself to them, so that all may see your progress. Pay close attention to yourself and to your teaching; continue in these things, for in doing this you will save both yourself and your hearers. (Church leaders are to lead by example, and not lording it over others.)

Chapter 5 gives instructions on how to treat different people within the church. Verses 1-8 say, Do not speak harshly to an older man, but speak to him as a father, to younger men as brothers, to older women as mothers, to younger women as sisters—with absolute purity. (Respect is important.) Honor widows who are really widows. If a widow has children or grandchildren, they should first learn their religious duty to their own family and make some repayment to their parents; for this is pleasing in God's sight. The real widow, left alone, has set her hope on God and continues in supplications and prayers night and day; but the widow who lives for pleasure is dead even while she lives. Give these commands as well, so that they may be above reproach. And whoever does not provide for relatives, and especially for family members, has denied the faith and is worse than an unbeliever. (Responsibility for each other in faith is a way of godliness.)

Verses 9-15 are about putting widows on the list. This is a reference to women who are taken care of by the church as they serve the church. She has to be sixty years old, married only once, and known for her good works. Younger widows are encouraged to remarry. Verse 16 says, If any believing woman has relatives who are really widows, let her assist them; let the church not be burdened, so that it can assist those who are real widows. (Again this age limit and limit of marriages is not a timeless law but one for that time, but there are some good principles here to pay attention to.)

Verses 17-20 say, Let the elders who rule well be considered worthy of double honor, especially those who labor in preaching and teaching; for the scripture says, "You shall not muzzle an ox while it is treading out the grain," and, "The laborer deserves to be paid." Never accept any accusation against an elder except on the evidence of two or three witnesses. As for those who persist in sin, rebuke them in the presence of all, so that the rest also may stand in fear.

The message is that preaching and teaching are so important that they must be paid a good wage. Also, when they are not true to their position, they must be disciplined. This is not only for the sake of justice but so those not in those positions can be taught that God does not take lightly the responsibilities Christ gives to both leaders and followers.

Verses 21-22 say, In the presence of God and of Christ Jesus and of the elect angels, I warn you to keep these instructions without prejudice, doing nothing on the basis of partiality. Do not ordain anyone hastily, and do not participate in the sins of others; keep yourself pure. No longer drink only water, but take a little wine for the sake of your stomach and your frequent ailments. (That is a challenge to those who say a true Christian never drinks any alcohol. Within the last few years it has been scientifically proven that some wine is a very healthy choice.)

Verses 24-25 say, The sins of some people are conspicuous and precede them to judgment, while the sins of others (even when not conspicuous) follow them there. So also good works are conspicuous; and even when they are not, they cannot remain hidden. (Christians are to be known for the good they do, not their sins.)

Chapter 6:1-5 says, Let all who are under the yoke of slavery regard their masters as worthy of all honor, so that the name of God and the teaching may not be blasphemed. Those who have believing masters must not be disrespectful to them on the ground that they are members of the church; rather they must serve them all the more, since those who benefit by their service are believers and beloved. Teach and urge these duties. Whoever teaches otherwise and does not agree with the sound words of our Lord Jesus Christ and the teaching that is in accordance with godliness, is conceited, understanding nothing, and has a morbid craving for controversy and for disputes about words. From these come envy, dissension, slander, base suspicions, and wrangling among those who are depraved in mind and bereft of the truth, imagining that godliness is a means of gain.

Although there is nothing in the Gospels about Jesus mentioning slavery these verses indicate he did talk about it. At this point being free from slavery was not a major issue, although slave traders are mentioned in the list of sins (1:10). Slaves, especially under Christians were treated well. Here slaves are encouraged to treat their masters in a positive manner. The key for a struggling church trying to get the message of Christ out to the people in their locality was not to do anything that upsets the stability of society, for that would give Christianity a bad name. At this point getting the message out about who Christ is and what he did is most important.

Verses 6-10 say, Of course, there is great gain in godliness combined with contentment; for we brought nothing into the world, so that we can take nothing out of it; but if we have food and clothing, we will be content with these. But those who want to be rich fall into temptation and are trapped by many senseless and harmful desires that plunge people into ruin and destruction. For the love of money is the root of all kinds of evil, and in their eagerness to be rich some have wandered away from the faith and pierced themselves with many pains. (The love of money, not money, has been the ruination of many, and has been a blemish on the church.)

Verses 11-12 say, But as for you, man of God, shun all of this; pursue righteousness, godliness, faith, love, endurance, gentleness. Fight the good fight of the faith; take hold of the eternal life, to which you were called and for which you made the good confession in the presence of any witnesses. (Godliness is a key word in Timothy.)

Verses 13-16 say, In the presence of God, who gives life to all things, and of Christ Jesus who in his testimony before Pontius Pilate made the good confession, I charge you to keep the commandment (probably love God and neighbor as self) without spot or blame until the manifestation of Jesus Christ, which he will bring about at the right time—he who is the blessed and only Sovereign, the King of kings and Lord of lords. It is he alone who has immortality and dwells in unapproachable light, whom no one has ever seen or can see; to him be honor and eternal dominion. Amen.

Verses 17-19 are God's message to those with wealth. They say, As for those who in the present age are rich, command them not to be haughty, or to set their hopes on the uncertainty of riches, but rather on God who richly provides us with everything for our enjoyment. They are to do good, to be rich in good works, generous, and ready to share, thus storing up for themselves the treasure of a good foundation for the future, so that they may take hold of the life that really is life. (Scripture never says it is wrong to be rich, but the wealthy are constantly challenged not to be greedy and to use their wealth for the common good in order to glorify God.)

Verses 20-21 say, Timothy, guard what has been entrusted to you. Avoid the profane chatter and contradictions of what is falsely called knowledge (Gnosticism or any philosophy that opposes who Christ is and his teachings); by professing it some have missed the mark as regards the faith. Grace be with you. The only true knowledge is that which comes through Jesus Christ.

The questions that must be asked to all are: What is your knowledge of Jesus Christ? Have you personally read and understood the four Gospels and the New Testament? If yes, what are you doing with it in your life and in the life of society? If you have not personally read them, why have you not read them?

As a way of review list some of the most important verses or thoughts in the letter of 1 Timothy.

THE SECOND LETTER
TO TIMOTHY

Paul writes to Timothy again in Ephesus. He reminds Timothy to stir into flame the gift God has given him. He says God did not give us the spirit of cowardice but rather the gift of power, love, and self control. So Paul tells him not to be ashamed of his testimony to our Lord or of him (Paul), a prisoner for Christ's sake, but to bear his share of hardship for the gospel with the strength that comes from God. Christ saved us and called us to a holy life through his grace. Paul tells him to take as his norm the sound words heard from him and guard the rich (apostolic) trust that has been given to him.

In chapter 2 he reminds him that if we die with Christ, we shall also live with him; if we persevere, we shall also reign with him. But if we deny him, he will deny us. If we are unfaithful, he remains faithful, for he can not deny himself. He tells him to remind the people to stop disputing about words, for it serves no useful purpose. He tells Timothy to be eager to present himself acceptable to God, a workman who causes no disgrace as he imparts the word of truth. Avoid profane idle talk, for such people will become more and more godless, and their teaching will spread like gangrene.

The Lord knows who are his, and let everyone who calls upon the name of the Lord avoid evil. Then Paul tells Timothy to turn from youthful desires and pursue righteousness, faith, love, and peace, along with those who call on the name of the Lord with purity of heart. Avoid foolish ignorant debates (good advice for Christians today) for they breed quarrels. Be gentle with everyone, be able to teach, be tolerant, correcting opponents with kindness. It may be God will grant them repentance and lead them to knowledge of the truth.

In chapter 3 he says there will be terrifying times in the last days. The last days have already begun. Compare verse 5 and Acts 2 :16-17. People will be self centered, lovers of money, proud, haughty, abusive, disobedient to their parents, ungrateful, irreligious, callous, implacable, slanderous, licentious, brutal, hating what is good, traitors, reckless, conceited, lovers of pleasure, rather than lovers of God, as they make pretense of religion but deny its power. Some are captivating women who are weighed down by sins, women always trying to learn but never able to reach the knowledge of truth. Men fit that category also. He tells them all who want to live religiously in Christ will be persecuted.

Paul tells them that all scripture is inspired by God and is useful for teaching, for refutation, for correction, and for training in righteousness, so that one who belongs to God may be competent, equipped for every good work. Does this say that every word is infallible and without error, along with the history and science of the Bible as taught by fundamentalists? We will discuss that later.

In chapter 4 Paul charges Timothy to proclaim the word; be persistent whether convenient or not convenient, convince, reprimand, encourage through all patience and teaching. For the time will come when people will not tolerate sound doctrine, but will have itching ears and follow their own desires. They will accumulate teachers to their own liking and stop listening to the truth. Then Paul tells them he is already being poured out as a libation, and that the time of his departure is at hand. He says he has competed well. He says that he has finished the race and kept the faith. From now on the crown of righteousness awaits him.

⌒∽⌒

Chapter 1:1-2 says, Paul, an apostle of Christ Jesus by the will of God, for the sake of the promise of life that is in Christ Jesus, To Timothy, my beloved child: Grace, mercy, and peace from God the Father and Christ Jesus our Lord. Verses 1-5 say, I am grateful to God—whom I worship with a clear conscience, as my ancestors did—when I remember you constantly in my prayers night and day. Recalling your tears, I long to see you so that I may be filled with joy. I am reminded of your sincere faith, a faith that lived first in your grandmother Lois and your mother Eunice and now, I am sure, lives in you. (This highlights the importance of parents and grandparents passing along their faith. As has been said Christianity is only one generation away from becoming extinct.)

Verses 6-7 say, For this reason I remind you to rekindle the gift of God that is within you through the laying on of my hands, for God did not give us a spirit of cowardice, but rather a spirit of power and of love and of self-discipline. Verses 8-10 say, Do not be ashamed, then, of the testimony about our Lord or of me his prisoner, but join with me in suffering for the gospel, relying on the power of God, who saved us and called us with a holy calling, not according to our works but according to his own purpose and grace. This grace was given to us in Christ Jesus before the ages began, but it now has been revealed through the appearing of our Savior Jesus Christ, who abolished death and brought life and immortality to light through the gospel.

God graces his people with the call to holiness, and part of that holiness involves relying on God's power to stand with him in his interests and purposes and be willing to suffer for those interests and purposes when challenged.

In verses 11-12 Paul says, For this gospel I was appointed a herald and an apostle and teacher, and for this reason I suffer as I do. But I am not ashamed, for I know the one in whom I have put my trust, and I am sure that he is able to guard until that day what I have entrusted to him. (Paul has the faith that God will use his gifts until the time for Paul is finished.) In verse 13 Paul says, Hold to the standard of sound teaching (the apostolic teachings) that you have heard from me, in the faith and love that are in Christ Jesus. Guard the good treasure entrusted to you, with the help of the Holy Spirit living in us. (This is God's purpose for all, especially the leaders of the church.)

Verses 15-18 say, You are aware that all who are in Asia have turned away from me, including Phygelus and Hermogenes. May the Lord grant mercy to the household of Onesiphorus, because he often refreshed me and was not ashamed of my chain; when he arrived in Rome, he eagerly searched for me and found me—may the Lord grant that he will find mercy from the Lord on that day! And you know very well how much service he rendered in Ephesus. (We will read more about Onesiphorus in Philemon.)

⚬⚬⚬

Chapter 2:1-2 says, You then, my child, be strong in the grace that is in Christ Jesus; and what you have heard from me through many witnesses entrust to faithful people who will be able to teach others as well. (As a priority find people to teach God's word who will have the ability to teach others.)

Verse 3 says, Share in suffering like a good soldier of Christ Jesus.

(Notice how often suffering is mentioned. This is not the experience of most Christians in the United States. Does the reader think that says anything about American Christianity? Why or why not?)

Verses 4-7 say, No one serving in the army gets entangled in everyday affairs; the soldiers aim is to please the existing officer. And in the case of the athlete, no one is crowned without competing according to the rules. It is the farmer who does the work who ought to have the first share of the crops. Think over what I say, for the Lord will give you understanding in all things. (The examples of the soldier, athlete, and farmer have the same point. They all work hard with singleness of purpose and in the process discipline themselves as they endure all things negative in order to receive the reward.)

Verses 8-10 say, Remember Jesus Christ, raised from the dead, a descendent of David—that is my gospel, for which I suffer hardship, even to the point of being chained like a criminal. But the word of God is not chained. Therefore endure everything for the sake of the elect, so that they may also obtain the salvation that is in Christ Jesus, with eternal glory. (Paul tells Timothy to be like the soldier, athlete, and farmer and endure with patience as he teaches God's word.)

Verses 11-13 say, The saying is sure: If we have died with him, we will also live with him; if we endure, we will also reign with him; if we deny him he will also deny us; if we are faithless, he remains faithful—for he cannot deny himself. (He will deny us if we do not live with him, reign with him in the kingdom he came to establish, or remain faithful, but he will wait for us to return to him if we happen to fall away from him. The Scriptures do not teach the fundamentalist teaching of once saved always saved. That teaching is true only if one remains faithful.)

Verses 14-15 say, Remind them of this, and warn them before

God that they are to avoid wrangling over words (majoring in minors), which does no good but only ruins those who are listening. Do your best to present yourself to God as one approved by him, a worker who has no need to be ashamed, rightly explaining the word of truth.

The task of teaching and preaching is difficult work that demands discipline, courage, and much study. At the heart it involves the explanation of God's word. The purpose is not speculative theology, but sound apostolic theology and morality found in and based upon God's word.

Verses 16-18 say, Avoid profane chatter (opposed to the word of truth), for it will lead people into more and more impiety, and their talk will spread like gangrene. Among them are Hymenaes and Philetus, who have swerved from the truth by claiming that the resurrection has already taken place. They are upsetting the faith of some. (They believe in a spiritual resurrection in this life and possibly in the next life but not a bodily resurrection in the next life. The foundation of apostolic teaching is both a spiritual resurrection meaning a changed life as one follows the teachings of Christ and then to be followed by a judgment and a bodily resurrection.)

Verses 19-21 say, But God's firm foundation stands, bearing the inscription: "The Lord knows who are his," and, "Let everyone who calls on the name of the Lord turn away from wickedness." In a large house there are utensils not only of gold and silver but also of wood and clay, some for special use, some for ordinary. All who cleanse themselves of the things I have mentioned will become special utensils dedicated and useful to the owner of the house, ready for every good work. (God needs special utensils as a channel for the advancement of his kingdom, God's good future breaking into the earth, until he comes again to make all things perfect.)

Verses 22-26 say, Shun youthful passions and pursue

righteousness, faith, love, and peace, along with those who call on the Lord with a pure heart. Have nothing to do with stupid and senseless controversies; you know that they breed quarrels. And the Lord's servant must not be quarrelsome but kindly to everyone, an apt teacher, patient, correcting opponents with gentleness. God may perhaps grant that they will repent and come to know the truth, and that they may escape from the snare of the devil, having been held captive to him to do his will.

According to the writer the devil is using those who are teaching religious things that are opposed to the apostolic teachings. Timothy is to patiently continue teaching God's word, praying that his opponents will see God's truth and repent. Notice the importance put on sound teaching in this book of Timothy.

Chapter 3:1-5 says, You must understand this, that in the last days distressing times will come. For people will be lovers of themselves, lovers of money, boasters, arrogant, abusive, disobedient to their parents, ungrateful, unholy, inhuman, implacable, slanderers, profligates, brutes, haters of good, treacherous, reckless, swollen with conceit, lovers of pleasure rather than lovers of God, holding to the outward form of godliness but denying its power. Avoid them! (These words could describe every age. As the following indicates, the writer is saying this last age is upon us now.)

Verses 6-7 say, For among them are those who make their way into households and captivate silly women, overwhelmed by their sins and swayed by all kinds of desires, who are always being instructed and can never arrive at a knowledge of the truth. (It sounds like men and women today who are always being instructed, but it does not take hold because their desires, both sexual and non-sexual, are more important.)

Verses 8-9 say, As Jannes and Jambres opposed Moses, so these people, of corrupt mind and counterfeit faith, also oppose the truth. But they will not make much progress, because, as in the case of those two men, their folly will become plain to everyone. (Jewish tradition says that Jannes and Jambres were Pharoah's magicians.) Verses 10-12 say, Now you have observed my teaching, my conduct, my aim in life, my faith, my patience, my love, my steadfastness, my persecutions and suffering the things that happened to me in Antioch, Iconium, and Lystra. What persecutions I endured! Yet the Lord rescued me from all of them. (Paul's reason for mentioning this follows in verse 12.) Indeed, all who want to live a godly life in Christ Jesus will be persecuted.

Verses 13-15 say, But wicked people and imposters will go from bad to worse, deceiving others and being deceived. But as for you, continue in what you have learned and firmly believed, knowing from whom you learned it, and how from childhood you have known the sacred writings that are able to instruct you for salvation through faith in Christ Jesus. All scripture is inspired by God and is useful for teaching, for reproof, for correction, and for training in righteousness, so that everyone who belongs to God may be proficient, equipped for every good work.

Scripture is inspired (meaning God breathed like Gen 2:7) by God for salvation even though it is written in human words. The question is what is inspired? Is every word inspired and inerrant? It does not say every word is inerrant as the fundamentalists believe; it simply says that Scripture is inspired for salvation. It is this writer's opinion that what is inspired is the meaning or the theology behind the words. The words are simply the human instruments used to point to Christ and describe the meaning behind the words. It is obvious for thinking people that the purpose of the Bible is not to detail exact history or science, even though the core of history is there. It is the record of God's historical people, but primarily a record of their theology. Theology defined means the faith of God's people seeking understanding. It is a record inspired by God as it uses humans and their imperfect words, words that can never totally convey the full implication of God's teachings. Nor was it ever meant to be a recipe book for every thing that can happen to an individual while on earth, even though it does present guidelines on thinking through whatever happens. That is why the writer of 1 Cor 12:13 says, For now we see in a mirror, dimly, but then we will see face to face. Now I know only in part; then I will know fully, even as I have been fully known.

Chapter 4:1-2 says, In the presence of God and of Christ Jesus, who is to judge the living and the dead, and in view of his appearing and his kingdom, I solemnly urge you: proclaim the message; be persistent whether the time is favorable or unfavorable; convince, rebuke, and encourage, with the utmost patience in teaching. (Again the emphasis is on teaching.) Verses 3-5 say, For the time is coming when people will not put up with sound doctrine, but having itching ears, they will accumulate for themselves teachers to suit their own desires, and will turn away from listening to the truth and wander away to myths. (The reference is to the Gnostics and their mythology.) As for you, always be sober, endure suffering, do the work of an evangelist, carry out your ministry fully.

Itching ears and pride have been the problem since the beginning with Adam and Eve. Humans have a tendency to ignore God, when it is not in their particular interest; they listen to themselves instead of God, and then they find someone who tells them what they want to hear, which was very easy to find in the world then and also today.

Verse 6 says, As for me, I am already being poured out as a libation, and the time of my departure has come. (He is saying his suffering is about to end because he is about to be put to death.) Verses 7-8 say, I have fought the good fight, I have finished the race, I have kept the faith. From now on there is reserved for me the crown of righteousness, which the Lord, the righteous judge, will give me on that day, and not only to me but to all who have longed for his appearing. (This crown of righteousness is the reward the righteous judge will give to those who are steadfast in God's purposes and for enduring the suffering that comes with it.)

Verses 9-11 say, Do your best to come to me soon, for Demas (Philemon 24, Col 4:14), in love with this present world, has deserted me and gone to Thessalonica; Crescens has gone to Galatia, Titus to Delmatia. (After being in Crete Titus went to Dalmatia on the Adriatic coast.) Only Luke is with me. Get Mark and bring him with you, for he is useful in my ministry. (The breach they initially had in Acts 15:36-41 has been healed.) Verses 12-15 say, I have sent Tychicus (Acts 20:4, Col 4:7, Eph 6:21, Titus 3:12) to Ephesus. When you come, bring the cloak that I left with Carpus at Troas, also the books, and above all the parchments. Alexander the coppersmith did me great harm; the Lord will pay him back for his deeds. You also must beware of him, for he strongly opposed our message.

Verses 16-18 say, At my first defense no one came to my support, but all deserted me. May it not be counted against them! But the Lord stood by me and gave me strength, so that through me the message might be fully proclaimed and all the Gentiles might hear it. So I was rescued from the lion's mouth. The Lord will rescue me from every evil attack and save me for his heavenly kingdom. To him be the glory for ever and ever. Amen. (Being rescued from the lions could be a reference to the Coliseum in Rome where Christians were thrown to the lions for the entertainment of the crowds. It is also an OT metaphor for a violent death.)

Verses 19-22 say, Greet Prisca and Aquila, and the household of Onesiphorus. Erastus remained in Corinth; Trophimus (Acts 20:4-5, Acts 21:27-29) I left ill in Miletus. Do your best to come before winter. Eubulus sends greetings to you as do Pudens and Linus and Claudia and all the brothers and sisters. The Lord be with your spirit. Grace be with you.

Prisca and Aquila assisted Paul in Corinth (Acts 18:2-3) and Ephesus (Acts 18, 19:26, 1 Cor 16:19). They risked death to save his life, and all the Gentile communities are indebted to them (Rom 16:3-5). Erastus was the city treasurer in Corinth (Rom 16:24, 19:22). Trophimus from Asia accompanied Paul from Greece to Troas (Acts 20:4-5). Linus may have been the second pope in Rome (according to Irenaeus) and tradition has Claudia as the mother of Linus.

As a way of review list some of the most important verses or thoughts in the letter of 2 Timothy.

THE LETTER TO TITUS

Paul writes to Titus who is leading the church on the island of Crete. He writes for the sake of the truth of Christ. Paul left Titus in Crete to appoint presbyters in every town. In chapter one he list some qualifications for bishops that are similar to the ones mentioned to Timothy. It seems presbyters (elders) and bishops are the same. It may be that a bishop was the leading presbyter. Paul tells Titus to hold fast to the true message, so he will be able to exhort with sound doctrine and refute opponents. The book of Titus is similar to Timothy.

Beyond defining who Christ is, sound doctrine seems more related to ethics than to what is called doctrine today, although both to some extent seem to be included. Paul says there are many rebels, idle talkers, and deceivers, especially of the false teachers. He says they are upsetting whole families by teaching for sordid gain (greed) what they should not. Paul says to admonish them so they may be sound in the faith instead of paying attention to Jewish myths, genealogies and regulations from people who have repudiated the truth. Their minds and consciences are tainted. These people claim to know God, but by their deeds they deny him.

In chapter 2 Paul tells him to say what is consistent with sound doctrine, that older men should be temperate, dignified, self controlled, sound in faith, love, and endurance. Sound doctrine primarily centers on moral behavior. Older women should be reverent in their behavior, not slanderers, not addicted to drink (alcoholic), teaching what is good, so that they may train younger women to love their husbands and children, to be self controlled, chaste, good homemakers, under the control of their husbands (not bringing shame upon their husbands), so that the word of God may not be discredited.

Paul says to urge the young men to control themselves, be a model of good deeds, with integrity in teaching, dignity, and sound speech that can not be criticized so that the opponent will be put to shame without anything bad to say about us. Slaves are to be under the control of their masters, not talking back to them, or stealing from them, exhibiting good faith so as to adorn the doctrine of God in every way. The hope is that the slave masters will want to know about Christ. For the grace of God trains us to reject godless ways and worldly desires, and to live temperately, justly, and devoutly in this age as we wait the blessed hope. Since Christianity is a small minority, they are not to act in a way contrary to godly behavior that turns people away from being exposed to Christ. Then he tells Titus to correct wrong with all authority; let no one look down on you.

In chapter 3 Paul tells Titus to remind them to be under the control of magistrates and be obedient to every good enterprise. Of course they are to first obey God not humans (Acts 5:29). He reminds them we were all once foolish slaves to various desires and pleasures living in malice and envy, hateful of ourselves and others. But when the kindness and love of our Savior appeared not because of any righteous deeds we did but because of his mercy, he saved us through the bath of rebirth and renewal by the Holy Spirit whom he richly poured out on us through Jesus Christ our Savior, so that we might be justified by his grace and become heirs in hope of eternal life. Paul tells Titus to devote himself to good works that are beneficial to others and avoid foolish arguments about the law, for they are useless and futile. He is told to realize those who do so are perverted, sinful, and stand condemned.

⤥⤦

Chapter 1:1-4 says, Paul a servant of God and an apostle of Jesus Christ, for the sake of God's elect and the knowledge of the truth that is in accordance with godliness, in the hope of eternal life that God, who never lies, promised before the ages began—in due time he revealed his word through the proclamation with which I have been entrusted by the command of God our Savior, To Titus my loyal child in the faith we share: Grace and peace from God the Father and Christ Jesus our Savior. (The church is God's elect, the chosen people, chosen through Christ.)

Verses 5-9 say, I left you behind in Crete for this reason, so that you should put in order what remained to be done, and should appoint elders in every town, as I directed you: someone who is blameless, married only once, whose children are believers, not accused of debauchery and not rebellious. For a bishop, as God's steward, must be blameless; he must not be arrogant or quick tempered or addicted to wine (alcoholic) or violent or greedy for gain; but he must be hospitable, a lover of goodness, prudent, upright, devout, and self-controlled. He must have a firm grasp of the word that is trustworthy in accordance with the teaching, so that he may be able both to preach with sound doctrine and refute those who contradict it. (Elder and bishop seem to be the same. Possibly the bishop was the leading elder.)

Again as in Timothy these are guidelines applied in the spirit of the law, not hard and fast laws. Being able to preach and teach and refute those who reject sound doctrine is important. As usual sound doctrine basically refers to who Christ is and what he did and most important the moral behavior he taught. The letter contrasts elders and false teachers.

Verses 10-12 say, There are also many rebellious people, idle talkers, and deceivers, especially those of the circumcision, they must be silenced since they are upsetting whole families by teaching for sordid gain what is not right to teach. (The false teachers must have been Jews who became Christian Gnostics.) It was one of them, their very own prophet, who said, "Cretans are always liars, vicious brutes, lazy gluttons." (How is that for stereotyping? This writer doubts that the people of Crete would accept that statement. This is quoted from the Cretan poet Epimenides.)

Verses 13-14 say, That testimony is true. (He is probably saying this quote from Epimenides is true about these particular false teachers.) For this reason rebuke them sharply, so that they may become sound in the faith, not paying attention to Jewish myths or to commandments of those who reject the truth. (The false teachers were probably the same as those in Timothy.) Verses 15-16 say, To the pure all things are pure, but to the corrupt and unbelieving nothing is pure. Their very minds and consciences are corrupted. They profess to know God, but they deny him by their actions. They are detestable, disobedient, unfit for any good work. (Consciences become corrupted by false teachers, those teaching contrary to the teachings of Christ and the apostles.)

❧

Chapter 2:1-2 says, But as for you, teach what is consistent with sound doctrine. Tell the older men to be temperate, serious, prudent, and sound in faith, in love, and in endurance. Likewise tell the older women to be reverent in behavior, not to be slanderers or slaves to drink; they are to teach what is good, so that they may encourage the young women to love their husbands, to love their children, to be self-controlled, chaste, good managers of the household, kind, being submissive (subject) to their husbands, so that the word of God may not be discredited. (Eph5:21 states that husbands and wives are to subject themselves to each other with respect. Husbands are to love their wives as Christ loved the church and gave himself up for it. In interpreting Scripture, one must be not only aware of the context but cognizant of the whole Bible.)

Verses 6-8 say, Likewise, urge the younger men to be self-controlled. Show yourself in all respects a model of good works, and in your teaching show integrity, gravity, and sound speech that cannot be censured; then any opponent will be put to shame, having nothing evil to say of us. (All this goes back to verse 5, so that the word of God not be discredited.) Verses 9-10 say, Tell slaves to be submissive to their masters and to give satisfaction in every respect; they are not to talk back, not to pilfer, but to show complete and perfect fidelity, so that in everything they may be an ornament to the doctrine of God our Savior.

Christians were a minority, so at this point they are being told not to do anything that hurts their witness to Christ (5). This is always a sound teaching, but it becomes a little different when Christians become a majority. Then the seeds within the whole message can begin to bloom and those more mature in the faith can grow deeper into the more complex things of faith.

It is possible that the message here is to those like in 1 Tim 6:1-2 who had masters who were also Christian. It is stated that slavery is a yoke and in 1 Tim 1:10 slave trading is listed as a sin. Slavery is not being approved, but the message is how to behave if you are a slave while Christianity is a minority. Do not do anything that discredits the word in the society where one lives. Let time endure while people who eventually accept Christ have time to be taught God's will and the deeper meaning of Christ's teachings.

Verses 11-13 say, For the grace of God has appeared, bringing salvation to all, training us to renounce impiety and worldly passions, and in the present age to live lives that are self-controlled, upright, and godly, while we wait for the blessed hope and the manifestation of the glory of our great God and Savior, Jesus Christ. (The following verses 14-15 give the reason for these teachings.) He it is who gave himself for us that he might redeem us from all iniquity and purify for himself a people of his own (Ezek 37:23, 1 Pet 2:9) who are zealous for good deeds. Declare these things; exhort and approve with all authority. Let no one look down on you.

Chapter 3:1-4 says, Remind them to be subject to rulers and authorities, to be obedient, to be ready for every good work, to speak evil of no one, to avoid quarreling, to be gentle, and to show every courtesy to everyone. For we ourselves were once foolish, disobedient, led astray, slaves to various passions and pleasures, passing our days in malice and envy, despicable, hating one another. (Titus 1:9 does say to refute those who contradict the faith. So do that in a non-quarreling way, while not speaking evil and showing courtesy. Christ teaches to love one's enemies. This is not a feeling but a way of acting. They are to first obey God if there is a conflict with governing authorities.)

Verses 4-5 say, But when the goodness and loving kindness of God our Savior appeared, he saved us, not because of any works of righteousness that we had done, but according to his mercy, through the water of rebirth (Jn 3:5) and renewal of the Holy Spirit. (The water of rebirth is the instrument God normally uses to channel the

Holy Spirit and the work of the Holy Spirit, Acts 2:38, Acts 22:16, Eph 5:26, and to *begin* the process of being adopted children of God. It is the grace and work of the Holy Spirit the entire way, for after the salvation process begins, the Spirit bears fruit for God.)

Verses 6-8 say, This Spirit he poured out on us richly through Jesus Christ our Savior, so that, having been justified by his grace, we might become heirs according to the hope of eternal life. The saying is sure, I desire that you insist on these things, so that those who have come to believe in God may be careful to devote themselves to good works, these things are excellent and profitable to everyone. (The Spirit then continues the process as God's people let God continue his work in and through them for the glory of God and the advancement of the kingdom.)

Verses 9-11 say, But avoid stupid controversies, genealogies, dissensions, and quarrels about the law, for they are unprofitable and worthless. After a first and second admonition, have nothing to do with anyone who causes divisions, since you know that such a person is perverted and sinful, being self-condemned.

The problem throughout the history of the church is where and how that line is to be drawn. The disunity of Christianity divided by many hundreds of divisions shows that his people either ignored this teaching, or they did not know the difference between what is adiaphora, meaning what does not matter, and what does matter under the law of freedom. We would have fewer divisions if we would allow everything outside the doctrine of Christ, which includes who he is and what he did and his teachings on living life, be adiaphora. That would not have eliminated all problems, but certainly would have diminished many of them.

Verses 12-15 say, When I send Artemis to you, or Tychicus (Acts 20:4, Eph 6:21, Col 4:7, 2 Tim 4:12), do your best to come to me at Nicopolus, for I have decided to spend the winter here. Make every effort to send Zenas the lawyer and Apollos (Acts 18:24, 1 Cor 1:12, 16:12) on their way, and see that they lack nothing. And let people learn to devote themselves to good works in order to meet urgent needs, so that they may not be unproductive. All who are with me send greetings to you. Greet those who love us in the faith. Grace be with all of you.

As a way of review list some of the most important verses or thoughts in the letter to Titus.

THE LETTER TO PHILEMON

Paul and Timothy write to Archippus and Apphia and to the church at their house located in Colossae (Asia Minor-Turkey). Onesimus the slave of Archippus had run away, and in the meantime heard Paul teach and became a follower of Christ. Meanwhile Paul calls himself an old man who is in prison for the cause of Christ. Paul tells them (primarily Philemon) about Onesimus and informs them that Onesimus has been a big help to him. Paul tells them he is sending him back to them, but says he could really use him. Paul says he is no longer a slave because he is for both of them more than a slave, for he is their brother, a man in the Lord. Paul says if they regard him (Paul) as a brother, welcome Onesimus as a brother also. Paul then tells them he knows they will do even more for Onesimus than Paul requests.

In a day where slavery was normal, Paul put into motion the idea that love eliminates any form of slavery. He had already stated in 1 Tim 1:10 slave trading is a sin. This is an example of how the kingdom of God, God's good future, is breaking into the world in different places at different rates. Too bad it took the issue of slavery and women so long to break into America. The spin off from those issues still haunts us.

Chapter 1:1-3 says, Paul, a prisoner of Christ Jesus and Timothy our brother, To Philemon our dear friend and co-worker, to Apphia our sister, to Archippus our fellow soldier, and to the church in your house: Grace to you and peace from God our Father and the Lord Jesus Christ. (The early Christians met in homes, Rom 16:5, 1 Cor 16:19, Col 4:15. This writer wonders at times if the church would not have been better off in some way staying as house churches. What does the reader think?)

Verses 4-7 say, When I remember you in my prayers, I always thank my God because I hear of your love for all the saints and your faith toward the Lord Jesus. I pray that the sharing of your faith may become effective when you perceive all the good we may do for Christ. I have indeed received much joy and encouragement from your love, because the hearts of the saints have been refreshed through you, my brother. (Paul wants Philemon and the church to act out of good will, so he establishes their good will at the beginning of the letter.)

Verses 8-12 say, For this reason, though I am bold enough in Christ to command you to do your duty (through the power of his apostleship), yet I would rather appeal to you on the basis of love—and I, Paul do this as an old man, and now also as a prisoner of Christ Jesus. I am appealing to you for my child, Onesimus (name means useful), whose father I have become during my imprisonment. Formerly he was useless to you, but now he is indeed useful both to you and me. I am sending him, that is, my own heart back to you.

I wanted to keep him with me, so that he might be of service to me in your place during my imprisonment for the gospel; but I preferred to do nothing without your consent, in order that your good deed might be voluntary and not something forced. Perhaps this is the reason he was separated from you for awhile, so that you might have him back forever, no longer as a slave but more than a slave, a beloved brother—especially to me but how much more to you, both in the flesh and in the Lord. (This is the seed that moves a serious Christian to liberate his slaves. Loving your neighbor means treating them as you would want to be treated if in their position.)

Verses 17-20 say, So if you consider me your partner, welcome him as you would welcome me. If he has wronged you in any way, or owes you anything, charge that to my account. I, Paul, am writing this with my own hand: I will repay it. I say nothing about you owing me even your own self. Yes, brother, let me have this benefit from you in the Lord. Refresh my heart in Christ. Confident in your obedience, I am writing to you, knowing that you will do even more than I say. (How could he deny Paul's request after this letter? Could we call this schmoozing?)

Verses 22-25 say, One thing more—prepare a guest room for me, for I am hoping through your prayers to be restored to you. Epaphras, my fellow prisoner in Christ Jesus, sends greetings to you. And so do Mark, Aristarchus, Demas, and Luke, my fellow workers. The grace of the Lord Jesus be with your spirit.

Paul shows respect for order and a stable society and prefers to let God's word work in the hearts of people in society, and especially the church. He does not directly challenge slavery, but previously he called slave trading a sin (1 Tim 1:10). Paul does direct Philemon to the higher law, the law of love and compassion, the law of doing to others what you would want done to you, if in the same situation. He encourages Philemon to accept Onesimus as a brother in Christ. This is how he puts into effect his teaching in Gal 3:28: There is no longer Jew or Greek, there is no longer slave or free, there is no longer male and female; for all of you are one in Christ.

As a way of review list some of the most important verses or thoughts in the letter to Philemon.

THE LETTER TO THE
HEBREWS

Throughout most of history the Apostle Paul was considered the author, but today very few scholars agree, and there is no agreement on who did write this letter. The writer had to be a Hebrew writing to Hebrews, for he is very familiar with ancient Israel, Jerusalem, the temple and Old Testament worship. Chapter 1 begins by saying that in times past God spoke in partial and various ways to our ancestors through the prophets, but in these last days he speaks to us through his Son, who is the imprint of his very being and who sustains all things by his mighty word. When he had accomplished purification from sins, he took his seat at the right hand of the Majesty on high (Dan 7:13-14). He is far superior to the angels, for the angels are to worship him. Angels are ministering spirits sent to serve for the sake of those who are to inherit salvation.

In chapter 2 the writer says God testified for Jesus by signs, wonders, various miracles, and gifts of the Holy Spirit. Jesus the pioneer of salvation was made perfect through his suffering. Through death he destroyed the one who had power over death, the devil. He had to become like his brothers in every way that he might be a merciful and faithful high priest before God to expiate the sins of the people. Because he himself was tested through what he suffered, he is able to help those who are being tested.

In chapter 3 the writer says Moses was faithful to God, but Christ is superior to Moses and worthy of more glory. God said in reference to the people Moses led, because I was provoked with them, I swore in my wrath that they shall not enter my rest. The writer says take care that none of you have an evil and unfaithful heart so as to forsake the living God. Do not become hardened by the deceit of sin. We are partners of Christ if only we hold firm until the end.

Chapter 4 says let us be on our guard while the promise of entering his rest, the promised land, remains. Since it remains that some will enter his rest, and some in the past did not because of disobedience, God spoke through David when he said, today when you hear his voice do not harden your hearts. A Sabbath rest still remains for the people of God. Let us strive to enter that rest so that no one may fall after the same example of disobedience.

Indeed the word of God is living, sharper than any two edged sword, penetrating between soul and spirit able to discern reflections and thoughts of the heart. No one is concealed from him, and everything is exposed to the eyes of him to whom we must give an account. Therefore since we have a great high priest, who has passed through the heavens, Jesus, the Son of God, let us hold fast to our confession. For we do not have a high priest who is unable to sympathize with our weaknesses, but one who has been tested in every way and without sin. So let us confidently approach the throne of grace to receive mercy and to find grace for timely help.

In chapter 5 we are told the OT priests died a physical death, but Jesus was made a priest forever. He learned obedience from what he suffered, and when he was made perfect, he became the source of eternal salvation for all who obey him. He tells them that by this time they should have become teachers, but you need someone to teach you again the basic elements of the utterances of God.

In chapter 6 he says let us leave behind the basic teachings about Christ and advance to maturity. For those who once held the faith but now are again crucifying the Son of God, there is nothing you can do. If they are producing thorns and thistles in their lives they will be rejected and burned, so do not become sluggish but be imitators of those who through faith and patience are inheriting the promises.

Chapter 7 says that the OT priesthood was imperfect. Because the OT priesthood was imperfect, the perfect Jesus is the new priest, and with the change in priesthood there is a change in the law. The old law brought nothing to perfection, so Jesus became the guarantee of a better covenant. Therefore he is able to save those who approach God through him since he lives forever to make intercession for them. It is fitting that we should have such a high priest, holy, innocent, undefiled, and separated from sinners, higher than the heavens. He has no need as the OT priests did to offer sacrifices day after day for their own sins then the sins of the people. He did that once for all when he offered himself, for this is a Son who has been made perfect forever.

Chapter 8 says the main point is this, we have such a high priest who has taken his seat at the right hand of the throne of majesty in heaven, a minister of the sanctuary and the true tabernacle that the Lord, not man, has set up. The OT worship was just a shadow of the true faith. Jesus is the mediator of a better covenant enacted on better promises. The prophets foretold of a new and better covenant. The old has been made obsolete and close to disappearing.

Chapter 9 describes well the worship under the first covenant, but he says when Christ came as high priest he entered once and for all with his own blood thus obtaining eternal redemption. If the blood of goats and bulls can sanctify those who are defiled so that their flesh is cleansed how much more will the blood of Christ who through the eternal spirit offered himself unblemished to God to cleanse our consciences from dead works to worship the living God.

For this reason he is the mediator of a new covenant, but a will takes place only upon the death of the testator. According to the law almost everything is purified by blood, and without the shedding of blood, there is no forgiveness. Once for all he has appeared at the end of the ages to take away sin. Just as it is appointed that humans die once and after this the judgment, so also Christ offered once to take away the sins of many and will appear a second time not to take away sin but to bring salvation to those who eagerly await him.

Chapter 10 says in the OT sacrifices there was only a yearly remembrance of sins, for it is impossible for the blood of bulls and goats to take away sins, so Christ was prepared to come and do the will of God. He came to take away the first to establish the second. By this will we have been consecrated through the offering of the body of Jesus Christ once for all. He also says their sins and their evil doing I will remember no more. Where there is forgiveness of these there is no longer an offering for sin. Therefore, through the blood of Jesus we have confidence of entrance into the sanctuary.

Consider how to encourage one another to good works and do not forsake the assembling together as some. If we sin deliberately (if the way of Christ is rejected) after receiving knowledge of truth, there no longer remains a sacrifice for our sins but a fearful prospect of judgment and a flaming fire that consumes. The Lord will judge his people, and it is a fearful thing to fall into the hands of the living God. He who is to come will come. He shall not delay.

Chapter 11 is about the heroes of faith, but first faith is defined.

It is the realization of what is hoped for and evidence of things not seen; by faith we understand the universe was ordered by the word of God, so what is visible came into being by what is invisible. Then the writer makes it plain as the writer of James does (2:14-26) and (Rom 2:6-13) that without obedience there is no faith.

By faith Abel offered a sacrifice greater than Cain. By faith Enoch pleased God and was taken up so that he did not see death. Without faith it is impossible to please God, for anyone who approaches God must believe he exists and that he rewards those who seek him. By faith Noah warned about what was not seen and built an ark. By faith Abraham obeyed when he was called to leave and go to a new land. By faith he received power to procreate even though he was far past the age and while Sarah was sterile. All these died in faith. By faith Moses was hidden by his parents for 3 months after his birth, and they were not afraid of Pharaoh's edict. By faith Moses refused to be known as Pharaoh's son, for he chose to be ill treated along with the people of God. The chapter continues like this showing that real faith is a faith that acts.

In chapter 12 the writer says since we are surrounded by such a great cloud of witnesses, let us persevere in running the race keeping our eyes on Jesus the perfecter of our faith. In your struggle against sin you have not yet resisted to the point of shedding blood. Strive for peace with everyone, and for that holiness without which no one will see the Lord. We who are receiving the unshakeable kingdom should have gratitude with which we should offer worship pleasing to God in reverence and awe.

In chapter 13 the writer says let mutual love continue, and do not neglect hospitality, for through it some have unknowingly entertained angels. Let marriage be honored and the marriage bed undefiled, for God will judge the immoral and adulterers. Let your life be free of the love of money. Then he says to remember your leaders who spoke the word of faith to you and imitate their faith. Jesus Christ is the same yesterday, today, and forever, so do not be carried away with strange teachings. Let us continually offer God a sacrifice of praise, the fruit of lips that confess his name. Let us now go through the chapters verse by verse.

Chapter 1:1-2 says, Long ago God spoke to our ancestors in many and various ways by the prophets, but in these last days he has spoken to us by a Son, whom he appointed heir of all things, through whom he also created the worlds. (All the speaking in the past by the prophets by the many and various ways through the Old Testament was to lead to Christ, who is the very image of God and the fulfillment of God's purposes.)

Verses 3-4 say, He is the reflection of God's glory and the exact imprint of God's very being, and he sustains all things by his powerful word. When he had made purification for sins, he sat down at the right hand of the Majesty on high, having become as much superior to angels as the name he has inherited is more excellent than theirs. (Some false teachers influenced by Gnosticism were saying that Jesus was an angel or just a spiritual being, and that he did not have a real body. Therefore he did not rise with a physical body.)

Verses 5-12 say, For which of the angels did God ever say, "You are my Son; today I have begotten you"? Or again, "I will be his Father, and he will be my Son"? And again, when he brings the firstborn into the world, he says, "Let all God's angels worship him." Of the angels he says, "He makes his angels winds, and his servants flames of fire." But of the Son he says, "Your throne, O God, is for ever and ever, and the righteous scepter is the scepter of your kingdom. You have loved righteousness and hated wickedness; therefore God, your God, has anointed you with the oil of gladness beyond your companions." And, "In the beginning you founded the earth, and the heavens are the work of your hands, they will perish, but you remain; they will all wear out like clothing; like a cloak you will roll them up, and like clothing they will be changed. But you are the same, and your years will never end." But to which of the angels has he ever said, "Sit at my right hand until I make your enemies a footstool for your feet"? And are not all angels spirits in the divine service, sent to serve for the sake of those who are to inherit salvation?

Here we learn of the superiority of Christ over the angels and learn the purpose and differences of both. Jesus is God's unique Son and everything created will eventually be put in submission to him. Angels are spirits in divine service sent to those who will inherit salvation. Notice salvation is inherited. It is a gift. As human families stay loyal to the family, they inherit possessions. As members of God's family stay loyal to God and his purposes, they will inherit salvation. But if one drops out of the family, there will be nothing to inherit. This is the idea of calling Jesus the firstborn. The Hebrew use of the word is to signify the nature of inheritance. The firstborn receives the inheritance. Now it is through Jesus that one inherits salvation.

Chapter 2:1-4 says, Therefore we must pay greater attention to what we have heard, so that we do not drift away from it. For if the message declared through angels was valid (law of Moses), and every transgression or disobedience received a just penalty, how can we escape if we neglect so great a salvation? It was declared first through the Lord (the message of Jesus), and it was attested to us by those who heard him, while God added his testimony by signs and wonders and various miracles, and by gifts of the Holy

Spirit, distributed according to his will. (God testifying to Jesus is a primary purpose of the miracles and gifts of the Holy Spirit.)

Verses 5-9 say, Now God did not subject the coming world, about which we are speaking, to angels. But someone has testified somewhere, "What are human beings that you are mindful of them, or mortals that you care for them? You have made them for a little while lower than the angels; you have crowned them with glory and honor, subjecting all things under their feet." (This is a quote from Ps 8:4-6, which agrees with the Septuigint or Greek text not the Hebrew text.) Now in subjecting all things to them, God left nothing outside their control. As it is, we do not yet see everything in subjection to them, but we do see Jesus, who for a little while was made lower than the angels, now crowned with glory and honor because of the suffering of death, so that by the grace of God he might taste death for everyone.

Verses 10-13 say, It was fitting that God, for whom and through whom all things exist, in bringing many children to glory, should make the pioneer of their salvation (Jesus) perfect through sufferings. (To make perfect is a characteristic of this letter, 5:9, 7:19, 7:28, 9:9, 10:1, 10:14, 11:40, 12:23.) For the one who sanctifies and those who are sanctified all have one Father. For this reason Jesus is not ashamed to call them brothers and sisters, saying, "I will proclaim your name to my brothers and sisters, in the midst of the congregation I will praise you." And again, "I will put my trust in him." And again, "Here am I and the children whom God has given me."

With the death and resurrection of Jesus, his followers will be mystically united to the Father through the Son by the power of the Holy Spirit. This makes them adopted sons and daughters of God and no longer slaves to the law.

Verses 14-18 say, Since, therefore, the children share flesh and blood, he himself likewise shared the same things (became human), so that through death he might destroy the one who has the power of death, that is, the devil, and free those who all their lives were held in slavery by the fear of death. For it is clear he did not come to help angels, but the descendants of Abraham. Therefore he had to become like his brothers and sisters in every respect, so that he might be a merciful and faithful high priest in the service of God, to make a sacrifice of atonement for the sins of the people. Because he himself was tested by what he suffered, he is able to help those who are being tested.

Christ makes atonement for sin, so that all who have sinned can be at one with God, and as his people continually stay washed in Christ's blood, they remain purified and one with God. Jesus became a human being to overcome Satan and free humanity from death (Rom 6:23). Revelation 21:27 states that nothing unclean will enter heaven, nor anyone who practices abomination or falsehood, but only those who are written in the Lamb's book of life. From the beginning of the Old Testament through to the end of the New Testament sin is the problem, and to enter into eternal life it must be atoned for. This is why Jesus is so important to Christians. No other religious leader in history atoned for humanities' sin and then rose from the dead, and then had his resurrection attested to by hundreds of people.

Chapter 3:1-6 says, Therefore, brothers and sisters, holy partners in a heavenly calling, consider that Jesus, the apostle and high priest of our confession, was faithful to the one who appointed him, just as Moses also "was faithful in all God's house." Yet Jesus is worthy of more glory than Moses, just as the builder of a house has more honor than the house itself. For every house is built by someone, but the builder of all things is God. Now Moses was faithful in

all God's house as a servant, to testify to the things that would be spoken later. Christ, however, was faithful over God's house as a Son, and we are his house if we hold firm the confidence and the pride that belongs to hope.

Both Jesus and Moses were faithful to their tasks, but Jesus has a higher calling and is superior to Moses. Moses was a servant in God's house, but Jesus is a Son, the foundation stone of God's house. The faithful people of God are now built into God's house through Christ (1 Peter 2:4-10).

Verses 7-11 say, Therefore, as the Holy Spirit says, "Today if you hear his voice, do not harden your hearts as in the rebellion, as on the day of testing in the wilderness, where your ancestors put me to the test, though they had seen my works for forty years. Therefore I was angry with that generation, and I said, 'They always go astray in their hearts, and they have not known my ways.' As in my anger I swore, 'They will not enter my rest.' "

Verses 12-15 say, Take care, brothers and sisters, that none of you have an evil, unbelieving heart that turns away from the living God. But exhort one another every day, as long as it is called "today," so that none of you may be hardened by the deceitfulness of sin. For we have become partners of Christ, if only we hold our first confidence firm to the end. As it is said, "Today, if you hear his voice, do not harden your hearts as in the rebellion." (This certainly destroys the idea some teach that once you are saved, you are always saved. That teaching is true only if you stay firm until the end.)

Verse 16-19 say, Now who were they who heard and yet were rebellious? Was it not all those that left Egypt under the leadership of Moses? But with whom was he angry forty years? Was it not those who sinned, whose bodies fell in the wilderness? And to whom did he swear that they would not enter his rest, if not to those who were disobedient? So we see that they were unable to enter because of unbelief. (The rest is eternal life. Is not the message quite clear? God's people who he set free from Egypt did not enter the promised land because they were disobedient.)

❧

Chapter 4:1-3 says, Therefore, while the promise of entering his rest is still open, let us take care that none of you should seem to have failed to reach it. For indeed the good news came to us just as to them; but the message they heard did not benefit them, because they were not united by faith with those who listened. For we who have believed enter that rest, just as God has said, "As in my anger I swore, 'They shall not enter my rest,' " though his works were finished at the foundation of the world.

Verses 4-7 say, For in one place it speaks about the seventh day as follows, "And God rested on the seventh day from all his works." And again in this place it says, "They shall not enter my rest." Since therefore it remains open for some to enter it, and those who formerly received the good news failed to enter because of disobedience, again he sets a certain day—"today"—saying through David much later, in the words already quoted, "Today if you hear his voice, do not harden your hearts." (Much of this is based on Psalm 95:7-11. Entering the promised land under Joshua was only a type, a symbol, of the true rest to come, which is eternal life.)

Verses 8-11 say, For if Joshua had given them rest, God would not speak later about another day. So then a sabbath rest remains for the people of God; for those who enter God's rest also cease from their labors as God did from his. Let us therefore make every effort to enter that rest, so that no one may fall through such disobedience as theirs.

Verses 12-13 say, Indeed, the word of God is living and active, sharper than any two-edged sword, piercing until it divides soul from spirit, joints from marrow; it is able to judge the thoughts and intentions of the heart. And before him no creature is hidden, but all are naked and laid bare to the eyes of the one to whom we must render an account. (The point is that God's word is not a dead letter; it is alive and working. Therefore let God's word read you (speak to you), and then after you hear it, read and meditate on it, and ask yourself what God's word is saying to you about you?)

Verses 14-16 say, Since, then, we have a great high priest who has passed through the heavens, Jesus, the Son of God, let us hold fast to our confession. For we do not have a high priest who is unable to sympathize with our weaknesses, but we have one who in every respect has been tested as we are, yet without sin. Let us therefore approach the throne of grace with boldness, so that we might receive mercy and find grace to help in time of need. (The Jesus who overcame can help his people overcome.)

Chapter 5:1-6 says, Every high priest chosen from among mortals is put in charge of things pertaining to God on their behalf, to offer gifts and sacrifices for sins. He is able to deal gently with the ignorant and wayward, since he himself is subject to weakness; and because of this he must offer sacrifice for his own sins as well as those of the people. And one does not presume to take this honor, but takes it only when called by God, just as Aaron was. So also Christ did not glorify himself in becoming a high priest, but was appointed by the one who said to him, "You are my Son, today I have begotten you"; as he says also in another place, "You are a priest forever, according to the order of Melchizedek." (The Father made the Son the eternal priest. We do not know much about Melchizedek other than he was an eternal priest and Abraham paid

him a tithe. Gen 1:18-20 and Ps 110:4 are the only places outside of Hebrews that he is mentioned.)

Verses 7-10 say, In the days of his flesh, Jesus offered up prayers and supplications, with loud cries and tears, to the one who was able to save him from death, and he was heard because of his reverent submission. Although he was a Son, he learned obedience through what he suffered, and having been made perfect (at the cross), he became the source of eternal salvation for all who obey him, having been designated by God a high priest according to the order of Melchizedek.

Verses 11-14 say, About this we have much to say that is hard to explain, since you have become dull of understanding. For by this time you ought to be teachers, you need someone to teach you again the basic elements of the oracles of God. You need milk, not solid food; for everyone who lives on milk, being still an infant, is unskilled in the word of righteousness. But solid food is for the mature, for those whose faculties have been trained by practice to distinguish good from evil. (The author is unhappy with the spiritual immaturity of these people. Milk stands for the basic teachings of the faith, while solid food represents the deeper understanding of Christ's teachings.)

Chapter 6:1-2 says, Therefore let us go on toward perfection, leaving behind the basic teaching about Christ, and not laying again the foundation: repentance from dead works and faith toward God, instruction about baptisms, laying on of hands, resurrection of the dead, and eternal judgment. (These are the six basics that the Christian church the Hebrew writer is addressing could not get beyond. He is not saying to forget them but get into some of the more mature teachings in order to grow in the faith.)

Verses 3-6 say, And we will do this, if God permits. For it is impossible to restore again to repentance those who have been once enlightened, and have tasted the heavenly gift, and have shared in the Holy Spirit, and have tasted the goodness of the word of God and the powers of the age to come, and then fallen away, since on their own they are crucifying again the Son of God and are holding him up to contempt. (In context with the whole Bible this means it is impossible to restore them if they refuse to repent and return. See 2 Peter 2:21-22. God never takes away a person's free will.)

Verses 7-8 say, Ground that drinks up the rain falling on it repeatedly, and that produces a crop useful to those for whom it is cultivated, receives a blessing from God. But if it produces thorns and thistles, it is worthless and on the verge of being cursed; its end is to be burned over. (The author is not saying they can not repent (Jas 5:19-20), but he is saying apostates are like the ground that produces thorns and thistles; they will be burned up.)

Verses 9-12 say, Even though we speak in this way, beloved, we are confident of better things in your case, things that belong to salvation. For God is not unjust; he will not overlook your work and the love you have showed for his sake in serving the saints, as you still do. And we want each one of you to show the same diligence so as to realize the full assurance of hope to the very end, so that you may not become sluggish, but imitators of those who through faith and patience inherit the promise. (Faithfulness linked with love leads to the confidence of hope, if they remain steadfast in the faith.)

Verses 13-16 say, When God made a promise to Abraham, because he had no one greater by whom to swear, he swore by himself, saying, "I will surely bless you and multiply you." And thus Abraham, having patiently endured, obtained the promise. Human beings, of course, swear by someone greater than themselves, and an oath given as confirmation puts an end to all dispute.

Verses 17-20 say, In the same way, when God desired to show even more clearly to the heirs of the promise the unchangeable character of his purpose, he guaranteed it by an oath, so that through two unchangeable things, in which it is impossible that God would prove false, we who have taken refuge might be strongly encouraged to seize the hope set before us. We have this hope, a sure and steadfast anchor of the soul, a hope that enters the inner shrine behind the curtain, where Jesus, a forerunner on our behalf, has entered, having become a high priest forever according to the order of Melchizedek.

The inner shrine is the Holy of Holies of the tabernacle, which was restricted to the high priest alone. The inner shrine is now heaven, which Christ has entered, and now all enter that inner shrine through Christ.

Chapter 7:1-3 says, This "King Melchizedek of Salem, priest of the Most High God, met Abraham as he was returning home from defeating the kings and blessed him"; and to him Abraham apportioned "one-tenth of everything." His name, in the first place, means "king of righteousness"; next he is also king of Salem, that is, "king of peace." Without father, without mother, without genealogy, having neither beginning of days nor end of life, but resembling the Son of God, he remains a priest forever.

Verses 4-10 say, See how great he is! Even Abraham the patriarch gave him a tenth of the spoils. And those descendants of Levi who receive the priestly office have a commandment in the law to collect tithes from the people, that is, from their kindred, though these also are descended from Abraham. But this man who does not belong to their ancestry, collected tithes from Abraham and blessed him who had received the promises. It is beyond dispute that the inferior is blessed by the superior. In the one case, tithes are received by those who are mortal; in the other, by one of whom it is testified that he lives. One might even say that Levi himself, who receives tithes, paid tithes through Abraham, for he was still in the loins of his ancestors when Melchizedek met him. (The whole process of reasoning is to demonstrate that Melchizedek is superior to both Abraham and the Old Testament priests that came from Levi.)

Verses 11-14 say, Now if perfection had been attainable through the levitical priesthood—for the people received the law under this priesthood—what further need would there have been to speak of another priest arising according to the order of Melchizedek, rather than one according to the order of Aaron? For when there is a change in the priesthood, there is necessarily a change in the law as well. Now the one of whom those things are spoken belonged to another tribe, from which no one has ever served at the altar. For it is evident that our Lord was descended from Judah, and in connection with that tribe Moses said nothing about priests.

The Levitical priesthood is inadequate because it is only temporary. On the other hand a priest like Melchizedek is eternal. Our Lord was descended from Judah, not Aaron, and with a change in the priesthood came a change in the law. This is the point of verses 15-19. A priest resembling Melchizedek is eternal according to Psalm 110:4, and the office is neither inherited nor transmitted. Verses 18-19 say, There is, on the one hand, the abrogation of an earlier commandment because it was weak and ineffectual (for the law made nothing perfect); there is, on the other hand, the introduction of a better hope, through which we approach God.

Verses 20-22 say, This was confirmed with an oath; for others who became priests took their office without an oath, because of the one who said to him. "The Lord has sworn and will not change his mind, 'You are a priest forever' "—accordingly Jesus has also become the guarantee of a better covenant. Further more, the former priests were many in number, because they were prevented by death from continuing in office; but he holds his priesthood eternally, because he continues forever. Consequently he is able for all time to save those who approach God through him, since he always lives to make intercession for them.

Unlike the Levitical priests, Jesus was appointed with a divine oath for this better covenant. In this new and better covenant all who come to him are saved by him, and he is there to make intercession for them. Even though Christ is the mediator, the people of Christ can ask anyone on earth or heaven to pray to him for them.

Verses 26-28 say, For it was fitting that we should have such a high priest, holy, blameless, undefiled, separated from sinners, and exalted above the heavens. Unlike the other high priests, he has no need to offer sacrifices day after day, first for his own sins, and then for those of the people; this he did once for all when he offered himself. For the law appoints as high priests those who are subject to weakness, but the word of the oath, which came later than the law, appoints a Son who has been made perfect forever. (The whole chapter is to show why the priesthood of Jesus is superior to the Old Testament priesthood.)

Chapter 8:1-5 says, Now the main point in what we are saying is this: we have such a high priest, one who is seated at the right hand of the throne of the Majesty in the heavens, a minister in the sanctuary and the true tent that the Lord, and not any mortal, has set up. For every high priest is appointed to offer gifts and sacrifices; hence it is necessary for this priest also to have something to offer.

Now if he were on earth, he would not be a priest at all, since there are priests who offer gifts according to the law. They offer worship in a sanctuary that is a sketch and shadow of the heavenly one; for Moses, when he was about to erect the tent, was warned, "See that you make everything according to the pattern that was shown you on the mountain."

Verses 6-7 say, But Jesus has now obtained a more excellent ministry, and to that degree he is the mediator of a better covenant, which has been enacted through better promises. For if that first covenant would have been faultless, there would have been no need to look for a second one.

The idea is that we have a high priest who is also the enthroned King ministering on our behalf in the heavenly sanctuary. The tabernacle constructed by Moses was a sketch and shadow of the heavenly one. Jesus who made the perfect sacrifice has now instituted the better covenant, for the first covenant was only temporary.

Verses 8-9 say, God finds fault with them when he says: "The days are surely coming, says the Lord, when I will establish a new covenant with the house of Israel and with the house of Judah; not like the covenant that I made with their ancestors, on the day when I took them by the hand to lead them out of the land of Egypt; for they did not continue in my covenant, and so I had no concern for them, says the Lord.

Verses 10-13 say, This is the covenant that I will make with the house of Israel after those days, says the Lord: I will put my laws in their minds and write them on their hearts, and I will be their God, and they shall be my people. And they shall not teach one another or say to each other, 'Know the Lord,' for they shall all know me, from the least of them to the greatest. For I will be merciful toward their iniquities, and I will remember their sins no more." In speaking of a "new covenant," he has made the first one obsolete. And what is obsolete and growing old will soon disappear. (The new covenant prophesied by Jeremiah (Jer 31:31-34) makes known a future new order as he shows the old will be replaced with the beginning of a new priesthood.)

Chapter 9:1-5 says, Now even the first covenant had regulations for worship and an earthly sanctuary. For a tent was constructed, the first one, in which were the lampstand, the table and the bread of the Presence; this is called the Holy Place. Behind the second curtain was a tent called the Holy of Holies. In it stood the golden altar of incense and the ark of the covenant overlaid on all sides with gold, in which there were a golden urn holding the manna, and Aaron's rod that budded, and the tablets of the covenant; above it were the cherubim of glory overshadowing the mercy seat. Of these things we cannot speak now in detail. (These are all described in the book of Exodus.)

Verses 6-10 say, Such preparations having been made, the priests go continually into the first tent to carry out their ritual duties; but only the high priest goes into the second, and he but once a year, and not without taking the blood that he offers for himself and for the sins committed unintentionally by the people. By this the Holy Spirit indicates that the way into the sanctuary has not yet been disclosed as long as the first tent is still standing. This is a symbol of the present time, during which gifts and sacrifices are offered that cannot perfect the conscience of the worshiper, but deal only with food and drink and various baptisms, regulations of the body imposed until the time comes to set things right. (All of this was temporary. The Levitical sacrifices can not cleanse the inner guilt that results from sin. The time to set things right will be inaugurated by Christ and the new covenant.)

Verses 11-14 say, But when Christ came as a high priest of the good things that have come, then through the greater and perfect tent, not made with hands, that is, not of this creation, he entered once for all into the Holy Place, not with the blood of goats and calves, but with his own blood, thus obtaining eternal redemption. For if the blood of goats and bulls, with the sprinkling of the ashes of a heifer, sanctifies those who have been defiled so that their flesh is purified, how much more will the blood of Christ, who through the eternal Spirit offered himself without blemish to God, purify our conscience from dead works to worship the living God!

The animal sacrifices basically only purified the flesh related to the purification laws, but the sacrifice of Christ purifies the whole person. The atonement process under the old covenant is being compared to the atonement of Christ and the new covenant and found wanting.

Verse 15 says, For this reason he is the mediator of a new covenant, so that those who are called may receive the promised eternal inheritance, because a death has occurred that redeems them from the transgressions under the first covenant. (Under the old covenant sins were just temporarily put on hold from year to year.)

Verses 16-22 say, Where a will (covenant) is involved the death of the one who made it must be established. For a will takes effect only at death, since it is not in force as long as the one who has made it is alive. Hence not even the first covenant was inaugurated without blood. For when every commandment had been told to all the people by Moses in accordance with the law, he took the blood of calves and goats, with water and scarlet wool and hyssop, and sprinkled both the scroll itself and all the people saying, "This is the blood of the covenant that God has ordained for you." And in the same way he sprinkled with the blood both the tent and all vessels used in worship. Indeed, under the law almost everything is purified with blood, and without the shedding of blood there is no forgiveness of sins. (Covenants must be ratified by blood.)

Verses 23-28 say, Thus it was necessary for the sketches (shadow) of the heavenly things to be purified by these rites, but the heavenly things themselves need better sacrifices than these. For Christ did not enter a sanctuary made by human hands, a mere copy of the true one, but he entered into heaven itself, now to appear in the presence of God on our behalf. Nor was it to offer himself again and again, as the high priest enters the Holy Place year after year with blood that is not his own; for then he would have had to suffer again and again since the foundation of the world. But as it is, he has appeared once for all at the end of the age to remove sin by the sacrifice of himself. And just as it has been appointed for mortals to die once, and after that the judgment, so Christ, having been offered once to bear the sins of many, will appear a second time not to deal with sin, but to save those who are eagerly waiting for him.

Under the old covenant sacrifices had to be offered daily and once a year on the Day of Atonement, but under the new covenant only one sacrifice is needed for all time. The atonement of Christ is the perfect atonement. After that the one sacrifice is simply made present to us. Under both covenants sin is a major issue that must be dealt with.

⚘

Chapter 10:1-4 says, Since the law has only a shadow of the good things to come and not the true form of these realities, it can never, by the same sacrifices that are continually offered year by year, make perfect those who approach. Otherwise would they not have ceased being offered, since the worshipers, cleansed once for all, would no longer have any consciousness of sin? But in these sacrifices there is a reminder of sin year after year. For it is impossible for the blood of bulls and goats to take away sins. (The annual offering of animals under the old covenant is not the reality that takes away sins. It only deals with sin temporarily.)

Verses 5-10 say, Consequently, when Christ came into the world, he said, "Sacrifices and offerings you have not desired, but a body you have prepared for me; in burnt offerings and sin offerings you have taken no pleasure. Then I said, 'See, God, I have come to do your will, O God' (in the scroll of the book it is written of me)." When he said above, "You have neither desired nor taken pleasure in sacrifices and offerings and burnt offerings and sin offerings" (offered according to the law), then he added, "See, I have come to do your will." He abolishes the first in order to establish the second. And it is by God's will that we have been sanctified through the offering of the body of Jesus Christ once for all. (God's people are both justified, made right with God, brought together as one, and sanctified, made holy, by Christ. The Old Testament sacrificial system of offerings is ended with the sacrifice of Jesus.)

Verses 11-14 say, And every priest stands day after day at his service, offering again and again the same sacrifices that can never take away sins. But when Christ had offered for all time a single sacrifice for sins, "he sat down at the right hand of God," and since then has been waiting "until his enemies would be made a footstool for his feet." For by a single offering he has perfected for all time those who are sanctified.

Christ not only came to provide that single and final offering for sin but came to establish the kingdom of God. The kingdom has broken into the world, and the process of putting all things under his feet has begun. It will be finished when he comes the second time, and all things are put under his feet and perfected.

Verses 15-18 say, And the Holy Spirit also testifies to us, for after saying, "This is the covenant that I will make with them after those days, says the Lord: I will put my laws in their hearts, and I will write them on their minds," he also adds, "I will remember their sins no more." Where there is forgiveness of these, there is no longer any offering for sin. (Citing Ps 110:1 the author emphasizes Jesus superiority to the Levitical priests as he sits at God's right hand waiting for his enemies to be put in submission to him.)

Verses 19-22 say, Therefore, my friends, since we have confidence to enter the sanctuary by the blood of Jesus, by the new and living way that he opened for us through the curtain (that is, through his flesh) and since we have a great priest over the house of God, let us approach with a true heart in full assurance of faith, with our hearts sprinkled clean from an evil conscience and our bodies washed with pure water.

The great high priest that we approach with a true heart is Christ. It is he who purifies us of an evil conscience. Having our bodies washed with pure water is a reference to baptism. There is no question that baptism is called for by all who approach Christ. Baptism is the channel by which the Holy Spirit adds one to the body of Christ and then works the works of God for the glory of God.

Verses 23-25 say, Let us hold fast to the confession of our hope without wavering, for he who has promised is faithful. And let us consider how to provoke one another to love and good deeds, not neglecting to meet together, as is the habit of some, but encouraging one another, and all the more as you see the Day approaching.

Three responsibilities are mentioned: To hold fast to our public confession of hope, to encourage each other to love and do good deeds, and to meet together for worship and learning.

Verses 26-31 say, For if we willfully persist in sin (ignoring these responsibilities) after having received the knowledge of the truth, there no longer remains a sacrifice for sins, but a fearful prospect of judgment, and a fury of fire that will consume the adversaries. Anyone who has violated the law of Moses dies without mercy "on the testimony of two or more witnesses." How much worse punishment do you think will be deserved by those who have spurned the Son of God, profaned the blood of the covenant by which they were sanctified, and outraged the Spirit of grace? For we know the one who said, "Vengeance is mine, I will repay." And again, "The Lord will judge his people." It is a fearful thing to fall into the hands of the living God. (This sounds quite serious. Does the reader think most people take these verses seriously?)

Verses 32-36 say, But recall those earlier days when, after you had been enlightened, you endured a hard struggle with sufferings, sometimes being publically exposed to abuse and persecution, and sometimes being partners with those so treated. For you had compassion for those who were in prison (for the cause of the faith), and you cheerfully accepted the plundering of your possessions, knowing that you yourselves possessed something better and more lasting. Do not, therefore, abandon that confidence of yours; it brings a great reward. For you need endurance, so that when you have done the will of God, you may receive what was promised. (Throughout the book obedience and the endurance of faith is stressed.)

Verses 37-39 say, For yet "in a very little while, the one who is coming will come and will not delay; but my righteous one will live by faith. My soul takes no pleasure in anyone who shrinks back." But we are not among those who shrink back and so are lost, but among those who have faith and so are saved.

According to the writer of Hebrews those who do not endure in the faith, who turn away from Christ, and the responsibilities he gives them will be lost. Again it is important to hold fast to the confession of our hope without wavering, to provoke one another to love and good deeds, and to not neglect meeting together as stated in verses 23-25.

⟡⟡⟡

Chapter 11:1-3 says, Now faith is the assurance of things hoped for, the conviction of things not seen. Indeed, by faith our ancestors received approval. By faith we understand that the worlds were prepared by the word of God, so that what is seen was made from things that are not visible.

Basic faith is belief in God and his word without having proof beyond doubt. Faith acts on God's word, even though God has not individually appeared and spoken to the person. The rest of the chapter demonstrates with many of the Old Testament heroes just how faith works.

Verses 3-6 say, By faith Abel offered to God a more acceptable sacrifice than Cain's. Through this he received approval as righteous, God himself giving approval to his gifts; he died, but through his faith he still speaks. By faith Enoch was taken so that he did not experience death; and "he was not found, because God had taken him." For it was attested before he was taken away that "he had pleased God." And without faith it is impossible to please God, for whoever would approach him must believe that he exists and that he rewards those who seek him. (Again faith is seeking God and trusting in his word without having absolute proof that there is a God.)

Verses 7-10 say, By faith Noah, warned by God about events as yet unseen, respected the warning and built an ark to save his household; by this he condemned the world and became an heir to the righteousness (relationship with God) that is in accordance with faith. By faith Abraham obeyed when he was called to set out for a place that he was to receive as an inheritance; and he set out, not knowing where he was going. By faith he stayed for a time in the land he had been promised, as in a foreign land, living in tents, as did Isaac and Jacob, who were heirs with him of the same promise. For he looked forward to the city that has foundations whose architect and builder is God. (The city is the heavenly Jerusalem, 12:22, Gal 4:26, Rev 21:2. This indicates, contrary to many scholars, that there were those Old Testament people who believed in eternal life.)

Verses 11-12 say, By faith he (Abraham) received power of procreation, even though he was too old—and Sarah herself was barren—because he considered him faithful who had promised. Therefore from one person, and this one as good as dead, descendants were born, "as many as the stars of heaven and as the innumerable grains of sand by the seashore." (Abraham was hundred and Sarah ninety when they had a child.)

Verses 13-16 say, All of these died in faith without having received the promises, but from a distance they saw and greeted them. They confessed that they were strangers and foreigners on the earth, for people who speak in this way make it clear that they are seeking a homeland. If they had been thinking of the land that they had left behind, they would have had opportunity to return. But as it is, they desire a better country, that is, a heavenly one. Therefore God is not ashamed to be called their God; indeed, he has prepared a city for them.

Verses 17-22 say, By faith Abraham, when put to the test, offered up Isaac. He who had received the promises was ready to offer up his only son, of whom he had been told, "It is through Isaac that descendants shall be named for you." He considered the fact that God is able to even raise someone from the dead—and figuratively speaking, he did receive him back. (God accepted a ram in place of his son.) By faith Isaac invoked blessings for the future on Jacob and Esau. By faith Jacob, when dying, blessed each of the sons of Joseph, "bowing in worship over the top of his staff." By faith Joseph, at the end of his life, made mention of the exodus of the Israelites and gave instructions about his burial.

Verses 23-31 say, By faith Moses was hidden by his parents for three months after his birth, because they saw that the child was beautiful; and they were not afraid of the king's edict. By faith Moses, when he was grown up, refused to be called a son of Pharoah's daughter, choosing rather to share ill-treatment with the people of God than to enjoy the fleeting pleasures of sin. He considered abuse suffered for the Christ (see 1Cor 10:3-4) to be greater wealth than the treasures of Egypt, for he was looking forward to the reward. By faith he left Egypt, unafraid of the king's anger; for he persevered as though he saw him who is invisible. By faith he kept the Passover and the sprinkling of blood, so that the destroyer of the first born would not touch the firstborn of Israel. By faith people passed through the Red Sea as if it were dry land, but when the Egyptians attempted to do so, they were drowned. By faith the walls of Jericho fell after they had been encircled for seven days. By faith Rahab the prostitute did not perish with those who were disobedient, because she had received the spies in peace.

Verses 32-38 say, And what more should I say? For time would fail me to tell of Gideon, Barak, Samson, Jephthah, of David and Samuel and the prophets—who through faith conquered kingdoms, administered justice, obtained promises, shut the mouths of lions, quenched raging fire, escaped the edge of the sword, won strength out of weakness, became mighty in war, put foreign armies to flight. Women received their dead by resurrection. Others were tortured, refusing to accept release, in order to obtain a better resurrection. Others suffered mocking and flogging, and even chains and imprisonment. They were stoned to death, they were sawn in two (tradition says this was Isaiah), they were killed by the sword, they went about in skins of sheep and goats, destitute, persecuted, tormented—of whom the world was not worthy. They wandered in deserts and mountains, and in caves and holes in the ground. (All of this is a long list of faith in action. Biblically faith without obedient action is not faith.)

Verses 39-40 say, Yet all these, though they were commended for their faith, did not receive what was promised, since God had provided something better so that they would not, apart from us, be made perfect. (The heroes of the Old Testament obtained their reward only after the saving work of Christ was accomplished. Thus they already enjoy what Christians who are still struggling do not yet possess in its fullness, Mt 27:50-53.)

Chapter 12:1-3 says, Therefore, since we are surrounded by so great a cloud of witnesses, let us also lay aside every weight and the sin that clings so closely, and let us run with perseverance the race that is set before us, looking to Jesus the pioneer and perfecter of our faith, who for the sake of the joy that was set before him endured the cross, disregarding its shame, and has taken his seat at the right hand of the throne of God (Dan 7:13-14). Consider him who endured such hostility against himself from sinners, so that you may not grow weary or lose heart. (The call is to endure suffering when persecuted in the faith by looking to Jesus as your model.)

Verses 4-6 say, In your struggle against sin you have not yet resisted to the point of shedding your blood (as Jesus did). And you have forgotten the exhortation that addresses you as children—"My child, do not regard lightly the discipline of the Lord, or lose heart when you are punished by him; for the Lord disciplines those whom he loves, and chastises every child whom he accepts."

The writer is saying that as they endure with discipline they will mature and become stronger Christians. Johnson (1999, 472-473) says that a nuance of the Greek word for discipline is education. Discipline here is not punishment but a learning experience. The human experience of suffering shapes Christians in the pattern of him who learned to be the Son through suffering. It is the process of learning to become children of God as Jesus did through obedience. As most students know learning can be a form of suffering.

Verses 7-11 say, endure trials for the sake of discipline. God is treating you as children (meaning a child of God); for what child is there whom a parent does not discipline. If you do not have that discipline in which all children share, then you are illegitimate and not his children. Moreover, we had human parents to discipline us, and we respected them. Should we not be even more willing to be subject to the Father of spirits and live? For they disciplined us for a short time as seemed best to them, but he disciplines us for our good in order that we may share his holiness. Now, discipline always seems painful rather than pleasant at the time, but later it yields the peaceful fruit of righteousness to those who have been trained by it. (Here discipline seems to be punishment, but it is learning how to be more holy.)

The writer seems to be saying that if the follower of Jesus does not live the faith and receive the suffering that the world gives to those who seriously live and stand for the ways of Christ, then that follower will become a dead branch (Jn 15:1-11) and never really grow in Christ.

Verses 12-13 say, Therefore lift your drooping hands and strengthen your weak knees, and make straight paths for your feet, so that what is lame may not be put out of joint, but rather be healed. (The following are a few things a child of God must do.)

Verses 14-17 say, Pursue peace with everyone, and the holiness without which no one will see the Lord. See to it that no one fails to obtain the grace of God; that no root of bitterness springs up and causes trouble, and through it many become defiled. See to it that no one becomes like Esau, an immoral and godless person, who sold his birth rite for a single meal. (He exchanged his future blessing for immediate satisfaction.) You know that later, when he wanted to inherit the blessing, he was rejected for he found no chance to repent, even though he sought the blessing with tears. (It was too late to change his father's mind. He had chosen a life of godlessness. Is this saying that there is a time when it is too late to repent?)

In verses 18-25 the two covenants are contrasted and the Hebrews are encouraged for as verses 22-25 say, But you have come to Mount Zion and the city of the living God, the heavenly Jerusalem, and to innumerable angels in festal gathering, and to the assembly of the first born who are enrolled in heaven, and to God the judge of all, and to the spirits of the righteous made perfect, and to Jesus, the mediator of a new covenant, and to the sprinkled blood that speaks of a better word than the blood of Abel. See that you do not refuse the one who is speaking; for if they did not escape when they refused the one who warned them on earth, how much less will we escape if we reject the one who warns from heaven! (This is a warning not to reject the word of God.)

Verses 26-29 say, At that time his voice shook the earth; but now he has promised, "Yet once more I will shake not only the earth but also heaven." This phrase, "Yet once more," indicates the removal of what is shaken—that is, created things—so that what cannot be shaken may remain. (Only the eternal will remain.) Therefore, since we are receiving a kingdom that cannot be shaken, let us give thanks, by which we offer to God an acceptable worship with reverence and awe; for indeed our God is a consuming fire. (This is a primary reason to always worship God in reverence and awe in what we do and in the assembly of God's people. Does the reader believe that most of God's people worship in reverence and awe?)

Chapter 13:1-3 says, Let mutual love continue. Do not neglect to show hospitality to strangers, for by doing that some have entertained angels without knowing it. (Are angels who look like humans at work in this world?) Remember those who are in prison, as though you were in prison with them; those who are being tortured, as though you yourselves were being tortured. (From this does it seem that God approves the torturing of prisoners?)

Verse 4 says, Let marriage be held in honor by all, and let the marriage bed be kept undefiled; for God will judge fornicators and adulterers. (It seems to this writer that the modern day church rarely, if ever, mentions fornication and adultery in its sermons (homilies). If sex is ever mentioned the emphasis seems to be only on homosexuality. Of these three issues, which one is least likely to be an issue of people sitting in the pews?)

Verses 5-6 say, Keep your lives free from the love of money, and be content with what you have, for he has said, "I will never leave you or forsake you." So we can say with confidence, "The Lord is my helper; I will not be afraid? What can anyone do to me?" (Again this writer asks, of these four issues, fornication, homosexuality, adultery, and the love of money, which is probably violated most by people sitting in church pews? The least? Which one does the church talk about the most? The least? How often does it talk about the others? Why?)

Verse 7 says, Remember your leaders, those who spoke the word of God to you; consider the outcome of their way of life, and imitate their life. (In most cases that is good advice.) Verses 8-10 say, Jesus Christ is the same yesterday, today, and forever. Do not be carried away by all kinds of strange teachings; for it is well for the heart to be strengthened by grace, not by regulations about food, which have not benefitted those who observe them. (Faithfulness is characterized by the teaching of Jesus not by these false teachers coming in to make Jesus what he is not and to make people obey certain food laws when he abolished all the food laws.)

Verses 12-14 say, Jesus also suffered outside the city gate (Jerusalem) in order to sanctify (make holy) the people by his own blood. Let us then go to him outside the camp (of Jerusalem) and bear the abuse he endured. For here we have no lasting city, but we are looking for the city that is to come (heavenly Jerusalem).

Verses 15-16 say, Through him, then, let us continually offer a sacrifice of praise to God, that is, the fruit of lips that confess his name. Do not neglect to do good and to share what you have, for such sacrifices are pleasing to God. (How much is this latter statement a part of the American capitalistic economic theory?)

Verse 17 says, Obey your leaders and submit to them, for they are keeping watch over your souls and will give an account. Let them do this with joy and not with sighing—for that would be harmful to you. (Is the writer of Hebrews calling for blind obedience? How do you know?)

Verses 18-19 say, Pray for us; we are sure that we have a clear conscience, desiring to act honorably in all things. I urge you all the more to do this, so that I may be restored to you very soon. (The follower of Christ is to always be a person of honorable character.)

Verses 20-22 are a doxology: Now may the God of peace (not war and guns), who brought back from the dead our Lord Jesus, the great shepherd of the sheep, by the blood of the eternal covenant, make you complete in everything good so that you may do his will, working among us that which is pleasing in his sight, through Jesus Christ, to whom be the glory forever and ever. Amen.

Verses 22-25 say, I appeal to you, brothers and sisters, bear with my word of exhortation, for I have written you briefly. I want you to know that our brother Timothy has been set free; and if he comes in time, he will be with me when I see you. Greet all your leaders and all the saints. Those from Italy send you greetings. Grace be with all of you.

As a way of review list some of the most important verses or thoughts in the letter to the Hebrews.

THE LETTER OF JAMES

The book is written by James who calls himself a slave of God and Jesus Christ. This James is probably the brother of Jesus, who became the leader in the Jerusalem church. It is a book that is blessed with sayings of Christian wisdom often strung out with no apparent order. Chapter 1 begins by saying count it all joy when you suffer various trials, for the testing of faith produces perseverance and perseverance leads to perfection. If any lack wisdom, ask in faith without doubting and God will grant it. Doubters will not be granted wisdom for they are unstable in their ways. James says blessed are those who persevere in temptation, for they will receive the crown of life. Keep in mind God tempts no one. All are tempted when lured and enticed by their own desires. Desire conceives and brings forth sin, and when sin reaches maturity, it brings forth death.

James reminds them that all good gifts come from the Father, so do not be deceived. He willed to give us birth by the word of truth that we may be a first fruits of his creatures. They should be quick to hear but slow to speak, and slow to be angry, for neither accomplishes the righteousness of God. So, put away all sin and humbly welcome the word that is planted in you and is able to save your souls. Be doers of the word not just hearers. Those who look into the perfect law of freedom and persevere as a doer who acts, and he will be blessed in what he does. But if anyone thinks he is religious and does not bridle his tongue, he deceives his heart, and his religion is in vain. Religion that is pure is to care for those in need like widows and orphans and to keep oneself unstained by the world.

In chapter 2 James says show no partiality between rich and poor, and do not be discriminating against the poor, judging with evil designs. God has chosen those who are poor in the world to be rich in faith and heirs of the kingdom. He asks them, is it not the rich who are oppressing you? If you show partiality toward the rich, you are committing sin, for whoever keeps the whole law but falls short in one thing, you have become guilty in respect to all of it. Therefore show mercy not judgment to those who are not the wealthy and powerful, to those who are not the elites. Judgment will be without mercy to those who do not show mercy, for mercy will triumph over judgment.

Then James says what good is it if someone says he has faith but does not have any works with it? Can that faith save him? If those who have no food or clothing and you do not do what you can for those in need, what good is that? So, also, faith of itself, if it does not have works, is dead. I will demonstrate my faith by my works.

Then James says you do well if you believe, but even the demons believe. You want proof that faith without works is useless? Was not Abraham our father justified by works when he offered his son Isaac upon the altar. You see that his faith was active with his works, and faith was completed by his works. Thus the scripture was fulfilled that says, Abraham believed God, and it was credited to him as righteousness, and he was called the friend of God. See how a person is justified by works and not by faith alone. Rahab the harlot was also justified by works when she welcomed the messengers and

THE LETTER OF JAMES

sent them by a different route. For just as a body without a spirit is dead, so also faith without works is dead. James is countering those distorting the teachings of Paul and John who were saying that all one has to do is to believe and nothing else in order to find salvation. The issue is still around in the times we live in today.

In chapter 3 James says not many should become teachers, for you will be judged more strictly, for we all fall short in many respects. He relates this to the power of speech that teachers have because people come to them to learn truth. He talks about the power and danger of the tongue which is difficult to control. He compares the tongue with the small rudder in a ship that does the guiding. James says consider how a spark can set a forest ablaze. The tongue is like that; it is a small fire that can defile the whole body. Human beings seem to be able to tame everything but the tongue. He calls it a restless evil full of deadly poison, for with it we bless the Lord and curse humans.

Then James says follow wisdom from above in a life of humility. Be pure, peaceable, gentle, compliant, full of mercy, and good fruits, be sincere, and sow the fruit of righteousness in peace, and cultivate peace. Get rid of bitter jealousy and selfish ambition which is earthly, unspiritual, and demonic for they produce nothing but disorder and every foul practice.

In chapter 4 James says where do wars and conflicts come from? Is it not from your passions? You covet but do not possess. You kill and envy, but you can not obtain, so you fight and wage war. You ask for the wrong things. You ask to have things to fulfill your passions. You are like adulterers. Do you not know to be a lover of the world is enmity with God? Whoever wants to be a lover of the world is an enemy of God. God resists the proud and gives grace to the humble, so submit yourself to God. Humble yourself before the Lord, and he will exalt you.

James says, purify your hearts, you of two minds, and draw near to God. Do not speak evil of one another and judge one another; be doers of the law not judges. One who knows the right thing to do and does not do it, commits sin. Remember you are a puff of smoke who appears briefly, then disappears, so do not be so arrogant to say tomorrow or the next day or the next year I am going to do business here or there and make a profit. You have no idea what your life will be tomorrow, for you do not have the control you think you have.

In chapter 5 he warns the rich who have stored up their treasures in wealth and things, for he says they will rot away. He says you who got rich by withholding the workers' wages, who have lived on earth in luxury and pleasure; you have fattened your hearts for the day of slaughter. By doing so you have condemned and murdered the righteous one. Then to his brothers he says be patient, make your hearts firm, for the Lord will come. The judge is standing at the gates. Persevere as Job did. The Lord is merciful and compassionate. James then establishes what the church calls the anointing of the sick. Finally, he tells them to confess their sins to one another and pray for one another that you may be healed, for the fervent prayer of a righteous person is powerful. He reminds them that if one strays from the truth, work to bring him back in order to save his soul.

Chapter 1:1-4 says, James, a servant of God and of the Lord Jesus Christ, To the twelve tribes in the Dispersion: Greetings. My brothers and sisters, whenever you face trials of any kind, consider it nothing but joy, because you know that the testing of your faith produces endurance; and let endurance have its full effect, so that you may be mature and complete, lacking in nothing.

It is important to note that the thinking of people in those times compared to modern times is quite different, which is a major reason so many have a difficult time relating to the Bible's message. We live in a time of basic comfort and in an age of materialism and consumerism. How many people in our prosperous country, in a time when a false prosperity gospel is rampant, can say, count it all joy when you suffer for Christ? To the disciples in those times learning the way of Christ was remaining obedient under persecution.

Verses 5-8 say, If any of you is lacking in wisdom, ask God, who gives to all generously and ungrudgingly, and it will be given you. But ask in faith, never doubting, for the one who doubts is like a wave of the sea, driven and tossed by the wind; for the doubter, being double-minded and unstable in every way, must not expect to receive anything from the Lord. (The wisdom of God is Jesus Christ, 1 Cor 1:30. Instead of seeking first the wisdom of the world, seek God's wisdom, trust it, and put it into action.)

Verses 9-11 say, Let the believer who is lowly boast in being raised up, and the rich in being brought low, because the rich will disappear like a flower in the field. For the sun rises with its scorching heat and withers the field; its flower falls, and its beauty perishes. It is the same way with the rich; in the midst of a busy life, they will wither away.

The Bible says very little that is encouraging to those who are rich. They are constantly told to accept the mind set of Christ and to use their wealth for the benefit of Christ and the common good. The emphasis is on the fact that God has allowed them to gain the wealth. It is not on how superior they are because they gained the wealth. There are those politicians in America who would call this teaching "class warfare."

Verses 12-16 say, Blessed is anyone who endures temptation. Such a one has stood the test and will receive the crown of life that the Lord has promised to those who love him. No one, when tempted, should say, "I am being tempted by God"; for God cannot be tempted by evil and he himself tempts no one. But one is tempted by one's own desire, being lured and enticed by it; then, when that desire has conceived, it gives birth to sin, and that sin, when it is fully grown, gives birth to death. Do not be deceived, my beloved. (Temptation is sure to come, but it is our desires that tempt us not God. This may also be said in relation to the preceding paragraph and the subject of riches.)

Verses 17-21 say, Every generous act of giving, with every perfect gift, is from above, coming down from the Father of lights, with whom there is no variation or shadow due to change. In fulfillment of his own purpose he gave us birth by the word of truth, so that we would become a kind of first fruits of his creatures. You must understand this, my beloved: let everyone be quick to listen, slow to speak, slow to anger; for your anger does not produce God's righteousness. Therefore rid yourselves of all sordidness and rank growth of wickedness, and welcome with meekness the implanted word that has the power to save your souls. (The emphasis is on letting the word of God work in and through the followers of Christ.)

Verses 22-25 say, But be doers of the word, and not merely hearers who deceive themselves. For if any are hearers of the word and not doers, they are like those who look at themselves in a mirror, for they look at themselves and, on going away, immediately forget what they were like. But those who look into the perfect law, the law of liberty, and persevere, being not hearers who forget but doers who act—they will be blessed in their doing. (It is the law of liberty because it frees us from self and sin that controls us.)

The letter of James will repeat this message throughout the book. The followers of Christ will hear God's word and do what it says. They will not just hear it. The church has many who follow this teaching, but it also has too many who hear God's word, but then do what they want. The law of Christ is called the perfect law because his teachings are to lead one to the eventual perfection that can only come in and through Christ.

Verses 26-27 give an example. If any think they are religious, and do not bridle their tongues but deceive their hearts, their religion is worthless. Religion that is pure and undefiled before God, the Father, is this: to care for orphans and widows in their distress, and to keep one unstained by the world. (Pure religion is more than hearing God's word and participating in devotional exercises. It is to care for those in need and distress. In the ancient world widows and orphans represented those most in need and in distress.)

Chapter 2:1-4 says, My brothers and sisters, do you with your acts of favoritism really believe in our Lord Jesus Christ? For if a person with gold rings and in fine clothes comes into your assembly, and if a poor person in dirty clothes also comes in, and if you take notice of the one wearing the fine clothes and say, "Have a seat here, please," while to the one who is poor you say, "Stand there," or, "Sit at my feet," have you not made distinctions among yourselves, and become judges with evil thoughts? (The idea is that when the rich are preferred over the poor, one has not either heard or paid attention to the teachings of Jesus.)

Verses 5-7 say, Listen, my beloved brothers and sisters. Has not God chosen the poor of the world to be rich in faith and to be heirs of the kingdom that he has promised to those who love him? But you have dishonored the poor. Is it not the rich who oppress you? Is it not they who drag you into court (or before Congress and state legislatures to defeat you)? Is it not they who blaspheme the excellent name that was invoked over you? (Does the reader think this continues today even by people who call themselves Christians, or is this done only by those who are not Christians?)

Verses 8-13 say, You do well if you really fulfill the royal law according to scripture, "You shall love your neighbor as yourself." But if you show partiality, you commit sin and are convicted by the law as transgressors. For whoever keeps the whole law but fails on one point has become accountable for all of it. For the one who said, "You shall not commit adultery," also said, "You shall not murder." Now if you do not commit adultery but if you murder, you have become a transgressor of the law. So speak and so act as those who are to be judged by the law of liberty. For judgment will be without mercy to anyone who has shown no mercy; mercy triumphs over judgment.

That is quite a strong message for many of us today who show very little compassion or mercy toward the disadvantaged and certainly do not want to take their part or stand for them in public. This includes those in Congress and state legislatures.

Verses 14-17 say, What good is it, my brothers and sisters, if you say you have faith but do not have works? Can faith save you? If a brother or sister is naked and lacks daily food, and one of you says to them, "Go in peace; keep warm and eat your fill," and yet you do not supply their bodily needs, what good is that? So faith by itself, if it has no works, is dead. (All through the gospels Christ calls his people to meet the basic needs of people, their need for food, clothing, and healing, both spiritual and physical.)

Verses 18-24 say, But someone will say, "You have faith and I have works." Show me your faith apart from your works, and I by my works will show you my faith. You believe that God is one; you do well. Even the demons believe—and shudder. Do you want to be shown, you senseless person, that faith apart from works is barren? Was not our ancestor Abraham justified by works when he offered his son Isaac on the altar? You see that faith was active along with his works, and faith was brought to completion by the works. Thus the scripture was fulfilled that says, "Abraham believed God, and it was reckoned to him as righteousness," and he was called the friend of God. You see that a person is justified by works and not by faith alone.

Just belief is of no value, for even the demons believe. Faith must be brought to completion to be considered real faith and to have the faith that saves. Justification begins with belief, but it must be brought to completion. Verses 25-26 say, Likewise, was not Rahab the prostitute also justified by works when she welcomed the messengers and sent them out by another road? For just as the body without the spirit is dead, so faith without works is also dead. (God's grace brings about both faith and works in and through his people, and that is the grace that saves.)

Chapter 3:1 says, Not many of you should become teachers, my brothers and sisters, for you know that we who teach will be judged with greater strictness. (This sets up the following concerning the use and control of the tongue.) Verses 2-5 say, For all of us make many mistakes. Anyone who makes no mistakes in speaking is perfect, able to keep the whole body in check with a bridle. If we put bits into the mouths of horses, to make them obey us, we guide their whole bodies. Or look at ships: though they are so large that it takes strong winds to drive them, yet they are guided by a very small rudder wherever the will of the pilot directs. So also the tongue is a small member, yet it boasts of great exploits.

How great a forest is set ablaze by a small fire! And the tongue is a fire. The tongue is placed among our members as a world of iniquity; it stains the whole body, sets on fire the cycle of nature, and is itself set on fire by hell. For every species of beast and bird, of reptile and sea creature, can be tamed by the human species, but no one can tame the tongue—a restless evil, full of deadly poison. With it we bless the Lord and Father, and with it we curse those who are made in the likeness of God. From the same mouth come blessing and cursing. (That is probably true of most of us either in thought or deed.) My brothers and sisters, this ought not to be so. Does a spring pour forth from the same opening both fresh and brackish water? Can a fig tree, my brothers and sisters, yield olives, or grapevine figs? No more than can salt water yield fresh. (The use and abuse of the important role of teaching in the church are related to the good and bad use of the tongue or the use and control of the tongue. Of course this applies not only just to teachers but to all humans.)

Verses 13-18 say, Who is wise and understanding among you? Show by your good life that your works are done with gentleness born of wisdom. But if you have bitter envy and selfish ambition in your hearts, do not be boastful and false to the truth. Such wisdom does not come down from above, but is earthly, unspiritual, devilish. For where there is envy and selfish ambition, there will also be disorder and wickedness of every kind. But the wisdom from above is first pure, then peaceable, gentle, willing to yield, full of mercy and good fruits, without a trace of partiality or hypocrisy. And a harvest of righteousness is sown in peace for those who make peace.

This author believes that the whole chapter is primarily about what makes a good and bad teacher in the eyes of God. The tongue must be under control and the emphasis is to be on teaching God's word and the overall intention of God's word, and not the words of the teacher or human thoughts. The teacher should be gentle not arrogant, not boastful, envious, or full of selfish ambition, not a hypocrite, or one who shows partiality. The teacher should be spiritual, filled with God's wisdom and should never falsify God's truth or wisdom. The teacher should also be a person who does not create conflict and is willing to yield to the thoughts and beliefs of others, but also compare them to God's wisdom. And when the teacher applies God's word to every day life, it must be done with the right intention whether it is popular or not. Even so, the teacher is to be a person of peace, mercy, compassion, and a producer of good fruit.

～○∽

Chapter 4:1-4 says, Those conflicts and disputes among you, where do they come from? Do they not come from your cravings that are at war within you? You want something and do not have it; so you commit murder. And you covet something and cannot obtain it; so you engage in disputes and conflicts. You do not have because you do not ask. You ask and do not receive, because you ask wrongly, in order to spend what you get on your pleasures. Adulterers! Do you not know that friendship with the world is enmity with God? Therefore whoever wishes to be a friend with the world becomes an enemy with God.

All our disputes, conflicts, and wars come from our selfish greed, coveting, our uncontrolled passions, and friendship with the world and its things. There are basically two sets of values: God's and the world's. One leads to peace, and the other leads to conflict.

Verses 5-10 say, Or do you suppose it is for nothing that the scripture says, "God yearns jealously for the spirit that he has made to dwell in us"? But he gives all the more grace; therefore it says, "God opposes the proud, but gives grace to the humble." Submit yourself therefore to God. Resist the devil, and he will flee from you. Draw near to God, and he will draw near to you. Cleanse your hands, you sinners, and purify your hearts, you double minded.

Lament and mourn and weep. Let your laughter be turned into mourning and your joy into dejection. Humble yourself before the Lord, and he will exalt you.

Can you imagine the reactions of many in today's world if these verses were given in this manner to today's people that sit in our modern day churches? How about this one: Cleanse your hands, you sinners, and purify your hearts, you double minded. Resist the devil. This author wonders how the people would react to this in a sermon or homily. How does the reader think they would react?

Verses 11-12 say, Do not speak evil against one another, brothers and sisters. Whoever speaks evil against another or judges another, speaks evil against the law and judges the law, you are not a doer of the law but a judge. There is one lawgiver and judge who is able to save and to destroy. So who, then, are you to judge your neighbor? (This obviously has reference to slander and to those who judge the motivations of others as well as their salvation, for in other places evil is to be judged and defeated.)

Verses 13-16 say, Come now, you who say, "Today or tomorrow we will go to such and such a town and spend a year there, doing business and making money." Yet you do not even know what tomorrow will bring. What is your life? For you are a mist that appears for a little while and then vanishes. Instead you ought to say, "If the Lord wishes we will do this or that." As it is, you boast in your arrogance; all such boasting is evil. (This is about the sovereignty of God. It is God who permits or does not permit. When God showers us with blessings, his people need to humble themselves and thank him for allowing it to happen.) Verse 17 says, Anyone, then, who knows the right thing to do and fails to do it, commits sin. (According to this, is there anyone who is not a sinner needing the grace of God's forgiveness? Does the reader think Americans in general believe this?)

Chapter 5:1-6 says, Come now, you rich people, weep and wail for the miseries that are coming to you. Your riches have rotted, and your clothes are moth-eaten. Your gold and silver have rusted, and their rust will be evidence against you, and it will eat your flesh like fire. You have laid up treasures for the last days. Listen! The wages of the laborers who mowed your fields, which you kept back by fraud, cry out, and the cries of the harvesters have reached the ears of the Lord of hosts. You have lived on earth in luxury and in pleasure; you have fattened your hearts in a day of slaughter. You have condemned and murdered the righteous one, who does not resist you. (Christ again is put to death by our actions.)

There goes James with his class warfare again. Is there any wonder that it is easy to find quite a few in America who do not like James? There are even churches that refuse to deal with the letter of James. It is important to note that this teaching by James goes back to the Old Testament prophets.

Many comfortable people and well-off business people and top administrators sitting in pews blame the poor for their situation. They want to keep wages down. They oppose middle class and lower class workers making a living wage because it may drop their profits. They do everything in their power to oppose a living wage. They believe the tax structure should benefit them as opposed to the people in the classes below them. They cry class warfare at those who expect them to pay the same percentage of taxes the middle class pays. How does the reader think these people would react to a religious leader expounding on these verses in church? Probably the same way many are reacting today. They would probably cry out that the religious leader is a socialist who is against capitalism, when the issue is not capitalism but fairness, corruption, greed, and an unjust wage system, and what most benefits the common good.

Verses 7-8 say, Be patient therefore, beloved, until the coming of the Lord. The farmer waits for the precious crop from the earth, being patient with it until it receives the early and the late rains. You also must be patient. Strengthen your hearts for the coming of the Lord is near. (In other words accomplish your purposes the right way. Does the coming of the Lord mean the second coming, or the time Christ will act through his people to make the kingdom of God grow like a mustard seed on this earth?)

Verses 9-13 say, Beloved, do not grumble against one another (help one another). See the judge is standing at the doors! As an example of suffering and patience, beloved, take the prophets who spoke in the name of the Lord. (They did not remain silent, they spoke God's word and acted, and, of course, they suffered.) Indeed we call blessed those who showed endurance. You have heard of the endurance of Job, and you have seen the purpose of the Lord, how the Lord is compassionate and merciful. (Compassion and mercy toward the struggling are the qualities God's people, rich or not, are to have.)

Verse 12 says, Above all, my beloved, do not swear, either by heaven or earth or by any oath, but let your "Yes" be yes and your "No" be no, so that you may not fall under condemnation. (In other words be a person of truth, so you do not have to be put under oath for people to believe what you say.)

Verses 13-16 say, Are any among you suffering? They should pray. Are any cheerful? They should sing songs of praise. Are any among you sick? They should call for the elders (presbyters) of the church and have them pray over them, anointing them with oil (used as a medicine and for anointing) in the name of the Lord. The prayer of faith will save the sick, and the Lord will raise them up; and anyone who has committed sins will be forgiven. Therefore confess your sins to one another, and pray for one another, so that you may be healed. The prayer of the righteous is powerful and effective.

Roman Catholics and Protestants differ on their interpretation of these verses. The Catholics make a sacrament from this, which was formerly called Extreme Unction. Today it is called the Sacrament of the Sick, and most often it is used for the dying. Most Protestants do not anoint with oil. Those that do anoint with oil do it anytime a person is sick and requests it. It is not just for the dying.

Verses 17-18 say, Elijah was a human being like us, and he prayed fervently that it might not rain, and for three years and six months it did not rain on the earth. Then he prayed again, and the heaven gave rain and the earth yielded its harvest. (This is an example of the prayer of a righteous man.)

Verses 19-20 say, My brothers and sisters, if anyone among you wanders from the truth and is brought back by another, you should know that whoever brings back a sinner from wandering will save the sinner's soul from death and will cover a multitude of sins. (Is this part of the Catholic idea of penance?)

This ends the letter of James. As a way of review list some of the most important verses and thoughts James made.

THE FIRST LETTER OF PETER

The book states it is from Peter, written to those located in modern day Turkey (Pontus, Galatia, Cappadocia, Asia, and Bithynia). It is interesting to note that Peter is writing to churches that were basically located in areas where Paul worked. To those churches in chapter 1 he writes blessed be God the Father of our Lord Jesus Christ, who in his great mercy, gave us a new birth through a living hope, through the resurrection of Jesus Christ, to an inheritance that is imperishable and undefiled kept in heaven for you, who by the power of God is safeguarded through faith, to a salvation that is ready to be revealed in the final time. Rejoice in this even though for a little while you must suffer through various trials so that the genuineness of your faith may prove to be for praise, glory, and honor, at the revelation of Jesus Christ as you attain the goal of your faith, the salvation of your souls.

He tells them that the prophets, hundreds of years before, prophesized for you the future sufferings of Christ, and the grace that would be yours, through the Spirit of Christ that is working in them (Daniel, Jeremiah, Isaiah, Zechariah, Psalms). Therefore set your hopes on this grace and live soberly, for he who has called you to be holy is holy. Remember you were ransomed from your previous, futile conduct by the precious blood of Christ. Since you have purified yourself by obedience of the truth, love one another from a pure heart. You have been born anew, not from perishable but from imperishable seed, through the living and abiding word of God. All flesh is like the flowers and the grass that withers away, but the word of the Lord remains forever. This is the word that has been proclaimed to you.

In chapter 2 Peter says rid yourself of all malice and deceit, insincerity, envy, and slander. Long for pure spiritual milk that you may grow into salvation. Come to him, a living stone, rejected by human beings, but chosen and precious in the sight of God, and like living stones let yourself be built into a spiritual house to be a holy priesthood to offer spiritual sacrifices acceptable to God through Jesus Christ. The stone which the builders rejected (the majority of Jews) has become the cornerstone (Jesus is the cornerstone). They stumble by disobeying the word.

But Peter says to whom he writes, you are a chosen race, a royal priesthood, a holy nation, a people of his own, so that you may announce the praises of him who called you out of darkness into his wonderful light. Once you were no people, but now you are God's people. You had not received mercy but now you have. He then urges them to keep away from worldly desires that wage war against their soul. He tells them to maintain good conduct so that when those who speak evil of you may see your good works. He tells them to do good and be subject to government who punishes evil doers and approves those who do good so foolish people may be silenced. According to Romans 13:1-7 government has been created by God in order to serve his purposes. Peter tells them to be free without using freedom as a pretext for evil, but be slaves of God. He tells slaves to bear their suffering as Christ did. He will give them grace to do so. His point is not to return evil for evil. His example is theirs to follow.

In chapter 3 he gives advice to wives, which is similar to what is found in Ephesians and Timothy. His advice on Christian conduct for all is also similar. He tells them to always have an answer or explanation for those who ask you for the reason you have the hope you have, but do it with gentleness and reverence, keeping your conscience clear so that when you are maligned those who defame your good conduct in Christ may themselves be put to shame, for it is better to suffer for doing good than evil.

Peter reminds them that Christ suffered also, but was brought to life in the spirit, in which he went to preach to the spirits in prison who had once been disobedient. God had patiently waited for repentance from the people in the days of Noah and the building of the ark, but only eight were saved through water. This saving through the water prefigured baptism which saves you now. It is not a removal of dirt from the body, but an appeal to God for a clear conscience through the resurrection of Jesus Christ, who has gone to heaven and is at the right hand of God with angels, authorities, and powers subject to him. Water by itself does nothing, but what is active is the Holy Spirit that is channeled through the water. The New Testament considers baptism as important which is contrary to the teaching of many today, including some churches.

In chapter 4 Peter states that since Christ suffered in the flesh, arm yourself with the same attitude, for whoever suffers in the flesh has broken with sin. He reminds them they no longer live in the sins of the pagans who live in debauchery, evil desires, drunkenness, orgies, carousing, and idolatry and harass the believers for not doing as they do. He says these pagans will give an account of themselves to the just judge.

Peter tells them to be hospitable to one another, let your love be intense and share your gifts to benefit one another, and whoever preaches, let it be with the words of God, and whoever serves, let it be with the strength God supplies, so that in all things God may be glorified through Jesus Christ to whom belongs glory and dominion forever.

Then he says do not be surprised if trial by fire comes. If you are insulted for the name of Christ, blessed are you. Make sure you do not suffer for doing wrong, for judgment will begin with the house of God, and if it begins with us, how will it end for those who do not obey the gospel of God? If the righteous are barely saved what will it be like for the godless and sinners? The idea that judgment begins with God's people, and God's people are barely saved is not the message one hears today in most churches.

In chapter 5 advice is given to the presbyters to tend the flock as God would have you and not for shameful profit but willingly. Be examples to your flock, and when the chief shepherd comes you will be given a crown of glory. Peter tells younger members to be subject to your presbyters (elders), and all of you clothe yourself in humility, for God opposes the proud. So humble yourself, be sober and vigilant, and cast all your worries upon him because he cares for you. Remember your opponent the devil is prowling around like a roaring lion looking for someone to devour. Resist him steadfast in the faith knowing that your fellow believers throughout the world undergo the same sufferings. The God of all grace will strengthen you. He ends by saying the chosen one at Babylon (Rome) sends you greetings, so does Mark.

Chapter1:1-2 says, Peter, an apostle of Jesus Christ, To the exiles of the Dispersion (those outside the Holy Land) in Pontus, Galatia, Cappadocia, Asia, and Bithynia, who have been chosen and destined by God the Father and sanctified (made holy) by the Spirit to be obedient to Jesus Christ and to be sprinkled with his blood

(forgiven of sin): May grace and peace be yours in abundance. (All who respond to God's grace through Christ are God's chosen ones. The Christ is the one chosen by the Father, Eph 1:1-14.)

Verses 3-5 say, Blessed be the God and Father of our Lord Jesus Christ! By his great mercy he has given us a new birth (the opportunity to be born of God) into a living hope through the resurrection of Jesus Christ from the dead, and into an inheritance that is imperishable, undefiled, and unfading, kept in heaven for you, who are being protected by the power of God through faith for a salvation ready to be revealed in the last time.

The resurrection of Jesus Christ is the living hope of the follower of Christ. The living hope is that as long as one stays in faith no one can interfere with the eternal salvation Christ obtained for them through the cross.

Verses 6-9 say, In this you rejoice, even if now for a little while you have had to suffer various trials, so that the genuineness of your faith—being more precious than gold that, though perishable, is tested by fire—may be found to result in praise and glory and honor when Jesus Christ is revealed. Although you have not seen him, you love him; and even though you do not see him now, you believe in him and rejoice with an indescribable and glorious joy, for you are receiving the outcome of your faith, the salvation of your souls.

The early Christians knew very little about sitting in the comfort of a pew. Notice how practically all the New Testament books mention suffering. They understood that through suffering for Christ, faith grows to a higher maturity, even though in the process some may lose their faith. But those who endure will grow deeper in Christ and in the process save their souls. God allows followers to suffer for him as he suffered as proof of the quality of their faith.

Verses 10-12 mention the Old Testament prophets, who had

the Spirit of Christ within them as they testified by the power of the Holy Spirit to the suffering the Christ to come would go through for those of us living in this age. Verses 13-16 say, Therefore prepare your minds for action; discipline yourselves; set all your hope on the grace that Jesus Christ will bring you when he is revealed. Like obedient children, do not be conformed to the desires that you formerly had in ignorance. Instead, as he who called you is holy, be holy yourselves in all your conduct; for it is written, "You shall be holy, for I am holy." (Becoming holy is being obedient to Jesus Christ not to our desires that enslave us.)

Verses 17-21 say, If you invoke as Father the one who judges all people impartially according to their deeds, live in reverent fear during the time of your exile (from the promised land or heaven). You know that you were ransomed from the futile ways inherited from your ancestors, not with perishable things like silver or gold, but with the precious blood of Christ, like that of a lamb without defect or blemish. He was destined before the foundation of the world, but was revealed at the end of the ages for your sake. Through him you have come to trust in God, who raised him from the dead and gave him glory, so that your faith and hope are set on God.

Christ was predestined before the world began. He was chosen by God to be the one through whom all humans may become God's chosen, his adopted children. But being God's chosen must be followed up by the chosen's obedience to Christ, for as (17) says all will be judged impartially by their deeds. One can not enter into eternal life without being obedient to Christ. This means allowing God's grace to live in and through the believer by the power of the Holy Spirit.

Verse 22 says, Now that you have purified your souls by your obedience to the truth so that you have genuine mutual love, love one another deeply from the heart. (Purifying the soul by obedience to the truth begins with baptism (Acts 2:38) then loving from the heart is to follow, which generally begins by doing to others as you would have them do to you.) Verses 23-25 say, You have been born anew, not of perishable but of imperishable seed, through the living and enduring word of God. For, "All flesh is like grass and all its glory like the flower of grass. The grass withers, and the flower falls, but the word of the Lord endures forever." That word is the good news announced to you. (Being born anew comes from the Holy Spirit working through the word of God.)

Chapter 2:1-3 says, Rid yourselves, therefore, of all malice, and all guile, insincerity, envy, and all slander. Like newborn infants, long for the pure, spiritual milk, so that by it you may grow into salvation—if indeed you have tasted that the Lord is good. (Notice God's people are to grow into salvation by eliminating from themselves those things that are not of God. In the process they are to learn what is desirable from God's word.)

Verses 4-8 say, Come to him, a living stone, though rejected by mortals yet chosen and precious in God's sight, and like living stones, let yourself be built into a spiritual house, to be a holy priesthood, to offer spiritual sacrifices acceptable to God through Jesus Christ. For it stands in scripture: "See I am laying in Zion a stone, a cornerstone chosen and precious; and whoever believes in him will not be put to shame." To you then who believe, he is precious; but for those who do not believe, "The stone that the builders rejected has become the very head of the corner," and "A stone that makes them stumble, and a rock that makes them fall." They stumble because they disobey the word as they were destined to do.

People have the choice of either being built upon the foundation stone of Christ by obeying his word or by choosing not to build their life upon that stone and being disobedient to his word. If one builds a life on the foundation stone of Christ, then that person becomes part of a holy priesthood, offering spiritual sacrifices through Christ to the Father (Mt 7:21-29). That person now allows Christ to live in them and through them.

Verses 9-10 say, But you are a chosen race, a royal priesthood, a holy nation, God's own people, in order that you may proclaim the mighty acts of him who called you out of darkness into his marvelous light. Once you were not a people, but now you are God's people; once you had not received mercy, but now you have received mercy.

In the Old Testament God chose a nation. In the New Testament God chooses a church to which all nations are invited through which they become chosen, holy, God's very own people, and priests to proclaim the mighty acts of God. Christ and his followers are now a spiritual temple that takes the place of the Old Testament temple. Instead of God's presence being in the Holy of Holies in the temple, it now resides in his people. The people of God are the temple of God revealing the presence (Shechinah) of God.

Verses 11-12 say, Beloved, I urge you as aliens and exiles to abstain from the desires of the flesh that wage war against the soul. Conduct yourselves honorably among the Gentiles, so that, though they malign you as evil doers, they may see your honorable deeds and glorify God when he comes to judge.

One's life is a witness to God, or it is a witness to the world. If it is half a witness to God and half a witness to the world, it is a duplication of the syncretism called a false, pagan religion found throughout the Old Testament.

Verses 13-17 say, For the Lord's sake accept the authority of every human institution, whether of the emperor as supreme, or of governors, as sent by him to punish those who do wrong and to praise those who do right. For it is God's will that by doing right you should silence the ignorance of the foolish. As servants of God live as free people, yet do not use your freedom as a pretext for evil. Honor everyone. Love the family of believers. Fear God. Honor the emperor.

Government does much good as well as protecting law abiders from those who violate the law. So honor and respect the government leaders in the good they accomplish. But always remember if there is a conflict between what government does and what God teaches, we must obey God rather than human authority (Acts 5:29).

Verses 18-21 say, Slaves, accept the authority of your masters with all deference, not only those who are kind and gentle but also those who are harsh. (See 1 Tim 6:1-5, Titus 2:9, Philemon, Eph 5:6-7, and Col 4:1 for previous comments on slavery in New Testament times.) For it is a credit to you if, being aware of God, you endure pain while suffering unjustly. If you endure when you are beaten for doing wrong, what credit is that? But if you endure when you do right and suffer for it, you have God's approval. For to this you have been called, because Christ also suffered for you, leaving you an example, so that you should follow in his steps.

This advice was given to slaves at a time when Christians were in a minority, and there was no chance of slavery being eliminated. It is possible that most people did not even think about it since slavery had existed since early ancient history. So, at this point, very little could be done about the evils of slavery. Therefore advice is given to help one survive a bad situation. The encouragement is for the time being be like Christ and suffer as he did for wrong doing not deserved.

Verses 22-25 say, "He (Jesus) committed no sin, and no deceit was found in his mouth." When he was abused, he did not return abuse; when he suffered, he did not threaten; but he entrusted himself to the one who judges justly. He himself bore our sins in his body on the cross, so that, free from sins, we might live for righteousness; by his wounds you have been healed. For you were going astray like sheep, but now you have returned to the shepherd and guardian of your souls.

Because of what Christ has done for his people, they are to live for his righteousness and as verse 21 says, follow in his steps. In the process he will continue to shepherd and be the guardian of your soul. Following in his steps, not only means bearing the fruit of God's virtues and rejecting the vices, but also making his priorities your priorities and standing with and for those he stood with.

Chapter 3:1-2 says, Wives, in the same way, accept the authority of your husbands, so that even if some of them do not obey the word, they may be won over without a word by their wife's conduct, when they see the purity and reverence of your lives.

Again keep in mind the minority status of Christianity in a pagan society where the purpose is not to upset the stability of a society so much that it turns people away from hearing about who Christ is and what his message says. Also see comments on husband-wife relationships in (1 Cor 11:1-16, 13:4-7, 14:26-40, Eph 5:21-33, Gal 3:28-29, Col 3:18).

Verses 3-7 say, Do not adorn yourselves outwardly by braiding your hair, and by wearing gold ornaments or fine clothing; rather, let your adornment be the inner self with the lasting beauty of a gentle and quiet spirit, which is very precious in God's sight. It was in this way long ago that the holy women who hoped in God used to adorn themselves by accepting the authority of their husbands. Thus Sarah obeyed Abraham and called him lord. You have become her daughters as long as you do what is good and never let fears alarm you. Husbands, in the same way, show consideration for your wives in your life together, paying honor to the woman as the weaker sex (physically), since they too are also heirs of the gracious gift of life—so that nothing may hinder your prayers. (The idea is to respect each other as their culture understands respect.)

See comments on this subject in 1 Tim 2:8-15, and the passages mentioned in the previous paragraph. It must be kept in mind that these are not timeless laws, but temporary teachings geared to the survival of a minority group of people, whose higher goal is to spread the message of who Christ is, what he did, along with his basic teachings to a society that has no idea what Christianity is about. It is up to people living in this century to discern the principles within these teachings that may have value. For example how a person dresses, and how males and females or husband and wife treat each other says much about their devotion to Christ.

Verses 8-15 say, Finally, all of you, have unity of spirit, sympathy, love for one another, a tender heart, and a humble mind. (These are positive qualities for a child of God.) Do not repay evil for evil or abuse for abuse; but, on the contrary, repay with a blessing. It is for this that you were called—that you might inherit a blessing. For "Those who desire life and desire to see good days, let them keep their tongues from evil and their lips from speaking deceit; let them turn away from evil and do good; let them seek peace and pursue it. For the eyes of the Lord are on the righteous, and his ears are open to their prayer. But the face of the Lord is against those who do evil." (God will hear the prayer of the righteous and bless them.)

Verses 13-16 say, Now who will harm you if you are eager to do what is good? But even if you do suffer for doing what is right, you are blessed. Do not fear what they fear, and do not be intimidated, but in your hearts sanctify Christ as Lord. Always be ready to make your defense to anyone who demands from you an accounting for the hope that is in you; yet do it with gentleness and reverence. Keep your conscience clear, so that when you are maligned, those who abuse you for your good conduct in Christ may be put to shame. (Do what is right and good, and always be ready to explain in a gentle and reverent way, not a confrontational way, why you are a person of honor and character. Bless people by your life and your words, and if you suffer, remember that Christ suffered also.)

Verses 17-22 say, For it is better to suffer, if suffering should be God's will, than to suffer for doing evil. For Christ also suffered for sins once for all, the righteous for the unrighteous, in order to bring you to God. He was put to death in the flesh, but made alive in the spirit, in which also he went and made proclamation to the spirits in prison, who in former times did not obey, when God waited patiently in the days of Noah, during the building of the ark, in which a few, that is, eight persons, were saved through water. And baptism, which this prefigured, now saves you—not as a removal of dirt from a body, but as an appeal to God for a good conscience, through the resurrection of Jesus Christ, who has gone into heaven and is at the right hand of God, with angels, authorities, and powers made subject to him.

Who the spirits Christ proclaimed to, and what he said to them is basically impossible to know. Were they the disobedient who died in the time of Noah and the flood, and if so, what did he say to them?

The reason for mentioning the eight persons saved through water is to emphasize the importance of water baptism. No matter how much certain people say water baptism is not important, the New Testament says over and over it is important. Now baptism itself does not for all time automatically save anyone, but God has chosen to work through water baptism with the power of the Holy

Spirit as one appeals to God for a good conscience. Yes, some who do not come to God seriously just get a bath. But water baptism has a spiritual effect for those who take their devotion to God seriously. Baptismal transformation in the New Testament means the end of life in the flesh and the beginning of life in the Spirit according to the will of God. Although the New Testament seems to indicate that immersion in water upon a person who understands was the norm, baptism upon an infant certainly conveys that God's gift is purely by his grace.

Chapter 4:1-6 says, Since therefore Christ suffered in the flesh, arm yourselves also with the same intention . . . so as to live for the rest of your earthly life no longer by human desires but by the will of God. You have already spent enough time in doing what the Gentiles (pagans) like to do, living in licentiousness, passions, drunkenness, revels, carousing, and lawless idolatry. They are surprised that you no longer join them in the same excesses of dissipation, and so they blaspheme. But they will have to give an accounting to him who stands ready to judge the living and the dead. For this is the reason the gospel was proclaimed even to the dead, so that, though they had been judged in the flesh as everyone is judged, they might live in the Spirit as God does.

Does that mean that when Christ went to those who were dead (judged in the flesh) from the time of Noah and the flood (3:18), they are now given a final judgment? And what does it mean that they might live in the spirit? Did the eight saved through water rise to eternal life, while the disobedient rose to eternal punishment? Or did they all rise to eternal life? Did he proclaim the gospel to all of them so that they may choose Christ for their salvation? Or is it just teaching the principle that all will be judged by Christ? These are just some of the questions scholars ask, but no one has the answer.

Verses 7-11 say, The end of all things is near; therefore be serious and discipline yourselves for the sake of your prayers. Above all, maintain constant love for one another, for love covers a multitude of sins. Be hospitable to one another without complaining. Like good stewards of the manifold grace of God, serve one another with whatever gift each of you has received. Whoever speaks must do so as one speaking the very words of God; whoever serves must do so with the strength that God supplies, so that God may be glorified in all things through Jesus Christ. To him belong the glory and the power forever and ever. Amen.

Verses 12-16 say, Beloved, do not be surprised at the fiery ordeal (persecutions) that is taking place among you to test you, as though something strange were happening to you. But rejoice in so far as you are sharing Christ's sufferings, so that you also may be glad and shout for joy when his glory is revealed. If you are reviled for the name of Christ, you are blessed, because the spirit of glory, which is the Spirit of God, is resting in you. But let none of you suffer as a murderer, a thief, a criminal, or even as a mischief maker. Yet if any of you suffer as a Christian, do not consider it a disgrace, but glorify God because you bear his name.

To suffer because of one's stand for and with Christ was the norm in the early days of Christianity. The question the reader needs to think through is: Why did the governing authorities so severely persecute the early Christians so that for many being a martyr was almost the norm? There are two major reasons they were persecuted by non-Jews, the Gentiles. First, the kingdom Christ came to initiate is a way of life that challenged the way of life of the world's kingdoms. Second, it challenged the religion of the gods and the emperors who claimed to be a god. These gods had religious centers that were very closely tied into economics and commerce, and when people's profits may be diminished, there will surely be problems (Acts 17:1-15). Some of the Jews persecuted the early Christians because they considered them followers of a false prophet who were following a false messiah.

Verses 17-19 say, For the time has come for judgment to begin with the household of God; if it begins with us, what will be the end for those who do not obey the gospel of God? "And if it is hard for the righteous to be saved, what will become of the ungodly and sinners?" Therefore, let those suffering in accordance with God's will entrust themselves to a faithful Creator, while continuing to do good.

The Scripture says that judgment begins with God's people, and it is even hard for the righteous to be saved. Is that not contrary to the message of many religious teachers today? This writer has heard them constantly teach that all you have to do is believe in Jesus (Jn 3:16) then you can never even lose your salvation. That message is quite opposite of what this writer sees throughout both the Old and New Testaments.

⌒⌒⌒

Chapter 5:1-3 says, Now as an elder myself and a witness to the sufferings of Christ (Peter was with Christ), as well as one who shares in the glory to be revealed, I exhort the elders among you to tend the flock of God that is in your charge, exercising the oversight, not under compulsion but willingly, as God would have you do it—not for sordid gain but eagerly. Do not lord it over those in your charge, but be examples to the flock. (Lead by example, and not by dictatorial power.)

Verses 4-7 say, And when the chief shepherd appears, you will win the crown of glory that never fades away. In the same way you who are younger must accept the authority of the elders. And all of you must clothe yourselves in humility in your dealings with one another, for "God opposes the proud, but gives grace to the humble." Humble yourselves therefore under the mighty hand of God, so that he may exalt you in due time. Cast all your anxiety on him because he cares for you.

Elders (presbyters) have authority and power, but they are to be humble and use it in a way that respects all involved as they lead by example. Then those who are younger will learn by the example of their elders. But if there is a confrontation, the elders have the power of decision making.

Verses 8-11 say, Discipline yourselves, keep alert. Like a roaring lion your adversary the devil prowls around, looking for someone to devour. Resist him, steadfast in the faith, for you know that your brothers and sisters in all the world are undergoing the same kinds of suffering. And after you have suffered for a little while, the God of all grace, who has called you to his eternal glory in Christ, will himself restore, support, strengthen, and establish you. To him be the power forever and forever. (The devil is an active force, always looking for someone to sneak up on and cause havoc.)

Verses 12-14 say, Through Silvanus (Silas), whom I consider a faithful brother, I have written this short letter to encourage you and to testify that this is the true grace of God. Stand fast in it. Your sister church in Babylon (Rome), chosen together with you, sends you greetings; and so does my son Mark. Greet one another with a kiss of love. Peace to all of you who are in Christ.

This ends the letter of 1 Peter. As a way of review list some of the most important verses or thoughts made by Peter.

THE SECOND LETTER OF PETER

Second Peter attempts to refute those distorting apostolic teaching, especially that there will be no final judgment and that the world will not end. Some of the information is similar to Jude. Peter says in chapter 1 that God's divine power has given us everything needed for life and godliness through the knowledge of God. He even has given us a share in God's divine nature. So Peter says make every effort to supplement faith with virtue, virtue with knowledge, knowledge with self control, self control with endurance, endurance with devotion, devotion with mutual affection, and mutual affection with love. They will keep you from being unfruitful. Anyone who lacks them is blind and shortsighted.

Peter encourages them to make their call and election firm, for in doing so you will never stumble. As long as I am alive I will remind you to be firm in the truth, the apostolic teachings. We did not follow cleverly designed myths, but made known to you what we saw with our eyes. We heard God's voice saying, this is my Son in whom I am well pleased at the mountain of transfiguration.

Moreover we possess the prophetic message that is reliable. You will do well to be attentive to it. First of all know this: there is no prophecy of scripture that is a matter of personal interpretation, for no prophecy of scripture ever came through human will, but rather by human beings moved by the Holy Spirit directed under the influence of God. (His point is the Scriptures are from God not humans.)

In chapter 2 there is a warning about false teachers who introduce destructive heresies even denying Christ who ransomed them bringing swift destruction on themselves. This is obviously a brand of Gnosticism. Many will follow their licentious ways and because of them the way of truth will be reviled. In their greed they will exploit you with fabrications, but their destruction is sure to come.

If God did not spare the angels when they sinned, condemning them to the chains of *tartoros*, handing them over to judgment, and if he did not spare the ancient world even though he spared Noah with seven others, and if he condemned the cities of Sodom and Gommorah, even though rescuing Lot a righteous man oppressed by the licentious conduct of unprincipled people, then the Lord knows how to rescue the righteous while keeping the unrighteous under punishment for the day of judgment, and especially those who follow the flesh with its depraved desire.

Bold and arrogant are these false teachers. They are like irrational animals born by nature for destruction, who revile things they do not understand, and in their destruction they will be destroyed. Thinking daytime revelry a delight, their eyes are full of adultery and insatiable for sin. They seduce unstable people, and their hearts are trained in greed. Abandoning the straight road, they have gone astray. These people are waterless springs, mists driven by wind, for them the gloom of darkness is reserved. They talk empty bombast, they promise people freedom though they themselves are slaves of corruption, for a person is a slave to what overcomes him. They were once followers of Christ, but have fallen away becoming entangled in defilements, and now their last condition is worse than the first. The dog has returned to its own vomit; the pig has returned to its own mud.

In chapter 3 he says in the last days scoffers will come to scoff, living according to their own desires, and asking where is the promise of his coming. They forget that the world was once destroyed by water. The present heavens and earth have been reserved by the same word for fire, kept for the day of judgment and of destruction for the godless. But do not ignore this one fact: With the Lord one day is like a thousand years and a thousand years like one day. The Lord does not delay his promise as some regard delay, but he is patient not wishing that any should perish but that all should come to repentance. But the day of the Lord will come like a thief in the night, and then the heavens will pass away with a mighty roar, and the elements will be dissolved by fire, and the earth and everything done on it will be found out.

Therefore conduct yourselves in holiness and devotion. According to his promise we await a new heaven and new earth in which righteousness dwells. As you await these things be found without spot or blemish before him at peace. Consider the writings of Paul speaking of these things. In them there are some things hard to understand that the ignorant and unstable distort to their own destruction, just as they do other scriptures. Then Peter says you have been forewarned, so be on your guard not to be led by the unprincipled and to fall from your own stability. Grow in the grace and knowledge of Jesus Christ. To him be glory.

Chapter1:1-4 says, Simeon Peter, a servant and apostle of Jesus Christ, To those who have received a faith as precious as ours through

the righteousness of our God and Savior Jesus Christ: May grace and peace be yours in abundance in the knowledge of God and of Jesus Christ our Lord. His divine power has given us everything needed for life and godliness, through the knowledge of him who called us by his own glory and goodness. Thus he has given us, through these things, his precious and very great promises, so that through them you may escape from the corruption that is in the world because of lust, and may become participants of the divine nature. (Those who have become born of God become participants of the divine nature by living in God and letting God live in them, see John chapter 15.)

Verses 5-9 say, For this very reason, you must make every effort to support your faith with goodness, and goodness with knowledge, and knowledge with self-control, and self-control with endurance, and endurance with godliness and godliness with mutual affection and mutual affection with love. For if these things are yours and are increasing among you, they keep you from being ineffective and unfruitful in the knowledge of our Lord Jesus Christ. For anyone who lacks these things is near sighted and blind, and is forgetful of the cleansing of past sins.

Faith should lead to virtues and values that please God. Anyone with goodness, knowledge (of God), self-control, endurance, godliness, mutual affection, and love will be effective for God and lead a fruit filled life.

Verses 10-11 say, Therefore, brothers and sisters, be all the more eager to confirm your call and election, for if you do this, you will never stumble. For in this way, entry into the eternal kingdom of our Lord and Savior Jesus Christ will be richly provided for you.

Followers of Christ confirm their faith by doing what Christ calls them to do, and each Sunday they confirm their faith by worshiping, listening to God's word, and participating in the Eucharist (Holy Communion).

Verses 12-15 say, Therefore I intend to keep on reminding you of these things, though you know them already and are established in the truth that has come to you. I think it right, as long as I am in this body, to refresh your memory, since I know my death will come soon, as indeed our Lord Jesus Christ has made clear to me (Jn 21:18-19). And I will make every effort so that after my departure you may be able at any time to recall these things.

Verses 16-18 say, For we did not follow cleverly devised myths when we made known to you the power and coming of our Lord Jesus Christ, but we had been eyewitnesses of his majesty. For he received honor and glory from God the Father when that voice was conveyed to him by the Majestic Glory, saying, "This is my Son, my Beloved, with whom I am well pleased." We ourselves heard this voice come from heaven, while we were with him on the holy mountain. (This is a reference to the transfiguration, Mt 17:1-8. Apostolic tradition is not based on clever myths as Gnosticism and the pagan religions are but on the experience of eyewitnesses.)

Verses 19-20 say, So we have the prophetic message more fully confirmed. You will do well to be attentive to this as to a lamp shining in a dark place, until the day dawns and the morning star rises in your hearts. (Christ the morning star, Rev 22:16, brings light and hope.) First of all you must understand this, that no prophecy of scripture is a matter of one's own interpretation, because no prophecy ever came by human will, but men and women moved by the Holy Spirit spoke from God. (Peter confirms the inspiration of the Scriptures. They are not the thoughts of humans but the thoughts of God put in human language.)

Chapter 2:1-3 says, But false prophets also arose among the people, just as there will be false teachers among you, who will secretly

bring in destructive opinions. They will even deny the Master who bought them—bringing swift destruction on themselves. Even so, many will follow their licentious ways, and because of these teachers the way of truth will be maligned. And in their greed they will exploit you with deceptive words. Their condemnation, pronounced against them long ago, has not been idle, and their destruction is not asleep. (Notice the problem in some way is greed. They deny Christ, at least the Christ of the apostolic tradition, and they distort the truth of God's word because they prefer their evil ways.)

Verses 4-10 say, For if God did not spare the angels when they sinned, but cast them into hell (Greek word is tartaros, and not the usual word translated for hell, hades, or sheol) and committed them to chains of deepest darkness to be kept until the judgment; and if he did not spare the ancient world, even though he saved Noah, a herald of righteousness, with seven others, when he brought a flood on a world of the ungodly; and if by turning the cities of Sodom and Gomorrah to ashes he condemned them to extinction and made them an example of what is coming to the ungodly; and if he rescued Lot, a righteous man greatly distressed by the licentiousness of the lawless . . . then the Lord knows how to rescue the godly from trial, and to keep the unrighteous, under punishment until the day of judgment—especially those who indulge their flesh in depraved lust, and who despise authority. (God's past judgments indicate what is in store for these false prophets who indulge their flesh, not just sexual, and reject the authority of the apostles.)

Verses 11-16 say, Bold and willful, they are not afraid to slander the glorious ones, whereas angels, though greater in might and power, do not bring against them a slanderous judgment from the Lord. These people, however, are like irrational animals, mere creatures of instinct, born to be caught and killed. They slander what they do not understand, and when those creatures are destroyed, they also will be destroyed, suffering the penalty for doing wrong. They count it a pleasure to revel in the daytime. They are blots and blemishes, reveling in their dissipation while they feast with you. They have eyes full of adultery, insatiable for sin. They entice unsteady souls. They have hearts trained in greed. Accursed children! They have left the straight road and have gone astray, following the road of Balaam son of Bosor, who loved the wages of doing wrong, but was rebuked for his own transgression; a speechless donkey spoke with a human voice and restrained the prophet's madness (see Numbers 22).

Verses 17-22 say, These are waterless springs and mists driven by a storm; for them the deepest darkness has been reserved. For they speak bombastic nonsense, and with licentious desires of the flesh they entice people who have just escaped the defilements of the world through the knowledge of our Lord and Savior Jesus Christ, they are again entangled in them and overpowered, the last state has become worse for them than the first. For it would have been better for them never to have known the way of righteousness than, after knowing it, to turn back from the holy commandment that was passed on to them. It has happened to them according to the true proverb, "The dog turns back to its own vomit," and, "The sow is washed only to wallow in the mud."

These false prophets were once a part of the apostolic tradition, but then rejected it, and are now teaching a distortion of God's truth. They were probably teachers of a form of Gnosticism or even a mixture of Gnosticism, Judaism, and the pagan mystery religions with Christianity.

Chapter 3:1-3 says, This is now, beloved, the second letter I am writing to you; in them I am trying to arouse your sincere intention by reminding you that you should remember the words spoken

in the past by the holy prophets, and the commandments of the Lord and Savior Jesus Christ spoken through your apostles. (He is reminding them to pay attention to Scripture both old and new.)

Verses 3-6 say, First of all you must understand this that in the last days scoffers will come, scoffing and indulging their own lusts and saying, "Where is the promise of his coming? For ever since our ancestors died, all things continue as they were from the beginning of creation!" They deliberately ignore this fact, that by the word of God heavens existed long ago and an earth was formed out of water and by means of water, through which the world of that time was deluged with water and perished.

According to Peter in Acts 2:17 the last days began on the Day of Pentecost. Therefore Peter is referring to his present time as the last age; therefore, his reference is to the false prophets who are infiltrating the churches to whom Peter is writing.

Verses 7-10 say, But by the same word the present heaven and earth have been reserved for fire, being kept until the day of judgment and destruction of the godless. But do not ignore this one fact, beloved, that with the Lord one day is like a thousand years, and a thousand years is like one day. The Lord is not slow about his promise, as some think of slowness, but is patient with you, not wanting any to perish, but all to come to repentance. But the day of the Lord will come like a thief, and then the heavens will pass away with a loud noise, and the elements will be dissolved with fire, and the earth and everything that is done on it will be dissolved.

This will be a transformation, not a destruction with violence. Fire in Scripture is used to reveal God's presence, to judge, and to purify. The idea is that there will be judgment and a final transformation, but the reader who is in Christ need not fear it. If it does come in the lifetime of the reader they will not experience anything violent; they will simply be transformed, and the world will become a new heaven and new earth. (Remember the fire of Moses was a different type of fire.)

Verses 11-13 say, Since all these things are to be dissolved in this way, what sort of persons ought you to be in leading lives of holiness and godliness, waiting for and hastening the coming of the day of God, because of which the heavens will be set ablaze and dissolved and the elements will melt with fire? But in accordance with his promise, we wait for new heavens and a new earth, where righteousness is at home. (This is a reference to the kingdom made perfect for eternity, see 1 Cor 15:20-28.)

Verses 14-16 say, Therefore, beloved, while you are waiting for these things, strive to be found by him at peace, without spot or blemish, and regard the patience of our Lord as salvation. So also our beloved brother Paul wrote to you according to the wisdom given him, speaking of this as he does in all his letters. There are some things in them hard to understand, which the ignorant and unstable twist to their own destruction, as they do the other scriptures. (Paul was even difficult for Peter to read, even as those looking to ignore God's word were able to distort it. Does the reader think that this goes on even today? Do people twist the Scriptures to fit their pre-conceived beliefs?)

Verses 17-18 say, You therefore, beloved, since you are forewarned, beware that you are not carried away with the error of the lawless and lose your own stability. (The lawless do anything they feel like doing.) But grow in the grace and knowledge of our Lord and Savior Jesus Christ. To him be the glory both now and to the day of eternity.

Growing in the grace and knowledge of Christ is a life long pursuit. It means to worship God, continually hearing God's word and participating in Holy Communion (Eucharist), and then constantly reading and meditating on God's word.

This ends the letter of 2 Peter. As a way of review list some of the most important verses and thoughts of Peter.

THE FIRST LETTER OF JOHN

Early Christians said the three letters from John were written by the Apostle John. Later it was said that the letters were written by disciples within his school at a later time. Others say they were written by an elder/presbyter named John. Like most of the New Testament books, it is difficult to prove who wrote them. Even so authorship has nothing to do with inspiration of the Scriptures.

The foundation of Christian ethics and morality is in the book of 1 John as it centers upon the concept of love, a topic dear to the heart of the apostle. Chapter 1 begins by focusing on the fact that Jesus had a real physical body which was denied by some of the false teachers. Showing that Jesus had a physical body is important for teaching about a bodily resurrection. John says, He who was from the beginning was made visible, and we saw him, heard him, and touched him. We testify to it and proclaim to you the eternal life that was with the Father and made visible to us, so that you may have fellowship with us and our fellowship is with the Father and his Son, Jesus Christ.

This is the message we have heard from him and proclaim to you: God is light, and in him there is no darkness. If we say we have fellowship with him and walk in darkness, we lie. If we walk in the light as he is in the light, then we have fellowship with one another, and the blood of his Son cleanses us from all sin. If we say we are without sin, we deceive ourselves and the truth is not in us. If we acknowledge our sins, he is faithful and just and will forgive our sins and cleanse us of every wrong doing. If we say we have not sinned, we make him a liar, and his word is not in us.

In chapter 2 John says when we sin we have an advocate with the Father, Jesus Christ, the righteous one. He is the expiation for our sins. The way we may be sure that we know him is to keep his commandments. Whoever says I know him but does not keep his commandments is a liar, and the truth is not in him. But whoever keeps his word, the love of God is truly perfected in him.

This is the way we may know we are in union with him: whoever claims to abide in him ought to live just as he lived. Whoever says he is in the light yet hates his brother is still in darkness, and the darkness has blinded him. John says I am writing to you because your sins have been forgiven, because you have conquered the evil one, because you know the Father, because you know him who is from the beginning, because you are strong and the word of God remains in you.

Do not love the world or the things in the world. If anyone loves the world, the love of the Father is not in him. Sensual lust, enticement for the eyes, and a pretentious life are not from the Father but the world. Yet the world and its enticements are passing away, but whoever does the will of God remains forever.

John says it is the last hour because many antichrists have already appeared. They went out from us, but they were not really of us. If they were of us, they would not have deserted us. Who is the liar? Whoever denies that Jesus is the Christ, and whoever denies the Father, is the antichrist.

So let what you have heard from the beginning remain in you, then you will remain in the Father and the Son. And this is the promise he made us: eternal life. Do not let others deceive you. The anointing you received from him remains in you, so that you do not need others to teach you. His anointing teaches you about everything and is true, so remain in him so that when he appears, we may not be put to shame. Anyone who acts in righteousness as he is righteous is begotten by him.

In chapter 3 John says God loves us so much that he calls us his children, and the reason the world does not know us is that it did not know him. The Son of Man was revealed to destroy the works of the devil, and the children of God, and the children of the devil are made plain. We are either children of righteousness or children of sin. No one can walk in sin and be a child of God. God's children love one another, unlike Cain who belonged to the evil one by killing his brother. He did this because his works were evil and those of his brother were righteous. So, do not be amazed if the world hates you.

We know we have passed from death to life because we love our brothers. Everyone who hates his brother is a murderer and no murderer has eternal life in him. We know love because he laid down his life for us; therefore we ought to lay down our lives for our brothers. If someone has worldly means and sees a brother in need and refuses him compassion how can the love of God remain in him? Let us love not in word or speech but in deed and truth. If our hearts condemn us we are not in the truth. If they do not condemn us we have confidence before God. Those who keep his commandments remain in him and he in them, and the way we know that he remains in us is from the Spirit he gives us.

In chapter 4 John says test the spirits to see if they belong to God because many false prophets have gone into the world. This is how you can know the Spirit of God: every spirit that acknowledges that Jesus Christ came in the flesh belongs to God.

The spirit of antichrist is already in the world, and every spirit that does not acknowledge Jesus does not belong to God. You have conquered them, for the one that is in you is greater than the one that is in the world. They and their teaching belong to the world, and the world listens to them. We belong to God, and anyone who knows God listens to us. Anyone who does not belong to God refuses to hear us.

This is how we know the spirit of truth and the spirit of deceit. Everyone who loves is begotten by God and knows God. Whoever is without love does not know God, for God is love. In this way the love of God was revealed to us: God sent his only Son to the world that we might have life through him. In this is love, not that we loved him, but that he loved us and sent his Son as an expiation for our sins. If God so loved us, we must love one another. This is how we know that we remain in him and he in us, that he has given us his Spirit. If anyone says he loves God but hates his brother, he is a liar, for whoever does not love a brother he can see, can not love God who he can not see.

In chapter 5 John says we know that we love God if we keep his commandments. Whoever is begotten of God conquers the world, and the victory that conquers the world is our faith. God has testified in behalf of his Son through the water (in baptism), the blood (in the cross from which he was raised) and the Holy Spirit (which now testifies). And this is the testimony God has given about his Son: God gave us eternal life, and this life is in his Son. Whoever possesses the Son has life; whoever does not possess the Son of God does not have life. Then he says all wrong doing is sin, but there is a sin that is not deadly, and there is a sin which is deadly. We know that no one begotten of God lives in sin. God protects those and the evil one can not touch him.

Chapter 1:1-4 says, We declare to you what was from the beginning, what we have heard, what we have seen with our eyes, what we have looked at and touched with our hands, concerning the word of life—this life was revealed, and we have seen it and testify to it, and declare to you the eternal life that was with the Father and revealed to us—we declare to you what we have seen and heard so that you also may have fellowship with us; and truly our fellowship is with the Father and with his Son Jesus Christ. We are writing these things so that our joy may be complete. (John writes to show that this Jesus the Messiah was truly a human person, even God's unique Son. He uses the five senses to describe that he is real and not like a ghost as some of the Gnostics are saying.)

Verses 5-7 say, This is the message we have heard from him and proclaim to you, that God is light and in him there is no darkness at all. If we say that we have fellowship with him while we are walking in darkness, we lie and do not do what is true; but if we walk in the light as he himself is in the light, we have fellowship with one another, and the blood of Jesus his Son cleanses us from all sin.

Is he saying that through coming together in the worship experience, they continued to receive forgiveness of sins? Acts 2:41-42 is an example of what was a priority when they assembled together. The baptized devote themselves to the apostles' teaching and fellowship, to the breaking of bread (Eucharist), and the prayers.

Verses 8-10 say, If we say we have no sin, we deceive ourselves, and the truth is not in us. If we confess our sins, he who is faithful and just will forgive our sins and cleanse us from all unrighteousness. If we say we have not sinned, we make him a liar, and the word is not in us. (Too many people do not take Christ seriously either because they really do not believe their sin is a serious problem, or they do not believe they sin.)

✦

Chapter 2:1-6 says, My little children, I am writing these things to you so that you may not sin. But if anyone does sin, we have an advocate with the Father, Jesus Christ the righteous; and he is the atoning sacrifice for our sins, and not ours only but also for the sins of the whole world. Now by this we may be sure that we know him, if we obey his commandments. Whoever says, "I have come to know him," but does not obey his commandments, is a liar, and in such a person the truth does not exist; but whoever obeys his word, truly in this person the love of God has reached perfection. By this we may be sure that we are in him: whoever says, "I abide in him," ought to walk just as he walked.

Those who say they are followers of Christ and do not obey his commands are not really followers, even if they say they are, and if they are not making his priorities their priorities, they are not his followers.

Verses 7-11 say, Beloved, I am writing you no new commandment, but an old commandment that you have had from the beginning; the old commandment is the word that you have heard. Yet I am writing you a new commandment that is true in him and in you, because the darkness is passing away and the true light is already shining. (Christ is the new and living example of what the old commandment is to look like.) Whoever says, "I am in the light," while hating a brother or sister, is still in the darkness. Whoever loves a brother or sister lives in the light, and in such a person there is no cause for grumbling. But whoever hates another believer is in the darkness, walks in the darkness, and does not know the way to go, because the darkness has brought on blindness.

Verses 12-14 say, I am writing to you, little children (the whole Christian group), because your sins are forgiven on account of his name. I am writing to you, fathers (the aged), because you know him who is from the beginning. I am writing to you, young people, (those younger than the aged) because you have conquered the evil one. I write to you, children, because you know the Father. I write to you, fathers, because you know him who is from the beginning. I write to you, young people, because you are strong and the word of God abides in you, and you have overcome the evil one.

Verses 15-17 say, Do not love the world or the things in the world. The love of the Father is not in those who love the world; for all that is in the world—the desire of the flesh, the desire of the eyes, the pride in riches—comes not from the Father but from the world. And the world and its desire are passing away, but those who do the will of God live forever. (Those who live for the things of the world and its wealth have their first love as the world; their first love is not God.)

Verses 18-19 say, Children, it is the last hour. (It is the last age.) As you have heard that antichrist is coming, so now many antichrists have come. From this we know it is the last hour. (The antichrists have already come.) They went out from us, but they did not belong to us; for if they had belonged to us, they would have remained with us. But by going out they made it plain that none of them belongs to us. (The antichrists were at one time declared Christians.)

Verses 20-25 say, But you have been anointed by the Holy One, and all of you have knowledge. I write to you, not because you do not know the truth, but because you know it, and you know that no lie comes from the truth. Who is the liar but the one who denies that Jesus is the Christ (Messiah)? This is the antichrist, the one who denies the Father and the Son. No one who denies the Son has the Father; everyone who confesses the Son has the Father also. Let what you had from the beginning abide in you. If what you heard in the beginning abides in you, then you will abide in the Son and in the Father. And this is what he has promised us, eternal life. (See the Gospel of John chapter 15.)

Verses 26-27 say, I write these things to you concerning those who would deceive you. As for you, the anointing that you received from him abides in you, and so you do not need anyone to teach you. But as his anointing teaches you about all things, and is true and is not a lie, and just as it has taught you, abide in him. (Christians have received the anointing grace of the Holy Spirit, therefore they can discern the truth, Jer 31:31-34, 1 Cor 2:15-16, Jn 14:26.)

They do not need outsiders to teach them the things of God. The anointing is the mark of knowledge about who God is and the mark of new life. It demonstrates that one is abiding in Christ through the Holy Spirit. Verses 28-29 say, And now, little children, abide in him, so that when he is revealed we may have confidence and not be put to shame before him at his coming. If you know that he is righteous you may be sure that everyone who does right has been born of him.

An emotional encounter where one experiences being born again is not the criteria. Billy Graham, probably the world's number one promoter of a born again experience, said that his wife never had the born again experience, for she said she never knew a time when she did not believe she was a child of God. Even so, for many there comes a time in life that one must decide the path they will follow. Still this may simply be a rational reasoned decision and not an emotional experience.

✧

Chapter 3:1-3 says, See what love the Father has given us, that we should be called children of God; and that is what we are. The reason the world does not know us is that it did not know him. Beloved, we are God's children now; what we will be has not been revealed. What we do know is this: when he is revealed, we will be like him, for we will see him as he is. And all who have this hope in him purify themselves, just as he is pure. (Because his followers have been born of God, when Christ comes, they will be like him in that they will live eternally.)

Verses 4-10 say, Everyone who commits sin is guilty of lawlessness; sin is lawlessness. You know that he was revealed to take away sins, and in him there is no sin. No one who abides in him sins (or practices or lives in sin); no one who sins has either seen him or known him. Little children, let no one deceive you. Everyone who does what is right is righteous, just as he is righteous. Everyone who commits sin is a child of the devil; for the devil has been sinning from the beginning. The Son of God was revealed for this purpose, to destroy the works of the devil. Those who have been born of God do not sin (do not practice sin), because God's seed abides in them (the Holy Spirit); they cannot sin (live in sin), because they have been born of God. The children of God and the children of the devil are revealed in this way: all who do not do what is right are not from God, nor are those who do not love their brothers and sisters. (You will know them by the fruit they bear, see John 15.)

Verses 11-15 say, For this is the message you have heard from the beginning, that we should love one another. We must not be like Cain who was from the evil one and murdered his brother. And why did he murder him? Because his own deeds were evil and his brother's righteous. Do not be astonished, brothers and sisters, that the world hates you. We know that we have passed from death to life because we love one another. Whoever does not love abides in death. All who hate a brother or sister are murderers, and you know that murderers do not have eternal life abiding in them. We know love by this, that he laid down his life for us—and we ought to lay down our lives for one another. How does God's love abide in anyone who has the world's goods and sees a brother or sister in need and yet refuses to help?

Love is defined by the actions of 1 Cor 13:4-7 and the actions of Christ. Love and compassion for our fellow humans and especially those in need are to be major characteristics of a follower of Christ. Does the reader see that in the Christians he knows? How about the church? How about the politicians and business leaders the reader knows, who say they are Christians? On what actions or lack of actions is your opinion based?

Verses 18-22 say, Little children, let us love, not in word or speech, but in truth and action. And by this we will know that we are of the truth and will reassure our hearts before him whenever our hearts condemn us; for God is greater than our hearts, and he knows everything. Beloved, if our hearts do not condemn us, we have boldness before God; and we receive from him whatever we ask, because we obey his commandments and do what pleases him.

Verses 23-24 say, And this is his commandment that we should believe in the name of his Son Jesus Christ and love one another, just as he has commanded us. All who obey his commandments abide in him, and he abides in them. And by this we know that he abides in us, by the Spirit that he has given us. (The Spirit produces love, compassion, and the desire to not only do the teachings of Christ but to think and act like him. The choice is the Spirit of Christ or the spirit of the world.)

Chapter 4:1-3 says, Beloved, do not believe every spirit, but test the spirits to see if they are from God; for many false prophets have

gone out into the world. By this you know the spirit of God; every spirit that confesses that Jesus Christ has come in the flesh (has a physical body) is from God, and every spirit that does not confess Jesus is not from God. And this is the spirit of the antichrist, of which you have heard that it is coming; and now it is already in the world.

The false prophets are the antichrists that have gone into the world. They teach Jesus is just a spirit, a ghost like creature. These people were also called Docetic Gnostics. People are to test the teachings of others by comparing what they teach with the apostolic teachings.

Verses 4-6 say, Little children, you are from God, and have conquered them; for the one who is in you is greater than the one who is in the world. (With the Spirit of God in you, there is no need to worry about being overcome by evil.) They are from the world; therefore what they say is from the world, and the world listens to them. We are from God. Whoever knows God listens to us, and whoever is not from God does not listen to us. From this we know the spirit of truth and the spirit of error. (Christians believe the truth of God and what he teaches is found in the apostolic teachings now found in Scripture.)

Verses 7-10 say, Beloved, let us love one another, because love is from God; everyone who loves is born of God and knows God. (When truly born of God, Christ's followers let his love live in and through them.) Whoever does not love does not know God, for God is love. God's love was revealed among us in this way: God sent his only Son into the world so that we might live through him. In this is love, not that we loved God but that he loved us and sent his Son to be the atoning sacrifice for our sins. (There are a few churches today who no longer teach that Christ is the atoning sacrifice for sin. They teach that he is simply a great moral leader.

Would the writer of John call the leaders of those churches false prophets, even antichrists?)

Verses 11-16 say, Beloved, since God loved us so much, we also ought to love one another. No one has ever seen God; if we love one another, God lives in us, and his love is perfected in us. By this we know that we abide in him and he in us, because he has given us of his Spirit. And we have seen and do testify that the Father has sent his Son as the Savior of the world (not just individuals but the world and its structures). God abides in those who confess that Jesus is the Son of God, and they abide in God. So we have known and believe the love God has for us. God is love, and those who abide in love, abide in God, and God abides in them.

This is the goal of the follower of Christ: To let Christ live in them and through them as people of compassion and love allowing God's love and compassion to be perfected in them. Jesus came to establish the kingdom of God. Before he rose at the *Ascension*, he told his followers to go into the world baptizing and teaching *all* that he commanded. All includes spreading the kingdom he came to establish, the kingdom that would grow like a mustard seed. Jesus did not just talk about individual salvation. In fact he rarely mentioned that. He talked about the kingdom, the kingdom of God that has broken into the world and will be perfected at his final coming. Jesus is not just about reforming and saving individuals, but is also about reforming and saving the world and its structures that will finally be perfected at his coming.

Verses 17-18 say, Love has been perfected among us in this: that we may have boldness on the day of judgment, because, as he is, so are we in the world. (In other words his followers are to become like Christ, standing for the things he stood for and acting like he acted in the situations that come to them.) There is no fear (of judgment) in love, but perfect love casts out fear; for fear has to do with punishment, and whoever fears has not reached perfection in love.

Many of his followers continue to fear because they know they do not have Christ's love and compassion living in them. They still hang on to love of the self, the world, and all its enticements and false promises.

Verses 19-21 say, We love because he first loved us. Those who say, "I love God," and hate their brothers or sisters, are liars; for those who do not love a brother or sister whom they have seen, cannot love God whom they have not seen. The commandment we have from him is this: those who love God must love their brothers and sisters also. (Love in the Bible is not defined as a feeling, but as action such as doing to others as you would have them do to you, and then modeled by Jesus' words and actions.)

Chapter 5:1-5 says, Everyone who believes that Jesus is the Christ has been born of God, and everyone who loves the parent loves the child. (If God is loved, then his children are to be loved also.) By this we know that we love the children of God, when we love God and obey his commandments. For the love of God is this, that we obey his commandments. And his commandments are not burdensome, for whatever is born of God conquers the world. And this is the victory that conquers the world, our faith. Who is it that conquers the world but the one who believes that Jesus is the Son of God? (Faith is the acceptance of Jesus' true character, and children of God are identified by their faith, which involves obedience to his commands, and love for God and all of God's children.)

Verses 6-8 say, This is the one who came by water and blood, Jesus Christ, not with the water only but with the water and the blood. And the Spirit is the one that testifies, for the Spirit is the truth. There are three that testify: the Spirit and the water and the blood, and these three agree. (The water refers to baptism; the blood refers to Christ's death on the cross. The Spirit is the Holy Spirit, which was at work in the life, death, and resurrection of Jesus, and is at work in those baptized into Christ.)

Verses 9-13 say, If we receive human testimony, the testimony of God is better; for this is the testimony of God that he has testified to his Son. (He has done this by raising him from the dead and by the Holy Spirit.) Those who believe in the Son of God have the testimony in their hearts. (God through the Holy Spirit has sent Christ to live in their hearts.) Those who do not believe in God have made him a liar by not believing in the testimony that God has given concerning his Son. And this is the testimony: God gave us eternal life, and this life is in his Son. Whoever has the Son has life; whoever does not have the Son does not have life. I write these things to you who believe in the Son of God, so that you may know that you have eternal life.

The true follower of Christ says the following: We know that we have eternal life, if our heart has the Spirit of Christ living in it, and we know that is so when we think like Christ, stand for those Christ stood for, and act as Christ would act in the life situations that are presented to us and come before us. It is then that we can know that by God's grace and mercy we will have eternal life.

Verses 14-18 say, And this is the boldness we have in him, that if we ask anything according to his will, he hears us. And if we know that he hears us in whatever we ask, we know that we have obtained the requests made of him. If you see your brother or sister committing what is not a mortal sin, you will ask, and God will give life to such a one—to those whose sin is not mortal. There is a sin that is mortal; I do not say that you should pray about that. All wrongdoing is sin, but there is sin that is not mortal. We know that those who are born of God do not sin. (They do not practice or live in sin.), but the one who is born of God protects them, and the evil one does not touch them.

It seems as though mortal sin is on those who have rejected Christ and the purpose of the cross, and then the Holy Spirit. This sin will not be forgiven. Sin that is not mortal seems to be the sin that those who have chosen Christ commit as they fall short of the mark. These sins can be forgiven through confession, prayer (1:8-10, 2:1-2) and Holy Communion (Mt 26:26-28).

Verses 19-21 say, We know that we are God's children, and that the whole world lies under the power of the evil one. And we know that the Son of God has come and has given us understanding so that we may know him who is true; and we are in him who is true, in his Son Jesus Christ. He is the true God and eternal life. Little children, keep yourself from idols. (Idols are anything of the world that is a rival of the one God and keeps one from being a true follower of Christ.)

This ends the letter of 1 John. As a way of review list some of the most important verses or thoughts made by John.

THE SECOND LETTER OF JOHN

The elder (presbyter) writes to the chosen lady which is the church. He says many deceivers have gone into the world, who do not acknowledge Christ coming in the flesh (the Incarnation); such is the deceitful one, the antichrist. Anyone so progressive to not remain in the teachings of Christ does not have God. If anyone comes and does not have the doctrine of the Father and Son, do not welcome them. There is only one chapter in this book.

Verses 1-3 say, The elder to the elect lady (the church) and her children, whom I love in the truth, and not only I but also all who know the truth, because of the truth that abides in us and will be with us forever: Grace, mercy, and peace will be with us from God the Father and from Jesus Christ, the Father's Son, in truth and love.

Verses 4-6 say, I was overjoyed to find some of your children walking in the truth, just as we have been commanded by the Father. But now, dear lady, I ask you, not as though I were writing you a new commandment, but one we have had from the beginning, let us love one another. And this is love, that we walk according to his commandments; this is the commandment just as you have heard it from the beginning—you must walk in it.

Verses 7-8 say, Many deceivers have gone out into the world, those who do not confess that Jesus Christ has come in the flesh; any such person is the deceiver and the antichrist! (These were mainly the Gnostics who believed that Jesus was not flesh and blood, but only a spirit.) Be on guard, so that you do not lose what we have worked for, but may receive a full reward.

Verses 9-11 say, Everyone who does not abide in the teaching of Christ, but goes beyond it, does not have God; whoever abides in the teaching has both the Father and the Son. (The teaching is that Christ came in the flesh as a human and is God's Son.) Do not receive into the house or welcome anyone who comes to you and does not bring this teaching; for to welcome is to participate in the evil deeds of such a person. (The idea is do not welcome into the church those who claim to be of the apostolic teaching if they teach that Jesus did not come in the flesh.)

Verses 12-13 say, Although I have much to write to you, I would rather not use paper and ink; instead I hope to come to you and talk with you face to face, so that our joy may be complete. The children of your elect sister send you their greetings.

THE THIRD LETTER OF JOHN

J ohn is encouraged by Gaius who is walking in the truth and helping some traveling disciples as they spread God's word. He writes about Diotrephes who loves to dominate and does not acknowledge John and is spreading evil about him as well as not accepting the apostolic missionaries. John says that he will deal with him later.

Verses 1-4 say, The elder (presbyter) to the beloved Gaius whom I love in the truth. Beloved, I pray that all may go well with you and that you may be in good health, just as it is well with your soul. I was overjoyed when some of the friends arrived and testified to your faithfulness to the truth, namely how you walk in the truth. I have no greater joy than this, to hear that my children are walking in the truth.

Verses 5-8 say, Beloved, you do faithfully whatever you do for the friends, even though they are strangers to you; they have testified to your love before the church. You will do well to send them on in a manner worthy of God; for they began their journey for the sake of Christ, accepting no support from non-believers. Therefore we ought to support such people, so that we may become co-workers with the truth.

Verses 9-10 say, I have written something to the church; but Diotrephes, who likes to put himself first, does not acknowledge our authority (apostolic authority). So if I come, I will call attention to what he is doing in spreading false charges against us. And not content with those charges, he refuses to welcome the friends, and even prevents those who want to do so and expels them from the church.

Verses 11-12 say, Beloved, do not imitate what is evil but imitate what is good. Whoever does good is from God; whoever does evil has not seen God. Everyone has testified favorably about Demetrius and, so has the truth itself. We also testify for him, and you know that our testimony is true.

Verses 13-15 say, I have much to write to you, but I would rather not write with pen and ink; instead I hope to see you soon, and we will talk together face to face. Peace to you. The friends send you their greetings. Greet the friends there, each by name.

This ends the letters of 2 and 3 John. As a way of review list some of the more important verses or thoughts made by John.

THE LETTER OF JUDE

Jude is 1 chapter with 25 verses. The writer is Jude a slave of Christ and brother of James. Traditionally this has been said to be the brother of Christ, but there is no proof for or against this. The letter is very similar to 2 Peter. He says may mercy, peace, and love be yours in abundance. He says to contend for the faith that was once and for all handed down through the saints, the holy ones. There have been intruders, godless persons who pervert the grace of God into licentiousness, and who deny Christ.

He says I want to remind you that the Lord who saved his people from Egypt later destroyed those who did not believe. Also the angels who deserted their proper dwelling have been kept in eternal chains for judgment. Likewise Sodom and Gomorrah and those who indulged in sexual promiscuity and practiced unnatural vice (homosexuality) serve as an example by undergoing a punishment of eternal fire. These dreamers also defile the flesh, scorn lordship and revile glorious beings. They revile what they do not understand. Woe to them! The Lord will execute judgment on all their godless deeds and harsh words the godless sinners have uttered against him. They are complainers and disgruntled who live by their desires. Their mouths utter bombast as they fawn over people to gain advantage.

The apostles told you that in the last time there will be scoffers who will live according to their own godless desires. They cause division, living on the natural plane devoid of the Spirit. But you, build yourself up in the most holy faith; pray in the Spirit. On those who waver have mercy. Save others by snatching them out of the fire.

❧

Verses 1-2 say, Jude, a servant of Jesus Christ and brother of James, To those who are called, who are beloved in God the Father and kept safe for Jesus Christ: May mercy, peace, and love be yours in abundance.

Verse 3 says, Beloved, while eagerly preparing to write to you about the salvation we share, I find it necessary to write and appeal to you to contend for the faith that was once for all entrusted to the saints.

God's people already have the inspired faith. There will be no more inspired faith other than the apostolic faith, but there was illumination then and will be illumination throughout history. The Spirit will illuminate God's people and help them understand better the teachings, so they are better able to apply the teachings to the new situations they find themselves in down through history.

Verses 4-8 say, For certain intruders have stolen in among you, people who long ago were designated for this condemnation as ungodly, who pervert the grace of our God into licentiousness and deny our only Master and Lord Jesus Christ. Now I desire to remind you, though you are fully informed, that the Lord, who once for all saved a people out of the land of Egypt, afterward destroyed those who did not believe. And the angels who did not keep their own position, but left their proper dwelling, he has kept in eternal chains in deepest darkness for the judgment of the great Day. Likewise

Sodom and Gomorrah and the surrounding cities, which, in the same manner as they, indulged in sexual immorality and pursued unnatural lust, serve as an example by undergoing a punishment by eternal fire. Yet in the same way these dreamers also defile the flesh, reject authority, and slander the glorious ones.

There were different kinds of Gnostics. These Gnostics believed they could do anything they wanted, for they did not believe the flesh was real, or at least of no value. The only thing that was real was the spirit. Therefore it was acceptable to engage in licentiousness.

Verses 9-13 say, But when the archangel Michael contended with the devil and disputed about the body of Moses, he did not dare to bring a condemnation of slander against him, but said, "The Lord rebuke you!" (This is taken from Jewish tradition.) But these people slander whatever they do not understand, and they are destroyed by those things that, like irrational animals, they know by instinct. Woe to them! For they go the way of Cain (Gen 4:1-16) and abandon themselves to Balaam's error for the sake of gain (Numbers chapters 22, 23, 31), and perish in Korah's rebellion (Numbers 16). These are blemishes on your love-feasts, while they feast with you without fear, feeding themselves. (Apparently, they were within the assembly, and they were either promoting or indulging in the same orgies found in the pagan religions.) They are waterless clouds carried along by the winds; autumn trees without fruit, twice dead, uprooted; wild waves of the sea, casting up the foam of their own shame; wandering stars, for whom the deepest darkness has been reserved forever. (These heretics slander spiritual truths they do not understand; they will perish because they follow their animal passions. Their shame is cast up like the waves of the sea cast up their foam onto the sand.)

Verses 14-15 say, It was also about these that Enoch, in the seventh generation from Adam prophesied, saying, "See, the Lord is coming with ten thousands of his holy ones, to execute judgment on all, and to convict everyone of all the deeds of ungodliness that they have committed in such an ungodly way, and of all the harsh things that ungodly sinners have spoken against him." (This is quoted from the book of Enoch, a book not included in the Bible.) Verse 16 says, These are grumblers and malcontents; they indulge their own lusts; they are bombastic in speech, flattering people to their own advantage. (Jude is saying judgment is sure.)

Verses 17-19 say, But you, beloved, must remember the predictions of the apostles of our Lord Jesus Christ; for they said to you, "In the last time there will be scoffers, indulging their own ungodly lusts." It is these worldly people, devoid of the Spirit, who are causing divisions. (Jude believes they are in the last times, which is defined as the last age.)

Verses 20-23 say, But you, beloved, build yourselves up on your most holy faith; pray in the Holy Spirit; keep yourselves in the love of God; look forward to the mercy of our Lord Jesus Christ that leads to eternal life. And have mercy on some who are wavering; save others by snatching them out of the fire; and have mercy on still others with fear, hating even the tunic defiled by their bodies.

Verses 24-25 are a doxology, Now to him who is able to keep you from failing, and to make you stand without blemish in the presence of his glory with rejoicing, to the only God our Savior, through Jesus Christ our Lord, be glory, majesty, power, and authority, before all time and now and forever. Amen. This ends the letter of Jude. As a way of review list some of the most important verses or thoughts made by Jude.

REVELATION
(The APOCALYPSE)

The writer John, who is most likely the Apostle John sees everything in light of the Old Testament which he cites not by verse but by images over 250 times. It is thought that he is writing from the island of Patmos where he was banished because of what he was preaching and teaching. Most scholars date his writing around AD 95 during the time of the emperor Domitian, who demanded to be addressed as "lord and god." A minority of scholars date the writing before AD 70. Like most biblical books it is not easy to date them exactly or even to determine the exact author.

Revelation is a blend of three distinct literary types: apocalypse, prophecy, and letter. It shares its symbolism with other New Testament writings such as 2 Thess 2, Mk 13, Mt 24-25, Lk 21, also with the Old Testament such as Daniel, Zechariah, and aspects of Ezekiel, and a group of Hebrew writings known as the pseudepigrapha, a group of Jewish writings not in the Bible, but often claimed to be written by some biblical person. The testament of Abraham, 1 Enoch, and 4 Ezra are examples.

Revelation as apocalypse has some of the following characteristics:

(1) It looks forward to the time when God will bring a radical change or end in history where good will triumph, and evil will be judged.

(2) There are visions and dreams, and the language is cryptic having hidden meanings, that are mystical, and symbolic.

(3) Most of the images are fantasy such as a beast with seven heads and ten horns.

(4) There is a fondness for the symbolic use of numbers, animals, colors, and other images.

(5) It comes at a time of great persecution when much suffering is occurring and things look hopeless for believers.

(6) Readers are called to repent because of a coming judgment. There are many woes and warnings about unrighteousness as well as urging to righteous living.

(7) History is moving toward a new age, and there will be a discontinuity between the two ages, which is expressed in pessimism, degeneration, and domination by Satan and hostile powers of the current age. There does not seem to be much hope for the present compared to the age to come, which is characterized by a new creation, a new heaven and a new earth, a heavenly Jerusalem coming down from above, a paradise restored. The new age symbolizes an end of exile, sometimes an end of the old covenant, sometimes an end of the world. Read Acts 2:14-21 where the sun turning to darkness and moon to blood is used by Peter on the day of Pentecost as a fulfillment of the prophet Joel in 2:28-32. Notice the concept of end times is being used by Peter to mean the end of the old covenant and the beginning of the new. The new covenant age will then be called by New Testament writers as the end times meaning last age. For many readers that may be a totally new way to define end times.

(8) In apocalyptic literature there are messianic woes, judgment

on God's enemies, salvation for his people, and the end of the old age and beginning of the new that is marked by severe distress. This is usually symbolized by cosmic catastrophes like stars falling, changes in the moon and sun, earthquakes, wars, rumors of wars. These are all symbolic not to be taken literally. The messianic woes culminate in divine intervention, which brings in the new age, the age of bliss for the righteous remnant. The righteous dead are restored to life to share the blessings of the new age.

(9) The end is always near because of a particular crisis that is occurring and a longing for the new. Behind the evil stand the fallen angels and demons represented by Satan. The agent of the divine purpose is the Messiah who is called the Son of Man (Dan 7:13-14).

(10) God is in control and history is moving toward God's goal. Understanding apocalyptic literature is not easy, for even Daniel in the OT said he did not understand all that God was saying through him.

Revelation is also prophecy, but the emphasis is not on predicting what will happen in the far distant future which is what many associate with biblical prophecy. Biblical prophecy is more a prophetic word to the churches where Christ looks at them and compares what they are doing with what they should be doing. The problem is prophecy and apocalyptic literature often overlap, and it is difficult to know where the fine line is. The best we can say is that apocalyptic paints a broad picture while prophecy is more specific and focuses on issues of current justice and things that will occur very soon, not in the far distant future. Another interesting aspect of this literature is that many of the themes seem to repeat themselves throughout history.

When we interpret we must be careful to look at the original context and the original purpose of the letter and not spend too much time speculating. The purpose of the book is not to lay out in detail what is going to happen at the end of the world; that is not the real purpose of the writer.

There can be no arrogance in interpreting apocalyptic literature as is sometimes seen in modern day radio, television preachers, and writers comparing current events with the end times as they preach and write their novels. One example is an arrogance born of a doctrine of a rapture in which believers are removed from the scenes of persecution and suffering while the unsaved stay on earth and suffer. That teaching is contrary to Scripture which says that believers will suffer, and every eye will see him when he returns (1:7).

In the book of Revelation there are no scenes of cars crashing into one another because their drivers have been blissfully raptured as well as some of the other nonsense spewed by these people and their prophecy conferences attempting to show that the end of the world is almost here. All one has to do is examine their literature and their date setting to see how wrong they have been down through the years.

They always know when Jesus' return is going to happen, even when Jesus did not know. These people have made millions on top of millions of dollars from biblically illiterate but good people. Most of these leaders probably believe what they are teaching, even though there is no basis for their fanciful thinking. No legitimate scholar from the Roman Catholics, the Orthodox, and mainline Protestant churches accept these wild theories produced mainly by some of the fundamentalist churches.

A current example is the popular *Left Behind* series, which has become the foundation of extreme right wing politics. It is best to stay away from these people who pretend to know more than Jesus. There are no Roman Catholic, Orthodox, or mainline Protestant scholars, that this author is aware of, who agree with that series. They all see it as a distortion of Scripture mainly because the method of interpretation used by most fundamentalists ignores the form of literature that distinguishes the book of Revelation.

Chapter 1:3 says blessed is the one who reads aloud and blessed are those who listen to this prophetic message and heed what is written in it, for the appointed time is near. In Scripture the appointed time is always near because from the time of Christ until the time he comes again we are in the last times, the last age, the end times. The call of God's people is to testify to the Lord Jesus by words and actions, and to be prepared, without spot or blemish, to do the things of God and to keep washed in the blood of the Lamb.

God will prevail. Good will prevail over evil in the end. There will be a final judgment, and those washed in the blood of the Lamb will be with him in the place of perfection where there will be no tears, no pain, or sorrow in the new heaven and new earth. Those who reject him and the blood that washes away all sin will be separated from him forever. This is a major theme to focus on.

The book of Revelation is apocalyptic poetry. This type of writing is not meant to be interpreted literally. The writer overwhelms the reader with visual images using symbols to express his thoughts. To turn this poetic vision into a system of charts that detail all the events of Christ's return at the end of this world distorts and does injustice to the nature of the literature.

John's primary purpose is to offer hope to those being persecuted for not offering worship to the emperor of Rome. The Roman emperors at the time claimed to be the son of god, lord and savior, bringing peace to the world and demanding worship, and those who refused suffered physical, mental, and economic persecution.

John is showing that the one God is in control and will prevail. The Son of God that brings peace to the earth, who is the real Lord and Savior is Jesus not the Roman emperor. God and his people will be victorious in the end. Injustice and evil will be judged and punished. So John encourages God's people to persevere in suffering and remain faithful.

The structure of the book consists of seven interlocking series of visions with each repeating the struggle of the believer, the church, and the judgment theme, and the inevitable victory of each from a different perspective. The process continually repeats itself as each cycle becomes more intense in a deeper and more progressive form than the previous one. This approach brings before the reader the symbol of triumph over oppression in the Old Testament, which is the seven branched menorah. Revelation may be seen as a Christian menorah symbolized by its seven fold structure.

There are 7 letters to 7 churches in chapters 2-3. There are 7 seals in chapters 6-8. There are 7 trumpet woes in chapters 8-11. There are 7 visions of the dragon's kingdom in chapters 12-13. There are 7 visions of worshipers of the Lamb and of the beast in chapter 14. There are 7 bowls of God's wrath in chapter 16. There are 7 visions of the fall of Babylon in chapters 17-19. There are 7 visions of the end of Satan's evil age and the beginning of God's righteous age in chapters 19-21.

It is obvious to serious observers of the book of Revelation that numbers are used as symbols. The following are the main numbers and what they represent. Three is the spiritual order. Four is the created order. Six is the height of imperfection. Seven, the sum of three and four is perfection or completeness. Ten is the perfect decimal or totality. Twelve, the product of three and four, is Israel or God's people. Three and one-half represents a form of evil. Three and one-half years (3 ½), twelve hundred sixty days (1260), forty two months (42), and one thousand years (1,000) symbolize the church age, the time between the first coming of Christ and the second coming of Christ which brings suffering to the serious believer.

In Revelation there is no important difference between 12, 144, 12,000, or 144,000. They all represent the people of God, with varying emphases on the totality and appropriate to the item counted or measured. The letters of the Hebrew alphabet were given numbers, giving each word a numerical value, which could also symbolize something. The symbolization of the numbers is important to understand in attempting to make sense of this book.

In all the New Testament letters there is a preview of each chapter before we enter into a verse by verse explanation. That will be omitted in the book of Revelation because of the nature of this introductory information and the nature of the book and its length. But we will go through each chapter and verse line by line. Let us begin.

Chapter 1:1-2 says, 'The revelation (Greek says apocalypse), of Jesus Christ which God gave him to show his servants what must soon take place; he made it known by sending his angel (messenger) to his servant John, who testified to the word of God and to the testimony of Jesus Christ, even to all that he saw.

The book of Revelation is about what will soon begin; it is not about everything readers would like to know concerning the end of the world and the detailed events leading to it. It is not about a future period immediately preceding the end of history. This is not a human message but a direct revelation, a revealing from God through Jesus Christ, through an angel, through John, through a reader, to the one who hears it. The book is to be read to people in the church, so they can hear it.

Verse 3 says, Blessed is the one who reads aloud the words of the prophecy, and blessed are those who hear and who keep what is written in it; for the time is near. (Again the time for all this to begin is near. This is the first of seven beatitudes in the book of Revelation. The others are 14:13, 16:15, 19:9, 20:6, and 22:7, 14. The message is not only to hear the book read but to do it or keep what is written in it.)

Verses 4-6 say, John to the seven churches that are in Asia: Grace to you and peace from him who is and who was and who is to come, and from the seven spirits who are before his throne, and from Jesus Christ, the faithful witness (Greek for witness is martyr), the first born of the dead (the first to rise from the dead enabling others to follow), and the ruler of the kings of the earth.

There were more than seven churches in Asia. The number seven in Hebrew symbolizes completeness, so he is writing a message that all the churches need to hear and pay attention to. The seven spirits probably are a reference to the complete or perfect Spirit of God, the Holy Spirit, thus the salutation is Trinitarian. Some scholars think it is a reference to Isa 11:1-5 and the manifold energies of the Spirit of God. The ruler of kings of the earth is God, especially Jesus through the Holy Spirit, for he is Lord of lords and King of kings. All the rulers of the world are responsible to him and will be judged by him. This would inspire confidence in those being treated cruelly by the Roman government. Verses 5-6 continue saying, To him who loves us and freed us from our sins by his blood, and made us to be a kingdom, priests serving his God and Father, to him be glory and dominion forever and ever. Amen.

God's people are his priests reigning with him now advancing the kingdom that Christ established while on earth. All through the Gospels Christ stressed the kingdom that he came to preach (Lk 4:43). Col 1:13-14 says, He has rescued us from the power of darkness and transferred us into the kingdom of his beloved Son, in whom we have redemption, the forgiveness of sins.

The kingdom is not totally invisible, for Jesus said it grows like a mustard seed. It is a real kingdom, advancing into the world, transforming the world and its structures. Jn 3:16 says, "God so loved the world . . ." God loves his creations both human and non-human and desires to renew them. So where Christ and his ways are made present the kingdom is present, and the renewal begins. Christ came not only to renew individuals but to renew the world and its structures through kingdom people who make Christ and his ways present to the world. Jesus calls his people to be his eyes, ears, mouth, hands, and feet continuing the mission he began. Then when he comes again, all things will be made perfect. We in America are so focused on individualism that the message about the world and its structures is missed and not taught in most churches. God created everything to benefit humans and glorify him, and all things are responsible to him.

At the coming of Christ, 1 Corinthians 15:24-28 says, Then comes the end, when he hands over the kingdom to God the Father, after he has destroyed every ruler and every authority and power. For he must reign until he has put all enemies under his feet. The last enemy to be destroyed is death. For God has put all things in subjection under his feet . . . When all things are subjected to him, then the Son himself will also be subjected to the one who put all things in subjection to him, so that God may be all in all.

Rom 8:18-25 says that even creation itself groans inwardly waiting for its final redemption. In Genesis God put the earth in the care of humankind and made them stewards of the earth, but instead of caring for it as God expected, more often than not, humans injure the earth. But these Scriptures say the earth as well as humans will be renewed and perfected. In the meantime the kingdom is to impact both individuals and the world.

Verses 7-9 say, Look! He is coming with the clouds; every eye will see him, even those who pierced him; and on his account all the tribes of the earth will wail. So it is to be. Amen. "I am the Alpha and the Omega," says the Lord God, who is and who was and who is to come, the Almighty.

Alpha is the Greek word for first; omega is the Greek word for last. God appearing symbolized by clouds usually is a reference to God making some form of judgment. The Bible is clear that Christ will return only once to judge all things, and submit the kingdom to the Father, and when he does, every eye will see him. That eliminates the so-called rapture where Christ secretly comes for some while the others are "left behind." There is also no mention of a thousand year reign after he comes. Most of the rapture people and those responsible for the *Left Behind* series of films and books, so popular with many fundamentalists, focus on fear and fatalism as opposed to the Bible's hope and transformation.

Verses 9-11 say, I, John, your brother who share with you in Jesus the persecution (tribulation) and the kingdom and the patient endurance, was on the island called Patmos because of the word of God, and the testimony of Jesus. I was in the spirit on the Lord's day, and I heard behind me a loud voice like a trumpet saying, "Write in a book what you see and send it to the seven churches, to Ephesus, to Smyrna, to Pergamum, to Thyatira, to Sardis, to Philadelphia, and to Laodicea."

Tradition says the Roman government banished John to the island of Patmos located in the Aegean Sea off the coast of Asia Minor (Turkey). He was banished there because of his preaching Christ and the kingdom. John was in the spirit on a Sunday, the day of worship. The Spirit overwhelmed his consciousness beyond his physical surroundings where he was immersed in a mystical experience with prophetic visions. He is told to write them in a book, and then send them to the churches.

Verses 12-16 say, Then I turned to see whose voice it was that spoke to me, and on turning I saw seven golden lampstands (the churches), and in the midst of the lampstands I saw one like the Son of Man (Jesus) clothed with a long robe and with a golden sash (suggesting his surpassing value) across his chest. (Christ is in the midst of his churches.) His head and his hair were white as white wool, white as snow (suggesting purity and wisdom); his eyes were like a flame of fire (piercing the minds and hearts of individuals and churches), his feet were like burnished bronze (suggesting stability and endurance), refined as in a furnace, and his voice was like the sound of many waters (suggesting majesty and authority). In his right hand he held seven stars (messengers or leaders of the church, see verse 20), and from his mouth came a sharp, two edged sword (the word of God that both saves and judges), and his face was like the sun shining with full force. (This is reminiscent of the transfiguration of the face of Moses when he came down from the mountain after being in the presence of God.)

Taken as a whole the picture of Christ presented here balances an overly familiar "buddy, buddy" image of Christ that is all too common in the church. Jesus walks with the church, but he is also the majestic, awe inspiring Son of God who is at the right hand of God ruling with the Father. John responds in fear and worship, and is overwhelmed, but he is comforted.

Verses 17-18 say, When I saw him, I fell at his feet as though dead. But he placed his right hand on me, saying, "Do not be afraid; I am the first and the last, and the living one. I was dead, and see, I am alive forever and ever; and I have the keys of Death and of Hades. (Because of the resurrection of Christ, he is the key to overcoming death.)

Verses 19-20 say, Now write what you have seen, what is, and what is to take place after this. As for the mystery of the seven stars that you saw in my right hand, and the seven golden lampstands: the seven stars are the angels of the seven churches, and the seven lampstands are the seven churches.

Angel means messenger and it is not always a reference to supernatural beings. Most likely the reference is to the elders or primary leaders of the churches. There are some who believe it may be a reference to the idea that each church has a guardian angel.

Chapter 2:1-3 says, "To the angel of the church at Ephesus write: These are the words of him (Christ) who holds the seven stars (leaders of the churches) in his right hand, who walks among the seven golden lampstands (churches): "I know your works, your toil and your patient endurance. I know that you cannot tolerate evil doers; you have tested those who claim to be apostles but are not, and have found them to be false. I also know that you are enduring patiently and bearing up for the sake of my name, and that you have not grown weary. (The church in Ephesus was morally and doctrinally sound.) But in (4-5) he says, I have this against you, that you have abandoned the love you had at first. Remember then from what you have fallen; repent, and do the works you did at first. If not, I will come to you and remove your lampstand from its place, unless you repent.

Their love had grown cold. Even though they were morally and doctrinally sound, they were not standing with those Christ stood with, nor were they working for their benefit (Jas 2:14-18, Mt 25:31-46). Christ is saying if they continue in the same vein, he will let the church close its doors. They had lost their love and passion for Christ and his works for the spiritually, physically, and materially needy.

The city of Ephesus was huge; it was the largest and most

important city in the province of Asia. The city was devoted to the cult of Artemis (Diana) and had a temple of the goddess that was regarded as one of the seven wonders of the ancient world. Fertility was a part of worship. In an agricultural society the crops needed sun and rain to grow. The people believed that as sexual intercourse at the temple took place, the gods would do the same, and this would bring the sun and rain to fertilize the crops. Much of their worship centered on orgies and sexual immorality. To the credit of the Ephesians those in the church remained pure in reference to those things.

Verses 6-7 say, "Yet this is to your credit: You hate the work of the Nicolaitans, which I also hate. (They believed the flesh did not matter; only the spirit mattered. Therefore they indulged in immorality, probably participating in the sexual orgies at the temple of Diana.) Let anyone who has an ear listen to what the Spirit is saying to the churches. To everyone who conquers, I will give permission to eat from the tree of life (represents eternal life) that is in the paradise of God (see Rev 22).

Verses 8-9 say, "And to the angel of the church in Smyrna write: 'These are the words of the first and the last, who was dead and came to life: I know your affliction and your poverty, even though you are rich. (Apparently they were not only doctrinally and morally sound but were passionately involved in the mission and works of Christ.) I know the slander on the part of those who say they are Jews and are not, but are a synagogue of Satan. (Jesus had said to them if you were Abraham's children, you would do the works of Abraham . . . Jn 8:39.)

Verses 10-11 say, "Do not fear what you are about to suffer. Beware, the devil is about to throw some of you into prison so that you may be tested and for ten days (a short period) you will have affliction. Be faithful unto death, and I will give you the crown of life. Let anyone who has an ear listen to what the Spirit is saying to the churches. Whoever conquers will not be harmed by the second death (the final end of sinners). The first death is physical on this earth; the second death is eternal separation from God.

Smyrna, modern Izmir, was the second largest city, reported as a most beautiful city, and noted for its sports and games. Cities were in competition with each other for these games, which were usually to honor the emperor. In the process they cost the people much money in taxes in order to conduct the games with great fanfare. Izmir is the only city of the seven still in existence. The famous bishop Polycarp was from here. He would later suffer as a martyr.

Verses 12-15 say, "And to the angel of the church in Pergamum write: These are the words of him who has the sharp two-edged sword (God's word that saves and condemns): I know where you are living, where Satan's throne is. Yet you are holding fast to my name, and you did not deny your faith in me even in the days of Antipas my witness, my faithful one who was killed among you, where Satan lives. But I have a few things against you: you have some there who hold to the teaching of Balaam, who taught Balak to put a stumbling block before the people of Israel, so that they would eat food sacrificed to idols and practice fornication. So you also have some who hold to the teachings of the Nicolaitans. (Even though the two groups had different doctrines, both groups ate foods offered to idols and participated in the sexual orgies at pagan temples.)

Verses 16-17 say, "Repent then. If not I will come to you soon and make war against them with the sword of my mouth (the word of God). Let anyone who has an ear listen to what the Spirit is saying to the churches. To everyone who conquers I will give some of the hidden manna (food for eternity), and I will give a white stone, and on the white stone is written a new name that no one knows except the one who receives it.

The white stone was admission into events. Here it symbolizes admission into eternal life. The church is being chastised for not getting rid of the false teachers and for not disciplining those living in sin. The temptation to ignore false teaching has always been in the church, but many churches have not figured out what differences are permitted to exist, and which are adiaphora (unimportant). It must also be noted that when Christ threatens to act and make a judgment in history it is called a coming of the Lord; it obviously is not the final coming or final judgment. This concept is missed by most of the "Jesus is coming now" people.

Pergamum was the capitol of Asia Minor and the main seat of Roman government. It must be remembered that the emperor was to be worshiped, and places to worship the emperor were all through the area. The city had the second largest library in the world, second only to Alexandria of Egypt.

Verses 18-21 say, "And to the angel of the church in Thyatira write: These are the words of the Son of God, who has eyes like a flame of fire, and whose feet are like burnished bronze: I know your works—your love, faith, service, and patient endurance. I know that your last works are greater than your first. But I have this against you: you tolerate that woman Jezebel, who calls herself a prophet and is teaching and beguiling my servants to practice fornication and to eat food sacrificed to idols. I gave her time to repent, but she refuses to repent of her fornication.

Thyatira was a commercial center that had many trade guilds. Each guild had a patron god they worshiped. Worshiping the god of the trade union was a requirement for being hired, and worship was often accomplished through fertility rites and sexual immorality. As previously mentioned in an agricultural society many thought rain would come to grow the crops if the worshipers would unite in fornication. This would cause the gods to do the same causing the rain to come and fertilize the crops. Jezebel was probably one of these sacred prostitutes at one of the temples who had become a follower of Christ, and then a prophet, but she refused to eliminate eating the food of idols and the practice of the fertility rites. She was probably teaching that practicing both religions was acceptable. This was a constant problem throughout the Old Testament. It was called syncretism where both the one God and the gods were worshiped. God allows this to continue for awhile in order to give her a chance to repent.

Verses 22-23 say, "Beware, I am throwing her on a bed, and those who commit adultery with her I am throwing into great distress, unless they repent of her doings; and I will strike her children dead. (Probably means they will be declared by his messengers, the apostles, to be without eternal life.) And all the churches will know that I am the one who searches minds and hearts, and I will give to each of you as your works deserve. (Here the reference is to works that oppose God's teachings. Works are important in the judgments of Christ as we have seen throughout the New Testament.)

Verses 24-29 say, "But to the rest of you in Thyatira, who do not hold this teaching, who have not learned what some call 'the deep things of Satan,' to you I say, I do not lay on you any other burden; only hold fast to what you have until I come. (Lydia, a dealer in purple cloth, and a convert of Paul in Philippi was from Thyatira, Acts 16:14.) To everyone who conquers and continues to do my works until the end, I will give authority over nations; to rule them with an iron rod, as when clay pots are shattered—even as I also received authority from my Father. (They will reign with Christ.) To the one who conquers I also give the morning star. Let anyone who has an ear listen to what the Spirit is saying to the churches. (In Rev 22:16 Jesus is the morning star. Again, as stated judgment includes one's works. What one does is important.)

It is important to note that most of these churches had problems; none of them was really perfect. People in today's churches flirt with paganism when they create modern day gods such as self, ego, greed, money, sex, sports, the flag or country, their culture, or whatever it may be as first in importance over the things of God. They also flirt with paganism when they become involved with the New Age practices, the occult, Ouija boards, astrology, psychics, and other such activities.

⌘

Chapter 3:1-3 says, "And to the angel of the church in Sardis write: These are the words of him (Christ) who has the seven spirits of God (Holy Spirit) and the seven stars (church leaders): I know your works; you have the name of being alive, but you are dead (spiritually). Wake up, and strengthen what remains and is on the point of death (their spiritual health), for I have not found your works perfect (mature) in the sight of my God. Remember then what you received and heard; obey it, and repent. If you do not wake up, I will come like a thief, and you will not know at what hour I will come to you.

Sardis receives no praise. Only its reputation is good, the church is close to its spiritual death. It was the capital of the ancient kingdom of Lydia. King Croesus, who was known for his great wealth resided there. The city was famous for its wealth and luxuries, but the city was fading and like the church was trying to live on its former reputation. Christ threatens to come and close the church doors if they do not soon repent and become alive again. In the New Testament Christ comes in historical judgments that are not a reference to his second coming.

Verses 4-6 say, "Yet you have a few persons in Sardis who have not soiled their clothes (by becoming dead spiritually); they will walk with me, dressed in white (purity), for they are worthy. If you conquer (sin and Satan), you will be clothed like them in white robes (washed by the blood of the Lamb), and I will not blot your name out of the book of life; I will confess your name before my Father and the angels. Let anyone who has an ear listen to what the Spirit is saying to the churches.

This shows, again, that followers of Christ retain their free will and can reject Christ, even after they have been his follower. But as long as one remains a follower and continues to receive forgiveness and walk with him in his name, Christ will confess their name before the Father. Possibly many of the believers in Sardis no longer met to hear, study, and discuss God's word. Whenever a church cuts down on those things or eliminates them, they and the people become spiritually dead as far as Christianity is concerned. Sardis had the reputation of being alive, but they were dead. The church at Philadelphia, the next church mentioned, was the opposite. It had the reputation of being weak, but it was spiritually alive.

Verses 7-8 say, "And to the angel of the church in Philadelphia write: These are the words of the holy one, the true one (the Messiah, the Christ), who has the key (of the kingdom) of David, who opens and no one will shut. I know that you have but little power, and yet you have kept my word and have not denied my name. (Therefore the power of God will preserve them unto eternal life.)

Verses 9-11 say, "I will make those of the synagogue of Satan who say that they are Jews and are not, but are lying—I will make them come and bow down before your feet, and they will learn that I have loved you. Because you have kept my word of patient endurance, I will keep you from the hour of trial that is coming on the whole world to test the inhabitants of the earth. I am coming soon; hold fast to what you have, so that no one may seize your crown.

Protection is promised, but not a rapture or evacuation from being persecuted. I am coming soon probably has reference to Christ acting in history as he promised when he talked about Jerusalem and the temple being destroyed in AD 70. Remember Christ acting in history is usually a reference to his acting from heaven in judgment, not the coming end.

As in Smyrna (2:9) those persecuting the church appear to have been local Jews. In Christ's eyes they were not real Jews, for as he said in Jn 8:39, if they were, they would be doing the works of Abraham. The hour of trial coming upon the known world was probably attacks by different Roman emperors who demanded to be worshiped, which resulted in thousands of Christian martyrs. Whatever it was, it was to occur to those people in those times. The message is to stand fast, for in so doing the crown of life would be received.

Verses 12-13 say, "If you conquer, I will make you a pillar in the temple of my God; you will never go out of it. I will write on you the name of my God, and the name of the city of my God, the new Jerusalem that comes down from my God out of heaven, and my own new name. Let anyone who has an ear listen to what the Spirit is saying to the churches.

The church is the pillar of God (1 Cor 3:16, Eph 2:20-22, 1 Tim 3:15, 1 Pet 2:5). Having the name of the Father and the Son written on one is like a slave bearing the name of his master. We will see that one is sealed by God or the mark of the beast. Paul equates this with being sealed by the Holy Spirit (Eph 1:13, 4:30). The message is that those who trust and remain steadfast during all the tribulation will receive eternal life. For true believers their first and primary citizenship is in heaven (Phil 3:20); it is not in the state or nation in which they live. That citizenship is secondary to their heavenly citizenship.

Verses 14-17 say, "And to the angel of the church in Laodicea write: The words of the Amen (Christ is the Amen, 2 Cor 1:20), the faithful and true witness, the origin of God's creation. (Christ is the source of all creation, Jn 1:3, Col 1:15-18.) I know your works; you are neither cold nor hot. So, because you are lukewarm, and neither cold nor hot, I am about to spit you out of my mouth. For you say, 'I am rich, I have prospered, and I need nothing.' (Here was a church who thought it had all things just right because it was wealthy and on the surface looked great. Apparently, because they had so much wealth, they thought God had blessed them for being such good Christians.) Verse 17 continues, You do not realize that you are wretched, pitiable, poor, blind, and naked.

The people being quite comfortable had become self-satisfied and complacent, which usually leads to a diminished zeal for the things of God. In thinking how wonderful they were, this author imagines they were quite shocked to learn that Christ had nothing positive to say about them. In fact he tells them they are so lukewarm that he was about to vomit them out. (Are there any churches like that today?)

Verse 18 says, "Therefore I counsel you to buy from me gold refined by fire so that you may be rich (character refined by affliction, for luxury is not known for its character building ability); and white robes to clothe you (purified from sin) and to keep the shame of your nakedness from being seen; and salve to anoint your eyes (what their medical school was well-known for) so that you may see. (He is suggesting that their wealth and comfort has blinded them, and they need to get their spiritual eyes healed and restored.) Verse 19 says, I reprove and discipline those whom I love. Be earnest therefore and repent.

Laodicea was very prosperous as a banking center and producer of black wool clothing and carpets. They were one of the wealthiest churches in Asia. Also located there was a famous medical school that was known for a medicine that aided eye ailments. The city's water supply came from hot springs about six miles away from the city. The water traveled through an aqueduct to Laodicea and by the time it got there the water was warm, neither hot nor cold.

Verse 20 says, "Listen! I am standing at the door, knocking; if you hear my voice and open the door, I will come in to you and eat with you, and you with me. (Jesus is saying you have locked me out of your assembly (church) so repent and open your doors, so I can come in again and be part of you. Dining with them probably has Eucharistic connotations.) Verses 21-22 say, To the one who conquers I will give a place with me on my throne, just as I myself conquered and sat down with my Father on his throne. Let anyone who has an ear listen to what the Spirit is saying to the churches."

Notice how confrontational Christ is, something that is rare to find in most modern churches because of the fear of offending the people and losing both them and their wealth. The approach of Jesus is to comfort the afflicted but also to afflict the comfortable in order to get them to change their thinking and ways to his thinking and ways. The issues found in these seven churches are the type of issues and problems found in the churches throughout history, even today.

Chapter 4:1-4 says, After this I looked, and there in heaven a door stood open! (This signifies God revealing himself.) And the first voice, which I had heard speaking to me like a trumpet, said, "Come up here, and I will show you what must take place after this." At once I was in the spirit, and there in heaven stood a throne, with one seated on the throne! And the one seated there looks like jasper and carnelian, and around the throne is a rainbow that looks like

emerald. (This is a vision of God in all his glory.) Around the throne are twenty-four thrones, and seated on the thrones (symbolizing that they are reigning with God) are twenty-four elders, dressed in white robes (the purified), with golden crowns (symbolizing victory) on their heads. (This represents all the redeemed of the Old and New Testaments, symbolized by those coming from the twelve tribes and the twelve apostles. They are reigning with God, Eph 1:20, 2:6, Rev 3:21, 20:6.)

Verses 5-8 say, Coming from the throne are flashes of lightning, and rumblings and peals of thunder (symbolizing God's power and majesty), and in front of the throne burn seven flaming torches, which are the seven spirits of God (Holy Spirit); and in front of the throne there is something like a sea of glass, like crystal (indicating the brilliance of God's glory).

Around the throne, and on each side of the throne, are four living creatures (cherubim-archangels, Ezek 10:15-20, who guard the holy things and attend God's presence), full of eyes in front and behind (to see everything): the first living creature like a lion (strength is like a lion), the second living creature like an ox (render service like the strength of an ox), the third living creature with a face like a human face (intelligence is like a human), and the fourth living creature like a flying eagle (move swiftly like an eagle). And the four living creatures, each of them with six wings, are full of eyes all around and inside. (They are God's eyes and ears.) Day and night without ceasing they sing, "Holy, holy, holy, the Lord God the Almighty, who was and is and is to come." (It is God who is worthy of worship, for he alone is holy, not the Roman emperor who was also demanding their worship.)

Verses 9-11 say, And whenever the living creatures give glory and honor and thanks to the one who is seated on the throne, who lives forever and ever, the twenty-four elders fall before the one who is seated on the throne and worship the one who lives forever and ever; they cast their crowns before the throne, singing, "You are worthy, our Lord and God, to receive glory, honor, and power, for you created all things, and by your will they existed and were created."

The purpose of all the heavenly beings and the redeemed is to worship the sovereign God in all his glory, for he is the creator of everything. It is important to realize this is a vision representing spiritual reality, not a description of the reality itself. It is all symbolic language conveying a very important spiritual message.

Chapter 5:1-5 says, Then I saw in the right hand of the one seated on the throne a scroll (the redemptive plan of God, Ezek 2:9-10) written on the inside and on the back sealed with the seven seals (nothing can be added to God's plan); and I saw a mighty angel proclaiming with a loud voice, "Who is worthy to open the scroll and break its seals?" And no one in heaven or on earth or under the earth was able to open the scroll or look into it. And I began to weep bitterly because no one was found worthy to open the scroll or look into it. Then one of the elders said to me, "Do not weep. See, the Lion of the tribe of Judah, the Root of David (the Messiah, Gen 49:9-10, 2 Sam 7:8-16), has conquered, so that he can open the scroll and its seven seals."

Verse 6 says, Then I saw between the throne and the four living creatures and among the elders a Lamb standing as if it had been slaughtered having seven horns and seven eyes, which are the seven spirits of God sent out into all the earth. (This is, the Son, who is the sacrificial Lamb, Jn 1:29, and the Holy Spirit. Seven horns symbolize being omnipotence, all powerful, and seven eyes symbolize being all knowing, omniscience.)

Verses 7-8 say, He went and took the scroll from the right hand of the one who was seated on the throne. When he had taken the scroll, the four living creatures (angels) and the twenty-four elders (people of God) fell before the Lamb, each holding a harp and golden bowls full of incense, which are the prayers of the saints. (This is the fulfillment of Daniel 7:9-14. Incense represents the prayers of the saints, the believers on earth. Keep in mind all of this is a symbolic vision.)

Verses 9-10 say, They sing a new song: "You are worthy to take the scroll and open its seals, for you were slaughtered and by your blood you ransomed for God saints from every tribe and language and people and nation; you have made them to be a kingdom and priests serving our God, and they will reign on earth."

Jesus is worthy to open the seals because he died on the cross for the sins of humankind, so that those washed in his blood can have eternal life. Those washed in the blood become his priests in his kingdom that he established on this earth and is growing like a mustard seed (Mt 13:31-33, Mk 4:30-32, Lk 13:18-21). They become his ears, voice, hands, and feet as they carry on his mission on earth making him present. Whenever Jesus and his values are made present on earth, the kingdom advances on earth like a mustard seed growing that begins as the tiniest of seeds. It is not a physical kingdom that is measured by boundaries but a spiritual kingdom making its impact upon this earth by its words and actions.

Verses 11-12 say, Then I looked, and I heard the voice of many angels surrounding the throne and the living creatures and the elders; they numbered myriads of myriads and thousands of thousands, singing with a full voice, "Worthy is the Lamb that was slaughtered to receive power and wealth and wisdom, and might and honor and glory and blessing!"

Verses 13-14 say, Then I heard every creature in heaven and on earth and under the earth and in the sea, and all that is in them, singing, "To the one seated on the throne and to the Lamb be blessing and honor and glory and might forever and ever!" And the four living creatures said, "Amen!" And the elders fell down and worshiped.

Worship and praise is offered to Jesus, the Lamb of God who takes away the sin of the world. These chapters teach that at the center of time and history is the throne of God, the Creator and the Lamb. The Lamb enables the plan of creation to be carried out (Dan 7:13-14, Isa 52-55). The Father, the Son, and the Holy Spirit rule the universe, and everything was created and exists to glorify the Father, Son, and Holy Spirit (Col 1:15-20). The Lamb is unfolding the Father's plan. His people reign with him while they are on earth. They rule with him as Christ through the Holy Spirit lives in and through them making him present as the kingdom makes its impact on a broken world.

Chapter 6:1-2 says, Then I saw the Lamb open one of the seven seals, and I heard one of the four living creatures call out, as with a voice of thunder, "Come!" I looked and there was a white horse! Its rider had a bow; a crown was given to him, and he came out conquering and to conquer.

19:11-13 the rider and horse are a reference to Christ. In this chapter we get a broad view of the history of the world. Christ, the gospel, and those reigning with him on earth continue the message into the world in the midst of evil and great tribulation until he comes again in the final coming. Some scholars do not believe this is a reference to Christ but a reference to war that has plagued the earth throughout its history. To this author, if it is a reference to physical war, it seems that the horse would not be colored white.

Verses 3-4 say, When he opened the second seal, I heard the

second living creature call out, "Come!" And out came another horse, bright red; its rider was permitted to take peace from the earth, so that people would slaughter one another; and he was given a great sword. (This horse symbolizes war and bloodshed.)

All throughout history God allows people to do evil against each other as well as against the church. Life on earth is continual war and rumors of wars. This symbolizes all the great evil leaders of history causing war for their own selfish ends. Jesus said in Mt 24:6 there will be wars and rumors of wars, and Mt 26:52 says that "all who take the sword will perish by the sword."

Verses 5-6 say, When he opened the third seal, he heard the third living creature call out, "Come!" I looked and there was a black horse! Its rider held a pair of scales in his hand, and I heard what seemed to be a voice in the midst of the four living creatures saying, "A quart of wheat for a day's pay, and three quarts of barley for a day's pay, but do not damage the olive oil and the wine!"

The black horse symbolizes famine, economic hardship, inflation, and disease that follow constant war. The oil and wine represent luxuries spared for the wealthy and those who support the efforts of continual war. The idea is that even in hard times the rich basically do quite well as do those who do evil compared to the masses of people.

Verses 7-8 say, When he opened the fourth seal, I heard the voice of the fourth living creature call out, "Come!" I looked and there was a pale green horse! Its rider's name was Death, and Hades followed with him; they were given authority over a fourth of the earth, to kill with sword, famine, pestilence, and by the wild animals of the earth.

Hades the place of the dead follows death in order to receive the dead. Since only a fourth of the earth is mentioned that indicates it is not always world-wide wars but that wars occur at different times in different places throughout history. There are others who interpret the last three horses as the persecution Christians suffer standing for those Christ stood with and promoting his kingdom and values in this broken world. Another group of interpreters believes the white horse symbolizes conquest and the rest of the horses symbolize that God uses this evil to judge the nations of the world throughout history and is a way to call them to repentance.

Verses 9-11 say, When he opened the fifth seal, I saw under the altar the souls of those who had been slaughtered for the word of God and for the testimony they had given; they cried out with a loud voice, "Sovereign Lord, holy and true, how long will it be before you judge and avenge our blood on the inhabitants of the earth?" (Many of the psalms ask the same thing.) They were each given a white robe (purity) and told to rest a little longer, until the number would be complete both of their fellow servants and of their brothers and sisters, who were soon to be killed as they themselves had been killed.

The picture of the martyrs presented here emphasizes the sacrificial character of their deaths. Their souls are under the altar where the blood of the sacrificial victims was poured in the Old Testament temple. The martyrs may represent all of God's people, for the New Testament assumes that God's people suffer because of God's word as well as for standing with those Jesus stood with.

Verses 12-17 say, When he opened the sixth seal, I looked, and there came a great earthquake; the sun became black as sackcloth, the full moon became like blood, and the stars of the sky fell to the earth as the fig tree drops its winter fruit when shaken by a gale. The sky vanished like a scroll rolling itself up, and every mountain and island was removed from its place. (All of this is apocalyptic symbolism, which is found throughout the Old Testament.) Then the kings of the earth and the magnates and the generals and the rich and the powerful, and everyone, slave and free, hid in the caves and among the rocks of the mountains, calling to the mountains and the rocks, "Fall on us and hide us from the face of the one seated on the throne and from the wrath of the Lamb; for the great day of their wrath has come, and who is able to stand?"

This is a preview of the end time judgment or the beginning of God's judgment of the wicked, and even though they tried to hide, there was no way to hide. As the old cliché goes, you can run, but you can not hide. John is given his first vision of the end and the wrath of God poured out on the evil doers. The Day of Judgment will be described in different ways and greater detail later, which is why its beginning is just previewed here. The vision here draws on Old Testament imagery. Old Testament prophecy commonly described social, political, and economic turmoil, and the judgment of nations in terms of cosmic cataclysms and foreign invasions. However taking the description as symbolic does not diminish the intended meaning.

Chapter 7:1-3 says, After this I saw four angels (destroying angels) standing at the four corners of the earth, holding back the four winds of the earth so that no wind could blow on earth or sea or against any tree. I saw another angel ascending from the rising of the sun, having the seal of the living God, and he called with a loud voice to the four angels who had been given power to damage earth and sea, saying, "Do not damage the earth or the sea or the trees until we have marked the servants of our God with a seal on their foreheads."

There is an interlude between the sixth and seventh seals. There will be two visions providing assurance that God's people will be secure from God's judgment. This is the answer to the question

John asked in the last chapter, "for the great day of their wrath has come, and who is able to stand?" The answer to who is able to stand is: those who have the seal of God on their forehead. Since this author has never seen anyone with a seal of God on the forehead, this symbolizes the Holy Spirit who enables one to believe, think, and act in a godly manner. Eph 1:13-14 says, In him you also, when you had heard the word of truth, the gospel of your salvation, and had believed in him, were *marked* with the seal of the promised Holy Spirit; this is the pledge of our inheritance toward redemption as God's own people, to the praise of his glory.

Verses 4-8 say, And I heard the number who were sealed, one hundred forty-four thousand, sealed out of every tribe of the people of Israel: Then twelve tribes are listed each with twelve thousand so that 12 x 12 x 1000 (the perfect decimal is cubed to indicate reduplicated completeness) make the 144,000. This symbolizes completeness or all the saved from the Old Testament people of God. The twelve listed are: Judah, Reuben, Gad, Asher, Naphtali, Manasseh, Simeon, Levi, Issachar, Zebulun, Joseph, and Benjamin. Manasseh replaced Dan because his territory was known for idol worship. Joseph replaces Ephraim because like Dan it was a territory known for idol worship. Some believe it represents all the redeemed, but in this situation, it may just represent the Old Testament people of God. That possibility exists because of what follows.

Verse 9 says, After this I looked and there was a great multitude that no one could count, from every nation, from all tribes and peoples and languages, standing before the throne and before the Lamb, robed in white, with palm branches in their hands.

The palm branches are a sign of victory and the white robes a sign of purity by being washed in the blood of Jesus. This probably symbolizes all the redeemed outside of the Old Testament people of God. The other possibility is that the 144,000 are all the redeemed from the twelve tribes and twelve apostles so that 12 x 12 x 1000 = 144,000, and verse 9 is simply pointing out that the numbers are so many that they can not be counted and the 144,000 is just symbolic. Which ever explanation the reader chooses all the redeemed of both groups are included one way or another.

Verses 10-12 say, They cried out in a loud voice, saying, "Salvation belongs to our God who is seated on the throne, and to the Lamb!" And all the angels stood around the throne and around the elders and the four living creatures, and they fell on their faces before the throne and worshiped God, singing, "Amen! Blessing and glory and wisdom and thanksgiving and honor and power and might be to our God forever and ever! Amen." (A constant theme is worship. People who do not worship do not really believe.)

Verses 13-17 say, Then one of the elders addressed me, saying, "Who are these robed in white, and where have they come from?" I said to him, "Sir, you are the one that knows." Then he said to me, "These are they who have come out of the great ordeal (the ordeal of life in this world); they have washed their robes and made them white in the blood of the Lamb. For this reason they are before the throne of God, and worship him day and night within the temple, and the one who is seated on the throne will shelter them. They will hunger no more and thirst no more; the sun will not strike them, nor any scorching heat; for the Lamb at the center of the throne will be their shepherd, and he will guide them to the springs of the water of life, and God will wipe away every tear from their eyes." (The imagery is from Isaiah. This is the promise for the redeemed, those who live for the things of God and worship him.)

❦

Chapter 8:1-3 says, When the Lamb opened the seventh seal, there was silence in heaven for about half an hour. (The silence is for a short time. This is the calm before the storm.) And I saw the seven angels who stand before God, and seven trumpets were given to them.

The call of the trumpets will serve as warnings in an effort to call the sinners to repentance. Preceding the first trumpet call, incense, representing Christ's intercession on behalf of the praying saints, goes up to heaven. Roman Catholics and the Orthodox believe this confirms their belief that the saints in heaven pray for those on earth. These prayers are answered in the form of calamities that follow.

Verses 3-5 say, Another angel with a golden censer came and stood at the altar; he was given a great quantity of incense to offer with the prayers of all the saints on the golden altar that is below the throne. And the smoke of the incense, with the prayers of the saints, rose before God from the hand of the angel. Then the angel took the censer and filled it with fire from the altar and threw it on the earth; and there were peals of thunder, rumblings, flashes of lightning, and an earthquake. (The prayers of God's people are answered just like in the Psalms. God is pouring out judgment upon the earth in the form of natural calamities.)

Verses 6-7 say, Now the seven angels who had the seven trumpets made ready to blow them. The first angel blew his trumpet, and there came hail and fire, mixed with blood, and they were hurled to the earth; and a third of the earth was burned up, and a third of the trees were burned up and all green grass was burned up.

Just like the plagues of Egypt, the judgments are intended as God's judgment on the wicked, not God's people. Limiting destruction to only one-third of the land means either that they will affect different places at different times, or they are warnings for the people to repent until the time that complete destruction will come as in the time of Noah. It is to warn people that eventually God's wrath will fall upon all who reject his ways.

Verses 8-9 say, The second angel blew his trumpet, and something like a great mountain, burning with fire, was thrown into the sea. A third of the sea became blood, a third of the living creatures in the sea died, and a third of the ships destroyed. (Could this be volcanic eruptions, tidal waves, typhoons, and hurricanes? The first trumpet affected the land; the second trumpet affected the sea. Since trade is accomplished by the sea, it appears that commerce is damaged.)

Verses 10-11 say, The third angel blew his trumpet, and a great star fell from heaven, blazing like a torch, and it fell on a third of the rivers and on the springs of waters. The name of the star is wormwood (an herb associated with bitterness and sorrow). A third of the waters became wormwood, and many died from the water, because it was made bitter. Natural resources are polluted. Inland waters are affected. Wormwood is used as a symbol of the perversion of justice, Amos 5:7, 6:12; of idolotry, Deut 24:17; of divine chastisement, Jer 9:14; and of bitter sorrow, Lam 3:19.

Verse 12 says, The fourth angel blew his trumpet, and a third of the sun was struck, and a third of the moon, and a third of the stars, so that a third of their light was darkened; a third of the day was kept from shining, and likewise the night.

As in the Old Testament cosmic disturbances are about days of judgment and change about to come. No part of the universe is left untouched, which means that even the righteous are affected by the calamities. This describes quite well what we all experience as we live on this earth. Some believe it is to remind people that a final judgment of individuals and what they are doing and causing to happen to the earth is sure to come. That only one-third is affected may be indicating that the worst is still to come.

Verse 13 says, Then I looked, and I heard an eagle crying with a loud voice as it flew in midheaven, "Woe, woe, woe to the inhabitants of the earth, at the blasts of the other trumpets that the three angels are about to blow!" (The impending judgment continues in the next chapter with the last three plagues that are especially grievous.)

Chapter 9:1-4 says, And the fifth angel blew his trumpet, and I saw a star that had fallen from heaven to earth, and he was given a key to the shaft of the bottomless pit; he opened the shaft of the bottomless pit, and from the shaft rose smoke like the smoke of a great furnace, and the sun and the air were darkened with the smoke from the shaft. Then from the smoke came locusts on the earth, and they were given authority like the authority of scorpions on the earth. They were told not to damage the grass of the earth or any green growth or any tree (which is what locusts usually damage), but only those people who do not have the seal of God on their forehead.

Keep in mind this is all poetic symbolism. The falling star (angel) represents Satan. God allows him to unleash his forces in a controlled way from the bottomless pit, so demons are released. Locusts and scorpions symbolize evil. Their influence upon each other creates spiritual darkness, blindness, delusion, and despair, which is suggested with the dark smoke coming from the pit bringing darkness to the light. This is to explain why the world is the way it is. Apocalyptic poetry is primarily about themes, concepts, and ideas; it is not for the purpose of describing literal history in detail.

Verses 5-6 say, They were allowed to torture them for five months (the limited time locust actually live meaning a short time), but not to kill them, and their torture was like the torture of a scorpion when it stings someone. And in those days people will seek death but will not find it; they will long to die, but death will flee from them. (The idea is that much agony and tribulation will be experienced. God's intention is probably to spur the unbelievers to repentance, and to remind believers that God is in control.)

Verses 7-11 say, In appearance the locusts were like horses equipped for battle. On their heads were what looked like crowns of gold; their faces were like human faces, their hair like women's hair, and their teeth like lions' teeth; they had scales like iron breastplates, and the noise of their wings was like the noise of many chariots with horses rushing into battle. They have tails like scorpions, with stingers, and in their tails is their power to harm people for five months. They have as king over them the angel of the bottomless pit; his name in Hebrew is Abaddon (means the destruction from the depths of the pit), and in Greek he is called Apollyon.

This imagery projects the brutality and ruthlessness associated with the barbarians or even the Roman army. Like scorpions they poison and terrorize humanity with their lies and cruelty. Here they are really symbolizing the demons and those controlled by demons led by Satan. (Jesus' point in many of his teachings was that their real enemy was not Rome, but Satan who was behind Rome.)

Verses 12-16 say, The first woe has passed. There are still two woes to come. Then the sixth angel blew his trumpet, and I heard a voice from the four horns of the golden altar before God, saying to the sixth angel who had the trumpet, "Release the four angels who are bound at the great river Euphrates." So the four angels were released, who had been held ready for the hour, the day, the month, and the year, to kill a third of mankind (a third meaning quite a bit). The number of the troops of cavalry was two hundred million (meaning alot); I heard their number.

Verses 17-19 say, And this is how I saw the horses in my vision: the riders wore breastplates the color of fire and of sapphire and of sulfur; the heads of the horses were like lions' heads, and fire and smoke and sulfur came out of their mouths. By these three plagues a third of humankind was killed, by the fire and smoke and sulfer coming out of their mouths. For the power of the horses is in their mouths and in their tails; their tails are like serpents, having heads; and with them they inflict harm. (God is allowing evil to create havoc upon an evil, decayed, and corrupt world. The horse is the biblical symbol for warfare, and warfare has throughout history inflicted misery upon civilization.)

Verses 20-21 say, The rest of humankind, who were not killed by these plagues, did not repent of the works of their hands or give up worshiping demons and idols of gold and silver and bronze and stone and wood, which cannot see or hear or walk. And they did not repent of their murders or their sorceries or their fornication or their thefts. (They are being compared to Pharaoh who did not repent when God allowed the plagues to afflict Egypt.)

Chapter 10:1-3 says, And I saw another mighty angel coming down from heaven, wrapped in a cloud, with a rainbow over his head (clouds and a rainbow are from around the throne of God); his face was like the sun, and his legs like pillars of fire. (The angel represents the holiness and sovereignty of the Father and the Son.) He held a little scroll open in his hand. (The little scroll represents the announcement of the final judgment.) Setting his right foot on the sea and his left foot on the land, he gave a great shout like a lion roaring. (The announcement affects the whole creation.)

Verse 4 says, And when he shouted, the seven thunders sounded. (The seven thunders represents the voice of God, Ps 29, Jn 12:27-31.) And when the seven thunders had sounded, I was about to write, but I heard a voice from heaven saying, "Seal up what the seven thunders have said, and do not write it down." (All the literal historical details of the final judgment are not to be told. Even Jesus did not know the exact time. It amazes this author how many of today's television and radio preachers and the authors of the *Left Behind* series know so much more than Jesus knew.)

Verses 5-7 say, Then the angel whom I saw standing on the sea and the land raised his right hand to heaven and swore by him who lives forever and ever, who created heaven and what is in it, the earth and what is in it, and the sea and what is in it: "There will be no more delay, but in the days when the seventh angel is to blow his trumpet, the mystery of God will be fulfilled, as he announced to his servants the prophets."

God is about to unleash his final judgment. Keep in mind these are interlocking visions where the unfolding of things is repeated over and over, and then further revealed with a deeper significance. All of these visions are not necessarily to be understood chronologically, but the only way John can write them is by putting one after another. Keep in mind he is revealing the mysteries of God, and mystery is not always understood rationally, especially with the use of apocalyptic poetry.

Verses 8-10 say, Then the voice that I had heard from heaven spoke to me again, saying, "Go, take the scroll that is open in the hand of the angel who is standing on the sea and on the land." So I went to the angel and told him to give me the little scroll; and he said to me, "Take it, and eat; it will be bitter to your stomach, but sweet as honey in your mouth." So I took the little scroll from the hand of the angel and ate it; it was sweet as honey in my mouth, but when I had eaten it, my stomach was made bitter.

The message is sweet because God is in control and in the end will make all things right. It is bitter because God's people will suffer much by standing with and for Christ during the church age. Also, it will be bitter for those who do not believe, and those who do not repent of sin because they love the ways of the world. Then in (11) he said to me, "You must prophesy again about many peoples and nations and languages and kings." (The second part of the book, chapters 12-20, will contain these prophecies.)

⮑ ⮐

Chapter 11:1-3 says, Then I was given a measuring rod like a staff, and I was told, "Come and measure the temple of God and the altar and those who worship there (the true worshipers), but do not measure the court outside the temple; leave that out, for it is given over to the nations, and they will trample over the holy city for forty-two months. And I will grant my two witnesses authority to prophesy for one thousand two hundred sixty days (1260 days = 42 months = 3 ½ years) wearing sackcloth.

This is a symbolic time period representing the time of authority given to hostile powers to create havoc among God's people. It is taken from Dan 7:25, 12:7, and refers to the three and a half years of terror under Antiochus Epiphanes when the temple was desecrated between 167-164 BC. The time periods for the trampling of the holy city by the Gentiles, the ministry of the two witnesses, the sojourn of the woman in the wilderness (12:6, 14), and the career of the beast (13:5) are equivalent; the time limit symbolizes the time of trouble and persecution. The two witnesses are wearing sackcloth to symbolize both repentance and sadness. The two witnesses symbolize the witnessing church, its missionary thrust, sent out two by two by Christ in the gospels. The duration of their ministry corresponds to the period in which the outer court and the holy city are trampled, which represents the whole church age.

Verses 4-6 say, These are the two olive trees and the two lampstands that stand before the Lord of the earth. And if anyone wants to harm them, fire pours from their mouth and consumes their foes; anyone who wants to harm them must be killed in this manner. They have authority to shut the sky, so that no rain may fall during the days of their prophesying, and they have authority over the waters to turn them into blood, and to strike the earth with every kind of plague, as often as they desire.

The two olive trees are reminiscent of Zerubbabel and Joshua (Zech 4:2-14), who were God's agents of restoration after the Babylonian exile. One was the political representative and the other the religious representative. The miracles mentioned recall those of Moses and Elijah suggesting that the authority and power once given to the law and the prophets is now given to the church, and its authority is the kingdom of God, which has both religious and political ramifications. Remember in the prayer of Jesus he taught his people to pray, your kingdom come, your will be done on earth as well as in heaven. The fire coming from their mouths symbolizes God's word. God told Jeremiah, "Behold, I will make my words in your mouth fire, and this people wood, and it shall devour them."

The book of Revelation has been so difficult for people because neither they, nor many of their ministers, have a very good understanding of the Old Testament or how to interpret apocalyptic literature. Therefore the book has been ignored or given fanciful interpretations that become total distortions from the intention of the writer of Revelation. Roman Catholic, Orthodox, mainline Protestant and a few Evangelical scholars agree that the many radio and television preachers and the example of the popular fundamentalist *Left Behind* series distort apocalyptic poetry by making it all literal.

Verses 7-8 say, When they have finished their testimony, the beast that comes up from the bottomless pit (antichrists powered by Satan) will make war on them and conquer them and kill them, and their dead bodies will lie in the street of the great city that is prophetically called Sodom and Egypt, where also their Lord was crucified.

The reference is to Jerusalem, who had become oppressive like Egypt and immoral like Sodom, which led to the destruction of their temple and great city. John says in 1 John 2:18 that many antichrists have already come. Much of the symbolism, other than from the Old Testament, is taken from the events that occurred from the crucifixion and resurrection to the time that Rome destroyed the temple and the city in AD 70.

Verses 9-10 continue, For three and a half days (a short period of time) members of the peoples and tribes and languages and nations will gaze at their dead bodies and refuse to let them be placed in a tomb; and the inhabitants of the earth will gloat over them and celebrate and exchange presents, because these two prophets had been a torment to the inhabitants of the earth.

There will be many martyrs because of the beast. The people of the earth rejoice because they do not like having their sin exposed, and they do not like being constantly confronted with a call to repentance. At this point the church appears dead, and the beast has prevailed. This has been the case numerous times throughout history.

This writer believes that it is highly possible the dead bodies are not a reference to the martyrs, for what actually produces a dead church are lukewarm believers who allow themselves and the church to be infiltrated by the world and its ways thus pushing Christ out. Then he has to stand outside knocking on the door hoping that the people will repent and let him in. Many times in history the church has seemed to be consumed and beaten by the world system, only to rise again. It is always a return to the word of God that brings about the revival. Today, we are again experiencing a time when the majority, even church people, are not really familiar with God's word in the Old and New Testaments. Karl Barth, the great German theologian during WW II warned that the real problem in the church is heresy, the corruption of its message, and not doubt, unbelief, or paganism (Church Dogmatics 1,1,36).

Verses 11-14 say, But after three and a half days, the breath of life from God entered them, and they stood on their feet, and those who saw them were terrified. Then they heard a loud voice from heaven saying to them, "Come up here." And they went up to heaven in a cloud while their enemies watched them. At that moment there was a great earthquake, and a tenth of the city fell; seven thousand people were killed in the earthquake, and the rest were terrified and gave glory to God in heaven. The second woe is passed. The third woe is coming very soon.

This symbolizes that the church is born again or resurrected from its spiritual death as it has been numerous times in history. Again, God lets natural calamities occur hoping that people will see that their life in this world is short and hoping many will come to repentance from their spiritual death. This has worked to some extent as it has at times throughout history, but this will only happen for awhile, for the time is short as the following conveys. The gates of hell will not prevail against the church.

Verse 15 says, Then the seventh angel blew his trumpet, and there were loud voices in heaven, saying, "The kingdom of the world has become the kingdom of our Lord and of his Messiah, and he will reign forever and ever." (What has been happening little by little like a mustard seed growing will be made complete at the final coming of Christ (1 Cor 15:20-28).

Verses 16-18 say, Then the twenty-four elders who sit on the thrones before God fell on their faces and worshiped God, singing, "We give you thanks Lord God Almighty, who are and who were, for you have taken your great power and begun to reign. The nations raged, but your wrath has come, and the time for judging the dead, for rewarding your servants, the prophets and saints and all who fear your name both small and great, and for destroying those who destroy the earth." (Is that a reference to those who through their greed are destroying the earth?) Then God's temple in heaven was opened, and the ark of the covenant was seen within the temple; and there were flashes of lightning, rumblings, peals of thunder, an earthquake, and heavy hail.

The temple of God is the body of Christ and all who are made part of that temple by receiving the forgiveness of sins (1 Peter 2:4-10). The ark of the covenant in the Most Holy Place symbolizes the presence of God. (See Hebrews 9 for a good explanation.) For God's people this symbolizes the privilege of perfect fellowship with God. For the unrepentant this pictures God's wrath. The various visions all cover the time John is living, and the symbolism is related to things happening in John's time. But the symbolism John is using is to tell us these things will continue in one way or another and occur over and over throughout time until the end. As the visions continue they are all interlocking, but they will become more intense, and more information will be added.

Chapter 12:1-2 says, A great portent appeared in heaven: a woman clothed with the sun, with a moon under her feet, and on her head a crown of twelve stars. She was pregnant and was crying out in birth pangs, in the agony of giving birth. (Genesis 37:9 describes and symbolizes Israel this way.) Verses 3-4 say, Then another portent appeared in heaven: a great red dragon (Satan, red from the blood of his violence), with seven heads and ten horns (universal power repeating itself, see Dan 1-9), and seven diadems on his heads (symbolizes the dominance of political power and the oppressive world leaders down through history). His tail swept down a third of the stars of heaven and threw them down to earth.

When he was cast out of heaven, he took quite a few of the angels in heaven with him (see verse 9; we call them demons, 2 Peter 2:4, Jude 6). Then the dragon stood before the woman who was about to bear a child, so that he might devour her child as soon as he was born.

Verses 5-6 say, And she gave birth to a son, a male child (Jesus the Messiah), who is to rule all the nations with a rod of iron. (The Old Testament people of God through the virgin Mary gave birth to the Messiah.) But her child was snatched away and taken to God and to his throne; and the woman fled into the wilderness, where she has a place prepared by God, so that there she can be nourished for one thousand two hundred sixty days.

Christ was raised from the dead, defeating Satan for God's people, and now in this last age, the church age, he rules through his people from the throne of God. In this last age, the church age, the time between the first coming of Christ and his second coming is also the time of tribulation. It is the time the church is involved in the mission it was given. The Old Testament people of God and the New Testament people of God have become the new Israel, and the old covenant has become the new covenant (Eph 2:11-22, Gal 3:6-29).

Verses 7-9 say, And war broke out in heaven, Michael and his angels fought against the dragon. The dragon and his angels fought back, but they were defeated, and there was no longer any place for them in heaven. The great dragon was thrown down, that ancient serpent, who is called the Devil and Satan, the deceiver of the whole world—he was thrown down to the earth, and his angels (now called demons) were thrown down with him.

Michael is the guardian angel of God's people (Dan 10:13, 12:1, Jude 9). He is a warrior angel. There is also a battle going on in the spiritual world. Revelation constantly shows that what is completed in heaven must know be completed on earth. For example the perfect kingdom that is in heaven has now been instituted on earth by Christ. His people have been given the mission to call people to the kingdom and make it present on earth. They do this by allowing Christ to live in and through them, thus making Christ and his kingdom present until he comes again to make all things perfect. This is God's mission to his people. There is a battle going on in both this physical world and the spiritual world.

Verses 10-11 say, Then I heard a loud voice in heaven, proclaiming, "Now have come the salvation and the power and the kingdom of our God and the authority of his Messiah, for the accuser of our comrades has been thrown down, who accuses them day and night before our God. But they have conquered him by the blood of the Lamb and by the word of their testimony, for they did not cling to life even in the face of death. (The accuser will not be successful for those washed in the blood of the Lamb.) Verse 12 says, Rejoice then, you heavens and those who dwell in them! But woe to the earth and the sea, for the devil has come down to you with great wrath, because he knows that his time is short!"

Christ has defeated Satan. He knows that his authority and power will not be forever, so he has doubled his effort. It is now the responsibility of his followers to do their part and bring defeat to him by advancing the kingdom into this world knowing that he and those on his side will do everything they can in order to thwart the advancement of God's kingdom.

Verses 13-14 say, So when the dragon saw that he had been thrown down to the earth, he pursued the woman who had given birth to the male child. (His goal is to provoke havoc and tribulation for the new Israel of God.) But the woman was given the two wings of the great eagle, so that she could fly from the serpent into the wilderness, to her place where she is nourished for a time, and times, and half time. (This symbolizes the church age, which is 42 months, 1260 days, or 3 ½ years. The woman's flight on the two wings of a great eagle recalls the same imagery used for Israel's protection in their flight from Egypt into the wilderness, Ex 19:4, Isa 40:31.)

Verses 15-17 say, Then from his mouth the serpent poured water like a river after the woman (false teaching, lies, worldly temptations as Jesus was tempted in the wilderness) to sweep her away with the flood. But the earth came to the help of the woman; it opened its mouth and swallowed the river that the dragon had poured from his mouth. (Satan did not succeed at that time.) Then the dragon was angry with the woman, and went off to make war on the rest of her children, those who keep the commandments of God and hold the testimony of Jesus.

It was just like the time of Jesus' temptation in the wilderness. Luke 4:16 says, When the devil had finished every test, he departed from him until an opportune time. Satan is not allowed to destroy the church, but he will create much havoc and tribulation. Again the comparison is with Egypt. Satan caused much evil tribulation, but in the end God's people were set free.

❦

Chapter 13:1-2 says, Then the dragon took his stand on the sand of the seashore. And I saw a beast rising out of the sea, having ten heads and seven horns; and on its horns were ten diadems (crowns), and on its heads were blasphemous names. And the beast that I saw was like a leopard, its feet were like a bear's, and its mouth was like a lion's mouth.

The beast from the sea is a composite of the beast from Daniel 2, 7, and 8. The sea represents chaos and sin. The beast represents the governments and nations of the world who create chaos and are used by Satan to disturb the world and the church. The seven heads symbolize the different forms the beast takes throughout history. The dragon (Satan) wears crowns on his heads while the beast's crowns are on his horns. This suggests that the self-centered, politically oppressive, economically exploitive governments, doing what they do in the name of God or the gods, derive their rule and power from Satan. The blasphemous names on the beast's heads tell us that certain rulers and governments throughout history usurp God's authority and demand for themselves what belongs only to God, which is worship or total allegiance. The flag becomes their symbol.

Verse 3 says, One of its heads seemed to receive a death-blow, but its mortal wound had been healed.

This is probably a reference to the Roman Emperor Domition ruling from 81-96 AD, who demanded to be worshiped and who revived the persecuting policies of Nero. The emperor Nero had made martyrs out of many thousands of Christians during his rule from 54-68 AD. It also may represent those "isms" in history that keep popping up throughout history that become the guiding light of people taking the place of God's light. They appear to run their course after awhile, but then pop up elsewhere or appear in another form. The isms are philosophies such as nationalism (extreme patriotism), socialism, communism, Nazism, even extreme capitalism. They are philosophies that become people's gods taking the place of God's light as their priority. Satan uses these to captivate people and control people in order to get them to deviate from God's course.

Verse 4 says, They worshiped the dragon, for he had given his authority to the beast, and they worshiped the beast, and who can fight against it? (This immediate reference is to the Roman emperor who demanded to be worshiped as a god. Who can resist the awesome political, economic, social, and military power of the beast is the question. Often having or keeping a job is related to what one worships. Throughout the Roman empire there were places to worship the emperor and the Roman gods. The trade guilds had their own gods but were also closely tied to emperor worship.)

Verses 5-8 say, The beast was given a month uttering haughty and blasphemous words, and it was allowed to exercise authority for forty-two months (symbolic of the Christian era). It opened its mouth to utter blasphemies against God, blaspheming his name and his dwelling, that is, those who dwell in heaven. Also it was allowed to make war on the saints and to conquer them. (Any power the beast has is only because God has permitted it.) It was given authority over every tribe and people and language and nation, and all the inhabitants of the earth will worship it, everyone whose name has not been written from the foundation of the world in the book of life of the Lamb that was slaughtered.

Verses 9-10 say, Let everyone who has an ear listen: If you are to be taken captive, into captivity you go; if you kill with the sword with the sword you must be killed. Here is a call for the endurance and faith of the saints. (Passive resistance and non-violence are God's way of responding to these oppressive governments who throughout history, usurp for themselves the authority that belongs to God, Mt 5, 6, 7.)

Verses 11-12 say, Then I saw another beast that rose out of the earth; it had two horns like a lamb and it spoke like a dragon. (Jesus called them wolves in sheep's clothing, Mt 7:15.) It exercises all the authority of the first beast on its behalf, and makes the earth and its inhabitants worship the first beast, whose mortal wound had been healed.

The beast represents false religion that serves the purpose of evil government. It begins with pagan religion serving the purposes of government. Instead of speaking God's values to the power structure, false prophets let power use them so they can benefit from power. This has occurred throughout history in many different forms. This gives free reign to the Hitlers, and the Stalins, plus the hundreds of dictators in the developing countries down through the years and even those in developed countries who worship their governments.

They put Christ in second place just as the pagans of the Old Testament worshiped both the one God and the pagan gods. They keep the name Christian and use it in a wrongful and evil way. Any nation's religion that marries nationalism or patriotism is no longer true religion. It subverts religion to power politics in such a way that Christianity becomes only an echo. Today this form of religion is usually called *civil religion.* Its great example in modern times was Nazi Germany.

These so-called Christians use their concept of religion or Christianity to preserve their concept of morality, their concept of what they believe government should do, their concept of what economics should be, and their concept of what the social order should be. Rather than being concerned with the kingdom of God and speaking truth to power they allow other interests to co-opt them. When this happens they become a form of government called for by the beast. This is further explained by the second beast. The first beast and the second beast become united with Satan in an unholy trinity to become the great whore.

Verses 13-15 say, It (the beast) performs great signs, even making fire come down from heaven to earth in the sight of all; and by the signs that it is allowed to perform on behalf of the beast, it deceives the inhabitants of the earth, telling them to make an image for the beast that had been wounded by the sword and yet lived; and it was allowed to give breath to the image of the beast so that the image of the beast could even speak and cause those who would not worship the image of the beast to be killed.

The symbolism is saying that many are fooled by the works and words of the two beasts, religion and government working together with Satan. The great signs performed are not miracles like Jesus performed, but miracles of daily accomplishments that impress humans. This author asks, is this possible even in the United States of America, or have we protected ourselves against anything like this from happening to us?

Verses 16-17 say, Also it causes all, both small and great, both free and slave, to be marked on the right hand or the forehead, so that no one can buy or sell who does not have the mark, that is the name of the beast or the number of its name.

The mark is not physical any more than the mark or seal of the Holy Spirit is for God's people. Though one knows a child of God by the fruit the Holy Spirit bears, one knows the mark of the beast by what it thinks (mark on forehead) and what one does (mark on right hand). Those marked by the beast, or those cooperating with the beast get all the economic advantages. Verse 18 says, This calls for wisdom: let anyone with understanding calculate the number of the beast, for it is the number of a person. Its number is six hundred sixty-six. Since 7 is the number of perfection 6 symbolizes imperfection. It is the number for the broken, imperfect human.

In the Hebrew language all numbers had significance. The number for the evil Roman emperor Nero was 666 which is the imperfect broken sin-filled human multiplied. Thielman (2005, 636) states, that when Nero Caesar is transliterated from the Greek into Hebrew, the Hebrew letters add up to 666. When the Greek letters for beast are put into Hebrew characters, it yields the same sum. Many evil leaders throughout history meet this antichrist criteria.

∽◯◡

Chapter 14:1-5 says, Then I looked, and there was the Lamb, standing on Mt Zion! (Zion symbolizes God's dwelling place.) And with him were one hundred forty-four thousand who had his name and his Father's name written on their foreheads. And I heard a voice from heaven like the sound of many waters and like the sound of loud thunder; the voice I heard was like the sound of harpists playing on their harps, and they sing a new song before the throne and before the four living creatures and before the elders. (The new song is the song of redemption that only the redeemed can sing.)

No one could learn that song except the one hundred forty-four thousand who have been redeemed from the earth. It is these who have not defiled themselves with women (adultery and fornicating in general, especially fornicating with the religious prostitutes of pagan religions), for they are virgins (purified); these follow the Lamb wherever he goes. (They give him their minds, hearts, and their will.) They have been redeemed from humankind as first fruits for God and the Lamb, and in their mouth no lie (false truth, which is adultery with the untruths of other religions) was found; they are blameless (with respect to believing in the beast).

The 144,000, the followers of the 12 tribes x 12 x 1000 the perfect decimal are either all the redeemed, or the first fruits of all the redeemed meaning all the Old Testament redeemed to be followed by all the redeemed in the Christian dispensation as in 7:1-10. It probably is a reference to all the redeemed, which would be the 12 tribes x the 12 apostles and their redeemed. The Jehovah Witnesses and their claim that only 144,000 will make up God's people in heaven and the rest of the righteous will be on earth is another example of literalism's distortion of God's word.

Verses 6-7 say, Then I saw another angel flying in midheaven, with an eternal gospel to proclaim to those who live on the earth— to every nation and tribe and language and people. He said in a loud voice, "Fear God and give him glory, for the hour of his judgment has come; and worship him who made heaven and earth, the sea and the springs of water." (The message is fear God, for judgment is coming.) Verse 8 says, Then another angel, a second, followed, saying, "Fallen, fallen is Babylon the great! She has made all nations drink of the wine of the wrath of her fornication." (Babylon symbolizes Rome and all like beasts of the unholy trinity down through history.)

Verses 9-11 say, Then another angel, a third, followed them, crying out with a loud voice, "Those who worship the beast and its image, and receive a mark on their foreheads or on their hands, they will also drink the wine of God's wrath, poured unmixed in the cup of his anger, and they will be tormented with fire and sulfer in the presence of his holy angels and in the presence of the Lamb. And the smoke of their torment goes up forever and ever. There is no rest day or night for those who worship the beast and its image and for anyone who receives the mark of its name."

Here is the announcement of eternal punishment for those who worship the beast and go along with its evil effect upon serious believers and the world. Again the mark of the beast on the head and hands is not a literal mark. It is a reference to the fact that minds and actions have been influenced by government and religion aligned together for their selfish interests as opposed to the interests of Christ. In this situation it is the Roman Empire, its ways, and its emperors, who are to be worshiped by the people under their jurisdiction.

Verses 12-13 say, Here is a call for the endurance of the saints (believers), those who keep the commandments of God, and hold fast to the faith of Jesus. And I heard a voice from heaven saying, "Write this: Blessed are the dead who from now on die in the Lord." "Yes," says the Spirit, "they will rest from their labors, for their deeds follow them." (The choice is between commitment to the ways of God or the ways of our worldly philosophies and ideologies. One leads to life, and the other leads to death.)

Verses 14-16 say, Then I looked, and there was a white cloud, and seated on the cloud was one like the Son of Man, with a golden crown on his head, and a sharp sickle in his hands! (He is King of kings and Lord of lords. Christ coming in clouds is always some kind of judgment whether it is within history or at the end of history.) Another angel came out of the temple, calling with a loud voice to the one who sat on the cloud, "Use your sickle and reap, for the hour to reap has come, because the harvest of the earth is fully ripe." So the one who sat on the cloud swung his sickle over the earth, and the earth was reaped. (It is the time for the final judgment; it is sheep and goat time, Mt 25:31-46, Mk 13:26-27, 14:62, 1 Thess 4:16-17, 1 Cor 15, Rev 11:11-12.)

Verses 17-20 say, Then another angel came out of the temple in heaven, and he too had a sharp sickle. Then another angel came out from the altar, the angel who has authority over fire, and he called with a loud voice to him who had the sharp sickle, "Use your sharp sickle and gather the clusters of the vine of the earth, for its grapes are ripe." So the angel swung his sickle over the earth and gathered the vintage of the earth, and he threw it into the great wine press of the wrath of God. And the wine press was trodden outside the city, and blood flowed from the wine press, as high as a horse's bridle, for a distance of about two hundred miles. (The Greek is 1600 stadia, which symbolizes the earth, 4 x 4 and wholeness 10 x 10.)

The wicked are pictured as grapes crushed in the wine press of God. The following explains the time of the end in more detail. Keep in mind that it is all symbolic poetry describing spiritual realities of what God is going to do. We must learn to receive God's message to us as he presents it in an imaginative and poetic manner.

Chapter 15:1-7 says, Then I saw another portent in heaven, great and amazing: seven angels and seven plagues, which are the last, for with them the wrath of God is ended. And I saw what appeared to be a sea of glass mixed with fire, and those who had conquered the beast and its image and the number of its name, standing beside the sea of glass with harps of God in their hands. (The sea of glass mingled with fire symbolizes God's transparent righteousness revealed in judgments upon the wicked.) And they sing the song of Moses, the servant of God, and the song of the Lamb: "Great and amazing are your deeds, Lord God the Almighty! Just and true are your ways, King of the nations! Lord, who will not fear and glorify your name? For you alone are holy. All nations will come and worship before you, for your judgments have been revealed."

The song of Moses (Ex 15) is a victory song as is the song of the Lamb. A just and holy God would not be just and holy if he allowed all the evil and wrong doing of the world to exist without making all things just and right.

Verses 5-8 say, After this I looked, and the temple of the tent of witness in heaven was opened, and out of the temple came the seven angels with the seven plagues, robed in pure bright linen, with golden sashes across their chests Then one of the four living creatures gave the seven angels seven golden bowls full of the wrath of God, who lives forever and ever; and the temple was filled with smoke from the glory of God and from his power, and no one could enter the temple until the seven plagues of the seven angels were ended.

The seven angels come ready to pour out the bowls of wrath. No one can enter the presence of God until the plagues are finished. No one can interfere with God's plan; intercession is no longer possible. The redeemed will not escape the tribulation by a rapture as the fundamentalists claim.

Chapter 16:1-7 says, Then I heard a loud voice from the temple telling the seven angels, "Go and pour out on the earth the seven bowls of the wrath of God." So the first angel went and poured his bowl on the earth, and a fowl and painful sore came on those who had the mark of the beast and who worshiped its image. The second angel poured his bowl on the sea, and it became like the blood of a corpse, and every living thing in the sea died. The third angel poured his bowl into the rivers and the springs of waters, and they became blood. And I heard the angels of the water say, "You are just, O Holy One, who are and were, for you have judged these things; because they shed the blood of saints and prophets, you have given them blood to drink. It is what they deserve!" And I heard the altar respond, "Yes, O Lord God, the Almighty, your judgments are true and just!"

God's divine retribution is called just because he did not overlook the injustice of the evil of personal sin of individuals and the social sin of nations and their institutions. The reader should note the similarity between these plagues and the plagues of Egypt. Furthermore, the similarities between the trumpets and the bowls tell us that the same event may be a warning (trumpets) for one person and a final judgment (bowls) for another.

Verses 8-11 say, The fourth angel poured his bowl on the sun, and it was allowed to scorch them with fire; they were scorched by the fierce heat, but they cursed the name of God, who had authority over these plagues, and they did not repent and give him glory. (People are hard headed in their beliefs and opinions, but God is in control.) The fifth angel poured his bowl on the throne of the beast, and its kingdom was plunged into darkness; people gnawed their tongues in agony, and cursed the God of heaven because of their pains and sores, and they did not repent of their deeds. (The sins of pride and arrogance control the people of the world.)

Verses 12-16 say, The sixth angel poured his bowl on the great river Euphrates, and its water was dried up in order to prepare the way for the kings of the east. (The Euphrates is the river from which Israel's ancient foes Assyria, Babylon, and Persia, came to defeat them.) And I saw three foul spirits like frogs coming from the mouth of the dragon, from the mouth of the beast, and from the mouth of the false prophet. These are demonic spirits, performing signs, who go abroad to the kings of the whole world, to assemble them for battle on the great day of God the Almighty. "See, I am coming like a thief! Blessed is the one who stays awake (alert) and is clothed, not going about naked and exposed to shame."

We in the United States also need to guard against approving or participating in the beastly activities of our own nation. Some examples are unjust wars, abandoning people in need of food, clothing, shelter, and health care for our idolatrous ways of selfish greed, consumerism, materialism, violence, and drugs.

Verse 16 says, And they assembled them at the place that in Hebrew is called Harmagedon.

This is spelled different ways in the manuscripts. It is also spelled Armageddon. It is probably a reference to Megiddo, the site of several important battles in Israel's history. For example Deborah and Barak led the Israelites to a victory at Megiddo and freed Israel from the domination of the Canaanites (Judges 5:19). The term became a symbolic way of referring to any battle by which God miraculously overcame the armies of those who oppressed his people. This is not intended to be a literal battle on this earth. It is a spiritual battle of apocalyptic poetry, symbolizing the defeat of all the enemies of God's people.

Verses 17-21 say, The seventh angel poured his bowl into the air, and a loud voice came out of the temple, from the throne, saying, "It is done!" And there came flashes of lightning, rumblings, peals of thunder, and a violent earthquake, such as had not occurred since people were upon the earth, so violent was that earthquake (Heb 12:26-29). The great city was split into three parts, and the cities of the nations fell. God remembered great Babylon and gave her the wine-cup of the fury of his wrath. And every island fled away, and no mountains were to be found; and huge hailstones, each weighing about a hundred pounds, dropped from heaven on people, until they cursed God for the plague of the hail, so fearful was that plague (Dan 2:34-35). (They blamed God, not themselves. It is the beginning of the transformation of the new heaven and new earth.)

Chapter 17:1-2 says, Then one of the seven angels who had the seven bowls came and said to me, "Come, I will show you the judgment of the great whore who is seated on many waters, with whom the kings of the earth have committed fornication, and with the wine of whose fornication the inhabitants of the earth have become drunk." (The great whore is Babylon that symbolizes Rome and all the nations of the world throughout history with activities and cultures opposed to the teachings of Christ.)

Verses 3-6 say, So he carried me away in the spirit into the wilderness (where the church is located, 12:6), and I saw a woman sitting on a scarlet beast (nations working together with Satan) that was full of blasphemous names, and it had seven heads and ten horns (nations with great power acting as Satan throughout history demanding worship). The woman was clothed in purple and scarlet, and adorned with gold and jewels and pearls, holding in her hand a golden cup full of abominations and the impurities of her fornication; and on her forehead was written a name, a mystery: "Babylon the great, mother of whores and of earth's abominations." (Babylon is another name for Rome; see 1 Peter 5:13.) And I saw that the woman was drunk with the blood of the saints and the blood of the witnesses to Jesus. When I saw her I was greatly amazed.

Babylon represents the world system of the ungodly, the type of culture that is contrary to the culture of the kingdom of God. In the time of the Roman empire when John was writing, many Christians were martyred. Throughout history the world system has done the same from time to time, but primarily it works by seductively pulling Christians into its fold by getting them to think and act as the world does instead of the way Christ thinks and acts. Again, the reference is to the German theologian Karl Barth, who said that the church's greatest threat is not unbelief or doubt but heresy, the corruption of its message.

Verses 7-8 say, But the angel said to me, "Why are you so amazed? I will tell you the mystery of the woman, and of the beast with seven heads and ten horns that carries her. The beast that you saw was, and is not, and is about to ascend from the bottomless pit and go to destruction. And the inhabitants of the earth, whose names have not been written in the book of life from the foundation of the world, will be amazed when they see the beast, because it was and is not and is to come.

Verses 9-14 say, This calls for a mind that has wisdom: the seven heads have seven mountains on which the woman is seated; also they are seven kings, of whom five have fallen, one is living, and the other has not yet come; and when he comes, he must remain only a little while. As for the beast that was and is not, it is an eighth but it belongs to the seven, and it goes to destruction. And the ten horns that you saw are ten kings who have not yet received a kingdom, but they are to receive authority as kings for one hour, together with the beast. These are united in yielding their power and authority to the beast; they will make war on the Lamb, and the Lamb will conquer them, for he is the Lord of lords and King of kings, and those with him are called and chosen and faithful."

Rome was located on seven hills. Ten represents all the kingdoms of the world presenting a culture contrary to the culture of the kingdom of God. The five fallen kings probably are a reference to Assyria, Babylon, Persia, Alexander the Great's Greek Empire, and Antiochus Epiphanes of the Selucids, who desecrated the Jewish temple. All of them forced Israel to live under their power. Rome would be the sixth empire that is. Then the seventh empire is the sum of all anti-Christian nations and their systems that rise between Rome and the eighth one to come. Then the eighth and final manifestation of the beast will rise, which is of the same nature as the seventh. With this beast will come Christ's final kingdom. It is possible that the kings could also be Roman kings leading to the fall of Rome and the ten kings referring to the ones like Rome that would follow throughout world history. Ten would be symbolic for the complete number. Either way the concept is the same. Christ will be victorious, which is the theme of this whole book giving hope to people in that time and our time.

Verses 15-16 say, And he said to me, "The waters that you saw, where the whore is seated, are peoples, and multitudes, and nations and languages. And the ten horns that you saw, they and the beast will hate the whore; they will make her desolate and naked; they will devour her flesh and make her burn up with fire. (This is probably a reference to civil war and nations turning on each other attempting to devour each other as they have throughout history.)

Verses 17-19 say, For God has put it into their hearts to carry out his purpose by agreeing to give their kingdom to the beast, until the words of God will be fulfilled. The woman you saw is the great city that rules over the kings of the earth. (As verse 17 says this is all designed by God working out his plan. At that time it was Rome, but many like Rome, anti Christian cultures and governments demanding total allegiance, were to come throughout history.)

Chapter 18:1-3 says, After this I saw another angel coming down from heaven, having great authority; and the earth was made bright by his splendor. He called out with a mighty voice, "Fallen, fallen is Babylon the great! (Babylon is a metaphorical name for all evil powers and their systems first represented by the city of Rome and its empire.) It has become a dwelling place of demons, a haunt of every foul and hateful bird, a haunt of every foul and hateful beast. For all the nations have drunk of the wine of the wrath of her fornication, and the kings of the earth have committed fornication with her, and the merchants of the earth have grown rich from the power of her luxury." (Keep in mind all of this throughout history usually takes the form of government working together with a form of false religion and being led by the working of Satan.)

Her charms engaged the political leaders of the world and her excessive lifestyle made the earth's merchants wealthy. There is no difference today, and rarely do the churches talk about how government and the wealthy work together to benefit themselves at the expense of those who are not wealthy, even though these economic issues are practically on every page of the Bible. A film that explicitly portrays this is *Inside Job* directed by Charles Ferguson and produced by Sony Pictures Classics. It is a documentary exposing the truth of the economic crisis of 2008. Another educational film worth viewing, also produced by Sony Pictures, is *The Ides of March* produced by George Clooney.

For some reason the church prefers to focus on other issues such as sexual issues and other issues that are never or rarely mentioned in the Bible. What an impact and change the church and its leaders could have in the world if they focused more on what is happening to those who are not powerful and not wealthy, like the working poor, the middle class, and the poor in general with the same zeal that they focus on issues the Bible rarely or never mentions.

The Old Testament prophets would be screaming at the way government benefits the wealthy and rich corporations at the expense of everyone else, and how business and profits have become god in our culture of commercialization, materialism, corruption, drugs and violence. Rarely, if ever, are these things mentioned from the pulpit. People in the pews and in most nations including our own have itching ears (2 Tim 4:3), and too many religious leaders are scratching them as they speak smooth things to us who are the comfortable.

Verses 4-8 say, Then I heard another voice from heaven saying, "Come out of her, my people, so that you do not take part in her sins, and so that you do not share in her plagues; for her sins are heaped high as heaven, and God has remembered her iniquities. Render to her as she herself has rendered, and repay her double for her deeds; mix a double draught for her in the cup she mixed. (She will receive perfect justice, exactly what her crimes deserve.) As she glorified herself and lived luxuriously, so give her a like measure of torment and grief. Since in her heart she says, 'I rule as a queen; I am no widow and will never see grief,' therefore her plagues will come in a single day—pestilence and mourning and famine—and she will be burned with fire; for mighty is the Lord God who judges her."

Throughout the Bible nothing positive is said about those who glorify themselves and live luxuriously. In fact every time the wealthy are mentioned in Scripture, they are warned that if they do not change their ways and care for those less fortunate, their souls will be in danger (Mt 25:41-36). Jesus in Lk 18:18-27 told a rich person to sell what he had and distribute it to the poor, after he asked what he could do to inherit eternal life. When he went away sorrowfully, Jesus told those around him that it was easier for a camel to go through the eye of a needle than for a rich person to enter the kingdom of God. Again the churches seem to ignore this message, which is on practically every page of the Bible probably because most of us sitting in the pews are the most comfortable of the world's people, and the religious leaders know it will upset some of the people.

The rest of the chapter is a lamentation over the fall of Babylon. Verses 9-10 say, And the kings of the earth (nations), who committed fornication and lived in luxury with her, will weep and wail over her when they see the smoke of her burning; they will stand far off, in fear of her torment, and say, "Alas, alas, the great city, Babylon, the mighty city! For in one hour your judgment has come!" (There have been many Babylons throughout history as well as now.)

Verses 11-14 say, And the merchants of the earth weep and mourn for her, since no one buys their cargo anymore, cargo of gold, silver, jewels, and pearls, fine linen, purple, silk and scarlet, all kinds of scented wood, all articles of ivory, all articles of costly wood, bronze, iron, and marble, cinnamon, spice, incense, myrrh, frankincense, wine, olive oil, choice flour and wheat, cattle and sheep, horses and chariots, slaves—and human lives. The fruit for which your soul longed has gone from you, and all your dainties and your splendor are lost to you, never to be found again!" (Most of these goods were luxuries illustrating the excesses of materialism in the society, even trading in slaves to get what they wanted to indulge themselves. There is much weeping for making money had become their god.)

Verses 15-20 say, The merchants of these wares, who gained wealth from her, will stand far off, in fear of her torment, weeping and mourning aloud, "Alas, alas, the great city, clothed in fine linen, in purple and scarlet, adorned with gold, with jewels, and with pearls! For in one hour all this wealth has been laid waste!" And all the shipmasters and seafarers, sailors and all whose trade is on the sea, stood far off and cried out as they saw the smoke of her burning, "What city was like the great city?" And they threw stones on their heads, as they wept and mourned, crying out, "Alas, alas, the great city, where all who had ships at sea grew rich by her wealth! For in one hour she has been laid waste. Rejoice over her, O heaven, you saints and apostles and prophets! For God has given judgment for you against her."

Note the anguish of those whose whole world collapsed with the fall of commerce in their materialist society. These words should trouble the citizens of a nation who value the strength of its economy over its moral character. Again see the film noted previously as one small example of life at the top.

Verses 21-24 say, Then a mighty angel took up a stone like a great millstone and threw it into the sea, saying, "With such violence Babylon the great city will be thrown down, and will be found no more; and the sound of harpists and minstrels and of flutists and trumpeters will be heard in you no more; and an artisan of any trade will be found in you no more; and the sound of the millstone will be heard in you no more; and the light of a lamp will shine in you no more; and the voice of bridegroom and bride will be heard in you no more; for your merchants were the magnates of the earth, and all nations were deceived by your sorcery. And in you was found the blood of prophets and of saints and of all who have been slaughtered on earth.

In Rome, Christians were herded into the Coliseum to become entertainment for the masses. These Christians who were clothed in animal skins were torn apart by hungry lions and wild dogs that were let loose on them. At other times they were dipped in tar and put on crosses and set on fire. During the time of Nero it was said at night the city of Rome was lit up by Christians dying on burning crosses. The people could not get enough of their luxuries, entertainment, and violence. Finally, in these verses we see symbolic action that represents the total destruction of the city, representing their nation and their culture.

Chapter 19:1-5 says, After this I heard what seemed to be the loud voice of a great multitude in heaven, saying, "Hallelujah! Salvation and glory and power to our God, for his judgments are true and just; he has judged the great whore who corrupted the earth with her fornication, and he has avenged on her the blood of his servants." Once more they said, "Hallelujah! The smoke goes up from her forever and ever." And the twenty-four elders and the four living creatures fell down and worshiped God who is seated on the throne, saying, "Amen. Hallelujah!" (The smoke going up forever symbolizes those in hell forever.)

This is the fifth time in the book of Revelation that we see the final judgment (6:12, 11:15, 14:11,16:17). As stated previously, Revelation presents a series of interlocking visions presenting the same thing over and over but then adding more detail and taking the message to a deeper level. Repetition is a style of Hebrew literature that also serves as an excellent teaching method, especially in a time when few could read and write.

Verses 5-8 say, And from the throne came a voice saying, "Praise our God, all you servants, and all who fear him, small and great." Then I heard what seemed to be the voice of a great multitude, like the sound of many waters and like the sound of many thunderpeals, crying out, "Hallelujah! For the Lord our God the Almighty reigns. Let us rejoice and exult and give him the glory, for the marriage of the Lamb has come, and his bride has made herself ready (the church); to her it has been granted to be clothed with fine linen, bright and pure—for the fine linen is the righteous deeds of the saints. (The wedding day is described where Christ comes to be with his people that will be with him forever.)

The betrothal period is the time on earth when one grants permission to Christ to live in and through the believer producing the fine linen of righteous deeds, and then at Christ's coming the marriage takes place. Verses 9-10 say, And the angel said to me, "Write this: Blessed are those who are invited to the marriage supper of the Lamb." And he said to me, "These are true words of God." Then I fell down at his feet to worship him, but he said to me, "You must not do that! I am a fellow servant with you and your comrades who hold the testimony of Jesus. Worship God! For the testimony of Jesus is the spirit of prophecy." (Only God is to be worshiped. It is God's word given by Jesus through the Holy Spirit to the prophets, which includes the words in this book.)

Verses 11-16 say, Then I saw heaven opened, and there was a white horse! Its rider is called Faithful and True, and in righteousness he judges and makes war. (This is spiritual warfare fought by the Lion of Judah.) His eyes are like a flame of fire, and on his head are many diadems; and he has a name that no one knows but himself. He is clothed in a robe dipped in blood (from the cross) and his name is called the Word of God. And the armies from heaven, wearing linen, white and pure, were following him on white horses.

From his mouth comes a sharp sword with which to strike down the nations, and he will rule them with a rod of iron; he will tread the wine press of the fury of the wrath of God the Almighty. On his robe and on his thigh he has a name inscribed, "King of kings and Lord of lords."

The sword in his mouth is the sword of the Spirit, the Word of God, that he uses to judge and to rule. To make all this literal, while ignoring the symbolic and the concept of the spiritual world and spiritual warfare, as some fundamentalist do in order to find Scripture to support their advocacy for war on other nations, is an outright distortion of the meaning and intention of Scripture.

Verses 17-18 say, Then I saw an angel standing in the sun, and with a loud voice he called to all the birds that fly in midheaven, "Come gather for the great supper of God, to eat the flesh of kings (oppressive government leaders), the flesh of captains (the greedy traders and merchants from the sea), the flesh of the mighty (the wealthy and powerful who lived for themselves and their interests), the flesh of horses and their riders (the war machine)—flesh of all, both free and slave, both small and great (the unredeemed)."

Verses 19-21 say, Then I saw the beast and the kings of the earth with their armies gathered to make war against the rider on the horse and against his army. And the beast (the governments of evil nations and their leaders) was captured, and with it the false prophet (false religion supporting the evil intentions of nations) who had performed in its presence the signs by which he deceived those who had received the mark of the beast (had the stamp of approval by the above) and those who worshiped its image. These two were thrown alive into the lake of fire that burns with sulfer. And the rest were killed (judged and sent to eternal separation from God) by the sword of the rider on the horse, the sword that came from his mouth; and all the birds were gorged with their flesh.

This is the victory of God. The beast and the false prophet are symbolic forms representing reality in this narrative of spiritual warfare. They are thrown into hell never again to appear outside of hell. The followers of the opposition are first slain, judged, by the word, (2 Thess 1:7-8), and then cast into the lake of fire (20:15, 2 Thess 1:9). Before being resurrected to damnation their bodies are subjected to the indignity of being eaten by birds as in Deut 28:6, 1 Sam 17:44-46, 1 Kings 14:11). Spiritual death is inflicted upon those hostile to God. Babylon is seen as the seductive world system of the beast and false prophet, described in terms of Rome, its chief expression in the time of John. This hostile power of evil is defeated by Christ through those who reign with him during this church age to be finally defeated when he comes to judge the living and the dead.

As a brief summary: The binding of Satan represents the victory of the cross over the powers of darkness accomplished at the cross for believers. The thousand years are symbolic of a long, indeterminate period, corresponding to the age of the church. It is also symbolized by 1260 days, 3 ½ years, and 42 months. A general resurrection and spiritual judgment of evil and good will occur at Christ's coming. There is no coming of Jesus, followed by a rapture, and then a thousand year reign of Christ. This theory can only be developed by distorting the symbolism and then making it all literal. Even then Scripture has to be twisted to get such a wild theory. Granted it does excite the emotions of those sitting in the pews, those who really do not understand the nature of apocalyptic poetry and methods of interpretation.

꙳

Chapter 20:1-3 says, Then I saw an angel coming down from heaven, holding in his hand the key to the bottomless pit and a great chain. He seized the dragon, that ancient serpent, who is the Devil and Satan, and bound him for a thousand years, and threw him into the pit, and locked and sealed it over him, so that he would deceive the nations no more, until the thousand years were ended. After that he must be let out for a little more.

As other numbers in this book are understood symbolically and not literally, so this period of a thousand years represents the fact that because of what Christ did on the cross, believers are aware of what Satan does and are able to overcome him. Satan is a spiritual being and is bound spiritually. The Scriptures normally understand numbers symbolically. The number "one thousand" means a long indefinite time (see Pss 50:10, 90:4, 91:7, Deut 7:9, Josh 23:10, Eccl 6:6, 2 Peter 3:8). One must be aware of those who read more into this passage than is warranted. Nothing is said about a literal thousand year reign on earth.

Satan is thrown into the abyss. The dragon is cast down to the earth (12:7-12) where he persecutes the church (12:13-17). He exercises his power through people and ungodly governments and their systems and with false religions that are united to them (13:1-18). Satan works through demonic powers under his control (9:1-11, 16:12-16). Note that Satan's activity is not completely curbed; it is curbed only by the gospel, meaning only as far as one is controlled by Christ, his message, and the kingdom of God. The statement in verse 3 that says after the thousand years Satan must be let out for a little while, probably means as Christ in Lk 18:8 says, And yet when the Son of Man comes, will he find faith on earth?

Verses 4-6 say, Then I saw thrones, and those seated on them were given authority to judge. I also saw the souls of those who were beheaded for their testimony to Jesus and the word of God. They had not worshiped the beast or its image and had not received its mark on their foreheads or their hands. They came to life and reigned with Christ for a thousand years (the church age). Then verse 5 says, the rest of the dead did not come to life until the thousand years ended. This is the first resurrection. Blessed and holy are those who share in the first resurrection. Over these the second death has no power (the first death is physical; the second death is being eternally separated from Christ), but they will be priests of God and of Christ, and they will reign with him a thousand years.

There were quite a few martyrs that John knew personally, for in his time it was a way the Romans were trying to eliminate Christians because they were teaching that the kingdom of God had broken into the earth with the advent of Jesus. They refused to worship the emperor and the government cult. The millennium (thousand years) is the time the saints reign with Christ. Christians already had been made a kingdom and priests to God (1:5-6). Therefore they reign with him now (5:10), and when they die, they go to reign with him in heaven. The millennium is the time of the first resurrection. Since there is only one physical resurrection, which will be at Christ's second coming, this resurrection must symbolize all born of God during the church age.

Otherwise it is saying only the martyrs are resurrected during the church age with everyone else resurrected at the second coming. Therefore, this author thinks that the first resurrection is those born of God in a spiritual resurrection. They are those who have been born of God living a resurrected life (Rom 6:4-11, Col 2:12-13, 3:1-4). The only physical resurrection is at the final judgment when all the dead are bodily raised. Then the end will come (1Cor 15:20-28, 51-52). In one and the same time the righteous and the wicked will be raised (Jn 5:28-29). This is difficult to comment on without any possibility of knowing for sure.

Verses 7-10 say, When the thousand years are ended, Satan will be released from his prison and will come out to deceive the nations at the four corners of the earth, Gog and Magog, in order to gather them for battle; they are as numerous as the sands of the sea. They marched up over the breadth of the earth and surrounded the camp of the saints and the beloved city. And fire came down from heaven and consumed them. And the devil who had deceived them was thrown into the lake of fire and sulfur, where the beast and the false prophet were, and they will be tormented day and night forever and ever.

As previously stated the loosening of Satan may just symbolize Lk 18:8, and the idea that real Christianity at that time will be rare. Gog and Magog refer to a nation who would attack God's people and in the process be miraculously overcome (Ezekiel 38-39). This prophesy was first fulfilled by the actions of Antiochus Epiphanes in the second century BC. The New Testament uses Antiochus' actions as a pattern of the final form of the antichrist or beast. Here the actions of Gog and Magog are used as a pattern for the final battle, which is a spiritual battle, not a literal physical battle on earth. The battle is called Armageddon (Rev 16:16).

Christ's second coming with fire is consistent with 2 Thess 1:7-8 and 2 Peter 3:10. These passages clearly indicate the earth will be transformed at Christ's second coming. Fire does not necessarily mean burned up. The fire appearing to Moses did not burn up the bush, and Scripture uses fire quite often to purify without burning anything up, which is why this author uses the term transformation. This along with 1 Cor 15:20-28 make the premillennialist understanding of a thousand year reign upon the earth after the second coming an impossibility. This fanciful theory is a creation of fundamentalists used to excite people and attract them into their churches. It has been repeated so often throughout the last one hundred fifty years that the people who preach it actually believe it was given to them by Christ himself. What is for sure is that with the casting of the devil into the lake of fire in verse 10 the destruction of evil is finished.

Verses 11-13 say, Then I saw a great white throne and the one who sat on it; the earth and the heaven fled from his presence, and no place was found for them. (There is no escaping the judgment.) And I saw the dead, great and small, standing before the throne, and books were opened. Also another book was opened, the book of life. And the dead were judged according to their works, as recorded in the books. (Again as consistently portrayed all the dead are judged according to their works.) And the sea gave up the dead that were in it, Death and Hades gave up the dead that were in them, and all were judged according to what they had done (Mt 16:27, 25:31-46, Rom 2:6, 2 Cor 5:10, Jas 2:14-26, Titus 1:16, 2:14).

St Augustine says, in his *Epistle* 194.5.19, "When God crowns your merits, he crowns nothing other than his own gifts. This is the idea that followers of Christ bear fruit because they have allowed Jesus by the power of the Holy Spirit to live in them and through them to bear fruit to eternal life. Verses 14-15 say, Then Death and Hades were thrown into the lake of fire. This is the second death, the lake of fire; and anyone whose name was not found written in the book of life was thrown into the lake of fire.

Chapter 21:1 says, Then I saw a new heaven and a new earth; for the first heaven and the first earth had passed away, and the sea (a symbol of evil, turbulence, and unrest) was no more (Isa 65:17, 66:22). (All creation will be transformed and renewed by the glory of God, Rom 8:19-21.)

Verses 2-4 say, And I saw the holy city, the new Jerusalem, coming down out of heaven from God, prepared as a bride adorned for her husband. And I heard a loud voice from the throne saying, "See, the home of God is among mortals. He will dwell with them as their God; they will be his peoples, and God himself will be with them; he will wipe every tear from their eyes. Death will be no more; mourning and crying and pain will be no more, for the first things have passed away."

Note that God comes down upon the transformed earth to dwell among the redeemed. They are not going "up" to heaven. At the transformation his people will meet him in the air, and then he will dwell with them in the new heaven (atmosphere) and earth, 1 Thess 4:14-17, Rev 21:10, where sin will be no more.

Verses 5-8 say, And the one who was seated on the throne said, "See, I am making all things new." Also he said, "Write this, for these words are trustworthy and true." Then he said to me, "It is done! I am the Alpha and the Omega, the beginning and the end. To the thirsty I will give water as a gift from the spring of the water of life. Those who conquer will inherit (a gift of inheritance) these things, and I will be their God and they will be my children. But as for the cowardly, the faithless, the polluted, the murderers, the fornicators, the sorcerers, the idolaters, and all liars, their place will be in the lake that burns with fire and sulfur, which is the second death." (The second death, symbolizing eternal separation from God, is contrasted to the water of life.)

Verse 9 says, Then one of the seven angels who had the seven bowls full of the seven last plagues came and said to me, "Come, I will show you the bride, the wife of the Lamb." (Verses 9-21 display the majesty of eternal life.) Verse 10 says, And in the Spirit he carried me away to a great, high mountain and showed me the holy city Jerusalem coming down out of heaven from God. (The mountain was the traditional place where visions from God were received. John's vision is built on that of Ezekiel 40 and Isaiah 60.) Verses 11-13 say, It has the glory of God and a radiance like a very rare jewel, like jasper, clear as crystal. It has a great, high wall with twelve gates, and at the gates twelve angels, and on the gates are inscribed the names of the twelve tribes of the Israelites; on the east three gates, on the north three gates, on the south three gates, and on the west three gates.

The gates remind us that God brought salvation to the whole world through Israel (see Gen 12:1-3, Jn 4:22, Lk 13:29). Verse 14 says, And the wall of the city has twelve foundations, and on them are the twelve names of the twelve apostles of the Lamb.

This recalls Paul's description of the church as the holy temple of God built on the foundation of the twelve apostles, Eph 2:21-22, Heb 11:10. The twelve tribes of Israel and the twelve apostles of the Lamb represent all the redeemed. Again, note the glory of God and the holy city descending (not ascending) making all things new with the new heaven and new earth to make their dwelling with the redeemed on the transformed earth.

Now we have the completion of the mission of Christ. He came the first time to institute the kingdom of God. In the prayer Jesus gave to his people in Mt 6:10 he says to pray, "Your kingdom come. Your will be done, on earth as it is in heaven." Before Christ ascended to heaven, he told his people to continue the mission until he comes again to make all things perfect, which is now being completed.

Verses 15-21 say, The angel who talked to me had a measuring rod of gold to measure the city and its gates and walls. The city lies foursquare, its length the same as its width; and he measured the city with its rod, fifteen hundred miles (Greek is 12,000 stadia, 3 x 4 x 1000); its length and width and height are equal. He also measured its wall, one hundred forty-four cubits by human measurement, which the angel was using. The wall is built of jasper (God is described as jasper in 4:3), while the city is pure gold, clear as glass. The foundations of the wall of the city are adorned with every jewel; the first was jasper, the second sapphire, the third agate, the fourth emerald, the fifth onyx, the sixth carnelian, the seventh chrysolite, the eighth beryl, the ninth topaz, the tenth chrysoprase, the eleventh jacinth, the twelfth amethyst. And the twelve gates are twelve pearls, each of the gates is a single pearl, and the street of the city is pure gold, transparent as glass.

The city is a cube, which is more evidence that a literal city is not meant, fifteen hundred miles in each direction. The Holy of Holies (the Most Holy place in the temple where God's presence dwelt) was also shaped like a cube. The reason, we are later told, is that there is no temple in the city because the city is itself a temple, God's dwelling place. God's people enjoy perfect fellowship with God for eternity. The gem stones are mixed with the imagery of the city suggesting the preciousness and purity of God and his people. The city and its streets are made of gold so pure that it is transparent. This symbolizes the result of God's refining process in the life of his people (see Job 23:10, Zechariah 13:9, Malachi 3:3, 1 Peter 1:7, Revelation 3:18). Keep in mind this is all apocalyptic poetry symbolizing concepts.

Verses 22-27 say, I saw no temple in the city, for its temple is the Lord God the Almighty and the Lamb. And the city had no need of sun or moon to shine on it, for the glory of God is its light, and its lamp is the Lamb. The nations will walk by its light, and the kings (those of the nations among the redeemed) of the earth will bring their glory into it. Its gates will never be shut by day—and there will be no night there. People will bring into it the glory and honor of the nations. But nothing unclean (sin) will enter it, nor anyone who practices abomination or falsehood, but only those who are written in the Lamb's book of life.

The only building the New Testament talks about is the temple building that is the people of God (Eph 2:19-22). Go to Isaiah 60 and compare it with the description of the new Jerusalem. People of every tribe, language, and nation will enter the city as they are in the process of doing during the 1000 years, 1260 days, 42 months, and 3 ½ years, all symbolizing the time between the first coming of Christ and the second coming. Verse 27 repeats the idea throughout the New Testament that nothing evil, like sin can enter. The reason, of course, is that no sin can enter all that has been purified and made perfect, for it would no longer be made perfect.

Chapter 22:1-5 says, Then the angel showed me the river of the water of life, bright as crystal, flowing from the throne of God and of the Lamb through the middle of the street of the city. On either side of the river is the tree of life with its twelve kinds of fruit, producing its fruit each month; and the leaves of the tree are for the healing of the nations. Nothing accursed will be found there any more (no more sin). But the throne of God and of the Lamb will be in it, and his servants will worship him; they will see his face, and his name will be on their foreheads. And there will be no more night; they need no light of lamp or sun, for the Lord God will be their light, and they will reign forever and ever.

The image of the river of life comes from Old Testament prophecy (Ezekiel 47:1-12, Zechariah 14:8, Joel 3:18). The river represents the pure and life-giving Holy Spirit flowing from the throne of God and the Lamb through the hearts and lives of his people. Now God's people eat freely from the tree of life that bears fruit every month of the year. The fruit of the trees that grow along the river of life heal and sustain eternal life. The nations symbolize the people of every language and people who are the redeemed from the nations.

Verses 6-7 say, And he said to me, "These words are trustworthy and true, for the Lord, the God of the spirits of the prophets, has sent his angel to show his servants what must soon take place. See, I am coming soon! Blessed is the one who keeps the words (teachings) of the prophecy of this book." (Blessed are the ones who keep the words, not those who spend all their time trying to know all the dates and details for the future history of the world and its end. Too many people are obsessed with speculations about Revelation rather than concentrating on keeping the words of this prophecy (1:3) by serving Christ and those he served.)

Verses 8-11 say, I, John, am the one who heard and saw these things. And when I heard and saw them, I fell down to worship at the feet of the angel who showed them to me; but he said to me, "You must not do that! I am a fellow servant with you and your comrades the prophets, and with those who keep the words of this book. Worship God!" And he said to me, "Do not seal up the words of the prophecy of this book, for the time is near. Let the evil doer still do evil, and the filthy still be filthy, and the righteous still do right, and the holy still be holy." (This command is in contrast to what God told Daniel in Dan 12:4. Daniel was told to seal up his prophecy, for the last days were yet to come, but we now live in the last days, which is the time between the first and second comings; see Acts 2:17.)

Verses 12-15 say, "See, I am coming soon; my reward is with me, to repay according to everyone's works. I am the Alpha and the Omega, the first and the last, the beginning and the end." Blessed are those who wash their robes, so that they will have the right to the tree of life and may enter the city by the gates. Outside are the dogs and sorcerers and fornicators and murderers and idolaters, and everyone who loves and practices falsehood.

In the last judgment everyone is judged by their works. The choice is not between works or no works; that is a false choice. Followers of Christ are saved by the grace of God as that grace does the works of Christ by the power of the Holy Spirit working in and through his people. If that is not happening, there will be no works accounted to the person at the judgment.

Verses 16-17 say, It is I, Jesus, who sent my angel to you with this testimony to the churches. I am the root and the descendant of David, the bright morning star." The Spirit and the bride say, "Come." And let everyone who hears say, "Come." And let everyone who is thirsty come. Let anyone who wishes take the water of life as a gift.

Numbers 22:16 foretells a star that would rise out of Jacob. And 2 Peter 1:19-20 says, So we have the prophetic message more fully confirmed. You will do well to be attentive to this as to a lamp shining in a dark place, until the day dawns and the morning star rises in your hearts. First of all you must understand this, that no prophecy of Scripture is a matter of one's own interpretation, because no prophecy ever came by human will, but men and women moved by the Holy Spirit spoke from God. (The point being made is that God is behind all of this; it is not being made up by humans.)

Verses 18-19 say, I warn everyone who hears the words of the prophecy of this book: if anyone adds to them, God will add to that person the plagues described in this book; if anyone takes away from the words of the book of this prophecy, God will take away that person's share in the tree of life and in the holy city, which are described in this book.

This is a warning not to pervert the message contained in this book. It is a warning not to change or ignore or eliminate the teachings and commands contained in this book. God also knew that the official copyists who preserve the written text for the Bible would be tempted to add their own explanatory notes, or leave out what they do not understand. God warns them not to make any attempt to add or take away from the original text.

Verses 20-21 say, The one who testifies to these things says, "Surely I am coming soon." Amen. Come, Lord! The grace of the Lord Jesus be with all the saints. Amen. (The Bible opens with creation and humanity in paradise. It ends with the new creation and new humanity at peace. The new creation once again rules over chaos.)

There are two legitimate ways to read the book of Revelation. The first one is to read it as a message to persons living in the early days of Christianity that announces God's judgment on the evil that is occurring to them living under the Romans in the Roman empire reassuring the faithful that God is in control of history and will make all things right in the end. He will judge evil and wrong doing and those who persevere and stay in Christ will be eternally with him. Revelation 1:1 tells us this message is to John about what must soon take place.

The second way to read Revelation is to look at the history of the world and compare it with the principles and themes behind the symbols and visions. This author believes integrating the two ways is the best way to understand the book of Revelation. The things that happen occur over and over in the generations throughout history. It is about what is happening on earth and about what is happening in heaven. Since the first coming of Christ until the second coming we are in the church age; therefore, the time is always near. The kingdom has broken into the earth, and our time on earth is not very long. The believers are praying, Your kingdom come. Your will be done on earth as it is in heaven. And they are being used as instruments of Christ to bring that prayer to fruition until he comes again to perfect all that is being done in his name. The Day is coming. There will be a new heaven and new earth when God will bring all things to perfection. So be prepared, for only the redeemed will live with him forever.

One final thought: Before ending the book of Revelation the writer pronounced seven blessings upon those who read the book. Those blessings are as follows.

1. Blessed is the one who reads aloud the words of the prophecy, and blessed are those who hear and who keep what is written in it; for the time is near (1:3). (We have been in the last age since the new covenant began.)

2. Blessed are the dead who from now on die in the Lord (14:13).

3. Blessed is the one who stays awake and is clothed, not going about naked and exposed to shame (16:15). (They are alert and clothed in Christ.)

4. Blessed are those who are invited to the marriage supper of the Lamb (19:9). (The marriage supper is a reference to both the Eucharist/Holy Communion and eternal life.)

5. Blessed and holy are those who share in the first resurrection (20:6). (The first resurrection is a spiritual one where one recognizes they are created by God for his purposes.)

6. Blessed is the one who keeps the words of prophecy (teaching) of this book (22:7).

7. Blessed are those who wash their robes (confess and keep purified of sin), so that they will have the right to the tree of life and may enter the city by the gates. Outside are the dogs and sorcerers and fornicators and murderers and idolaters, and everyone who loves and practices falsehood (22:14).

This ends the book of Revelation and the New Testament. As a way of review list some of the verses and thoughts that stood out to you in this final book of the New Testament.

BIBLIOGRAPHY OF SOURCES

Achtemeir, Paul J. *The Quest for Unity in the New Testament Church: A Study in Paul and Acts.* Philadelphia: Fortress Press, 1987.

Armstrong, Dave. *The Catholic Verses.* Manchester, NH: Sophia Institute Press, 2004.

Bailey, Kenneth E. *Through Peasant Eyes.* Grand Rapids: Eerdmans, 1980.

Baillie, D. M. *God Was in Christ.* New York: Charles Scribner's Sons, 1948.

Bainton, Roland. *Christian Attitudes Toward War and Peace.* Nashville: Abingdon Press, 1960.

Barbour, Ian G. *Issues in Science and Religion.* London: SCM, 1966.

Barclay, William. *The Mind of St. Paul.* New York: Harper and Row, 1958.

Barton, John. *Holy Writings, Sacred Text: The Canon in Early Christianity.* Louisville: Westminster John Knox, 1997.

Barr, James. *The Scope and Authority of the Bible.* Philadelphia: Westminster, 1980.

Beker, Christiaan. *Paul the Apostle: The Triumph of God in Life and Thought*. Philadephia: Fortress Press, 1980.

Bellah, Robert N., Richard Madsen, William M. Sullivan, Ann Swidler, and Steven M. Tipton. *Habits of the Heart: Individualism and Commitment in American Life*. Los Angeles and Berkeley: University of California Press, 1996.

Berkhof, Hendrikus. *Christ and the Powers*. London: SPCK, 1966.

Book of Concord: The Confessions of the Evangelical Lutheran Church. Editor Theodore G. Tappert. Philadelphia: Fortress Press, 1959.

Borg, Marcus J. *Jesus, A New Vision: Spirit, Culture, and the Life of Discipleship*. San Francisco: HarperCollins, 1987.

_____. *Reading the Bible Again for the First Time: Taking the Bible Seriously but not Literally*. San Francisco: HarperCollins, 2001.

_____. *The Heart of Christianity: Rediscovering a Life of Faith*. San Francisco: HarperCollins, 2003.

Borg, Marcus J., and John Dominic Crossan. *The First Paul: Reclaiming the Radical Visionary Behind the Churches Conservative Icon*. New York: HarperCollins, 2010.

Borg, Marcus J., and N. T. Wright. *The Meaning of Jesus: Two Visions*. San Francisco: HarperCollins, 1999.

Bowley, James E. *Living Traditions of the Bible: Scripture in Jewish, Christian, and Muslim Practice*. St. Louis, MO: Chalice Press, 1999.

Bristow, John Temple. *What Paul Really Said About Women*. San Francisco: HarperCollins, 1988.

Brown, Raymond E. *The Churches the Apostles Left Behind*. Mahweh, NJ: Paulist Press, 1984.

_____. *Responses to 101 Questions on the Bible*. Mahweh, NJ: 1990.

_____. *A Risen Christ in Eastertime: Essays on the Gospel Narratives of the Resurrection.* Collegeville, MN: Liturgical Press, 1991.

Brown, Robert McAfee. *The Spirit of Protesantism.* New York: Oxford University Press, 1965.

Bruce, F. F. *Apostle of the Heart Set Free.* Grand Rapids: William B. Eerdmans, 1977.

Brueggemann, Walter. *The Prophetic Imagination.* Philadelphia: Fortress Press, 1978.

Burgess, John P. *Why Scripture Matters: Reading the Bible in a Time of Church Conflict.* Louisville: Westminster John Knox Press, 1998.

Caird, G. B. *The Language and Imagery of the Bible.* London: Duckworth, 1980.

_____. *Principalities and Powers.* Oxford: Clarendon Press, 1956.

Calvin, John. *Institutes of the Christian Religion.* Editor John T. Mc Neill. Philadelphia: Westminster, 1960.

Catholic Study Bible of the New American Bible. Edited by Donald Senior, et al. New York: Oxford University Press, 1990.

Charlesworth, J. H., ed. *Jesus and the Dead Sea Scrolls.* New York: Doubleday, 1992.

Childs, Brevard S. *Biblical Theology of the Old and New Testaments: Theological Reflection on the Christian Bible.* Minneapolis: Fortress Press, 1992.

Collegeville Bible Commentary. Edited by Dianne Bergant, and Robert J. Karris. Collegeville, MN: The Liturgical Press, 1989.

Cone, James. *Risks of Faith: The Emergence of a Black Theology of Liberation.* Boston: Beacon Press, 1999.

Conybeare, W. J., and J. S. Howson. *The Life and Epistles of St. Paul.* New York: Scribner and Sons, 1968.

Countryman, William L. *Biblical Authority or Biblical Tyranny?* Harrisburg: Trinity International, 1994.

Crossan, John Dominic, and Jonathan R. Reed. *In Search of Paul: How Jesus' Apostle Opposed Rome's Empire with God's Kingdom.* San Francisco: HarperCollins, 2004.

Dunn, James D. G. *The Theology of Paul the Apostle.* Grand Rapids: William B. Eerdmans, 1998.

_____. *Unity and Diversity in the New Testament.* London: SCM, 1990.

_____. *The New Perspective on Paul.* Grand Rapids: William B. Eerdmans, 2005.

Ehrman, Bart D. *The New Testament: An Historical Introduction to the Early Christian Writings.* 2nd edition. New York: Oxford University Press, 2000.

_____. *Lost Scriptures: Books that Did Not Make It into the New Testament.* New York: Oxford University Press, 2003.

Fackre, Gabriel. *The Christian Story: A Narrative Interpretation of Basic Christian Doctrine, vol. 1.* Grand Rapids: William B. Eerdmans Publishing, 1996.

_____. *The Christian Story Authority of Scripture in the Church for the World, vol 2. Grand Rapids: William B. Eerdmans,* 1987.

Fee, Gordon. *God's Empowering Presence: The Holy Spirit in the Letters of Paul.* Peabody: Hendrickson, 1994.

Fee, Gordon D., and Douglas Stuart. *How to Read the Bible for All Its Worth.* Grand Rapids: Zondervan, 2003.

Fitzmyer, Joseph. *Pauline Theology: A Brief Sketch.* 2nd edition. Englewood, NJ: Prentice Hall, 1989.

Forell, George W. *The Protestant Faith.* Philadelphia: Fortress Press, 1975.

Frank, Harry Thomas. *Atlas of the Bible Lands.* Maplewood, NJ: Hammond Incorporated, 1990.

Furnish, Victor P. *The Moral Teachings of Paul: Selected Issue.* Revised edition. Nashville: Abingdon Press, 1985.

Grassi, Joseph A. *Rediscovering the Impact of Jesus' Death: Clues From the Gospel Audiences.* Kansas City: Sheed & Ward, 1987.

Gregg, Steve, ed. *Revelation: Four Views A Parallel Commentary.* Nashville: Thomas Nelson Publishers, 1997.

Griffith-Jones, Robin. *The Gospel According to Paul.* San Francisco: HarperCollins Publishers, 2004.

Hailey, Homer. *Revelation: An Introduction and Commentary.* Grand Rapids: Baker Book House, 1979.

Hare, Douglas R. A. *The Son of Man Tradition.* Minneapolis: Fortress Press, 1990.

Harper Collins Study Bible: New Revised Standard Version With the Apocryphal/ Deuterocanonical Books. Edited by Wayne A. Meeks, et al. New York: Harper Collins Publishers, 1993.

Harrington, Donald J. *Interpreting the New Testament.* Wilmington, DE: Michael Glazier, Inc., 1983.

Hays, Richard B. *Echoes of Scripture in the Letters of Paul.* New Haven: Yale University Press, 1989.

_____. *The Moral Vision of the New Testament: A Contemporary Introduction to New Testament Ethics.* San Francisco: Harper Collins, 1996.

Hauer, Christian, William A. Young. *An Introduction to the Bible: A Journey Into Three Worlds.* Englewood Cliffs, NJ: Prentice Hall, 1994.

Hauerwas, Stanley. *Unleashing the Scripture: Freeing the Bible From Captivity to America.* Nashville: Abingdon Press, 1993.

Hendricks, Obery M., Jr. *The Politics of Jesus.* New York: Doubleday, 2006.

Hendriksen, William. *More Than Conquerors: An Interpretation of the Book of Revelation.* Grand Rapids: Baker Book House, 1939.

Hobbs, Herschel H. *The Cosmic Drama.* Waco, TX: Word Books, 1971.

Horsley, Richard A. *Jerusalem in the time of Jesus: An Investigation into Economic and Social Conditions during the New Testament Period.* Philadelphia: Fortress Press, 1969.

_____. *Paul and Empire: Religion and Power in Roman Imperial Society.* Harrisburg, PA: Trinity Press International, 1997.

_____. *Paul and Politics.* Harrisburg: Trinity Press International, 2000.

_____. *Jesus and Empire: The Kingdom of God and the New World Disorder.* Minneapolis: Fortress Press, 2003.

_____. *Paul and the Roman Imperial Order.* Harrisburg, PA: Trinity Press International, 2004.

_____. *Covenant Economics: A Biblical Vision of Justice For All.* Louisville: Westminster John Knox Press, 2009.

Johnson, Luke Timothy. *The Writings of the New Testament: An Interpretation.* Minneapolis: Fortress Press, 1999.

Keck, Leander. *Paul and His Letters.* Philadelphia: Fortress Press, 1979.

Kee, Harold Clark. *Medicine, Miracle, and Magic in New Testament Times.* New York: Cambridge University Press, 1986.

Kung, Hans. *On Being a Christian.* Garden City, NY: Doubleday, 1984.

Ladd, George Eldon. *A Theology of the New Testament.* Grand Rapids: Eerdmans, 1974.

Lane, Thomas B. *Reading and Understanding the Old Testament: The Foundation of Judaism, Christianity, and Islam.* Parker, CO: Outskirts Press, 2010.

_____. *Reading and Understanding the Gospels: Who Jesus Is, What He Teaches, and the Beginning of Christianity.* Parker, CO: Outskirts Press, 2011.

Longnecker, Bruce W., ed. *Narrative Dynamics in Paul: A Critical Assessment.* Louisville: Westminster John Knox Press, 2002.

Major Themes in the Reformed Tradition. Edited by Donald K. McKim. Grand Rapids: Eerdmans Publishing, 1992.

Malina, Bruce. *The Social Gospel of Jesus: The Kingdom of God in Mediterranean Perspective.* Minneapolis: Fortress Press, 2001.

Maritain, Jacques. *Saint Paul: Selections From His Writings.* New York: McGraw-Hill, 1964.

Marty, Martin E., and R. Scott Appleby. *The Glory and the Power: The Fundamentalist Challenge to the Modern World.* Boston: Beacon Press, 1992.

_____. *Fundamentalisms Comprehended.* Chicago: University Chicago Press, 1993.

Martyn, J. Louis. *Theological Issues in the Letters of Paul.* Nashville: Abingdon Press, 1997.

McBrien, Richard P. *Catholicism.* New York: HarperCollins, 1994.

McFague, Sallie. *Models of God: Theology for an Ecological, Nuclear Age*. Philadelphia: Fortress Press, 1987.

Meeks, Wayne E. *The Writings of St. Paul*. New York: Norton, 1972.

_____. *The First Urban Christians: The Social World of the Apostle Paul*. New Haven: Yale University Press, 2003.

Morris, Leon. *The Revelation of St. John*. Grand Rapids: Eerdmans Publishing, 1969.

Most, William G. *The Thought of St. Paul: A Commentary on the Pauline Epistles*. Front Royal, VA: Christendom Press, 1994.

Mouw, Richard. *Politics and the Biblical Drama*. Grand Rapids: Eerdmans Publishing Co., 1976.

Murphy, Frederick J. *The Religious World of Jesus: An Introduction to Second Temple Palestinian Judaism*. Nashville: Abingdom Press, 1991.

Murphy-O'Connor, Jerome. *Paul: A Critical Life*. New York: Oxford Press, 1998.

New Jerome Biblical Commentary. Edited by Raymond E. Brown, Joseph R. Fitzmyer, and Roland E. Murphy. Englewood Cliffs: Prentice Hall, 1990.

New Oxford Annotated Bible With the Apocraphal/Dueterocanonical Books. Eds., Bruce M. Metzger, and Roland E. Murphy. New York: University Press, 1991.

New World Dictionary-Concordance to the New American Bible. Iowa Falls, IA: World Publishing, 1990.

NRSV Exhaustive Concordance: Includes the Apocryphal and Deuterocanonical Books. Nashville: Thomas Nelson Publications, 1991.

O'Collins, Gerald. *Interpreting the Resurrection:Examining the Major Problems.* New York: Paulist Press, 1988.

O'Donovan, Oliver. *The Desire of the Nations: Rediscovering the Roots of Political Theology.* Cambridge Uuiversity Press, 1996.

Ogletree, Thomas W. *The Use of the Bible in Christian Ethics.* Philadelphia:Fortress Press, 1983.

Pelikan, Jaroslav. *The Emergence of the Catholic Tradition (100-600).* Vol 1 of *The Christian Tradition: A History of the Development of Doctrine.* Chicago: University of Chicago Press, 1971.

Perkins, Pheme. *Reading the New Testament.* Mahwah, NJ: Paulist Press, 1988.

Pilch, John J. *Choosing a Bible Translation.* Collegeville, MN: Liturgical Press, 2000.

Polhill, John B. *Paul and His Letters.* Nashville: Broadman & Holman Publishers, 1999.

Presbyterian Understanding and Use of Holy Scripture. Louisville, KY: Office of the General Assembly, 1983.

Pontifical Biblical Commission. *The Interpretation of the Bible in the Church.* Washington, DC: U.S. Catholic Conference, 1994.

Ramsey, William M. *The Cities of St. Paul.* Grand Rapids: Baker Book House, 1960.

Rogers, Jack B., and Donald K. McKim. *The Authority and Interpretation of the Bible: An Historical Approach.* San Francisco: Harper & Row Publishers, 1979.

Rosenblatt, Marie-Eloise. *Paul the Accused: His Portrait in the Acts of the Apostles.* Collegeville, MN: Liturgical Press, 1995.

Sanders, E. P. *Paul.* New York: Oxford University Press, 1991.

_____. *Jesus and Judaism.* Philadelphia: Fortress Press, 1985.

_____. *Paul and Palestinian Judaism: A Comparison of Patterns of Religion.* Philadelphia: Fortress Press, 1977.

_____. *Paul, the Law, and the Jewish People.* Philadelphia: Fortress Press, 1983.

Schaff, Philip. *The Creeds of Christendom.* 3 vols. New York: Harper & Brothers, 1877.

Sider, Ronald J. *Rich Christians in an Age of Hunger.* Nashville: Word Publishing, 1997.

Smart, James. *The Strange Silence of the Bible in the Church.* Philadelphia: Westminster Press, 1970.

Spohn, William C. *What Are They Saying About Scripture and Ethics.* Mahwah, NJ: Paulist Press, 1995.

Stemberger, Gunter. *Jewish Contemporaries of Jesus: Pharisees, Sadducees, Essenes.* Minneapolis: Fortress Press, 1995.

Stendahl, Krister. *Meanings: The Bible as Document and as Guide.* Philadelphia: Fortress, 1984.

_____. *Paul Among Jews and Gentiles and Other Essays.* Philadelphia: Fortress Press, 1976.

Summers, Ray. *Worthy is the Lamb: An Interpretation of Revelation.* Nashville: Broadman Press, 1951.

Thielman, Frank. *Theology of the New Testament.* Grand Rapids: Zondervan, 2005.

Vatican Council ll: Dei Verbum (The Dogmatic Constitution on Divine Revelation). *The Documents of Vatican ll,* ed. W. M. Abbot. New York: Herder and Herder Association Press, 1966.

Verhey, Allen. *Remembering Jesus: Christian Community, Scripture, and the Moral Life.* Grand Rapids, MI: Wm. B. Erdmans Publishing Co., 2002.

Vine, W.E. *Vine's Expository Dictionary of Old and New Testament Words.* Nashville: Thomas Nelson, 1996.

Wakefield, Dan. *The Hijacking of Jesus: How the Religious Right Distorts Christianity and Promotes Prejudice and Hate.* New York: Avalon Publishing, 2006.

Wallis, Jim. *God's Politics: A New Vision for Faith and Politics in America.* San Francisco: Harper Collins, 2005.

Westerholm, Stephen. *Perspectives Old and New on Paul.* Grand Rapids: Eerdmans Publishing, 2003.

Wink, Walter. *Jesus and Nonviolence: A Third Way.* Minneapolis: Fortress Press, 2003.

Winter, Bruce. *The Book of Acts in its Ancient Literary Setting.* Grand Rapids: Eerdmans Publishing, 1993.

Witherington, Ben, III. *Women in the Ministry of Jesus: A Study of Jesus' Attitudes to Women and Their Roles as Reflected in His Earthly Life.* New York: Cambridge University Press, 1984.

_____. *The Paul Quest: The Renewed Search for the Jew of Tarsus.* Downers Grove, IL: Inter Varsity Press, 1998.

Wolterstorff, Nicholas. *Until Justice and Peace Embrace.* Grand Rapids: Eerdmans Publishing Co., 1983.

Wright, N. T. *Paul in Fresh Perspective.* Minneapolis: Fortress Press, 2005.

_____. *The Last Word: Beyond the Bible Wars to a New Understanding of the Authority of Scripture.* San Francisco: HarperCollins, 2005.

_____. *The Myth of the Millenium.* Louisville: John Knox Press, 1999.

_____. *The Climax of the Covenant: Christ and the Law in Pauline Theology.* Edinburgh: T. & T. Clark, 1998.

_____. *What Saint Paul Really Said: Was Paul of Tarsus the Real Founder of Christianity?* Grand Rapids: Eerdmans, 1997.

_____. *Jesus and the Victory of God: Christian Origins and the Question of God.* Minneapolis: Fortress Press, 1996.

_____. *The New Testament and the People of God.* Minneapolis: Fortress Press, 1992.

Yoder, John. *The Politics of Jesus.* Grand Rapids: William B. Eerdmans Publishing Co., 1972.

FROM THE AUTHOR

The author's teaching of the Bible, Religious Studies, and Theology over a forty year period has been done ecumenically in a public university, Penn State at Altoona; two Roman Catholic colleges, Mt Aloysius, and St Francis of PA; a public and Catholic high school, and in the United Church of Christ, the Christian Church (Disciples of Christ), and the Roman Catholic Church. At this writing he is teaching at the State College of Florida in Bradenton, Florida.

If we understand the Scriptures, there is room in Christ's church for all who believe and attempt to relate their imperfect lives to him. Life is a struggle to the Word and Spirit that comes from God and continues to work in the world. There is no group who perfectly understands. First Corinthians 13:12-13 says, For now we see in a mirror, dimly, but then we will see face to face. Now I know in part; then I will know fully, even as I have been fully known. May God's mercy and grace bless all of us who struggle in our understanding and spiritual growth along life's journey.

My prayer is the prayer of Jesus in John 17:17-23. Sanctify them in the truth; your word is truth. As you have sent me into the world, so I have sent them into the world. And for their sakes

I sanctify myself, so that they also may be sanctified in the truth. I ask not only on behalf of these, but also on behalf of those who will believe in me through their word, that they all may be one. As you, Father, are in me and I am in you, may they also be in us, so that the world may believe that you have sent me. The glory that you have given me I have given them, so that they may be one, as we are one, I in them and you in me, that they may be completely one, so that the world may know that you have sent me and have loved them even as you have loved me.

A BRIEF BIOGRAPHY

EDUCATION

- DMin, Pittsburgh Theological Seminary: Reformed Theology with an Emphasis in Comparative Christian Theology. Dissertation: Protestantism, Roman Catholicism, and the Orthodox: A Comparison of Christian Theology. Dissertation Directors: Dr. Charles Partee and Dr. John Mehl.

- PhD, Clayton University: Religious Studies/Counseling Psychology. Dissertation: Using Programmed Instruction in Teaching Religion and Counseling. Dissertation Directors: Dr. Harry Cargas, Roman Catholic author of 31 books and 2000 published articles, Dr. Barbara Finn, and Dr. Richard Foster, author of numerous books. (Clayton University associated with the Menninger Foundation closed its doors in 1989. Until that time it was listed in the U. S. Department of Education Handbook of Accredited Colleges and Universities.)

- MAT, Harding University: Biblical Studies.

- MEd, University of North Florida: Counseling.

- BSEd, Lock Haven University: Social Studies and English.

- Post Graduate Studies in Religion and Counseling Psychology at the University of Texas-El Paso, David Lipscomb University, Penn State University, and Indiana University (PA).

EMPLOYMENT

- Instructor of Religious Studies, and Chaplain in the Campus Ministry Program at Penn State University (Altoona Campus) teaching the following courses: Old and New Testaments, Comparative Christian Religions, World Religions, and Religion in America.

- Adjunct Professor of Scripture and Theology at Mt Aloysius College (PA).

- Adjunct Professor of Scripture and Theology at St. Francis University (PA).

- Adjunct Professor of Religious Studies at State College of Florida.

- Catholic High School Teacher, Counselor, teaching the following courses: Biblical Studies, Psychology, World History and Cultures, American History, Government, Economics, and English. Head basketball coach for the 1970 Bishop Guilfoyle High School (PA) state champions.

- Public High School Teacher, Counselor, Basketball and Baseball Coach teaching the following courses: Biblical Studies, World History and Cultures, American History, and English.

- Peace Corps in Senegal, French West Africa. Helped train their Olympic basketball team for the 1964 Olympics in Japan.

- Played professional baseball in the Cleveland and Minnesota minor league systems. On the Altoona (PA) NABF national championship team, getting the team's only hit in the tenth inning in a 1-0 win. The team was inducted into Blair County (PA) Hall of Fame. The following year was selected MVP of the national tournament as the team finished second in the national tournament for ages 14-19.

- Certified Psychologist, Teacher, and Counselor by the state of PA.

- Certified Counselor by the National Board of Certified Counselors.

- Over 40 years of teaching within the Roman Catholic Church, United Church of Christ, and the Christian Church (Disciples of Christ).

- Book Publication: *Reading and Understanding the Old Testament: The Foundation of Judaism, Christianity, and Islam*. Denver: Outskirts Press, 2010. The book is a text book for first level college students and a source for anyone desiring to expand their understanding.

- Book Publication: *Reading and Understanding the Gospels: Who Jesus Is, What He Teaches, and the Beginning of Christianity*. Denver: Outskirts Press, 2011. This book is a text book for first level college students and a source for anyone desiring to expand their understanding.

- Book Publication: *Reading and Understanding the Acts of the Apostles, the New Testament Letters, and the Book of Revelation*. Denver: Outskirts Press, 2012. This book is for the same audience as the first two books.

9 781432 794965